Banking and Finance Series

Monetary Economics

Banking and Finance Series

Monetary Economics

by

Brian Kettell, M.Sc. (Econ.)
Senior Lecturer, City of London Polytechnic

Graham & Trotman
A member of the Kluwer Academic Publishers Group
LONDON/DORDRECHT/BOSTON

First published in 1985 by

Graham & Trotman Limited
Sterling House
66 Wilton Road
London SW1V 1DE

Graham & Trotman Inc.
101 Philip Drive
Assinippi Park, Norwell
MA 02061, USA

Reprinted 1989

British Library Cataloguing in Publication Data

Kettell, Brian
Monetary economics
1. Money
I. Title II. Bell, Steven
332.4 HG221

ISBN-13: 978-0-86010-562-6 e-ISBN-13: 978-94-009-4960-7
DOI: 10.1007/ 978-94-009-4960-7

Contents

Series Foreword

The *Banking and Finance Series* has been written for students who are preparing for the Associateship of the Institute of Bankers. The structure of the series follows the syllabus closely. Although the emphasis is on the Institute of Bankers' examinations the series is also relevant to students for other professional examinations such as the different Accountancy Bodies, Chartered Secretaries, Diploma in Public Administration, undergraduate business courses, BTEC, BEC, HND, DMS, Stock Exchange courses, Association of Corporate Treasurers, Institute of Freight Forwarders, Institute of Export.

May 1985

Brian Kettell
Series Editor

Preface

This book has been written for students who are preparing for the Associateship of the Institute of Bankers. The structure of the book follows closely the syllabus for Monetary Economics, but is also relevant for some of the Stage I papers. In addition it is also directly relevant to the Monetary Economics Paper for the Association of Corporate Treasurers.

Although the emphasis has been on the Institute of Bankers examination the book covers the monetary economics courses taught in Advanced Level Economics, and is relevant to students for the finals of other professional examinations such as the different Accountancy Bodies, the Chartered Secretaries, and the Diploma in Public Administration.

Students studying undergraduate monetary economics at universities, polytechnics and colleges of further education will find it gives them a thorough background to many of the key issues currently surrounded with controversy within the profession. Issues such as the views of the "New Classicists" and the debate surrounding "rational expectations" and the role of the Public Sector Borrowing Requirement are introduced. A special section on "overshooting" gives the background to this controversial area. All these issues are treated in a clear, non-technical manner.

The system of monetary control within the United Kingdom has been subject to rapid change. The introduction of the Banking Act, the changing emphasis of monetary targets, the money market intervention system of the Bank of England and many other related issues have completely revolutionised the nature of the banking world (and incidentally have left most of the books on monetary economics completely outdated). In this book, these issues are all treated from the viewpoint of the underlying principles involved. Excessive cluttering up of the underlying themes with detailed discussion of historical developments has been reduced to a minimum, enabling the student to see the wood from the trees.

Particular emphasis is placed on an appreciation of what causes financial markets to change direction. A detailed examination of the factors explaining movements in money market rates and clearing bank base rates is included. The Eurocurrency market tends to be overlooked, or receive a cursory mention in many text books. This text makes it a central theme, in accordance with its keyrole in determining other money market rates. Its importance for recycling the OPEC balance of payments surplus resulting in the current international debt crisis is stressed. The critical relationship between eurocurrency rates spot and forward exchange rates is also emphasised. The determination and importance of foreign exchange rates, including the question of whether the United Kingdom should join the European Monetary System receive a detailed treatment.

May 1985 *Brian Kettell*

Acknowledgements

The author wishes to acknowledge the assistance of Steven Bell, B.Sc (Econ), M.S., Chief Economist and Assistant Director of Morgan Grenfell, who contributed Chapter 6.

The publishers are indebted to the following organisations for permission to reproduce previously published material:

Bank for International Settlements (BIS), Bank of England, Committee of London Clearing Banks, Federal Reserve Bank of New York, Financial Times, Gerrard & National, HMSO, IMF, Longman, Morgan Guaranty Trust Company, OECD, Prentice-Hall Inc.

This book is dedicated by Brian Kettell to his parents.

Chapter 1

The Concept of Money

MONEY – EVOLUTION AND FUNCTIONS

Many of the features of any financial system, irrespective of its stage of development, are taken for granted. We accept them without really thinking about them. Yet if we are to understand their importance we need to analyse precisely what the financial system does, how it works, and then possibly be in a position to say how it will change. Clearly there is nothing more important in the development of any complex financial system than the emergence of money. This is a very *slow* process and the forms of money have changed over time and indeed will change again in the future.

The early stages of commercial exchange consisted of barter, where a farmer of corn might exchange ten bushels of corn for an ox to grind his corn to make bread. Villagers would develop market places, where farmers and craftsmen could come to exchange their produce and gradually "rates of exchange" between various products would become established. The barter system farmer would have to maintain a huge list of exchange rates between his product and many others.

However, this system can be extremely inefficient and protracted. Generally, an individual has first to find the person who can produce the item he wishes to acquire and who must be prepared to swap it at that time after haggling for a mutually agreeable price. How long one may ask does the person who is individually gifted in the construction of artificial wooden legs have to search for a one-legged baker who will supply him with bread in exchange for one of his fine wooden legs? This problem is known as the "double coincidence of wants".

Deterioration, indivisibility and differences in quality of various bartered items make comparison and the setting of common exchange rates between goods, very difficult. The difficulties and inefficiency of the barter system led to the rather radical invention of money, to oil the wheels of the primitive system.

The value of all commodities which enter the sphere of influence of the new common unit of exchange, can now be converted into a price in terms of that unit. We can be justified in an economic sense to call this common unit, whether it be a cow, a shell, or a stone with a hole in it, money because it serves one of the basic functions of money, that of a "*medium of exchange*". It allows the producer of wooden legs to exchange his produce for money from the limbless and use that money to buy bread from the baker. This in turn provides the means for division of labour and specialisation within society thereby conferring enormous benefits.

As it is a standard by which other commodities may be judged and valued, money acts as a "*unit of account*", i.e. a yardstick in which the value of other commodities and services is measured. Consider the complexities and time involved in evaluating purchases of various types of materials for car manufacture and subsequent sales of cars other than in monetary terms. Thus, with a widely accepted "unit of account" markets can develop. Along with markets come prices which in turn provide the "signals" indicating either prices being too high or too low and thereby encouraging resources to move around accordingly. Indeed without true prices markets become singularly inefficient, e.g. as in Eastern Europe.

The units of money received for one's produce or services can be immediately exchanged for goods or they may be held in reserve. In this latter sense, money acts as a "*store of value*" or more accurately "liquid" store of value allowing an individual to overcome the problem of timing differences between receiving payment for goods or services and spending the money.

Thus money allows independence between the timing of receipts and the making of payments. An individual could buy some other assets such as antiques, but if the owner then wished to sell them he would be faced with the trouble of selling and the attendant risk in the amount he received for the antiques. Of course money is just one form in which wealth can be held (building society deposits are another), and this introduces a complexity for a government wishing to measure and control the money supply.

Finally money serves as a *standard for deferred payments and receipts*. Often goods are purchased now with a promise to pay at a later date. An example of this is the case of house purchase via a mortgage. The use of money facilitates this type of transaction. Indeed the ability to pay interest (and earn interest) on money enables units in society with surplus funds (surplus units) to lend money to units who need funds (deficit units). (The way this occurs is developed in Chapter 2.) Thus the development of borrowing and lending with contracts that involved the payment or the receipt of a stated sum of money would not be possible without money. And without borrowing and lending the whole manufacturing and distribution industries would not have evolved as we know them today.

FROM PAPER MONEY TO BANK DEPOSITS

The movement from barter to money in the United Kingdom was greatly facilitated by the introduction of paper money which essentially developed through the intervention of goldsmiths. Goldsmiths – craftsmen who worked with gold – naturally kept very secure safes in which to store their gold. The practice grew up among the public of storing their gold with the goldsmith for safe-keeping. In return, the goldsmith would give the depositor a receipt promising to hand over the gold on demand. If the depositor wished to make a large purchase, he could go to the goldsmith, reclaim his gold, and hand it over to the seller of the goods. The probabilities were that the seller would not require the gold, but would carry it back to the goldsmith for safe-keeping. Clearly, if people knew the goldsmith to be reliable, there was no need to go through the cumbersome and risky business of physically transferring the gold. The buyer need only transfer the goldsmith's receipt to the seller, who could accept it secure in the knowledge that the goldsmith would pay over the gold whenever it was needed. If the seller wished to buy a good from a third party who also knew the goldsmith to be reliable, this transaction too could be effected by passing the goldsmith's receipt from the buyer to the seller. The convenience of using these bits of paper instead of gold is obvious. So the first paper money was a promise to pay on demand so much gold, the promise being made first by goldsmiths and later by banks: As long as these institutions were known to be reliable, such pieces of paper would be "as good as gold". Such paper money was backed by precious metal and was convertible on demand into the metal.

For most transactions, individuals were content to use paper currency: It was soon discovered, therefore, by the goldsmiths that it was not necessary to keep an ounce of gold in the vaults for every claim to an ounce circulating as paper money. It was necessary to keep some gold on hand, because, for some transactions, paper would not do and in addition it was necessary to guard against withdrawals. If an individual wished to make a purchase from a distant place where the goldsmith was not known, he might have to convert his paper into gold and ship the gold. Further, if he was going to save up money for use in the distant future, he might not have perfect confidence in the goldsmith's ability to honour its pledge to redeem the notes in gold at that time. His alternative was to exchange his notes for gold and store the gold until he needed it. For these and other reasons at any one point in time, some holders of notes would be demanding gold in return for their notes. On the other hand, some of the customers would be receiving gold in various transactions and would be wanting to store this gold in the bank for safe-keeping. They would accept promises to pay (i.e. notes) in return. At any one time, therefore, some of the goldsmith's customers would be withdrawing gold, others would be depositing it, and the great majority would be carrying out their transactions using the goldsmith's paper notes without any need or desire to convert them into gold. Thus the goldsmith would be able to issue more money redeemable in gold than he actually had in gold in his vaults.

This would be a profitable thing to do, because the money can be used either to purchase securities that yield a return, or make interest-earning loans to households and firms. Eventually goldsmiths evolved into what we now know of as commercial banks.

The major problem of a fractionally backed currency (i.e. a currency not fully backed by gold) is that of maintaining its convertibility into the precious metal with which it is backed. In the past, the imprudent bank that issued too much paper money found itself unable to redeem its currency in gold when the demand for gold was even slightly higher than usual. This bank would then have to suspend payments, and all holders of its notes would suddenly find them worthless. The prudent bank, which kept a reasonable relation between its note issue and its gold reserve, found that it could meet the normal everyday demand for gold without any trouble. It was always the case with fractionally backed currency, however, that, if all note-holders demanded gold at once, they could not be satisfied. Thus, if ever the public lost confidence and en masse demanded redemption of their currency, the banks would be unable to honour their pledges, and the holders of their notes would lose everything. The history of nineteenth and early twentieth century banking is replete with examples of banks ruined by momentary runs on their cash and gold reserves. When this happened, the bank's depositors and the holders of its notes would find themselves holding worthless pieces of paper.

As time went on, note issue by commercial banks became less common and central banks took over a steadily increasing share of this responsibility. The gold standard was also abolished (this is discussed in detail in Chapter 9). The commercial banks retained the power to create money, but this was no longer done by printing paper money; instead deposit money was created (see Chapter 4). The modern bank deposit is the equivalent of the old bank note: a promise on the bank's behalf to pay out on demand the money of the time. The passing of the bank's note from hand to hand transferred ownership of the claim against the bank: this is now done by means of a cheque, which is merely an order to the bank telling it to transfer from one individual to another its obligation to pay cash. In the modern world the greater proportion of the money supply is the deposit money that is created by commercial banks. The cheque clearing system is described below.

THE CHEQUE CLEARING SYSTEM

One of the basic functions of the clearing banks is the provision of the country's main payments mechanism. Each year hundreds of millions of cheques are handled by the Bankers' Clearing House which also operates the Bank Giro by which payment can be made to any bank account in the United Kingdom. Through a separate limited company, Bankers' Automated Clearing Services, facilities are provided for the transfer of magnetic tapes containing details of customers' transactions. In addition each bank's clearing department handles a considerable volume of items passing between its own branches.

When the recipient of a cheque pays it into his or her own bank, it will be sent through the bankers' clearing house to the bank on which it is drawn. A simple example illustrates this (Figure 1.1). Settlement between the banks takes place when customer B's account is debited. A transfer between the two banks will take place by adjusting the account which they have with the Bank of England. Midland Bank will be better off and Lloyds Banks will be worse off after they have completed the transactions.

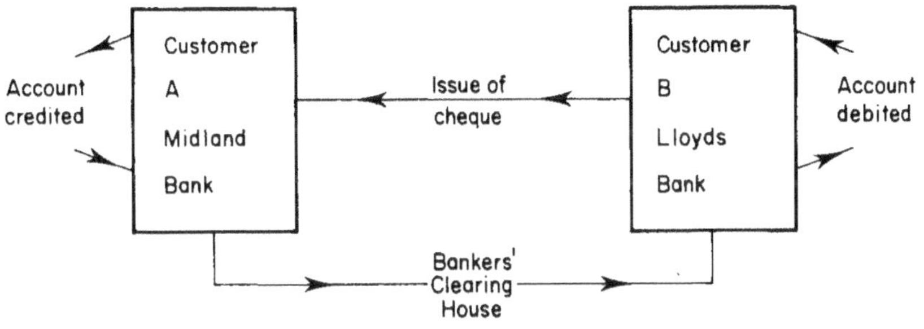

Fig. 1.1

On 9 February 1984 Clearing House Automated Payments Systems (CHAPS) started in London. CHAPS is the 1980s version of the Town Clearing which has handled high-value same-day settlements for inter-bank payments since Queen Victoria's time. Inevitably the messengers who scurry round the City just before cutting off time at 3 p.m. every week day are going to be replaced by the new ring of powerful computers with which the 12 settlement banks and their banker, the Bank of England, communicate with each other.

Each bank transmits and receives payment instructions through a so-called gateway computer, with common software for all. Messages, once accepted by the system as authentic are irrevocable. So CHAPS in effect allows banks to send guaranteed funds to each other for same day settlement.

THE CHARACTERISTICS OF MONEY

The four main characteristics which a commodity which is to serve as money are that it must act as a "medium of exchange"; a "unit of account", a "store of value" and as a "standard for deferred payments".

The particular commodity which is chosen as the unit of currency must fulfil, in order to perform the four functions above in an efficient manner, certain characteristics. In early societies the unit of currency would tend to possess its own innate value through satisfying physical needs (food or clothing), or by enabling one to produce goods or to satisfy psychological needs, e.g. precious or rare stones for jewellery. The basis of innate value is scarcity, in that there is not enough of the particular commodity to satisfy the desires of all the community and for which people are willing to pay a price.

Many commodities possess innate value but only a few are suitable as money. Suitability may be judged by five criteria:

(i) *Durability*. This characteristic is essential. Because of the timing difference between receipt of money and its use for payment the commodity chosen must be capable of surviving the intervening period.

(ii) *Stable supply and demand*. The commodity must maintain a certain level of scarcity in relation to other commodities in the market, otherwise its value might increase if it becomes more scarce, perhaps to such an extent that it renders it impractical, or if its supply increases, it would become worth less and less. This aspect has important applications concerning the price level and inflation.

(iii) *Homogeneity*. Each individual unit of the commodity should be as identical as possible to the next. Otherwise their relative values would differ according to their relative qualities, rendering the unit of currency unreliable because of the scope for fraud.

(iv) *Divisibility*. The commodity should be capable of being broken down into fractional units and equally capable of recombination. This is to enable transactions whose value is less than the value of one unit of the currency to take place. Otherwise such transactions would be impractical for the purchaser would have to buy inappropriately large quantities of the low priced good.

(v) *Portability*. Lastly, the commodity would ideally be of a convenient size and weight for an individual to carry with him between transactions.

Amongst man's choices of units of currency, metals such as gold and silver have stood out as the earliest most popular, permanent, and widespread form of money. Due to their psychological attractiveness, these were in great demand for making ornaments and jewellery. Both silver and gold are durable and their supply and demand is relatively stable; they are in general homogenous, though tests on their purity and quality would often be made. Both could be broken down into smaller units and are subsequently easily portable.

Gold and silver through their inherent value were easily recognised and accepted in many early economies. Once such an ideally suited form of currency was discovered and its use as money became more widespread, it became more and more widely accepted, exhibiting a "band-wagon", effect, as people found themselves, by growing weight of opinion, coerced into accepting that particular commodity as the unit of currency.

The commodity money system, i.e. using commodities and not bank accounts, existed for many thousands of years. It involved, however, the costs of production, transportation and storage of the commodity, all of which could be reduced by the use of non-commodity money and the resources thereby being released being used for the production of goods: i.e. instead of resources being used for gold mining they could be channelled into manufacturing.

With a greater degree of economic centralisation and the opportunity to economise on the above costs of commodity money, the banking system had the incentive to develop. Its development is a huge subject area in itself, but suffice it to say that it resulted in a monetary system where the money stock consists mainly of bank deposits, but with notes and coins in circulation.

These notes and coins, although they have no inherent value are still accepted as legal tender. This is because an authoritative system has developed to enforce its value by controlling and limiting its production (thereby controlling its value by controlling its supply) and by making it extremely difficult to forge. Such "representative money" has legal status conferred on it by the government of the country in which it was created.

As will be seen later, when looking at the monetary statistics, the principal form of money in the United Kingdom is bank deposits. Bank deposits are superior to notes and coins for several reasons. They are more secure and can be easily stored. Large transactions can be easily and cheaply transacted. Indeed with improvements in clearing systems between banks this latter development has become increasingly true.

However it is important to note that not all bank deposits are mediums of exchange. This is true only of those deposits which can be transferred directly in exchange for goods and services – that is current accounts. Banks also accept various other types of deposits where the customer agrees to leave the deposits at the bank for a specified period of time or at least to give adequate notice of withdrawal.

Financial assets have several attributes which might in principle be used as a basis for classification. Among these are:

(a) type of instrument i.e. is it a loan, a security, a deposit, etc

(b) marketability – is it easily sellable, e.g. true for a share but not for a building society deposit

(c) liquidity – what is the period for which an instrument remains in existence, i.e. is the remaining maturity short, medium, long or irredeemable. (The shorter the maturity the greater the liquidity and vice versa)

(d) capital certainty – to what extent can the full amount advanced be repaid.

(e) terms of payment of interest, fixed, variable, optional.

(f) terms of repayment of capital, instalment, fixed or variable

(g) types of record of the transaction, registered, unregistered.

(h) issuing sector – the sector for which the claim is a liability.

LIQUIDITY

However there are not just banks accepting deposits. Other institutions, known as non-bank financial intermediaries (NBFIs) also do so, e.g. building societies. It is important here to draw the line between "money" and "liquidity". An asset can be said to be more liquid the easier that it can be converted into cash (e.g. for use as a medium of exchange) at a known capital value and vice-versa. The less liquid an asset the higher will be the return from holding it in order to compensate the holder for the loss of liquidity. Individuals have a whole spectrum of financial assets and the assets which are most useful as media of exchange tend to be less profitable in terms of stores of value (and vice-versa).

However, it must be stressed that recent financial innovations are increasingly permitting investors to earn interest on deposits and also to write cheques on them. This means that some deposits can now be both stores of value and media of exchange.

The "*liquidity*" of an asset is a complex concept since it involves at least two sets of characteristics. The first is sometimes called the "*marketability*" of an asset, in the sense of the ease with which a holder of it if he needs to sell could obtain the highest price that anyone else is willing to pay. This is basically a matter of transaction costs which will depend on the number of individuals wishing to purchase/sell the asset during any period of time, and on the market organisation for the dissemination of information. The more perfect is a market, the smaller will be the transaction costs incurred in finding the highest bidder for an asset, and the greater will be the liquidity of the asset.

The second aspect of liquidity concerns the "*degree of uncertainty attaching to the price*" at which an asset can be sold. The smaller is that uncertainty, the more liquid is the asset. Uncertainty depends in part on the terms to maturity of an asset.

A popular form of asset is a bond – a security on which interest is paid at a fixed rate and is repaid when due (at its maturity) at face value. The interest rate on a bond varies inversely with the price of an asset. Unfortunately, this statement causes a vast amount of unnecessary confusion. Think of it this way: Paying £1,000 for a flat which you expect to rent for £100 p.a. produces a return of 10% on the money invested. If the rent remains fixed whilst the price of the flat increases then the rate of return will fall. The opposite will happen if the price of the flat decreases. There are a great many financial assets (such as government bonds) the nominal interest rates of which (the fixed £100 rent of the flat) are fixed but the capital values (market price of the flat) are not. So there is an inverse relationship between the price of an asset and its interest rate. Here however we are using the word interest rate as equivalent to "rate of return of investing a sum of money in a given asset". In Chapter 5 we discuss the whole question of interest rate determination in much more detail.

A short-term bond is more liquid than a long-term one, since the price of the former will be altered less by a given change in market interest rates. But the whole state of expectations, which is dependent on the chances of disturbances in particular markets or in the economy in general, helps to determine the liquidity of assets. For example the liquidity of all non-monetary assets will be reduced if there is a high probability that many individuals will want to sell them at the same time.

The existence of inflation does complicate the measurement of the extent to which different financial assets are a good store of value. The more (less) that the return on an asset is positive (i.e. it yields some rate of interest) the more (less) that it is a good store of value.

Many forms of money earn a zero rate of return in cash terms (a situation rapidly changing with increasing financial innovations) and in times of inflation their real return measured in terms of their command over goods and services will be negative. In order to measure the extent to which inflation erodes the purchasing power of money, statisticians have devised what are known as index numbers. These are discussed in more detail in Appendix 1. Chapter 5 describes one technique, index linking of financial assets, now being used in order to try to ensure that inflation fearing investors purchase government debt.

THE QUANTITY THEORY OF MONEY – THE BASIS OF MONETARISM

"Monetarist" economists emphasise that the government's monetary policy (i.e. controlling the supply of money in the economy) is more important for the management of the economy than fiscal policy (i.e. government policy on spending, taxation and borrowing). The fundamental idea behind "monetarism" although there are others which we discuss later, is that there is a close link between the amount of money in the economy and the level of prices. This relationship is based upon the quantity theory of money.

Misuse of the money supply can be illustrated by two spectacularly unstable episodes in economic history.

One involved the infamous German inflation in the years following the First World War. In December 1919, there were about 50 billion marks in circulation in Germany. Four years later, this figure had risen to almost 500,000,000,000 billion marks – or an increase of 10,000,000,000 times! Money became practically worthless and prices skyrocketed. Indeed, money lost its value so quickly that people were anxious to spend whatever money they had as soon as possible, while they could still buy something with it.

The second illustration involves the United States experience in the Depression of the 1930s. Economists are still debating the exact causes of that depression and their relative importance. But it can scarcely be denied that the misbehaviour of the monetary and banking system played a role. As the economy slid down into the depression, the quantity of money fell from $26.2 billion in mid 1929 to $19.2 billion in mid 1933 – or by 27%. By the time Roosevelt became President in 1933, many banks had closed their doors and many depositors had lost everything.

The quantity theory is essentially concerned with the demand for a stock of money in one's portfolio. People wish to hold money primarily to effect transactions in goods, services, and financial assets. In a modern economy we normally use the medium of money because it saves us the extensive costs of search and lengthy arguments of barter transactions. But this implies that, to avoid barter, we must maintain some quantity of money in our portfolio, since sales of goods and purchases are not nicely matched with one another in any given period of time.

The quantity of money we require in our portfolio will depend on many factors. Probably the most important will be the value of transactions concluded during a given time period. Other things being equal, the higher the value of transactions, the larger will be the quantity of money we shall wish to hold. The value of transactions consists of two elements – price and quantity; for a given quantity, the higher the price, the larger the amount of money one would wish to hold (and vice-versa).

Each of us, individually, makes a decision about the quantity of money he will hold in his portfolio. Each person adjusts the stock of money according to the value of the transactions which he wishes or expects to make during the ensuing time period. For any given value of transactions in the economy therefore, we could find the total demand for money by summing the demands of individuals. This gives us the aggregate demand for money.

Let us now assume that the aggregate amount of money demanded is greater than the supply of money that the government has made available (or printed). Using elementary economic analysis one would predict that as individuals desire more money in their portfolios of wealth than they currently have they would achieve this by selling goods in exchange for money and/or forego buying goods.

This will reduce the demand for goods and the price of goods will fall. If the production of physical goods does not change, the only effect will be on the level of prices. As prices diminish so will the demand for money as one's need for transactions balances is that much lower. Thus, when prices have been reduced so that at the lower value of transactions people are, in aggregate, just willing to hold the supply of money made available by the government, the price reductions will stop. Then the demand for money will be just equal to the supply and the system is back in equilibrium at a lower level of prices. So if the demand for money is greater than the supply of money there are forces in the economy which bring the two back together.

One may trace the effects of an excess supply of money in precisely the same way. Imagine that the government prints some extra pound notes and distributes them freely to everyone in the economy. Each of us would then find that he has too much money in his account relative to the value of his transactions. Consequently, he would reduce his money stock by buying goods. This would drive up the price of goods. Thus, the value of transactions would increase until people's demands for money were at such a level that they would be willing to hold the increased stock of money at this new high level of prices. Again there are forces bringing the demand for and supply of money back together.

These ideas underline the simplest version of the quantity theory. To further illustrate this point let us take some simple examples. First we need to define the major actors in the story:

M = Quantity of money in the hands of the public
P = Average level of prices
Q = Quantity of output

Thus PQ = national income measured in money terms. It is assumed here that the quantity of output and the quantity of income are interchangeable terms on the grounds that output (i.e. producing) generates income.

V = income velocity of money, that is, the average number of times that the money stock (M) is spent to buy final output during a year. Specifically, V is defined as being equal to PQ/M. An example will make the understanding of this clearer. Suppose that the money stock is £100 million in a given year. Assume that the national income in the same year is £400 million (PQ). This means that the given money supply, £100 million, has financed spending of £400 million. How is this possible? Well, when you spend money in a shop, the owner then spends it on re-stocking. His supplier in turn uses it to pay his supplier and so on. In this way the same amount of money finances expenditures of a larger amount. The extent to which money is spent in this way is measured by its velocity of circulation. In this example, velocity is equal to 4, i.e. PQ/M = £400 million/£100 million = 4. Thus, as V = PQ/M then rearranging the terms we derive the truism that MV = PQ.

In the hands of classical economists however, this truism became the basis of the quantity theory of money. The quantity theory of money is the proposition that velocity (V) is reasonably stable. Therefore, a change in the quantity of money (M) will cause the money national income (PQ) to change by approximately the same percentage. If, for example, the money stock (M) increases by 20% then classical economists argue that velocity (V) will remain reasonably stable. As a consequence nominal national income will rise by 20%. In addition they argue that over longer time periods output (Q) tends to be fairly fixed, depending on real factors such as the level of the capital stock, structure of the labour force, training and entrepreneurship rather than monetary disturbances. Therefore, the long run effect of a change in M is on P not Q. So MV (£480 million) equals PQ (£480 million) i.e. a 20% increase in the money supply causes prices to rise by 20%.

The success of this theory in predicting economic changes, discussed in more detail in Chapter 6, depends on the extent to which:

(a) the government can control the money supply;
(b) whether V is constant or not;
(c) whether Q is constant or not.

HOW MONEY AFFECTS THE ECONOMY – THE TRANSMISSION MECHANISM

It is not unreasonable to expect, that, since one of the main functions of money is to facilitate transactions, the desired amount of money balances will vary proportionally with the level of transactions, and therefore, with the level of income. If this relationship is fairly stable, say, one holds 10% of income on the *average* of any single time period in the form of money balances as opposed to any other type of assets, then if something causes these balances to increase then one will restore that 10% level by spending. As already discussed the fact that there is a stable relationship between money balances held by people and the level of their income is one of the key assumptions of the Quantity Theory. A different way of seeing this mechanism in action is to think of what you would do if a rich aunt left you £10,000 in her will (yes, I know it is a silly example but it works!). Would you keep £10,000 in the bank, building society or cash? Perhaps you would hold some of your legacy in one of these forms, but perhaps you would spend a part of it. And this is the point. Holding £10,000 in money balances does not provide the same pleasure or services as holding £9,000 in money balances and £1,000 in the form of new clothes, a new stereo set and a long holiday. In other words the £10,000 was too much money in the sense that it was too much of a particular asset. Now money is instantly transformed into goods and services. There is a perfect degree of substitutability between money and other things. This is another important aspect of the Quantity Theory. If money is substitutable for other goods then increases or decreases in the quantity of money are bound to be reflected in the demand for goods. Since on a quarter to quarter basis output of goods and services is unlikely to vary significantly, then these increases or decreases in demand will be reflected on changes in prices.

There is however a group of economists who argue that money has its main influence not on goods but on financial assets only. So the monetary transmission mechanism is the same as that described for the Quantity Theory approach but with the difference that people may well "buy" or "sell" (hold less) of other financial assets. This approach is called the *Keynesian Theory of the transmission mechanism* (after the economist J. M. Keynes).

If we have a series of goods which are close substitutes then increasing/decreasing the quantity of one good will affect the prices of the rest, as consumers shift their purchasers from one good to the other. To appreciate this point it is important to remember that the return on an asset varies inversely with its price (see p. 8 and App. 1 of Chap. 5).

There are of course a lot of assets, with fixed capital and interest rate values. A deposit with a building society of £100 will yield say 10% p.a. and since its capital value is fixed so is the rate of return – unless of course the building society changes the interest it pays its depositors.

Now if demand for a certain asset increases then there will be a downward pressure on the rate of return. If building societies are bulging with deposits they are *more* likely to *decrease* interest rates than increase them. If on the other hand the demand for, say, local authority bonds decreases then this will lead to an *upward* pressure on interest rates. So you can see what matters here is the differentials between the yields of different assets and the speed by which the interest rates (i.e. the rates of return) are adjusted. But interest rates are not only returns for investors, they are also costs for borrowers. So increases in the supply of money (the building society example) leading to a shift to other financial assets will also lead to a downward pressure on interest rates. Now certain classes of expenditure such as business investment, consumer spending on durables (and especially on housing) are fairly interest-rate elastic, i.e. they respond quickly to changes in interest rates. So, the argument here is that levels of aggregate demand and expenditure can be affected by changing the quantities of money and therefore by affecting interest rates which in their turn affect expenditures. Thus as the money supply rises Keynesians argue, returns on financial assets alter first, before expenditures as the monetarists claim.

We can, *crudely*, summarise the "transmission mechanism" of the Keynesian and Quantity Theory (sometimes called "Monetarist Approach") approaches as follows:

Keynesian

Changes in quantity of money → interest rate changes → changes in the level of expenditures which are affected by changes in interest rate.

Monetarist

Changes in the quantity of money → changes in expenditures (with likely effects on the price level especially in the short run).

You can see that there is an extra "link" in the Keynesian mechanism. If interest rates do not respond to changes in the quantity of money or if aggregate demand does not respond to changes in interest rates then varying the quantity of money will not have much effect on either prices or the level of aggregate demand. This is a very different view from that of the monetarists.

So whether variations in the quantity of money have their effects principally upon goods or financial assets depends on the respective degrees of substitutability. Monetarists consider money to be a unique financial asset distinguished by its ability to serve as the medium of exchange. Keynesians tend to view money as just another financial asset and see the key distinction between financial assets in general and goods. Chapter 6 discusses these views in much more detail.

THE MEASUREMENT OF THE MONEY SUPPLY

The money supply has assumed a much greater importance in macroeconomic policy in recent years. A similar trend has occurred in many countries and it has culminated in several countries, including the United Kingdom, in publicly announcing declared targets for monetary growth. The monetary aggregates are seen by financial markets as a barometer of the success of government financial policy and markets react if they suspect that the monetary policy is inconsistent with the declared target. The instruments through which monetary policy is pursued, such as interest rates and controls on the banking system are discussed further in Chapters 4 and 7.

In order to control a monetary aggregate it is necessary, naturally, to first define what exactly is money. This might, at first sight, seem a simple enough concept but in practice precise definition of exactly what constitutes "money" gives rise to certain difficulties. The most widely used criterion for choosing the appropriate definition of money is as a medium of exchange, that is to say as a generally accepted means of payment for goods and services, but there is considerable room for debate as to whether or not a particular financial asset performs this function. Moreover some financial assets such as bank time deposits are considered by some economists to be close substitutes for the media of exchange even if they cannot be used directly to finance transactions. No single definition of money therefore meets all requirements.

The authorities measure money in a number of ways. Very few people today would argue that the right measure is simply the notes which the Bank of England prints and the coins which it mints. The reason is that what most people use as money does not stop at the currency in circulation. Most of us are as happy to pay the bill at the Sainsbury's check-out with a cheque as with cash. Indeed, most transactions which take place in the economy are paid for not in cash (whatever your window cleaner thinks) but by transferring claims on the banks. That includes writing cheques.

The UK authorities monitor seven measures of the money supply: M_0, M_1, M_2, £M_3, M_3, Private Sector Liquidity (1) and Private Sector Liquidity (2). Before the March 1984 budget M_1, £M_3 and PSL_2 were officially targeted, i.e. the government announces desired rates of increase. The 1984 budget however introduced a new targeted monetary aggregate, M_0. At the same time £M_3 was also reaffirmed as being targeted. M_1 and PSL_2 were no longer to be officially targeted. However, in interpreting the behaviour of M_0 and £M_3 attention is still to be paid to other monetary indicators, in particular M_2 and PSL_2, interest rates and the exchange rate.

Domestic Credit Expansion (DCE) a monetary measure which was used in the fixed exchange rate era is discussed on pp. 25–26.

M_0

M_0 comprises notes and coins, both in circulation with the public and held in banks' tills, and banks' operational balances held with the Bank of England (see Table 1.1).

The reason why greater weight is being given to narrow monetary aggregates reflects recent experience. For although broad measures of money have frequently been subject to distortion and differences of interpretation, the Chancellor of the Exchequer, Nigel Lawson, in his 1983 Mansion House speech

Table 1.1
MO, the Wide Monetary Base

£ million

	Notes and coin in circulation outside the Bank of England				Bankers' deposits with Banking Department		Notes and coin in circulation outside the Bank of England		Bankers' operational deposits with the Banking Department	MO (Wide monetary base)	
	In circulation with the public		Held by banks (till money)								
	Unadjusted	Seasonally adjusted	Unadjusted	Seasonally adjusted	Operational deposits	Cash ratio deposits	Unadjusted	Seasonally adjusted		Unadjusted	Seasonally adjusted
	Amount outstanding						Average amount outstanding in month ended				
1982											
Jun 16	10,553	10,599	1,096	1,110	200	393	11,739	11,770	216	11,955	11,986
Jul 21	10,867	10,630	1,210	1,124	211	393	11,878	11,817	171	12,049	11,988
Aug 18	10,750	10,659	1,178	1,142	121	393	11,985	11,829	162	12,147	11,991
Sep 15	10,788	10,760	1,125	1,125	274	391	11,992	11,942	196	12,188	12,138
Oct 20	10,702	10,769	1,126	1,143	230	391	11,888	12,005	172	12,060	12,177
Nov 17	10,760	10,831	1,114	1,132	204	436	11,879	12,048	221	12,100	12,269
Dec 8	11,196	10,930	1,190	1,113	211	436	12,207	12,140	164	12,371	12,304
1983											
Jan 19	10,825	10,996	1,152	1,164	135	436	12,647	12,232	178	12,825	12,410
Feb 16	10,965	11,084	1,077	1,136	101	436	11,999	12,255	145	12,144	12,400
Mar 16	11,103	11,172	1,047	1,129	192	436	12,133	12,359	176	12,309	12,535
Apr 20	11,194	11,241	1,084	1,085	137	435	12,424	12,436	205	12,629	12,641
May 18	11,263	11,325	1,113	1,135	96	468	12,411	12,510	131	12,542	12,641
Jun 15	11,328	11,374	1,137	1,155	223	468	12,556	12,589	149	12,705	12,738
Jul 20	11,601	11,362	1,250	1,164	118	468	12,669	12,619	105	12,774	12,724
Aug 17	11,507	11,407	1,207	1,167	148	468	12,772	12,599	162	12,934	12,761
Sep 21	11,477	11,489	1,196	1,207	149	468	12,773	12,749	154	12,927	12,903
Oct 19	11,473	11,545	1,177	1,191	135	468	12,685	12,810	166	12,851	12,976
Nov 16	11,531	11,607	1,157	1,175	199	500	12,689	12,867	171	12,860	13,038
Dec 14	12,119	11,694	1,365	1,249	150	500	13,106	12,959	155	13,261	13,114
1984											
Jan 18	11,467	11,636	1,221	1,230	111	500	13,345	12,915	222	13,567	13,137
Feb 15	11,531	11,653	1,170	1,227	278	500	12,686	12,955	202	12,888	13,157
Mar 21	11,641	11,711	1,167	1,247	232	500	12,791	13,027	204	12,995	13,231
Apr 18	12,044	11,917	1,236	1,161	154	500	13,023	13,085	157	13,180	13,242
May 16	11,834	11,863	1,201	1,208	159	533	13,157	13,157	138	13,295	13,295
Jun 20	11,941	11,982	1,222	1,238	204	533	13,202	13,260	179	13,381	13,439

Source: Bank of England, *Quarterly Bulletin* (June 1984).
Reproduced by kind permission of the Bank of England.

pointed out that "it was the surge in the narrow aggregates in 1977 which was followed by the surge in inflation in 1979. And the deceleration in the growth of narrow money in 1979 and 1980 preceded the recent decline in inflation".

The other apparent reason put forward by the Chancellor for focusing on narrow money aggregates is because they "respond unambiguously to changes in short-term interest rates – with the broader measures much depends on the structure of rates". Empirical evidence suggests that the response of M_0 to interest rates changes is quite quick. So if interest rates rise M_0 falls and vice versa. With other measures such as £M_3 if the interest rates rise this could attract people to hold more of it.

M_1

M_1 is defined as notes and coins in circulation with the public plus private sector sterling current accounts (sight deposits). This is "money" in its most immediate form, an asset which can be readily exchanged for goods and services.

To arrive at an accurate figure for notes and current accounts held by the *public* two adjustments must be made in calculating M_1. First any inter-bank deposits are netted out: banks sometimes hold deposits with other banks and these are excluded. Secondly the double counting effect of *items of transit* must be eliminated. For instance, consider a cheque in the course of collection drawn on *Bank A*, transferred to a customer of Bank B, and presented for payment by Bank B; it may have been debited by Bank A, but not yet credited by Bank B.

Such a transaction would understate the volume of deposits or, in the case of overdrawn or loan accounts, overstate the volume of bank advances. In dealing with the net credit *minus* debit flow of items in transit, the Bank of England adopts the convention of deducting 60% from deposits and adding the remaining 40% to bank advances. M_1 also includes some non-current account deposits which cannot be used as a means of payment. These are large value (or wholesale) deposits held with banks mainly by companies and other large organisations. Though these deposits can be withdrawn at any time, they earn a good rate of interest and are held mainly as short-term investments rather than as "transactions balances".

From the point of view of monetary control the problem with M_1 is the growing element of it now accounted for by these interest-bearing sight deposits – over 25% of the total. As a result the authorities have continued searching for a monetary aggregate which accurately reflects transaction balances, i.e. spending power. This search culminated in M_0 being officially targeted and M_1 being relegated (see Table 1.2).

M_2 (Transaction balances)

M_2 includes cash in circulation with the public plus current account deposits and other deposits of less than £100,000 that can be withdrawn in less than one month held by the private sector with the banks (see Table 1.3). M_2 is a

Table 1.2
Money Stock
Amount outstanding at end of period

			UK private sector sterling sight deposits								
		Notes and coin in circulation with public	*Non-interest-bearing*	*60% of transit item*	*Interest-bearing*	*Total (adjusted for transit items)*	*Money stock M_1*	*UK private sector sterling time deposits*	*Money stock sterling M_3*	*UK private sector deposits in other currencies*	*Money stock M_3*
Unadjusted		1	2	3	4	5	6	7	8	9	10
1978	1	7,803	14,452	1,506	3,358	16,304	24,107	20,913	45,020	4,469	49,489
	2	8,084	14,631	1,510	3,348	16,469	24,553	22,093	46,646	5,123	51,769
	3	8,329	15,574	1,459	3,406	17,521	25,850	22,308	48,158	4,862	53,020
	4	8,733	16,122	1,462	3,971	18,631	27,364	23,215	50,579	4,799	55,378
1979	1	8,944	16,044	1,602	3,913	18,355	27,299	23,027	50,326	4,585	54,911
	2	9,065	16,605	1,840	3,822	18,587	27,652	25,197	52,849	5,043	57,892
	3	9,289	17,172	1,776	4,042	19,438	28,727	25,886	54,613	4,737	59,350
	4	9,511	17,706	1,680	4,319	20,345	29,856	27,374	57,230	5,202	62,432
1980	1	9,498	17,380	2,231	4,332	19,481	28,979	27,885	56,864	5,607	62,471
	2	9,568	17,508	2,084	4,521	19,945	29,513	31,503	61,016	5,604	66,620
	3	9,614	17,474	1,784	4,263	19,953	29,567	33,956	63,523	5,666	69,189
	4	10,239	18,221	2,003	4,587	20,805	31,044	36,766	67,810	6,189	73,999
1981	1	9,920	18,927	2,084	4,678	21,521	31,441	35,730	67,171	7,847	75,018
	2	10,008	19,494	1,970	5,007	22,531	32,539	38,810	71,349	9,564	80,913
	3	10,235	19,284	1,945	5,516	22,855	33,090	41,206	74,296	11,277	85,573
	4	10,824	19,118	2,077	6,587	23,628	34,452	42,704	77,156	9,872	87,028
		10,767	19,841	2,060	7,985	25,766	36,533	48,060	84,593	9,849	94,442
1982	1	10,355	19,745	2,038	8,279	25,986	36,341	47,964	84,305	10,384	94,689
	2	10,477	19,981	1,655	8,458	26,784	37,261	50,086	87,347	11,066	98,413
	3	10,748	20,845	2,047	8,659	27,457	38,205	50,671	88,876	11,765	100,641
	4	11,228	21,701	2,263	9,998	29,436	40,664	51,459	92,123	12,621	104,744
1983	1	11,774	22,428	2,803	10,308	29,933	41,707	52,387	94,094	13,566	107,660
		11,769	22,436	2,801	10,320	29,955	41,724	52,475	94,199	13,838	108,037
	2	11,402	22,385	2,210	11,247	31,422	42,824	54,718	97,542	13,353	110,895
	3	11,623	23,011	2,555	11,186	31,642	43,265	55,244	98,509	14,164	112,673
	4	11,906	23,919	2,297	11,700	33,322	45,228	56,632	101,860	16,263	118,123
1984	1	12,036	24,216	2,657	13,309	34,868	46,904	55,043	101,947	17,151	119,098

* Note that £M_3 and M_3 were redefined in March 1984.

Source: Bank of England, *Quarterly Bulletin* (June 1984).
Reproduced by kind permission of the Bank of England.

Table 1.3
Transactions Balances and Components of M_2

£ millions: *not seasonally adjusted*

	Notes and coin in circulation with public	*UK private sector sterling non-interest-bearing sight deposits with banks*	*Non-interest-bearing M_1 (columns 1 + 2)*	*Other UK private sector sterling retail deposits with banks*	*UK private sector retail shares and deposits with building societies*	*National Savings Bank ordinary account*	*M_2 (columns 3 + 4 + 5 + 6)*	*Public sector sterling retail deposits with banks*	*Overseas sterling retail deposits with banks*
	1	2	3	4	5	6	7	8	9
At mid-month									
1982 Sept. 15	10,788	17,355	28,143	28,265	46,496	1,728	104,632	740	2,436
Oct. 20	10,702	18,829	29,531	28,306	46,941	1,721	106,499	1,118	2,521
Nov. 17	10,760	17,886	28,646	28,391	47,367	1,763	106,167	936	2,504
Dec. 8	11,196	18,313	29,509	28,174	48,019	1,740	107,442	850	2,524
1983 Jan. 19	10,825	17,539	28,364	28,703	48,484	1,709	107,260	995	2,392
Feb. 16	10,965	17,327	28,292	28,784	48,791	1,773	107,640	1,071	2,642
Mar. 16	11,103	17,962	29,065	29,216	49,209	1,740	109,230	1,024	2,614
Apr. 20	11,194	18,609	29.803	29,591	49,580	1,753	110,727	1,169	2,620
May 18	11,263	18,415	29,678	29.903	49,846	1,769	111,196	998	2,738
June 15	11,328	18,564	29,892	30,259	50,389	1,751	112,291	1,160	2,637
July 20	11,601	18,978	30,579	30,512	50,546	1,749	113,386	1,193	2,741
Aug. 17	11,507	18,785	30,292	30,360	50,458	1,729	112,839	949	2,721
Sept. 21	11,477	18,876	30,353	30,176	50,672	1,742	112,943	864	2,732
Oct. 19	11,473	19,369	30,842	30,066	51,001	1,742	113,651	935	2,794
Nov. 16	11,531	19,264	30,795	30,089	51,200	1,745	113,829	1,045	2,669
	11,531	19,264	30,795	30,847	51,200	1,745	114,587	1,045	2,996
Dec. 14	12,119	19,990	32,109	30,218	53,920	1,750	117,997	899	2,999
1984 Jan. 18	11,467	19,319	30,786	30,340	55,503	1,765	118,394	1,072	3,124
Feb. 15	11,531	19,017	30,548	30,034	56,070	1,777	118,429	962	3,082

Source: Bank of England, *Quarterly Bulletin* (March 1984).

"new" monetary aggregate introduced by the Bank of England in 1982. M_2 differs from M_1 in two main ways which are designed to make M_2 a better measure of money held as transactions balances. First, wholesale sight deposits are excluded from M_2; as noted above these deposits are thought to be held more as short-term investments than as transactions balances.

Secondly, M_2 includes bank deposits up to £100,000 which, though they cannot be withdrawn immediately, can be withdrawn with little delay. This inclusion reflects the view that such deposits are very convenient for making transactions with.

The reason for excluding deposits of £100,000 and over is that most of these wholesale deposits are held mainly as investments. Deposits which can only be withdrawn after one month or longer are excluded because of the delay before they can be converted into the means of payment.

A weakness of M_2 is that it only includes bank deposits and does not cover deposits with building societies and other institutions that can be withdrawn swiftly.

Sterling M_3*

Sterling M_3 includes cash in circulation with the public together with all sterling deposits held by UK residents in the private sector with banks (note that sterling certificates of deposit, defined on page 85, are included as time deposits). Sterling M_3 is a "wider" aggregate than either M_1 or M_2 since it includes all types of sterling bank deposits held by UK residents. As we shall see, the authorities have considered sterling M_3 to be a particularly important aggregate in recent years.

M_3. This equals sterling M_3 plus all deposits held by UK residents in other currencies with UK banks (see Table 1.2).

Opinions differ as to which of the published monetary aggregates should be the main focus of money supply policy.

Those who believe that the medium of exchange concept of "money" is the most useful will probably attribute the greatest significance to M_0 or M_1. But the dividing line between "money" as a liquid asset available for potential future use is not a clear one, especially in the British system in which cheques can in effect be drawn on seven-day deposit accounts with only a minimal loss of interest, if any at all.

For a large part of the late 1970s and early 1980s the monetary authorities concentrated on controlling £M_3 as a means of reducing inflation. However, due to measuring difficulties, £M_3 became an increasingly unreliable indicator of "liquidity", i.e. potential spending power within the economy, and the authorities became increasingly doubtful about its reliability as an indicator of future trends in inflation.

*Prior to February 1984, Sterling M_3 included public sector deposits with UK banks.

One problem was that there was no clear economic distinction between certain assets included in £M_3 and some which were not. A three months certificate of deposit was included in £M_3 but a three months Treasury bill was not. In addition £M_3 became very sensitive to the banks' share of the home mortgage market. As bank lending for mortgages rose so did £M_3 as the banks bid for deposits to finance their bank lending but building society deposits and lending were moving in an opposite direction since individuals were not taking out building society mortgages and this was not reflected in £M_3. In addition as will be seen in later chapters, the behaviour of £M_3 was also distorted by the "corsets" imposed for three periods between 1973 and 1980 and the relaxation of exchange controls in 1979.

Partly for these reasons two new monetary aggregates were introduced in July 1980, Private Sector Liquidity 1 (PSL_1) and Private Sector Liquidity 2 (PSL_2). *PSL_1* equals the private sector's share of £M_3, i.e. public sector deposits are excluded, plus the private sector's holdings of other money marked instruments. PSL_1 includes "money" other money-market instruments and certificates of tax deposit. The second, wider, measure is labelled *PSL_2*. In addition to the wholesale items in PSL_1, it includes what might be described as retail liquidity of the personal sector in the form of more liquid building society shares and deposits and other similar forms of liquid savings instruments (see Table 1.4). The detailed components of PSL_1 and PSL_2 are broken down, by blocks, below:

(1) "Money"

Notes and coin in circulation	
Sterling bank deposits:	Sight
	Time
	Certificates of deposit

Notes and coins held by the public are the most liquid of all assets, with sight deposits with banks close behind. These two items comprise M_1. But the first block – "money" – also includes certificates of deposit, and time deposits apart from those of more than two years' original maturity (the only maturity breakdown available). The total of the "money" block thus differs from the usual wider measure of the money stock – sterling M_3.

(2) "Other money-market instruments"

These are defined in detail in Chapter 2 and comprise:

Treasury bills
Bank bills
Deposits with local authorities
Deposits with finance houses
TOTAL (GROSS)
less: Finance houses' holdings of "money"
Finance houses' holdings of other money-market instruments
TOTAL (NET)

This block includes other types of deposits held by persons and companies, including deposits with finance houses and local authorities, together with some negotiable paper with under one year of original maturity held predominantly by the corporate sector.

(3) Certificates of tax deposit

Certificates of tax deposit (CTD)
less: Holdings by building societies
TOTAL (NET)

CTDs are normally bought by companies against a known future tax liability, but provided there are continuing tax liabilities, a company's decision on surrendering them will be affected by relative interest rates in the same way as would its use of other liquid assets to meet the tax bill. On the other hand, although CTDs can be encashed on demand, there are substantial interest penalties, unless they are surrendered in payment of tax.

(4) Savings deposits and securities

These comprise:

Shares and deposits with building societies
Deposits with trustee savings banks
Deposits with the National Savings Bank
National savings securities
TOTAL (GROSS)
less: Savings institutions' holdings of "money"
Savings institutions' holdings of other money-market instruments
Building societies' deposits with other savings institutions
TOTAL (NET)

This block contains deposits with savings institutions, and certain national savings securities. These are predominantly held by persons. Building society shares and deposits are about one and a half times as large as personal bank deposits and are overwhelmingly the most important constituent of this block. Deposits with trustee savings banks (new department and ordinary accounts) and ordinary investment accounts with the National Savings Bank are also included. National savings securities comprise British savings bonds, premium bonds, and savings stamps and gift tokens. As with the previous block, deductions from the gross total are needed to avoid double counting. Savings institutions holdings of notes and coin, bank deposits and other money-market instruments are deducted, as are building society deposits with other savings institutions, to give the net total.

The UK monetary aggregates and the relationship between them are illustrated in Table 1.5 and Figure 1.2.

Table 1.4
Private Sector Liquidity, and Other Deposits

£ millions; percentages in italics

	Sterling M_3 less deposits of over 2 years original maturity and all public sector deposits		*Other money-market instruments*				*Savings institution deposits and securities*							
			Total bills	*Treasury bills*	*Bank with local authorities*	*Deposits*	*Total (net)*		*Building society shares, deposits and CDs*		*Trustee savings bank deposits*		*National savings deposits and securities*	
	Unadjusted	*Seasonally adjusted*					*Unadjusted*	*Seasonally adjusted*	*Unadjusted*	*Seasonally adjusted*	*Unadjusted*	*Seasonally adjusted*	*Unadjusted*	*Seasonally adjusted*
	1	2	3	4	5	6	7	8	9	10	11	12	13	14
Amounts outstanding														
At mid-month														
1983 Dec. 8	88,121	88,139	2,671	205	400	2,066	53,789	53,789	51,420	51,420			7,138	
1983 Jan. 19	88,476	88,723	2,541	196	370	1,975	55,181	54,998	52,088	51,905			7,276	
Feb. 16	88,284	89,314	2,654	267	328	2,059	56,349	56,404	52,391	52,446			7,473	
Mar. 16	88,804	90,371	2,783	272	440	2,071	57,268	57,355	52,983	53,070			7,471	
Apr. 20	91,677	92,012	3,295	261	717	2,317	58,091	58,249	53,571	53,729			7,518	
May 18	92,174	92,539	3,075	287	394	2,394	58,617	58,989	53,945	54,317			7,572	
June 15	93,368	93,748	3,090	305	583	2,202	59,547	59,474	54,987	54,914			7,595	
July 20	94,876	94,317	3,067	354	793	1,920	60,559	60,392	56,151	55,984			7,625	
Aug. 17	95,309	94,678	3,258	346	923	1,989	60,925	61,059	56,704	56,838			7,639	
Sept. 21	95,425	94,648	3,126	346	699	2,081	61,309	61,518	57,237	57,446			7,731	
Oct. 19	96,639	95,812	3,097	296	615	2,186	61,539	61,865	57,887	58,213			7,787	
Nov. 16	96,421	96,000	2,982	294	643	2,045	61,735	62,335	58,531	59,131			7,848	
Dec. 14	98,315	97,616	2,872	263	672	1,937	62,674	62,674	59,847	59,847			7,903	
1984 Jan. 18	97,746	97,848	2,729	273	474	1,982	64,405	64,247	61,330	61,172			7,795	
Feb. 15	97,011	97,947	2,678	313	363	2,002	66,150	66,310	62,408	62,568			8,121	

Source: Bank of England, *Quarterly Bulletins* (March 1984).
Reproduced by kind permission of the Bank of England.

Savings institution deposits and securities continued		*Certificates of tax deposit*			*PSL₁*	*PSL₂*	*Other shares and deposits with building societies*			
less *savings institutions holdings of liquid assets*		*Issues net of surrenders*		*Column 18* less *building society holdings*	*(columns 2 + 3 + 18)*	*(columns 2 + 3 + 8 + 19)*	*Total*	*Term shares with withdrawal facilities*	*Term shares without withdrawal facilities*	*SAYE deposits with building societies*
Unadjusted	*Seasonally adjusted*	*Unadjusted*	*Seasonally adjusted*	*Seasonally adjusted*	*Seasonally adjusted*	*Seasonally adjusted*				
15	16	17	18	19	20	21	22	23	24	25
4,769		2,246	2,063	1,818	92,873	146,417	15,839			
4,183		2,093	2,061	1,875	93,325	148,137	16,208			
3,515		2,012	2,183	1,999	94,151	150,371	16,352			
3,186		2,107	2,305	2,123	95,459	152,632	16,449			
2,998		2,183	2,305	2,123	97,612	155,679	16,491	10,666	5,556	269
2,900		2,156	2,253	2,071	97,867	156,674	16,505	10,776	5,458	271
3,035		2,119	2,135	1,953	98,973	158,265	16,519	10,849	5,397	273
3,217		2,039	1,979	1,797	99,363	159,573	16,633	10,997	5,361	275
3,418		1,966	1,929	1,747	99,865	160,742	16,174	11,082	5,356	276
3,659		2,033	1,943	1,742	99,717	161,034	17,246	11,534	5,433	279
4,135		2,209	2,067	1,849	100,976	162,623	17,804	12,063	5,461	280
4,644		2,248	2,147	1,915	101,129	163,232	18,241	12,505	5,452	284
5,076		2,254	2,096	1,843	102,584	165,005	18,556	12,824	5,444	288
4,900		2,149	2,162	2,040	102,739	166,864	18,740	13,042	5,408	290
4,379		1,798	2,035	1,892	102,660	168,827	18,880			

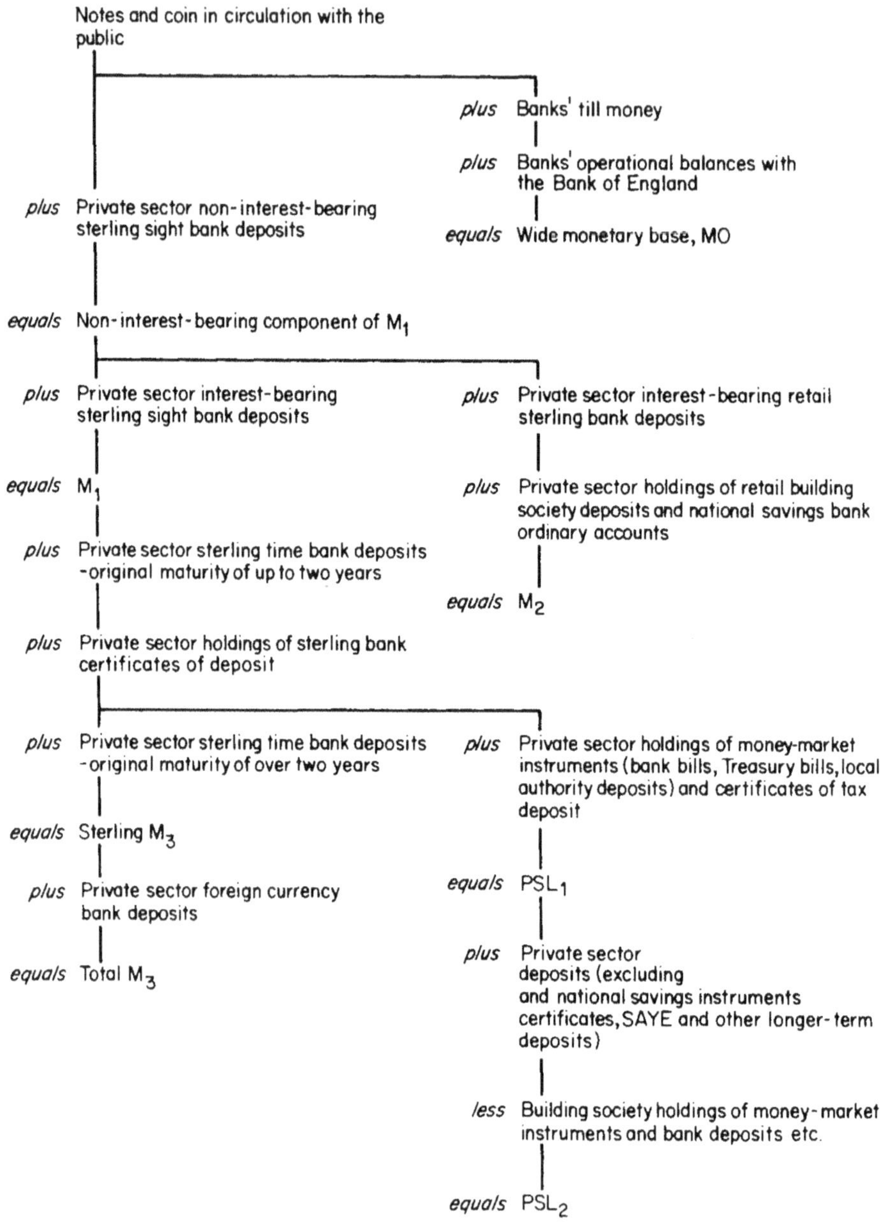

Fig. 1.2 Relationships among the monetary and liquidity aggregates and their components

Source: Bank of England, Quarterly Bulletin (March 1984)
Reproduced by kind permission of the Bank of England.

Table 1.5
The UK Monetary Aggregates

	M1	*M2*	*£M3 (1)*	*PSL1*	*PSL2*
A. Notes and coin	X	X	X	X	X
B. UK private sector bank deposits					
1. Maturity and interest					
(a) Non-interest bearing sight deposits	X	X	X	X	X
(b) Interest bearing checkable deposits	X	X	X	X	X
(c) Other interest bearing sight deposits	X		X	X	X
(d) Time deposits of less than one month (2)		X	X	X	X
(e) Time deposits of one month to two years (2)			X	X	X
(f) Time deposits of over two years (2)			X		
2. Size of deposit					
(a) Less than £100,000	X	X	X	X	X
(b) £100,000 and over	X		X	X	X
C. Other money market instruments (3)				X	X
D. Savings deposits and securities (4)					X

(1) M3 is the same as £M3, but includes foreign currency deposits of UK non-bank residents
(2) Including certificates of deposit
(3) Treasury bills, certificates of tax deposit, bank bills, and deposits with local authorities
(4) Shares and deposits with building societies, National Savings Bank deposits, and National Savings securities, excluding all assets not realisable within a year without significant loss.

DOMESTIC CREDIT EXPANSION

One of the problems with interpreting movements in the money supply is that if there is a large amount of sterling going overseas this will reduce measured money. Yet this is hardly a sign of a tightening of monetary conditions and far from signalling a reduction in inflation may well reflect fears of rising inflation.

In an attempt to abstract from external influences on the money supply, the IMF developed a concept known as domestic credit expansion (DCE). This is the government's fiscal deficits minus sales of public sector debt outside the banks plus bank lending in sterling to residents and non-residents alike. Or, equivalently, DCE equals the change in the money supply plus (minus) the balance of payments surplus (deficit) of the non-bank private sectors. If DCE is expanding fast but the money supply is not sterling must be draining away across the foreign exchanges.

When exchange rates are floating the Bank of England is not buying or selling sterling on the foreign exchanges. In this case the scope for a net inflow or outflow is more limited and the usefulness of DCE is diminished. However, under fixed exchange rates DCE is a rival to the quantity of money as an indicator of monetary ease or stringency. In his famous "letter of intent" in 1970 the Chancellor of the Exchequer affirmed that:

> "It is the Government's policy to ensure that the quarter by quarter course of domestic credit expansion as a whole, and of the Central Government borrowing requirement within it, is consistent with the intended result for the year as a whole and to take action as appropriate to this end."

And for the financial year ending in March 1970 the Chancellor's objective was to limit the DCE to not more than £400 million (compared with about £1,200 million in the financial year 1968–69).

The basic idea is that a DCE rule will give rise to a discipline that reflects the external balance just as the old gold standard system was supposed to have done. (See Chapter 10 for a discussion of the gold standard.) Suppose that the economy is nicely in equilibrium with stable prices and a balance of payments deficit of zero, and then imagine that the money stock is increased. People will spend more and so suck in more imports and export fewer goods, the balance of payments will turn to a deficit of, say, £100 million. Under a fixed exchange rate this deficit is financed by the Bank of England selling foreign currency and buying sterling. For a given DCE this will mean a reduction of £100 million in the money supply. A lower money supply depresses domestic demand reducing imports and increasing the scope for exports. In this way the deficit on the balance of payments is eliminated.

Domestic Credit Expansion as a measure of monetary ease or stringency is only valid under a fixed exchange rate system. As the United Kingdom has increasingly permitted the exchange to be flexible a DCE rule has become increasingly irrelevant.

A KEY ISSUE IN MONETARY THEORY

Before describing the instruments used for controlling monetary policy which we do later in the book, it is necessary to state a key issue of monetary theory. This is that if the authorities seek to fix the price of a commodity they cannot control the quantity of that product which is produced. Similarly, if the authorities wish to control the quantity of a product on any particular market they thereby lose control over the price at which that commodity is traded. Some simplified examples will make this clear.

If the authorities wish to control the price of money (the interest rate) then it cannot control the amount of money it creates. Assume that the interest rate which the government wishes to establish in the money markets is 15% and that the money supply and the money demand are equal. (At Point 0 in Figure 1.3).

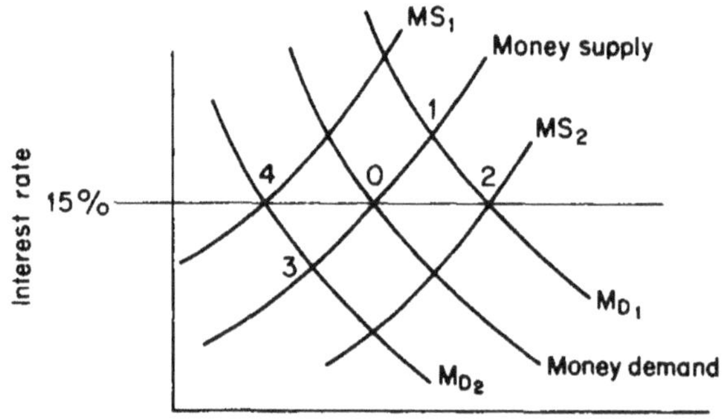

Fig. 1.3

However, now assume (for some reason) that the demand for money rises to, say, M_{D_1}. If the authorities did nothing, interest rates would rise as demand is greater than supply (Point 1).

However, the authorities do not wish interest rates to increase and so in order to accommodate the extra demand they increase the money supply to MS_2 thereby bringing interest rates back down again (Point 2). Again assume that the demand for money falls to M_{D_2} then again assuming that the authorities do nothing, interest rates will fall to Point 3. However, this is undesirable for the authorities wish interest rates to remain at 15%. The only way they can achieve this is by reducing the money supply to Point 4 thereby bringing interest rates back up again.

Conclusion. If the authorities seek to fix interest rates they lose control over the money supply.

Now let us examine the situation where the authorities wish to control the money supply at some level, say £1000 million over some time period.

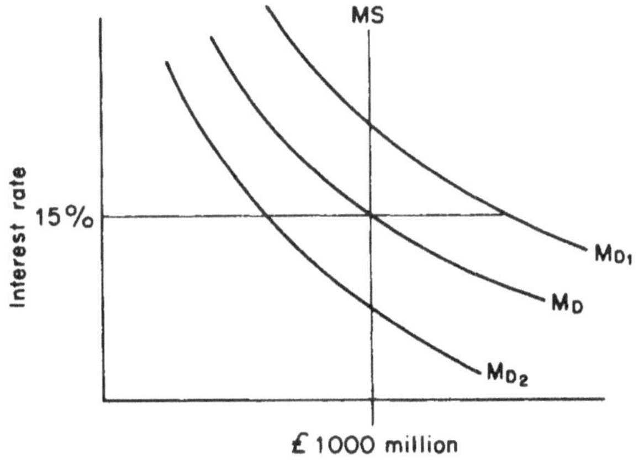

Fig. 1.4

Assume again that the money supply and the money demand are equal. Now assume that the demand for money rises to M_{D_1} in Figure 1.4. As the demand for money at the existing interest rate is greater than the supply of money then the interest rate will rise. Thus if the money supply is fixed by the authorities and the demand for money increases, then interest rates will rise. Again let us assume the opposite case in which the demand for money falls to M_{D_2}. At the interest rate of 15%, money supply is greater than money demand and interest rates will fall.

Conclusion. If the authorities seek to control the money supply they lose control over interest rates.

Thus the authorities must make a choice. For any given demand for money within the economy either the money supply could be set by the authorities, in which case they lose control over interest rates. Alternatively, interest rates could be fixed in which case the authorities lose control over the money supply. In recent history the authorities have moved from price fixing to quantity fixing. The different ways price fixing and monetary fixing can be achieved are discussed in Chapters 4 and 7.

APPENDIX 1

MEASURING CHANGES IN THE VALUE OF MONEY – PRICE INDEX NUMBERS

Attempts have been made to measure changes in the value of money by means of index numbers. In all cases the principle is the same: a base year is selected and the prices of a group of commodities in that year are noted. The index number for the base year is 100, and changes are shown as a percentage variation from the base. Thus a rise in prices of 10% as compared with a base year would give an index number of 110, and a fall of 5% an index of 95, the value of money, of course, changing in inverse proportion to the index number.

To see how it works, let us construct a simplified form of retail price index. Everyone's cost of living is the cost of the goods and services he buys in the course of living. One individual's cost is usually different from another's, but over society as a whole certain buying patterns become clear and by means of an ongoing survey of the ways in which several hundred typical families spend their money – the Family Expenditure Survey – the government continuously monitors what is being bought, in what quantities and at what prices. Apart from the prices, it becomes possible at any moment to conceive of a typical shopping basket of goods and services consumed by a family in a week. For our simplified example, let us suppose that this consists of the items and quantities in Table 1.6. The assumption is that the shopping basket remains the same but as the list of prices varies, not necessarily to the same extent for each item, we shall be able to watch for changes in total cost and make the desired comparisons. Every few years the Family Expenditure Survey may show that the standard basket is out of date; a new one can be specified and the monitoring of prices may re-commence on this new basis.

Table 1.6

Item	*Quantity*	*Price*	£ *Unit Price*	£ *Cost*
Beef	3 lb	30p/lb	0.30	0.90
Potatoes	8 lb	2p/lb	0.02	0.16
Fish	3 lb	25p/lb	0.25	0.76
Cigarettes	150	30p/20	0.015	2.25
Petrol	3 gal	40p/gal	0.40	1.20
Accommodation	1	£4.50/week	4.50	4.50
Heat and light	1	£2.50/week	2.50	2.50
				£12.26

Table 1.2 shows our initial prices and quantities, and multiplying price-per-unit by quantity we calculate the costs shown, with a weekly total of £12.26 for the basket. To construct the index this sum is to be called 100. The arithmetic of the transformation is, of course, to divide by the 12.26 and multiply by 100, a procedure to be used on all future total prices in the life of this index.

At a later date, still assuming that the contents and quantities in the basket are the same, prices might be those of Table 1.7. The total cost is now £16.31. Applying the transformation, we find:

$$\frac{16.31}{12.26} \times 100 = 133.03$$

so the new retail price index is 133.03. This is just an alternative way of saying that there has been a rise of 33.03% since this particular index began. If, still later, the total cost reaches £17.48, the index would be 142.58. This is 42.58% above the original cost.

Table 1.7

Item	*Quantity*	*Price*	£ *Unit Price*	£ *Cost*
Beef	3 lb	70p/lb	0.70	2.10
Potatoes	8 lb	3p/lb	0.03	0.24
Fish	3 lb	50p/lb	0.50	1.50
Cigarettes	150	35p/20	0.0175	2.62
Petrol	3 gal	55p/gal	0.55	1.65
Accommodation	1	£5.00	5.00	5.00
Heat and light	1	£3.20	3.20	3.20
				£16.31

Seen as a formula, the index we have looked at is:

$$\frac{\sum(\text{new unit price} \times \text{quantity})}{\sum(\text{original unit price} \times \text{quantity})} = 100$$

in short:

$$\frac{\sum p_0 q}{\sum p_1 q} = 100$$

q, the quantity, is taken at the original level, assumed unchanged, and to complete the logic in the formula, which is named after the economist Laspeyres,

$$\text{Laspeyres index} = \frac{\sum p_0 q_0}{\sum p_1 q_0} = 100$$

A Laspeyres index shows how the present cost of the original basket compares with its original cost. If the current purchasing pattern differs to an important extent from the original one, it may be advisable to change the basket. However, it is unwise to change the basis of an index too often, otherwise it cannot allow for the straightforward comparisons which are its primary purpose.

Where there are fairly frequent changes of quantities which would make a standard basket impracticable, an alternative approach is to use both current and original prices with current quantities. An index built in this way shows how the present cost of the present basket compares with the original cost of the present basket. This approach is named after one Paasche:

$$\text{Paasche index} = \frac{\sum p_0 q_1}{\sum p_1 q_1} = 100$$

The RPI, published each month by the Department of Employment, is the main measure used in the UK to record changes in the level of prices most people pay for the goods and services they buy. The prices of some 600 separate items are regularly collected and approximately 130,000 price quotations are used each month in compiling the index.

THE TAX AND PRICE INDEX

The RPI is affected by changes in indirect taxes, such as VAT and petrol duty but not by changes in income tax or national insurance contributions. The *tax and price index*, first published in August 1979, supplements the RPI in that it takes account of both changes in retail prices and in income tax and national insurance contributions, and may be used to measure changes in the purchasing power of gross (before tax) income for most taxpayers. In contrast, the RPI provides a basis for measuring changes in the purchasing power of net (after tax) income.

An excellent illustration of the use of price indices to illustrate the changing value of the pound, since 1920, is provided by Barclays Bank in Table 1.8.

MONETARY STATISTICS

Table 1.8
Purchasing Power of the Pound

Erosion of Purchasing Power (columns); Equivalent Purchasing Power (rows)

January	1920	1925	1930	1935	1940	1945	1950	1955	1960	1965	1970	1971	1972	1973	1974	1975	1976	1977	1978	1979	1980	1981	1982	1983
1920	100	125	135.5	157.2	128.4	111.4	98.0	75.9	66.0	58.3	45.6	41.9	38.8	36.0	32.1	26.8	21.7	18.6	16.9	15.5	13.1	11.8	10.3	9.9
1925	80.0	100	108.4	125.8	103.5	89.1	78.4	60.7	52.8	45.0	36.5	33.5	31.0	28.8	25.7	21.4	17.4	14.9	13.6	12.4	10.5	9.3	8.3	7.9
1930	73.8	92.3	100	116.0	95.5	82.2	72.4	56.0	48.7	41.5	33.7	30.9	28.6	26.6	23.7	19.8	16.0	13.7	12.5	11.4	9.7	8.5	7.6	7.3
1935	63.6	79.5	86.2	100	82.3	70.8	62.4	48.3	42.0	35.8	29.0	26.6	24.7	22.9	20.4	17.0	13.8	11.8	10.8	9.9	8.3	7.4	6.6	6.3
1940	77.3	96.6	104.7	121.5	100	86.1	75.8	58.7	51.0	43.5	35.3	32.3	30.0	27.8	24.8	20.7	16.8	14.4	13.1	12.0	10.1	9.0	8.0	7.6
1945	89.8	112.3	121.7	141.2	116.2	100	88.0	68.2	59.2	50.5	41.0	37.6	34.8	32.3	28.6	24.0	19.5	16.7	15.2	13.9	11.8	10.4	9.3	8.9
1950	102.0	127.5	138.2	160.4	132.0	113.6	100	77.4	67.3	57.4	46.5	42.7	39.5	36.7	32.6	27.3	22.2	19.0	17.3	15.8	13.4	11.8	10.5	10.1
1955	131.7	164.6	178.5	207.1	170.4	146.7	129.1	100	86.9	74.1	60.1	55.1	51.0	47.4	42.3	35.3	28.6	24.5	22.3	20.4	17.3	15.3	13.6	13.0
1960	151.6	189.5	205.4	238.4	196.1	168.8	148.6	115.1	100	85.3	69.2	63.4	58.6	54.6	48.7	40.6	32.9	28.2	25.7	23.5	19.9	17.6	15.7	14.9
1965	177.7	222.1	240.8	279.4	229.9	197.9	174.2	134.9	117.2	100	81.1	74.3	68.9	63.9	57.1	47.6	38.6	33.1	30.1	27.5	23.3	20.6	18.4	17.5
1970	219.2	274.0	297.0	344.7	283.6	244.1	214.9	166.4	144.6	123.4	100	91.7	85.0	78.5	70.4	58.7	47.6	40.8	37.1	34.0	28.7	25.4	22.7	21.6
1971	239.1	298.9	324	375.9	309.3	266.3	234.4	181.5	157.7	134.6	109.1	100	92.7	86.0	76.8	64.0	52.0	44.5	40.1	37.1	31.3	27.7	24.7	23.6
1972	258.0	322.5	349.6	405.7	333.6	287.3	252.9	195.9	170.2	145.2	117.7	107.9	100	92.6	82.9	69.1	56.1	48.1	43.7	40.0	33.8	29.9	26.7	25.4
1973	277.9	347.6	376.6	436.9	359.5	309.5	272.5	211.0	183.3	156.4	126.8	116.2	107.7	100	89.3	74.6	60.6	51.8	47.1	43.1	36.4	32.2	28.7	27.4
1974	311.3	389.1	421.8	489.5	402.7	346.7	305.2	236.4	205.3	175.2	142.0	130.2	120.7	112.0	100	83.3	67.7	58.0	52.8	48.3	40.8	36.1	32.2	30.7
1975	373.5	466.9	506.1	587.3	483.2	415.9	366.2	283.6	246.4	210.2	170.4	156.2	144.8	134.4	120.0	100	81.2	69.6	63.3	57.9	48.9	43.3	38.6	36.9
1976	460.1	575.1	623.4	723.4	595.7	512.4	451.1	349.4	303.5	258.9	209.9	192.4	178.3	165.6	147.8	123.2	100	85.7	78.0	71.3	60.3	53.3	47.6	45.4
1977	536.8	671	727.4	844.0	694.4	597.8	526.3	407.6	354.1	302.1	244.9	224.5	208.1	193.2	172.4	143.7	116.7	100	91.0	83.2	70.3	62.2	55.5	52.9
1978	590.1	737.6	799.6	927.8	763.4	657.1	578.5	448.1	389.2	332.1	269.2	246.8	228.7	212.3	189.6	158.0	128.3	109.9	100	91.5	77.3	68.3	61.0	58.2
1979	645.1	806.4	874.1	1014.3	834.5	718.4	632.5	489.8	425.5	363	294.3	269.8	250.0	232.1	207.2	172.7	140.2	120.2	109.3	100	84.5	74.7	66.7	63.6
1980	763.3	954.1	1034.3	1200.2	987.5	850.0	748.3	579.6	503.5	429.5	348.2	319.2	295.9	274.7	245.3	204.4	165.8	142.2	129.4	118.3	100	88.4	78.9	75.3
1981	863.4	1079.3	1169.9	1357.5	1116.9	961.5	846.5	655.6	569.5	485.9	393.9	361.1	334.7	310.7	277.4	231.2	187.7	160.8	146.3	133.8	113.1	100	89.3	85.1
1982	967.2	1209.0	1310.6	1520.8	1251.2	1077.1	948.2	734.4	638.0	544.3	441.2	404.5	374.9	348.0	310.7	259.0	210.2	180.2	163.9	149.5	126.7	112.0	100	95.4
1983	1014.1	1267.6	1374.1	1594.5	1311.9	1129.3	994.2	770.0	668.9	570.7	462.6	424.1	393.7	364.9	325.8	271.5	220.4	188.9	171.9	157.2	132.9	117.5	104.8	100

Source: Barclays Bank

Chapter 2

The United Kingdom Financial System

THE FUNCTIONS OF A FINANCIAL SYSTEM

The development of a financial system is closely related to the economy within which it evolves. There are certain features of an advanced economy which necessitate the evolution of a parallel financial system:

(a) increasing specialisation of people and therefore greater necessity for exchange;

(b) period of time for the results of production to appear on the market, e.g. agricultural products, consumer durables;

(c) need to provide resources for investment for future production;

(d) desire to save whilst still working, e.g. on the part of employees;

(e) desire to consume currently on the basis of *expected* future income.

The behaviour of financial institutions within the financial system is influenced by the structure of financial markets in which they participate, by the financial instruments in which they trade, and by the behaviour of the sectors of the economy from which they borrow and lend.

The financial system is a complex network embracing payments mechanisms and the borrowing and lending of funds. Though they also have other important functions, the key role played by the financial institutions in the system, is to act as financial intermediaries channelling funds from those with income in excess of their needs to those wishing to borrow.

A useful way to analyse a financial system is to distinguish between deficit and surplus economic units. A *deficit unit* has a desire to spend (i.e. make a claim on current output) more than its income in a given time period. A *surplus unit* has a desire to spend less than its income in a given time period.

This is done in two ways:

(1) *Directly* – surplus units hold claims on deficit units.

(2) *Indirectly* – by surplus units lending to financial institutions who then lend to deficit units.

The financial system deals in financial instruments or claims. These are all more or less sophisticated forms of IOUs – they are an asset of one party and a liability of another. In most instances the former party is entitled to repayment at a specified time, and also receives a promise of some interest, share of profits, or other service as compensation for his loan. For example, deposits are liabilities of banks or other institutions, are generally repayable on demand or in the fairly near future, and usually bear interest. Bank loans are often liabilities of ultimate borrowers, are frequently repayable by the end of some predetermined period, and carry an obligation to pay interest. Ordinary shares are liabilities of firms, which confer on their owners the right to a share of the profits earned but, in contrast with loans, do not have to be repaid.

One way in which financial institutions improve the terms facing borrowers is by transferring maturities i.e. they provide liquid liabilities which meet the needs of savers whilst employing their funds in the longer-term financial instruments which are more convenient for borrowers. Deposit-taking institutions like banks and building societies are able to do this because, although some individual depositors may be reducing their deposits, others will simultaneously be adding to theirs, and the institutions can rely on a considerable degree of stability in their deposit-base as a whole. It is therefore legitimate for them to regard at least a proportion of their deposits as available for long-term loans. Moreover, the existence of organised markets in which they can bid for large deposits provides banks with the assurance they need to make loan commitments.

Most financial institutions issue liabilities which are comparatively safe, but hold amongst their assets instruments on at least some of which there is a possibility of loss. To do this, they average risk and transform risk by taking the residual risk of loss on their own equity capital. For example, by making a large number of loans, and spreading them over a wide range of activities, banks try to ensure that their overall loss experience is small.

When a financial institution intermediates, it not only passes funds from lenders to borrowers, it usually also changes their terms and conditions. By aggregating small amounts of funds obtained from each of a large number of savers it is able to on-lend in larger packets, and as mentioned often to transform risk and maturity characteristics. The savings of many individuals when deposited with a building society, for example, go to make up a single house mortgage. By lending to a large number of house purchasers the building society pools and minimises the risk of loss, so that a depositor's funds are much safer than if they were lent directly for the same purpose; and while the depositor has access to his funds at short notice the building society can, provided it has a relatively stable deposit base in aggregate, lend to the house purchaser for a long period. Though building societies probably provide the extreme example, most institutions engage in maturity transformation to some extent, within limits set by differing prudential considerations. Also financial intermediaries are able to apply well established risk diversification techniques designed to reduce the risk of defaults.

The objectives of savers are various. Most want their money to be safe and some part at least to be readily available. Some save for the long term, and may be concerned primarily with preserving the real value of their wealth. Some feel able to take risks with part of their savings if there is a sufficient prospect of gain. But a high proportion of saving goes into deposits, that is liquid, secure financial instruments. Borrowers generally want access to funds for considerable periods, whether to finance current or capital expenditure, and some uncertainty and risk of loss is unavoidable. The financial institutions and markets help to reconcile these differing requirements, and thereby usually facilitate a higher level of saving and investment.

In analysing the flow of funds from savers (surplus units) to borrowers (deficit units) via the financial institutions it is customary to group the individual components of the economy into a number of sectors. These are relatively homogeneous groupings of economic units possessing similar characteristics and behaving in broadly similar ways – though not necessarily in exactly the same way; aggregation conceals a great diversity of individual behaviour. Moreover within one sector there may exist both net borrowers and net lenders; and in gross terms many economic units are both borrowers and lenders at the same time.

The sector financial accounts* compiled by the Bank of England and the Central Statistical Office present the statistics of lending and borrowing in the economy in a coherent framework. The economy is there divided into six main sectors, some of which can be further divided into sub-sectors, as follows:

Personal sector
Industrial and commercial companies
Public sector: General government:
  Central government
  Local authorities
  Public corporations
Monetary sector
Other financial institutions
Overseas sector

The personal sector includes all individuals resident in the UK. It also includes unincorporated businesses (because the transactions of these businesses cannot easily be separated from the purely personal transactions of their owners) and non-profit-making bodies such as charities, friendly societies, trades unions and universities. It is the personal sector which in

*A detailed description of the sector financial accounts is given in the Central Statistical Office's *Financial Statistics Explanatory Handbook* 1980 edition (HMSO, April 1981).

recent years has been responsible for the largest part of saving within the economy, i.e it is a surplus unit.

The industrial and commercial company sector consists of all companies not classified as financial institutions and so covers the extractive, manufacturing, distributive and service industries, including property companies. Subsidiaries and branches in the UK of foreign companies are included, but not subsidiaries and branches overseas of UK companies. Industrial and commercial companies carry out most of the private investment in the UK, and this sector is primarily concerned with the financing of industry and trade, i.e. it is a deficit unit.

The public sector consists of central government and the local authorities (called collectively "general government") and the public corporations (the nationalised industries and various other state-owned bodies). The public sector is financed on an integrated basis, with much of the financial needs of the local authorities and public corporations being met by borrowing from the central government which in turn borrows in the financial markets. It is therefore common within the financial accounts to present consolidated figures for this sector as a whole. The public sectoı is almost always in a deficit.

Each sector issues financial liabilities and holds financial assets which represent claims on the other sectors. In a modern financial system the range of these assets/liabilities is considerable. Usually each has its own characteristics reflecting the requirements of the lender and the borrower. The structure of the financial system is illustrated in Figure 2.1 below.

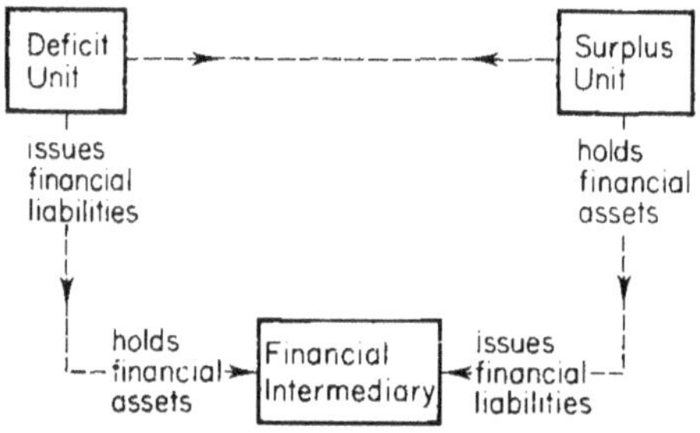

Fig. 2.1

The *changes* in a sector's position over time is shown in a *Flow of Funds* statement. A simple specimen matrix is shown in Table 2.1, with three sectors and three types of financial asset. The sum of surpluses and deficits must be zero. For each of the financial assets X, Y, Z, each sector has either made an acquisition, or incurred a liability, either by issuing a claim against itself, or by selling an existing claim against another sector. The sum of these transactions at the end of each line must also be zero. For each of the sectors A, B, C, the total of sources – financial surplus and increase in liabilities – must balance the total of uses – financial deficit and acquisition of assets. It should be noted that financial liabilities and assets have been given plus and minus

Table 2.1
Flow of Funds Matrix

	SECTOR A		*SECTOR B*		*SECTOR C*		
	Sources Liabilities	*Uses Assets*	*Sources Liabilities*	*Uses Assets*	*Sources Liabilities*	*Uses Assets*	
Financial balance	+200			-100		-100	0
Asset X	+100		+100			-200	0
Asset Y		-100		-100	+200		0
Asset Z		-200	+100		+100		0
	300	300	200	200	300	300	

Acquisition of assets and financial deficit = –
Increase in liabilities and financial surplus = +

signs respectively so that they can be more easily added to surpluses and deficits.

The main points about the Flow of Funds are:

(1) The rows show the particular form of asset/liability that is held/used.

(2) Columns show the financial activity of each sector and that the savings and investment in a sector can be different.

(3) The sum of changes in a row are zero.

(4) The sum of the columns is the size of the surplus or deficit for the sector.

Flow of funds are a very important method of analysing the behaviour of financial firms and financial markets as well as providing a useful tool for prediction.

Figure 2.2 illustrates which sectors have been in deficit and which in surplus in recent years. Appendix 1 illustrates the application of the flow of funds concept to the United Kingdom Financial System.

In order to best understand the roles played in channelling funds from borrowers to lenders, the United Kingdom financial system is divided by the monetary authorities into the Monetary Sector and Other Financial Institutions (OFIs).

THE MONETARY SECTOR

The definition of the monetary sector, introduced on 19 November 1981, and for banking statistics purposes taking effect from 1 January 1982, comprises the United Kingdom offices of institutions either recognised as banks or licensed to take deposits under the Banking Act 1979, together with the National Girobank, the Trustee Savings Banks, the Banking Department of the Bank of England, and those institutions in the Channel Islands and the Isle of Man which have opted to participate in the new monetary control arrangements introduced in August 1981. Recognised banks can, in turn, be subdivided into clearing banks, other banks, accepting houses, discount houses and foreign banks (see Figure 2.3).

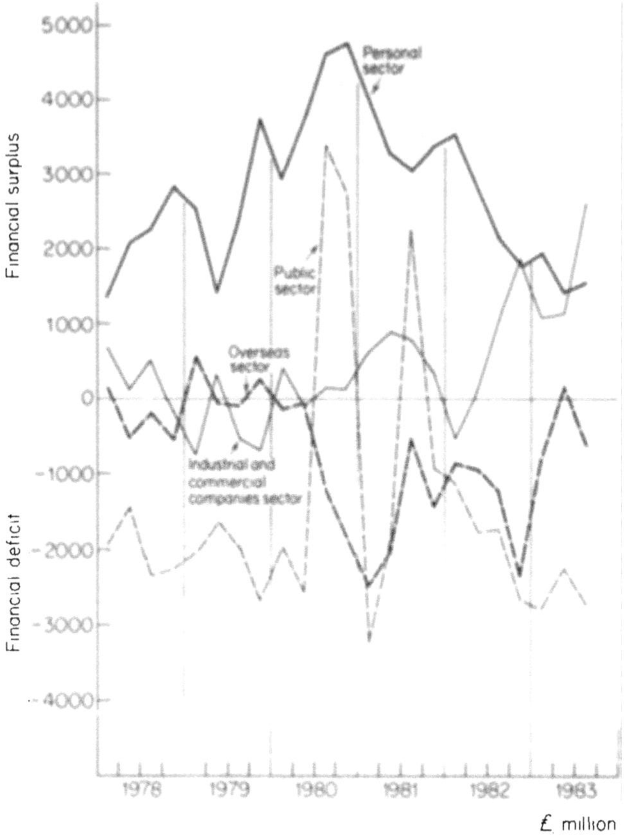

Fig. 2.2 Sector financial surplus/deficit

Source: *Economic Trends* 1983
Reproduced by kind permission of the Controller of Her Majesty's Stationery Office.

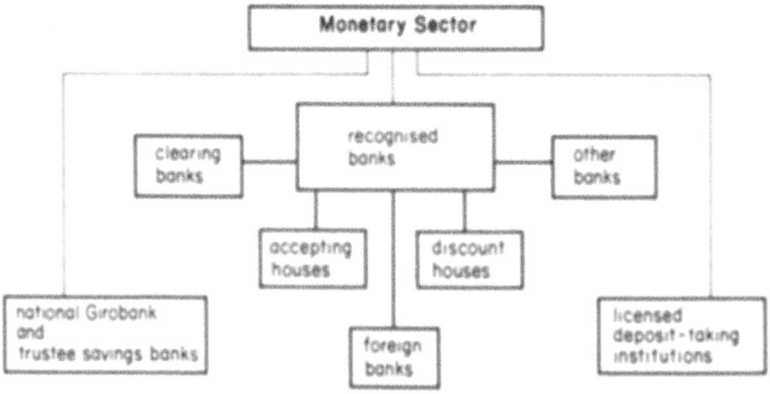

Fig. 2.3 The Monetary Sector

RECOGNISED BANKS

Clearing Banks

There are 450 institutions recognised as banks by the Bank of England. These include the clearing banks which have large branch networks, offer a wide range of services to both personal and business customer, and are the most important providers of cheque book and other payment services. The clearing banks are so called because they handle the exchange and settlement of cheques – "the clearing". They comprise:

- the London Clearing Banks, Barclays, Lloyds, Midland, National Westminster (the "Big Four"), Coutts & Co. (wholly-owned by National Westminster), and William & Glyn's;
- the Scottish Clearing Banks;
- the Northern Ireland Banks.

The common feature of the deposit-taking institutions is that they take deposits which are generally highly liquid and use them to make loans or to acquire other assets with longer average maturities, i.e which are less liquid.

There are a large number of commercial banks and they vary considerably in the range and scope of their operations. Their activities can be divided into retail and wholesale business.

Retail banking on the deposit side is mainly concerned with cash withdrawal and money transmission – usually the most important reason why people keep bank accounts. This requires a network of branches and is therefore mainly the province of the London and Scottish clearing banks, the Northern Ireland banks and certain other banks like the Co-operative Bank and the Yorkshire Bank who between them have a total of more than 13,000 outlets spread throughout the UK. Cash withdrawal and money transmission facilities are also provided by the National Girobank, which operates through some 21,000 Crown sub-post offices, and by the Trustee Savings Banks.

Wholesale banking involves the taking of large deposits, at higher rates of interest than those on deposit accounts, the deployment of liquid funds in money market instruments and the making of large loans and investments. Virtually all the commercial banks engage in some wholesale activities, and some, like the merchant banks and overseas banks, centre their business on them. In this type of business the banks have considerable freedom to vary the volume of liabilities they carry on their books, since they are usually able to increase the funds at their disposal when necessary by bidding for deposits at the going rate or by issuing negotiable time certificates of deposit (see p. 85). The scale of an individual bank's wholesale business will depend on its capital base, and the extent to which it is willing to hold assets of a longer maturity than its liabilities, as well as on its ability to seek out profitable lending business.

Every financial institution faces the task of prudent balance-sheet management – the maintenance, relative to the nature of their liabilities, of an appropriate mix between long-term assets (which generally carry a higher return), and short-term, more liquid assets. The problem, discussed later, for the deposit-taking institutions is that their deposits are generally short-term, while their loans are usually for significantly longer periods.

Traditionally the clearing banks have concentrated on providing short-term finance for working capital but they are now much more flexible in both the length and purpose of their lending. For instance, in the personal market the banks entered (and subsequently left) the mortgage market, offering secured loans for house purchase over periods up to 30 years, and over 40% of their non-personal lending is now medium term.

Licensed Deposit Taking Institutions, described in more detail on pp. 47–48 have special licences to take deposits from the public. They are generally smaller than the recognised banks and provide a narrower range of services. Most of the finance houses are licensed institutions.

Other Banks and Foreign Banks

Other Banks include those whose head offices are in Britain but whose main business is overseas. Foreign banks are geographically within the UK but are owned by foreigners.

Although other banks and foreign banks are a heterogeneous group they contrast in three main ways with the operation of clearing banks. First, the majority of their business is in foreign currency. There are differences within the individual groups of banks but the general principle that foreign currency deposits form the larger proportion of their business applies in all cases. Secondly, their involvement in the payments mechanism is minimal. Third, the size of their deposits is large, a minimum acceptable deposit being in the range of £50,000 to £100,000. They are therefore considered to be "wholesale" as opposed to retail bankers.

In contrast to the clearing banks, these banks are far more concerned with "matching" their asset and liability structures both with regard to their maturity and their currency. For example, if the bank accepts a dollar deposit expiring on 1 May 1986, it will endeavour to match this with a corresponding asset maturing on the same date.

The number of foreign banks in London has expanded rapidly in recent years (see Table 2.2). In 1960 the foreign banks directly represented numbered only 77. This figure grew to 100 during 1966, 200 during 1972, 300 during 1977, and reached 379 in 1981 and was over 450 by 1984. Foreign banks have been attracted to London as it is the centre of the Euro-currency market (see Chapter 11). US and Japanese banks are the most prevalent but, not surprisingly, there are increasing numbers from various European countries. The foreign banks' presence is not restricted to London and some of the banks are establishing networks of strategically placed offices in major cities. These include such centres as Aberdeen, in order to service the needs of the North Sea oil industry, and the large conurbations of Birmingham, Bradford and Liverpool, in order to cater for specific ethnic communities.

Representation takes different forms. Some banks operate through subsidiaries whilst others have opened branches in their own names. There are also large numbers of representative offices which do not transact banking business but act as a focal point for building up business relationships. Often a representative office is used as the first step towards setting up a branch operation.

Table 2.2
How London's Foreign Banking Community Has Grown

Year	*Directly represented**	*Indirectly represented†*	*Total*
1967	114	–	114
1968	135	–	135
1969	138	–	138
1970	163	–	163
1971	176	25	201
1972	215	28	243
1973	232	35	267
1974	264	72	336
1975	263	72	335
1976	265	78	343
1977	300	55	355
1978	313	69	382
1979	330	59	389
1980	353	50	403
1981	353	65	418
1982	379	70	449
1983	391	69	460

* Directly represented through a representative office, branch, or subsidiary.
† Other banks indirectly represented through a stake in a joint venture or consortium bank.

Source: *The Banker* (November 1983).

Foreign banks are also represented in London through 29 or so consortium banks. These are defined as banks which are owned by other banks but in which no one bank has a direct shareholding of more than 50%, and in which at least one shareholder is an overseas bank. One of the principal reasons why banks establish foreign networks is to service the requirements of their domestic customers' international operations, since even the largest banks in the world are not always able or willing to finance single-handed the increasingly large borrowing requirements of major multinational corporations. The consortium banks bring together leading banks from different countries, or from one country, combining resources and expertise predominantly to provide term loans in foreign currencies to corporate and public borrowers. They are also active in loan syndications, and some banks manage or underwrite international bond issues.

Accepting Houses

The accepting houses, otherwise known as merchant banks are diverse institutions dating back to the nineteenth century when they were simply merchant houses trading in various areas of the world. As they grew in reputation and stature, they found a remunerative source of business in accepting (i.e. adding their name to) bills of exchange issued by lesser known traders to finance trade which the latter had entered into. An acceptance is a guarantee provided by an accepting house against the default of the ultimate borrower. Through this means the London merchants adopted banking activities in the role of the accepting houses – hence the name, Accepting Houses Committee, for the representative body of 16 of the leading merchant banks. Traditionally the major banks have been centred in the heart of the City of London but in recent years provincial branches have been opened in such cities as Birmingham, Leeds, Manchester, Edinburgh and Glasgow, which are assuming increasing importance as financial centres.

The 16 members of the Accepting Houses Committee are as follows:

Baring Brothers & Co. Ltd.
Brown, Shipley & Co. Ltd.
Charterhouse Japhet PLC.
Robert Fleming & Co. Ltd.
Guinness Mahon & Co. Ltd.
Hambros Bank Ltd.
Hill Samuel & Co. Ltd.
Kleinwort, Benson Ltd.
Lazard Brothers & Co. Ltd.
Samuel Montagu & Co. Ltd.
Morgan Grenfell & Co. Ltd.
Rea Brothers PLC.
N. M. Rothschild & Sons Ltd.
J. Henry Schroder Wagg & Co. Ltd.
Singer & Friedlander Ltd.
S. G. Warburg & Co. Ltd.

Whilst the finance of international trade remains an important function of merchant banks, other activities have overtaken in significance their traditional acceptance business and they are now very much involved in other types of business. Indeed since the Bank of England increased its list of banks whose bills it is prepared to buy, as part of the new system of monetary controls brought in in August 1981 the accepting houses have faced severe competition in performing their traditional function.

The other types of business are quite diversified. First, they offer financial advice to customers, with respect to raising finance, dividend policies and also take-overs, both initiating such bids and offering defence against bids. Secondly, they are heavily involved in raising new capital by firms and offering advice on such matters as (i) drawing up the prospectus (ii) pricing new share issues and (iii) arranging for new issues to be underwritten. Thirdly, they manage portfolios on behalf of their customers though they rarely hold shares on their own account. They have also assisted in the establishment and management of unit trusts. Fourthly, they conduct ordinary banking business. A number of merchant banks now operate a current account service for their customers but their main deposit-taking activity is the acceptance of larger deposits for periods varying from one day to a year or more. They are very active in the money markets and have contributed greatly towards the success of negotiable certificates of deposit.

On the lending side they are active suppliers of corporate finance, concentrating on medium-term lending. In this connection, important aspects are the provision or arrangement of "nursery" finance for companies growing towards the size when they can consider a public flotation (they often advise companies joining the Unlisted Securities Market); medium-term finance for major UK exports backed by ECGD guarantee; and Euro-currency loans.

Fifthly, many merchant banks have diversified into other sectors of trade and commerce, both at home and abroad, either directly through subsidiaries or through substantial stakes in associated companies. Their activities in other sectors include equipment leasing, hire-purchase, factoring (the collecting of trade debts and financing their owners), insurance, insurance broking, shipping, property development and management.

Finally, different accepting houses undertake different specialist functions. Some are involved in the gold bullion market, others in commodity dealing, and financial advisory services such as the establishment of "currency funds". Table 2.3 illustrates the structure of their balance sheets.

Discount Houses

The London discount market, discussed in detail in Chapter 3 represents an integral part of the financial mechanism of the City of London and is basically concerned with borrowing and investing short-term money. The market consists of the 9 members of the London Discount Market Association (LDMA) together with a few small firms of bill brokers who, although not members of the LDMA, carry out similar activities. Each of the discount houses is owned and operated independently of other financial institutions, a situation which cannot be altered without official sanction. The majority of dealing is carried out by personal contact or telephone and despite the volume and complexity of the business the organisation of the discount houses is uncomplicated and comprises a small number of employees. The houses also have important subsidiaries which are active brokers in the various sterling and currency money markets.

The nine members of the London Discount Market Association are:

Alexanders Discount PLC.
Cater Allen PLC.
Clive Discount Co. PLC.
Gerrard & National PLC.
King & Shaxson PLC.
Gerald Quin, Cope & Co. PLC.
Seccombe Marshall & Campion PLC.
Smith St. Aubyn & Co. PLC.
The Union Discount Company of London PLC.

The discount houses borrow money from the clearing banks (money at call) and invest in short-term securities (treasury bills, commercial bills and gilt-edged securities). The profit of the discount houses come from two sources: (i) dealing profits and (ii) the margin between the yield on the securities and the cost of funds borrowed.

The discount houses provide services to banks, to the corporate sector and to the government. For the banks they provide an easy method for the disposal of

Table 2.3
Accepting Houses: Balance Sheet

Liabilities

	Sterling deposits							Other currency deposits					Sterling and other currencies	**Total liabilities/ assets**
	Total	*of which sight deposits*	*UK monetary sector*	*UK public sector*	*UK private sector*	*Overseas*	*Certificates of deposit*	**Total**	*UK monetary sector*	*Other United Kingdom*	*Overseas*	*Certificates of deposit*	*Items in suspense and transmission, capital and other funds*	
1983 Sept. 21	7,945	*1,746*	1,666	122	4,812	911	433	11,753	3,427	1,123	6,903	300	2,314	22,012
Oct. 19	8,401	*1,941*	1,615	129	5,219	938	500	11,923	3,554	1,260	6,811	297	2,428	22,752
Nov. 16	8,407	*1,935*	1,588	148	5,105	950	615	12,177	3,479	1,337	7,055	306	2,400	22,984
Dec. 14	8,415	*1,941*	1,557	120	5,177	995	566	12,604	3,902	1,462	6,910	330	2,457	23,476
1984 Jan. 18	8,512	*1,936*	1,476	143	5,362	1,054	477	12,534	3,721	1,391	7,098	324	2,426	23,472
Feb. 15	8,728	*2,151*	1,571	150	5,415	1,075	516	12,091	3,660	1,386	6,748	297	2,591	23,411
Mar. 21	8,833	*2,244*	1,650	124	5,313	1,086	660	12,860	3,916	1,583	7,059	303	2,594	24,287
Apr. 18	9,036	*2,237*	1,527	106	5,488	1,104	811	13,271	3,905	1,722	7,315	329	2,663	24,970
May 16	9,327	*2,447*	1,809	68	5,599	1,101	750	13,508	4,012	1,706	7,495	295	2,638	25,473

Sterling assets

	Notes and coin	*Balances Bank of England*		*Market loans*					*Bills*				*Advances*		
		Special and cash ratio deposits	*Other*	*Secured money with LDMA*	*Other UK monetary sector*	*UK monetary sector CDs*	*UK local authorities*	*Overseas*	*Treasury bills*	*Eligible local authority bills*	*Eligible bank bills*	*Other bills*	*UK public sector*	*UK private sector*	*Overseas*
1983 Sept. 21	1	16	1	203	3,034	962	612	243	1	1	56	7	111	2,552	792
Oct. 19	1	16	1	291	3,265	1,036	617	275	1	2	43	10	105	2,552	789
Nov. 16	1	18	1	257	3,051	1,141	615	238	4	3	69	6	103	2,530	819
Dec. 14	1	18	1	281	3,174	1,041	618	240	4	3	39	8	95	2,500	800
1984 Jan. 18	2	18	1	179	3,189	1,146	608	269	1	2	18	6	95	2,509	790
Feb. 15	2	18	1	213	3,171	1,371	596	215	2	2	29	8	96	2,517	814
Mar. 21	2	18	1	208	3,503	1,125	624	228	10	1	17	17	105	2,573	842
Apr. 18	2	18	1	229	3,228	1,293	686	258	5	2	90	13	108	2,603	888
May 16	1	19	2	213	2,837	1,079	704	303	4	1	27	11	103	2,583	838

	Sterling assets continued		Other currency assets											
	Investments		*Market loans and advances*							*Bills*	*Invest-ments*	*Sterling and other currencies: miscel-laneous assets*	*Accept-ances*	*Eligible liabilities*
	British govern-ment stocks	*Other*	**Total**	*of which advances*	*UK monetary sector*	*UK monetary sector CDs*	*UK public sector*	*UK private sector*	*Overseas*					
1983 Sept. 21	243	444	10,858	*4,079*	2,834	493	8	986	6,537	32	545	1,298	*2,822*	*3,597*
Oct. 19	276	464	10,823	*4,045*	2,087	439	9	961	6,607	38	556	1,589	*3,168*	*3,671*
Nov. 16	229	473	11,170	*4,172*	2,845	519	17	992	6,796	53	563	1,640	*3,048*	*3,782*
Dec. 14	233	510	11,803	*4,451*	2,929	622	19	1,090	7,143	70	556	1,482	*3,030*	*3,794*
1984 Jan. 18	241	572	11,652	*4,436*	2,978	553	17	1,069	7,036	85	522	1,565	*3,254*	*3,832*
Feb. 15	250	595	11,230	*4,396*	2,657	542	11	1,038	6,981	84	540	1,658	*3,357*	*3,832*
Mar. 21	242	578	11,746	*4,396*	3,086	500	8	1,122	7,031	55	636	1,757	*3,449*	*3,907*
Apr. 18	213	659	12,191	*4,361*	3,094	542	7	1,049	7,500	60	644	1,779	*3,509*	*4,180*
May 16	208	701	12,511	*4,378*	3,233	580	7	1,073	7,618	72	660	1,596	*3,540*	*4,116*

Source: Bank of England, *Quarterly Bulletin* (June 1984).
Reproduced by kind permission of the Bank of England.

surplus cash. If one bank has a surplus it can increase its loans of money at call. Conversely if another is short of cash it can withdraw call money from the market. Thus the market enables banks to economise on cash holdings.

For the company sector the houses' main function is the arrangement of borrowing facilities through discounting bills of exchange, whilst as a secondary function the houses offer various forms of short-term investments for company portfolios.

In the sphere of Government finance their major role is to cover in full the weekly treasury bill tender which is an essential part of the Government's short-term borrowing arrangements. They are also active dealers in short-dated Government stocks so that, in total, the houses provide the medium through which the Bank of England can influence movements in short-term interest rates. Additionally, the houses are active participants in the markets for local authority stocks and bonds.

Under the new monetary arrangements, introduced in August 1981, the system of operating monetary policy requires greater intervention in the money markets by the Bank of England and this requires an adequate supply of commercial bills. In this connection the Bank of England has extended the list of Banks whose acceptances are eligible for re-discount at the Bank of England, i.e. bills in which the Bank is prepared to deal. At the same time it was thought necessary to link eligibility to the existence of an adequate supply of funds for the discount market. Consequently each eligible bank has undertaken to ensure that it will maintain with the London discount houses and with approved money brokers and gilt-edged jobbers secured call money equal to (i) 5% of that bank's eligible liabilities; (ii) of the 5% not less than 2½% of that bank's eligible liabilities must be held with the LDMA.

The secondary market for negotiable dollar and sterling certificates of deposit is another sphere in which the houses play an active part and by providing ready marketability they have directly contributed to the success of this form of investment.

Savings Banks

The National Savings Bank was established in 1861 as the Post Office Savings Bank and is now the largest organisation of its kind in the world operating over 20 million active accounts, through the 20,000 or so post offices which handle savings bank business. There are two types of account – Ordinary and Investment. Relatively small withdrawals can be made on demand from Ordinary Accounts but Investment Account deposits are subject to one month's notice and consequently attract a higher rate of interest. The National Savings Bank is not part of the monetary sector.

The National Girobank was established in October 1968 as a sector of the Post Office Corporation to provide a simple money transmission service operated through the postal system and with cash facilities provided through post offices. It forms part of the new monetary sector as redefined in August 1981 and is subject to the new monetary control measures. The Girobank joined the London Bankers' Clearing House in March 1981.

Trustee Savings Banks (TSBs) originated as thrift institutions in the early nineteenth century and the movement, based on two fundamental principles of management by unpaid trustees and the automatic investment of deposits in public sector debt, although this latter principle no longer exists. They soon grew rapidly to cover the whole of the United Kingdom and the Channel Islands. Their establishments and operations are governed by a series of Trustee Savings Banks Acts; the most recent and most important being that of 1976.

During the 1960s the TSBs moved away from being simple depositories for savings towards becoming fully fledged banking institutions. Cheque accounts were introduced in 1965 and the TSB Unit Trust was launched in 1968. The Central Trustee Savings Bank was incorporated in 1973 as banker to the Trustee Savings Banks and their associated organisations. It provides banking, clearing and investment services to those bodies and, in 1975, became a functional member of the London Bankers' Clearing House. Central Trustee Savings Bank Ltd. is a wholly-owned subsidiary of Trustee Savings Bank (Holdings) Ltd., a holding company for the central operating companies of the TSB group. As banker to the regions TSBs the Central Trustee Savings Bank Ltd. is a recognised bank under the terms of the Banking Act 1979.

The Trustee Savings Banks group comprises 16 autonomous regional Trustee Savings Banks and a number of central companies providing specialised financial and banking services. The regional TSBs have a combined network of approximately 1,650 branches. The group is coordinated by the Trustee Savings Banks Act 1976 in which are vested regulatory powers. The regional TSBs form part of the new monetary sector and are subject to Treasury control, but are not, themselves, recognised banks or licensed deposit-takers under the Banking Act 1979, from which they were exempted. The Trustee Savings Banks are scheduled for "privatisation" in 1986.

Finance Houses — Licensed Deposit-takers

All finance houses, except those wholly financed by the parent company, are licensed deposit-takers. Finance houses are institutions which have traditionally been associated with hire-purchase and instalment credit. Other uses of funds take the form of providing loans to firms who hold stocks, to subsidiaries engaged in the factoring business and to provide assets leased out to companies. Sources of funds are (i) deposits (ii) discounted bills and borrowing and (iii) issued share capital.

They do not provide the full range of banking services required for recognised bank status. As LDTs they form part of the new monetary sector and have to conform with the new monetary control provisions introduced in August 1981. LDTs are further discussed on pp. 68–69.

The Finance Houses Association (FHA), established in 1945, now has 43 members who control 80% of instalment credit business in the UK, amounting in total to over £10 billion in 1981. The majority of the members are owned by banks or other financial institutions. All the main banks own at least one finance house, as is shown below:

Finance House	*Parent*
Lombard North Central	National Westminster
Mercantile Credit	Barclays
Lloyds and Scottish	Lloyds
Forward Trust Group	Midland
United Dominions Trust	Trustee Savings Bank
North West Securities	Bank of Scotland
St. Margaret's Trust	Williams & Glyn's

A large proportion of the deposits of finance houses come from banks and other financial institutions. Industrial and commercial companies are also large providers of funds. The majority of these funds are used to finance the purchase of new and second-hand cars and commercial vehicles. The remainder is accounted for by loans for consumer credit: home improvement, house purchase, finance for holiday and leisure activities, business gained by media advertising and direct mailing, and corporate sector business.

THE BANK OF ENGLAND

In the United Kingdom the term "Monetary Authorities" refers to the Bank of England and the Treasury, the government department directly concerned with monetary and financial policy. Statutory responsibility for monetary policy lies with the Treasury and by long-standing convention the Bank of England acts as the Treasury's agent in the execution of policy. In practice the two bodies work closely together. Whilst the objectives of monetary policy are an integral part of overall economic management, and as such are determined by the Treasury, the advice of the Bank is of considerable importance.

As regards the techniques of monetary control it is necessary to distinguish between the broader issues and the precise specification of the instruments to be used. Decisions on the former (e.g. whether to rely on market or direct controls), which may have important implications for the economy as a whole, are taken by the Treasury, though once again the Bank of England will be closely involved; on many occasions the advice of the Bank will be sufficiently authoritative to determine policy. Moreover the Bank of England, in view of its expertise and close contacts with the financial markets, is generally best placed to decide on the detailed mechanics of monetary control. And the Bank continues to enjoy a wide measure of discretion in its day-to-day operations in the money, gilt-edged and foreign exchange markets.

The Bank of England was established by charter in 1694 as a private concern and gradually assumed greater importance in the financial system over subsequent years. With its greater importance, its power to undertake independent actions became more limited and in 1946 it was nationalised. The day-to-day operation of the bank is vested in a court consisting of the Governor, the Deputy Governor, four executive directors and twelve part-time directors. In practice most decisions are taken by the Governor, Deputy Governor and the four executive directors.

The term of office of both the Governor and the Deputy Governor is five years. For the 16 directors it is four years, and they retire in rotation, four at the end of February each year; all are eligible for reappointment. The main office is in Threadneedle Street in the City of London and is often affectionately referred to as the "Old Lady of Threadneedle Street" to reflect the Bank's upright regard for prudent behaviour.

The departments and divisions of the bank are summarised in Figure 2.4 below:

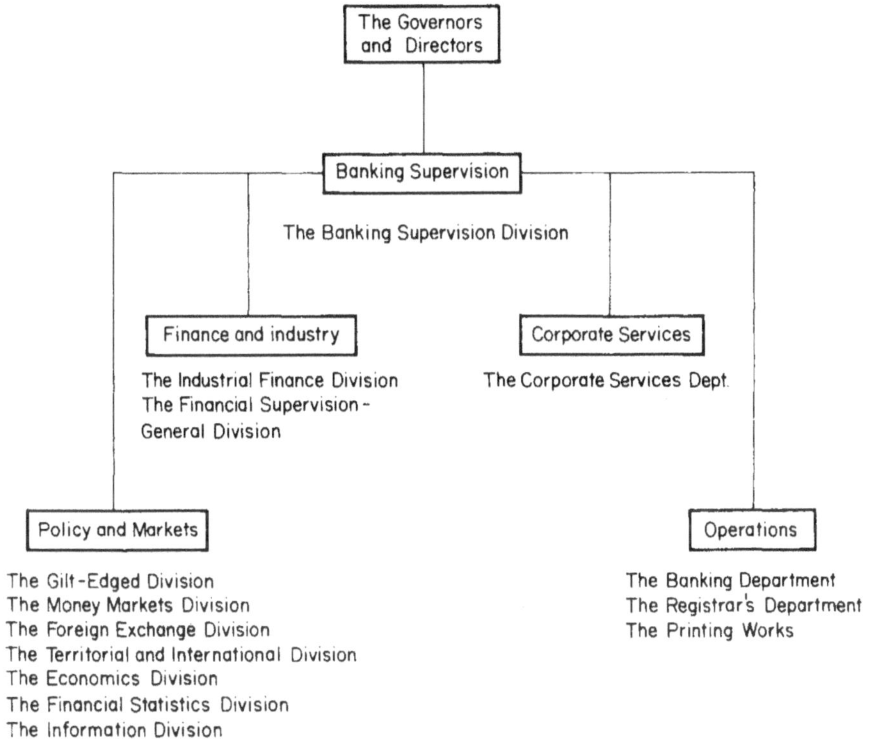

Fig. 2.4

Source: Bank of England

POLICY AND MARKETS

This section is concerned with domestic and external economic and financial policy and the associated market operations and research. There are a number of divisions within this area.

(i) *The Gilt-Edged Division* is concerned principally with all borrowing on behalf of the Government in the "gilt-edged" market and with other long-term borrowing operations. The gilt edged market is further discussed on p. 55.

(ii) *The Money Markets Division* is responsible for the Bank's daily operations in and lending to the discount market and generally supervises activities in the short-term money markets in sterling.

These two divisions carry out the Government's domestic policy through their operations in the respective markets and administer the system of controls over money supply and bank credit.

(iii) *The Foreign Exchange Division* is chiefly responsible for the foreign exchange and gold operations of the Government as well as of the Bank and its other customers and for the management of the UK reserves of foreign currency and gold.

(iv) *The Territorial and International Divisions* advise the Governors on all matters of external policy. They are responsible for keeping the Governors informed about economic and financial developments abroad and maintain close contact with overseas central banks and international organisations such as the IMF and the World Bank.

(v) *The Economics Division* analyses developments in the UK economy to inform and advise the Governors and formulate advice to them, particularly in the area of monetary and economic policies. It is also responsible for producing the Bank's Quarterly Bulletin.

(vi) *The Financial Statistics Division* collects information from the banks and others (mainly financial institutions) and assembles, analyses and comments on a wide range of financial statistics, for instance, on government financing, banking operations and capital markets. These statistics when aggregated are used both inside and outside the Bank.

(vii) *The Information Division* deals with all matters affecting the Bank's relationship with the Press and provides information to the general public.

CORPORATE SERVICES

The Corporate Services Department is responsible for the allocation of resources (including staff) and for the Bank's own finances and provides support services, such as computer services, to the rest of the Bank.

FINANCE AND INDUSTRY

(i) *The Industrial Finance Division* takes a close interest in the health of industrial and commercial companies and in the working of the financial system to meet their needs.

(ii) *The Financial Supervision – General Division* watches over developments in the markets for financial securities and the operations of the commodity markets.

BANKING SUPERVISION

The Banking Supervision Division is responsible within the formal framework of the Banking Act 1979 for ensuring that the UK banking system is run on a sound and healthy basis in order to protect depositors. It supervises about 590 recognised banks and licensed deposit-takers authorised to accept deposits from the public.

OPERATIONS

(i) *The Banking Department* provides banking services to the Bank's customers, who include the Government, commercial banks and overseas central banks, and the back-up services for the Bank's operations in the money, gilt-edged and foreign exchange markets. The Department is responsible for providing the public with new notes and withdrawing used notes from circulation via the main commercial banks. Its Head is known as the Chief Cashier and it is his signature which appears on the banknotes. There are seven branches outside London providing banking and note issue services. Supporting the work of the Industrial Finance Division, close contact is maintained at each branch and at the Glasgow Agency with the local business community to provide the Governors and Directors with an assessment of the state of the economy in the main industrial centres.

(ii) *The Registrar's Department* maintains registers of government and other stocks, makes interest payments, and handles the issue of new securities and the repayment of stocks as they fall due.

(iii) *The Printing Works* designs and prints banknotes and destroys them as they are withdrawn from circulation. It also prints other specialised documents, such as Treasury bills.

THE FUNCTIONS OF THE BANK OF ENGLAND

As a consequence of the 1844 Bank Charter Act the bank is required to prepare weekly accounts known as the Bank Return.

An appreciation of the functions of the Bank of England can be gleaned from an analysis of the Bank of England's balance sheet (see Table 2.4).

The balance sheet of the Bank of England is divided, for accounting purposes, into two departments – Issue Department and the Banking Department. The figures are taken from the Bank Return published each Thursday. In sector analysis, the Issue Department is included in central government, whereas the Banking Department is part of the monetary sector. This is partly because the Banking Department undertakes some fairly standard operations. The Exchange Equalisation Account, the government account which holds the official reserves of gold, convertible currencies and special drawing rights, is a Treasury account and is therefore not included in the table.

Table 2.4
Bank of England: Balance Sheet

£ millions

	Issue Department				Banking Department								
	Liabilities		*Assets*		*Liabilities*					*Assets*			
	Notes in circulation	*Notes in Banking Department*	*Government securities*	*Other securities*	**Total**	*Public deposits*	*Special deposits*	*Bankers deposits*	*Reserves and other accounts*	*Government securities*	*Advances and other accounts*	*Premises, equipment and other securities*	*Note and coin*
1983 Feb. 16	10,910	15	3,919	7,006	5,036	2,286	–	537	2,199	462	1,363	3,196	15
Mar. 16	11,008	17	3,655	7,370	4,737	1,912	–	628	2,182	424	1,399	2,897	17
Apr. 20	11,120	10	4,071	7,059	2,618	38	–	573	1,993	475	1,274	858	11
May 18	11,142	8	4,238	6,912	2,639	41	–	563	2,021	408	1,264	959	8
June 15	11,212	8	4,978	6,242	2,827	41	–	691	2,081	504	1,339	976	8
July 20	11,554	6	5,095	6,465	2,615	45	–	585	1,971	455	1,212	942	6
Aug. 17	11,436	4	5,394	6,046	2,590	42	–	615	1,918	466	1,137	983	4
Sept. 21	11,388	12	4,062	7,338	2,259	36	–	616	1,593	388	988	861	12
Oct. 19	11,347	13	3,705	7,655	2,218	38	–	602	1,563	458	854	893	13
Nov. 16	11,383	7	3,585	7,805	2,377	37	–	699	1,626	439	871	1,060	7
Dec. 14	12,152	8	4,669	7,461	2,356	44	–	650	1,648	383	947	1,018	8
1984 Jan. 18	11,363	7	2,161	9,209	1,977	45	–	611	1,307	455	627	888	7
Feb. 15	11,400	10	1,733	9,677	2,905	742	–	778	1,371	388	590	1,917	10

Source: Bank of England, *Quarterly Bulletin* (March 1984).
Reproduced by kind permission of the Bank of England.

Issue Department

Liabilities. The accounts of the Issue Department are concerned solely with the note issue. The department's only liabilities are Bank of England notes, including those held by the Banking Department (through which issues and withdrawals of notes are made).

Assets. Government securities include British government and government-guaranteed securities, Treasury bills, ways and means advances to the National Loans Fund, the historic liability of the Treasury of £11 million and any special Treasury liability.

Other securities include commercial bills, local authority bills, and, on occasion, local authority deposits and bonds, acquired in the course of market operations; and company securities and other miscellaneous securities. In recent years the pressures on the money markets have been enormous and the Issue Department has actively purchased large numbers of commercial bills (this is popularly known as the "bill mountain" and by mid-1985 stood at around £12 billion).

Banking Department

Through this department the Bank acts as banker to the Government, to banks, to overseas central banks and international organisations, and to a small number of other domestic institutions and private individuals including staff.

Liabilities. The total includes the Bank's capital of £14.6 million, held by the Treasury, which is not included in any of the sub-totals.

Public deposits are balances held by the central government at the Bank of England, including the accounts of the Exchequer, the National Loans Fund, the National Debt Commissioners and the Paymaster General, together with dividend accounts, accounts connected with tax collection and various other government funds.

Special deposits are forced loans by the banks to the Bank of England. They have been widely used as a monetary control measure. Interest is paid on special deposits at a rate adjusted weekly to the nearest 1/16% p.a. on the average rate for the latest Treasury bills issued.

Bankers' deposits. (Often referred to as Bankers' Balances). Up to 19 August 1981 these constituted the current account held at the Bank by the banks and discount houses. From the introduction of new arrangements for monetary control on 20 August 1981 they consist of operational deposits held mainly by the clearing banks, and non-operational cash ratio deposits for which recognised banks and licensed deposit-takers are liable.

Reserves and other accounts include deposit liabilities to overseas central banks, the dividend accounts of stocks managed by the Bank other than the direct obligations of the British Government, local authority and public corporation accounts.

Assets. Government securities include government and government-guaranteed securities.

Advances and other accounts include market advances to the discount market, loans to customers and support loans to deposit-taking institutions.

Premises, equipment and other securities includes equipment (at cost less accumulated depreciation) and premises (which have been valued professionally on the basis of an open-market value for existing use). Other securities include ordinary shares, local authority bills and bonds, and commercial bills.

THE BANKING ROLE

The Bank of England acts as a banker to the government, other banks, overseas central monetary authorities and institutions and a restricted number of private customers. This banking role is reflected in the liabilities and assets of the Banking Department listed in Table 2.4. As already mentioned public deposits represent the outstanding balance on the government's various bank accounts at the Bank of England. In addition to acting as banker to the government, any bank (subject to it possessing a satisfactory status), may keep an account at the Bank of England, and many do. All banks in the monetary sector *must*, however, hold accounts with the Bank of England.

Overseas monetary authorities also keep accounts at the Bank of England in order to settle indebtedness resulting from official intervention in the foreign exchange markets. In addition, as a legacy of the old sterling area, the Bank maintains the official reserves of certain countries. Finally a restricted amount of private banking business is carried out on behalf of customers including Bank employees. This is partly due to tradition but also serves the useful purpose of keeping the Bank in touch with the normal commercial business of banking.

The Banking Department's return is easy to interpret. As already stated the government's balances are shown as public deposits and the banks as bankers deposits. Reserves and other accounts include the Bank's reserves and the deposits of overseas monetary authorities and the private customers. Most of these funds are invested in government securities, though the bank makes advances to the monetary sector and holds a float of notes and coin.

THE NOTE ISSUE

The Issue Department's return is equally straightforward and shows that the note issue, its only liability, is backed in the main, by government securities and commercial bills. Although the management of the note issue is an important function performed by the bank in practice the notes are supplied simply on demand. If the general public wish to hold more currency (as happens, for example, just before Christmas) then the Bank will automatically increase the note issue. In this example cash is withdrawn from the banks and they replenish their stocks by running down their deposits at the Bank of England. Faced with a fall in its cash reserves the Bank will react by "selling" itself government securities and printing more notes.

The distinction between the Issue Department and the Banking Department is an accounting convention only.

THE GILT-EDGED MARKET

Included in the "gilt-edged market" are three main categories of fixed interest stocks;

(1) British Government stocks and those of public boards and nationalised industries;

(2) stocks of local authorities in Great Britain and Northern Ireland;

(3) stocks of Commonwealth central governments and corporations.

Category (1) accounts for around 94% of the market's overall value.

The highest degree of security attaches to those stocks where interest and repayment are guaranteed by the British Government and this substantially applies to its own stocks as well as those of public boards and nationalised industries, although this guarantee also extends to a few Irish stocks. Local authority stocks in Great Britain and Northern Ireland are not guaranteed by the Government, but, under the Local Government Act of 1933, it was laid down that interest on and repayment of such stocks was a charge on local authority revenues from all sources, including grants from the central government. Commonwealth stocks are not guaranteed by the British Government, although many of these stocks are managed by the Bank of England.

All issued British Government stocks have two principal features – a "coupon" and a redemption date (or dates). The "coupon" is the amount of interest paid (usually half-yearly except for Consols 2.5% where it is paid every quarter). The coupon a stock carries is generally indicative of the prevailing level of interest rates at the time it was issued. Because of the great fluctuation in interest rates in the postwar years coupons on existing stocks range from 2.5% to 15.5% – reflecting the cheap money of the immediate postwar period right up to the rampant inflation of most recent years.

With the exception of index-linked stocks British Government stocks are always redeemed at par value (£100) at a date fixed at the time of issue of the stock. This is the second principal feature of a gilt-edged stock; namely, it carries a redemption date – often two dates delineating a period during which the stock can be redeemed at the option of the Government and sometimes this period has been as long as ten years (e.g. Transport 3% 1978–88).

BALANCE SHEET MANAGEMENT OF THE CLEARING BANKS

Balance sheet management is influenced by three considerations. The need to:

(1) conform to government imposed controls;
(2) possess adequate liquidity to maintain confidence in banks;
(3) provide profits for the shareholders.

Banks are in business to borrow from groups with surplus funds and to lend to groups needing funds. However in deciding what types of assets to acquire they are subject to self-imposed controls and to government controls: the latter, as discussed in Chapters 4 and 7, have been subject to considerable change.

The key essential requirement for the role which deposit banks play in the payments mechanism is that their deposits (or, at least, that part of them which is transferable by cheque – the current accounts) should be widely accepted – without question as money. This requirement imposes on deposit banks the need to operate – and to be seen to operate – with extreme prudence.

The deposit banks have a large number of accounts (liabilities) most of which are quite small and they are nearly all withdrawable on demand or at quite short notice. Sterling deposits are divided into sight and time deposits. No notice is required to withdraw sight deposits but such deposits earn no rate of interest though a notional interest may be calculated and used to offset charges for operating the account. On the other hand time deposits earn a rate of interest but notice has to be given before withdrawal is permitted. In practice this requirement to give notice is often waived. Certificates of deposit arise when a deposit is made for a fixed term and the depositor receives a certificate which indicates the nature of the deposit. The holder of such a deposit can sell such a certificate in the financial markets if he wishes to regain his money before the end of the fixed term. Thus the deposit is fixed for a term as far as the bank is concerned but realisable before that date as far as the depositor is concerned.

The sterling assets in the consolidated balance sheet (Table 2.5) are arranged in descending order of liquidity. Liquidity is necessary because a very large proportion of sterling deposits are withdrawable on demand and most of the remainder within seven days' notice. Thus to maintain public confidence, the banks must always be able to meet withdrawals. Any failure or fear of failure to do so would lead to a "run" on the bank as depositors endeavoured to withdraw their deposits.

In order to meet the likely fluctuations in their deposit totals deposit banks need to hold a certain proportion of liquid assets which can be realised to meet withdrawals.* To demonstrate that their business is being conducted with extreme prudence, they need to hold further liquid assets beyond what is

*Since the late 1960s, the ability of the banks to bid for deposits to meet withdrawals (e.g. by issuing CDs) has enabled them to practise liability management. Thus instead of selling liquid assets the banks could "buy" deposits to replace withdrawals.

strictly necessary. (Remember from Chapter 1 that the more liquid the asset the lower is its return and vice versa.) These needs for extreme prudence result in the banks holding of very liquid assets being paralleled by holdings of other assets which although not perfectly liquid (and thereby yielding a higher return) can be readily sold to replenish their liquid assets, if necessary. (See pages 71–72 for further discussion of the need for "liquidity".)

On the *asset* side cash either in the till or at the Bank of England earns no interest. Money at call or short notice is money loaned out to certain financial institutions, mainly the discount houses, which can be recalled at extremely short notice, in some cases up to midday for return that day. The rate of interest on such loans is of course low, certainly below that earned on Treasury Bills. Other bills of exchange mainly consist of commercial bills, i.e. bills of exchange issued in connection with trade. Market loans are a new category of assets introduced in the new statistical series dating from 1975. These are loans made through the market, including money at call, to such bodies as discount houses, local authorities and various listed money brokers. This figure also includes the banks' holdings of certificates of deposits issued by other banks. The two remaining categories of sterling assets refer to loans and advances to customers and banks' holdings of stock. Loans and advances can be made in two ways: (i) by a loan for a fixed term i.e a loan which must be repaid on a specific date; and (ii) by an overdraft, i.e. the customer is permitted to overdraw his account up to a specified limit. The second method is traditionally more popular in the UK but term loans are also made. The overdraft system makes it difficult for the banks to control their lending where customers have unused overdraft facilities available and empirical studies confirm that significant unused facilities do exist. The advantage an overdraft offers to the customer is that interest is only paid to the extent that the loan is taken up.

The aim of profitability is self apparent. Profits are necessary to reward shareholders and provide reserves against the possibility of default on the bank's loans. The relationship between liquidity and profitability is illustrated, in a stylised form, in Figure 2.5. Table 2.5 illustrates the changing structure of the retail banks balance sheets.

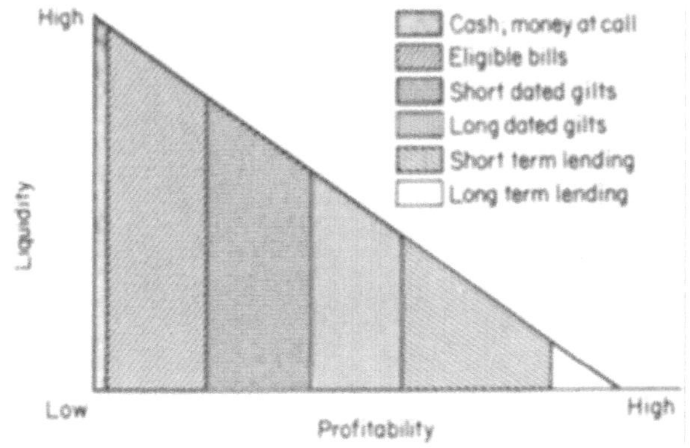

Fig. 2.5 The relationship between liquidity and profitability.

Table 2.5
Retail Banks Balance Sheet

£millions Liabilities

	Notes issued	Sterling deposits: Total	of which sight deposits	UK monetary sector	UK public sector	UK private sector	Overseas	Certificates of deposit	Other currency deposits: Total	UK monetary sector	Other United Kingdom	Overseas	Certificates of deposit	Sterling and other currencies: Items in suspense and transmission, capital and other funds	Total liabilities/assets
1983 Sept. 21	753	86,520	*31,585*	10,109	1,685	64,672	5,660	4,395	27,841	5,590	2,781	17,748	1,721	17,357	132,470
Oct. 19	768	87,280	*31,418*	9,748	1,638	65,235	5,856	4,803	28,937	5,743	2,875	18,677	1,643	18,051	135,036
Nov. 16	781	88,449	*32,118*	9,923	1,874	65,430	6,263	4,959	28,915	5,891	3,146	18,216	1,662	17,832	135,976
Dec. 14	836	88,921	*32,951*	10,125	1,767	65,790	6,250	4,989	30,412	6,408	3,243	18,000	1,961	17,943	138,112
1984 Jan. 18	788	89,085	*32,102*	9,815	2,020	65,888	5,978	5,384	29,314	5,766	3,232	18,633	1,683	17,712	136,900
Feb. 15	801	89,809	*32,126*	10,631	1,965	64,983	6,119	6,111	29,138	5,431	3,557	18,362	1,789	17,345	137,094
Mar. 21	818	90,068	*31,076*	10,357	2,010	65,437	6,524	5,739	29,349	5,211	3,593	18,729	1,816	18,456	138,691
Apr. 18	850	91,507	*31,179*	9,496	1,688	66,655	6,977	6,691	30,444	5,733	3,698	18,986	2,028	19,544	142,345
May 16	845	91,804	*21,882*	9,908	1,830	67,099	6,926	6,040	31,596	6,156	3,502	19,822	2,115	19,260	143,504

Sterling assets

	Notes and coin	Balances with Bank of England: Special and cash ratio deposits	Balances with Bank of England: Other	Market loans: Secured money with LDMA	Other UK monetary sector	UK monetary sector CDs	UK local authorities	Overseas	Bills: Treasury bills	Eligible local authority bills	Eligible bank bills	Other bills	Advances: UK public sector	UK private sector	Overseas
1983 Sept. 21	1,666	288	143	3,080	10,027	1,221	1,844	288	282	333	1,820	74	1,073	56,228	4,791
Oct. 19	1,651	288	128	3,506	9,572	1,395	1,847	251	303	354	2,023	80	1,013	56,857	4,784
Nov. 16	1,654	310	191	3,470	9,660	1,820	1,850	289	293	378	2,031	76	1,031	56,848	4,824
Dec. 14	1,915	310	141	3,975	10,215	1,600	1,840	350	246	338	1,898	81	968	57,085	4,859
1984 Jan. 18	1,749	310	102	3,213	9,969	1,619	1,799	299	250	281	1,760	83	952	58,136	4,969
Feb. 15	1,736	310	268	3,426	10,268	1,759	1,802	258	211	337	2,547	72	996	58,286	4,986
Mar. 21	1,723	310	224	3,850	10,226	1,705	1,846	350	165	345	2,802	75	•1,025	58,844	4,488
Apr. 18	1,819	310	146	3,963	10,115	1,960	1,843	401	219	265	1,734	74	977	59,752	4,993
May 16	1,780	321	139	3,231	10,471	1,721	1,885	424	198	161	2,400	74	963	60,205	4,971

	Sterling assets continued			Other currency assets										Sterling and other currencies: miscel-laneous assets	Acceptances	Eligible liabilities
	Banking Department lending to central government (net)	Investments		Market loans and advances							Bills	Invest-ments				
		British government stocks	Other	Total	of which advances	UK monetary sector	UK monetary sector CDs	UK public sector	UK private sector	Overseas						
1983 Sept. 21	406	5,485	3,175	27,718	*7,747*	10,932	353	74	2,444	13,915	61	1,451	11,016	*1,642*	*69,923*
Oct. 19	476	5,468	3,220	28,822	*7,722*	11,527	361	70	2,386	14,477	62	1,510	11,428	*1,866*	*70,574*
Nov. 16	451	5,417	3,241	29,028	*8,170*	11,286	275	73	2,709	14,685	59	1,525	11,532	*1,928*	*70,929*
Dec. 14	387	5,334	3,242	30,524	*8,591*	11,743	239	76	2,999	15,466	56	1,561	11,185	*2,020*	*71,057*
1984 Jan. 18	457	5,225	3,280	29,260	*8,519*	11,243	247	80	2,812	14,880	56	1,633	11,497	*2,110*	*72,152*
Feb. 15	-303	5,196	3,262	29,035	*8,730*	11,160	324	72	2,993	14,486	58	1,609	10,975	*2,304*	*72,145*
Mar. 21	-708	4,992	3,363	29,173	*9,001*	10,901	318	81	3,137	14,737	52	1,759	12,083	*2,254*	*72,202*
Apr. 18	474	5,045	3,396	30,535	*9,286*	10,943	276	100	3,212	16,003	52	1,763	12,507	*2,408*	*73,427*
May 16	200	5,056	3,391	31,843	*9,363*	11,627	254	93	3,192	16,678	53	1,782	12,232	*2,349*	*74,156*

Source: Bank of England, *Quarterly Bulletin* (June 1984).
Reproduced by kind permission of the Bank of England.

THE BALANCE SHEET ITEMS OF THE CLEARING BANKS: DEFINITIONS

The assets of the clearing banks indicate the uses to which the banks put the money deposited with them. The banks make profits by making a higher return on their assets than they need to pay to acquire liabilities. The principle assets and liabilities are described below. The principles determining asset and liability management were discussed above.

Assets

Notes and Coins

These are required to be kept in the bank tills in order to meet cash withdrawals.

Balances with the Bank of England

These can be of three types:

(i) *Cash ratio deposits.* The clearing banks have to lodge with the Bank of England non-operational, non-interest bearing deposits of ½% of their eligible liabilities.

(ii) *Special deposits.* Banks are liable for calls to lodge special deposits with the Bank of England. Interest is paid on special deposits at a rate adjusted weekly to the nearest 1/16% per annum on the average rate for Treasury bills issued at the weekly tender.

(iii) *Other.* These comprise balances with the Bank of England other than cash ratio and special deposits which are used for cheque clearing purposes.

Bills

These can be of various types.

(i) Treasury bills are three-month bills issued by the government.

(ii) Eligible local authority bills comprise UK local authority bills which are eligible for rediscount at the Bank of England.

(iii) Eligible bank bills comprise all bills which are payable in sterling and have been accepted by a reporting institution whose bills are eligible for discount at the Bank of England.

(iv) Other bills include ineligible local authority and bank bills.

Market Loans

These are short term loans to the money markets or to other banks, i.e. the inter-bank market.

Advances

These are loans and overdrafts to customers.

Investments

These are largely purchases of British Government stocks.

Liabilities

The major liabilities of the deposit banks are the deposits it receives from customers. These can be of two types:

(i) Sight deposits comprise balances which are transferable or withdrawable on demand without interest penalty. They include money at call (except where there is an agreement not to withdraw before a certain date or to call at a specific number of days' notice) and money placed overnight.

(ii) Time deposits comprise all other deposits (except certificates of deposit which are shown separately).

In addition, banks raise finance by issuing certificates of deposit. Naturally, the capital (shareholders' funds) is also included.

Eligible Liabilities

These comprise, in broad terms, sterling deposit liabilities, excluding deposits with an original maturity of over two years, plus any sterling resources obtained by switching foreign currencies into sterling. Inter-bank transactions (excluding cash ratio and special deposits with the Bank of England) are taken into the calculation of an individual institution's eligible liabilities.

OTHER FINANCIAL INSTITUTIONS (OFIs)

The OFI sector, as the name implies, comprise the remaining financial institutions (see Table 2.6). They are of various types which, though they are often competitors as borrowers or lenders, tend to operate in different markets.

The total assets of the major investing institutions and the major deposit institutions are given in Table 2.6. The commercial banks dominate the short end of the financial system with pension funds, life assurance companies and building societies dominating the long end of the system.

In contrast with clearing banks, other financial institutions have only a very limited role to play in the payments mechanism and in fact maintain their balances at deposit banks, not the Bank of England. Unlike the liabilities of clearing banks, those of OFIs are not generally accepted as a means of

Table 2.6

	Number of institutions	*Total assets at end of 1982*[1] *£ billion*
Finance houses and other consumer credit companies[2]	450	2.6
Building societies	210	74.5
Property unit trusts	33	1.6
Authorised unit trusts	614	7.7
Investment trusts	200	10.5
Insurance companies	900	96.9
of which: general funds		16.4
long-term funds[4]		80.5
Superannuation and pension funds	4,350[5]	84.3

1. Gross assets including physical assets.
2. Only those not included in the monetary sector.
3. Excludes about 1,500 companies which had each granted less than £50,000 credit in 1976.
4. Includes collecting friendly societies.
5. Includes about 3,500 small funds each with assets under £1 million in 1979.

Source: *Financial Statistics*.

payment. OFIs specialise in lending to certain sectors. The building societies lend to house buyers. Insurance companies, investment trusts, unit trust companies and superannuation funds invest more in longer-term securities such as long-dated gilts (see Table 2.7).

BUILDING SOCIETIES

Building societies are very actively involved in maturity transformation, i.e they provide liquid liabilities which meet the needs of savers whilst employing their funds in longer term financial instruments which are more convenient for borrowers (mortgages). They are non-profit making friendly societies.

Building societies operate in the traditional manner of financial institutions accepting deposits, virtually withdrawable on demand, from a wide range of small savers. They make loans for the purpose of house purchase for periods ranging from 15 to 25 years and are the dominant institution providing finance in the market for new or existing houses. The interest rate charged on mortgage loans is not fixed but is adjusted throughout the period of the mortgage. However, this entails administrative costs so they tend to change their rates less frequently than the changes which occur in other market rates. For this reason building society interest rates are said to be "sticky".

The dividing line between banks and building societies has in recent years become very blurred. Banks are now involved in house mortgages. Meanwhile the building societies are diversifying their deposit base by issuing CDs and also providing "chequeing facilities".

LIFE INSURANCE AND PENSION FUNDS

The business of insurance is that of spreading risk. Thus persons pay insurance companies a premium in return for the promise of a sum of money in the event of, for example, death, a car crash, fire, etc. Pension funds accept premiums now in return for the promise to pay a pension at a later date. Thus both types of business are faced with the twin problems of what to do with their funds and yet ensure ability to meet their commitments.

Life assurance fulfils two main functions. It provides insurance cover for a person's life and it is an important medium for saving. In the UK this second element is far more important than in many other countries, partly because of the greater freedom and opportunities given to life assurance companies in placing their funds and partly because of the tax advantages given to saving via life assurance. Pension funds also receive certain tax advantages. Pension provision involves the spreading of income over a lifetime – income received today is foregone and put aside to provide income during old age. It is therefore essentially a system of saving, albeit often involuntary, since many people are obliged to participate in their employer's pension scheme as a condition of employment.

Life assurance and pension funds originally tended to match the term of their lending very closely with that of their liabilities, so that assets (mainly gilts and other fixed-interest lending) matured with guaranteed money values at much the same time as liabilities became due for payment. This approach generally still holds good. But as more life assurance business is written on a with-profits basis, the life companies have placed greater emphasis on seeking as high a return as possible on their assets. Equities and properties, have therefore, become substantial proportions of their total portfolios. Pension funds incur liabilities which generally increase with wage and salary levels so that trustees have had a particular incentive to try to maintain the real value of their funds. For this reason they also turned in the 1960s to equities and property as a hedge against inflation.

Non-life or general insurance differs quite markedly from life assurance and pension business. The contract taken on by a general insurance company is essentially short-term and, while premiums are paid on a regular basis, the company only pays out in the event of certain circumstances occurring during a short period, usually a year. Insurance on a car, for example, normally lasts for one year and money is only paid out when there is an eligible claim. Some other categories of general business (for example marine or professional indemnity) produce claims which may arise some appreciable time after the premium has been received – even after the period of risk – and may take longer to settle. Accordingly the assets do not all need to be held in a very liquid form.

UNIT TRUSTS AND INVESTMENT TRUSTS

Unit trusts and investment trust companies provide for the collective placing of funds gathered together, mainly from individuals. Through them, an

Table 2.7
Sources of Uses and Funds of Other Financial Institutions

		Sources of funds														
			Deposits										Other liabilities			
		Total	Building societies	Trustee savings banks	NSB Investment account	Other	Bank borrowing	Unit trust units	Property unit trust units and LAMIT	Capital issues	Net inflow into Life assurance and pension funds	Official loans	UK	Overseas	Accruals adjustment	Residual
1979		19,311*	5,769	522	326	107	2,154	58	107	90	9,966	-4	130	-137*	520	-297*
1980		21,771	7,159	417	341	170	1,490	77	122	88	11,568	-4	193	-33	727	-544
1981		23,452	7,196	313		-96	2,001	456	221	244	12,640	-1	88	-60	184	266
1982		24,940	10,515				2,593	458	67	-3	12,803	-	68*	247	-156	-1,652
1983		29,816	12,056				2,288	1,316	89	128	14,010*	-	307*	982	-240	-1,120
1979	1	4,325*	1,206	216	99	-42	451	20	27	39	2,545	-1	96	-6*	-421	96*
	2	5,281	1,443	136	75	-9	973	12	36	12	2,380	-1	-86	59	203	48
	3	5,089	1,430	147	72	296	377	19	34	26	2,470	-1	119	-62	471	-309
	4	4,616	1,690	23	80	-138	353	7	10	13	2,571	-1	1	-128	267	-132
1980	1	4,428	1,207	135	76	-107	260	-9	9	25	2,705	-1	104*	-129	-414	567
	2	5,419	1,676	101	39	263	638	11	24	9	2,775	-1	111	-103	263	-387
	3	5,961	1,823	115	73	-132	305	14	32	-9	3,225	-1	-20	-2	494	44
	4	5,963	2,453	66	153	146	287	61	57	63	2,863	-1	-2	201	384	-768
1981	1	5,241	1,853	142		-205	746	133	55	132	3,230	-	57	-47	-898	43
	2	6,619	2,134	58		53	388	145	88	112	3,130	-	-7	165	347	6
	3	6,435	1,597	107		8	706	83	36	-4	3,235	-	28	-12	445	206
	4	5,157	1,612	6		48	161	95	42	4	3,045	-1	10	-166	290	11
1982	1	4,719	1,800				888	92	17	-2	3,686	-	-26	-443	-1,030	-263
	2	5,794	2,602				407	89	27	-3	2,724	-	-8	-322	225	53
	3	7,042	2,705				329	95	9	-20	3,350	-	65	260	498	-249
	4	7,385	3,408				969	182	14	22	3,043	-	37	752	151	-1,193
1983	1	5,840	1,907				603	329	16	-11	3,865	-	23	431	-1,430	107
	2	7,005	2,311				924	298	18	67	3,094	-	73	290	276	-346
	3	7,292	3,242				456	303	40	29	3,161	-	-34	-105	614	-414
	4	9,679	4,596				305	386	15	43	3,890*	-	245	366	300	-467
1984	1	8,166	3,610*				1,592	542*	20*	-4*	3,979	-	83	288	-1,093*	-851

Uses of funds

			Liquid assets		British government securities	Local authority longer term debt	UK company securities		Overseas securities			Loans and mortgages		Other financial assets		Land property and ground rents
									Company		Govern-ment securities					
		Total	Bank Deposits	Other			Ordinary shares	Other	Ordinary shares	Other		For house purchase	Other	UK	Overseas	
1979		19,311†	174	1,012	6,657	-113	2,051	-67	624	88	17	5,505	1,044	527†	427+	1,365
1980		21,771	1,671	357	5,546	188	2,431	-10	2,244	143	143	6,079	618	30	319	2,012
1981		23,452	1,983	-377	6,305	-369	2,388	115	2,470	275	172	6,601	656	689	356	2,188
1982		24,940	2,757	-370	4,692	359	2,474	449	2,980	285	809	8,153	391	711	-728	1,978
1983		29,816	2,754	268†	6,699†	-160†	2,019†	472†	2,660†	208	504†	11,194	1,082†	926	-328	1,518+
1979	1	4,325†	-331	715	1,508	-77	613	-34	80	23	11	1,306	148	78†	30†	255
	2	5,281	229	25	2,015	-55	655	-	67	14	-19	1,401	320	228	52	349
	3	5,089	-181	416	1,656	46	388	-22	144	35	-3	1,484	303	478	124	312
	4	4,616	457	-144	1,569	-27	395	-11	333	16	28	1,314	273	-257	221	449
1980	1	4,428	58	-53	1,417	130	336	-37	549	18	1	1,322	246	-119	60	500
	2	5,419	473	628	1,080	119	484	-11	414	40	16	1,331	365	11	15	454
	3	5,961	349	-70	2,230	-65	654	-4	577	48	60	1,622	-	67	53	440
	4	5,963	791	-148	819	4	957	42	704	37	66	1,804	7	71	191	618
1981	1	5,241	-355	-488	2,434	-150	504	-41	747	72	21	1,655	49	165	91	537
	2	6,619	502	113	1,652	-71	519	69	767	59	40	1,926	209	149	144	541
	3	6,435	1,119	197	1,099	-51	844	72	425	57	52	1,679	216	58	104	564
	4	5,157	717	-199	1,120	-97	521	15	531	87	59	1,341	182	317	17	546
1982	1	4,719	-232	125	1,565	7	470	120	683	115	150	1,305	68	137	-292	498
	2	5,794	916	-40	660	-33	737	110	547	93	222	2,021	110	172	-225	504
	3	7,042	944	-98	1,625	211	578	132	685	68	378	2,137	29	45	-219	527
	4	7,385	1,129	-357	842	174	689	87	1,065	9	59	2,690	184	357	8	449
1983	1	5,840	-651	190	896†	-151†	551	110	1,056	62	-11	2,812	123†	336	113	404
	2	7,005	1,061	-82	1,285	-49	453	197†	697	73	156	2,860	192	28	-204	338
	3	7,292	270	-12	2,549	-5	651	83	369	17	105	2,686	248	332	-343	342†
	4	9,679	2,074	172†	1,969	45	364†	82	538†	56	254†	2,836	519	230	106	434
1984	1	8,166	717	246	1,559	145	629	273	286	40†	200	2,985†	241	445	120	280

Source: *Financial Statistics*, (July 1984)

individual can obtain a share of a larger, more diversified portfolio than he could himself hold and also receives professional management-services. For providing these services the unit trust and investment company managers charge a fee. Unit trusts and investment trust companies operate as principals in the securities market (although the assets of unit trusts are held on their behalf by trustees), their portfolios consisting very largely of ordinary shares. Unit trusts issue equity claims on a proportionate part of their portfolio and investment trust companies issue shares in the company. The difference between their issued claims is therefore that the investor in a unit trust buys a proportion of the underlying assets, while the shareholder of an investment trust company buys shares in the company that owns the underlying assets.

Unit trusts are trusts in the legal sense. Investment trusts are limited companies, usually listed on the Stock Exchange and operating with both share and loan capital. Unit trusts are open-ended funds and their capital can be increased by issuing more units or decreased when holders want to redeem units. The unit-holder can always buy units from, or sell units to, the unit trust, which will, in turn, buy or sell securities according to the net inflow or outflow of funds (or draw on, or add to, its liquid assets.) Investment trust companies, on the other hand, are closed-ended funds and anyone wishing to buy their shares must, except when new issues are made, buy from an existing holder. Their share prices do not necessarily match the value of the underlying assets and in recent years have stood at a considerable discount to them. The price of shares in an investment trust reflects demand for its shares; the price of units, on the other hand, directly reflects the underlying value of the unit trust's portfolio. The shares of investment trust companies are often held by other institutions – perhaps looking for the benefits of diversification of management or an interest in a particular market sector which might not be readily available directly. Unit trust units are predominantly held by individuals; some are, however, held on behalf of individuals by life assurance companies running unit-linked assurance schemes.

THE 1979 UK BANKING ACT – THE BACKGROUND TO THE LEGISLATION

The UK was the only country in the world which had for centuries a highly developed banking system not comprehensively regulated under a Banking Act. Naturally this did not mean that regulation had been entirely absent. It was, however, conducted by informal means and by a disparate range of Acts of Parliament. Three developments occurring in the 1960s and 1970s however indicated the need for the financial system to be more explicitly regulated. These related to UK internal banking developments, UK external banking developments and the UK membership of the EEC.

Internally, from 1957 onwards, the fight against excessive internal demand and inflation and the balance of payments crises which it brought required repeated crash programmes of deflation. This always included a fierce quantitative and qualitative restriction of clearing bank advances. The clearing banks complained, not at the restrictions in themselves, but because the many hire-purchase finance houses were free of them and thus able to do the very business denied to the banks. The net was cast wider in later years, but the process of disintermediation (the process by which borrowing and lending bypasses the banks) had begun. As the years passed it spread and gave birth to many financial institutions on the fringe of the banking system proper, which were to cause much trouble in the mid-1970s.

External developments were linked to the growth of the new international capital markets based principally on the euro-dollar and, to a lesser extent, on some other currencies traded outside the bounds of their domestic origin and at rates of interest not tied to their domestic market but established internationally. As these markets grew, so it became necessary for banks who wished to do business in them to become more international in character. The British authorities have a special problem arising from the very attractiveness of the environment for banking business which they have created. There is, indeed no more attractive centre in the world from which to do international business. As a result, the influx of foreign banks in London during the past 15 to 20 years has been enormous, so that they now far outnumber the domestic banks.

Because of these domestic and international developments, the banking system which the Bank is required to regulate is vastly more diverse than the cosy little banking community that existed before the war.

Since 1973 the UK has been a member of the European Economic Community. Harmonisation of economic policy is already an acknowledged objective. Membership entails harmonisation in many fields of which banking is one. Whatever other considerations may have led the UK authorities to produce a banking Act, the inescapable need for it arises from the requirements of banking harmonisation within the Community. In short, all Community banks are required to be officially licensed before they can do banking business.

THE BANKING ACT 1979 – THE LEGISLATION

The act is not designed to regulate and control in detail every aspect of the business of banking.

The main purposes of the Act are:

(1) To prevent any bank or other financial institution, whether existing or newly formed, from accepting deposits without obtaining authority to do so from the Bank of England.

(2) To lay down the criteria which must be satisfied if such authority is to be received and retained.

(3) To provide statutory authority for the supervision by the Bank of England of the activities of all such institutions.

(4) To control the use of banking names and descriptions, limiting them in the main to recognised banks.

(5) To provide a measure of protection for depositors in licensed institutions through the medium of a Depositors' Protection Scheme.

The Banking Act provides for two forms of authorisation for deposit-taking institutions, namely that of:

(a) recognised bank; or

(b) licensed deposit-taker.

This division is not required by the EEC banking directive, but has been devised to enable the Bank of England to limit the use of banking names and descriptions, and to retain for recognised banks the informal type of supervision which it has hitherto exercised over them, while applying more rigorous controls over licensed deposit takers.

In order to qualify for recognised bank status an applicant would have to meet the following criteria:

(a) that the institution should enjoy and should have enjoyed for a reasonable period of time a high reputation and standing in the financial community;

(b) that the institutions should provide a wide range of banking services (or a highly specialised banking service), covering the following:

  (i) current and deposit account facilities or the acceptance of funds in the wholesale money markets;

  (ii) finance in the form of overdraft or loan facilities or the lending of funds in the wholesale money markets;

  (iii) foreign exchange services;

  (iv) finance through the medium of bills of exchange and promissory notes together with finance for foreign trade;

  (v) financial advice or investment management services and facilities for arranging the purchase and sale of securities.

Having listed the five basic banking services, the Act then goes on to give the Bank of England discretion to excuse the provision of one or two of the last three of them. Thus it might be possible to obtain recognition just by taking deposits, making loans and providing one other of the five basic services. Finally, it is possible to qualify for recognition, not by providing the five services but by demonstrating that, as the Act puts it, a "highly specialised banking service" is provided. However, it is understood that this provision would be used in the case of the discount houses. So the hurdles for the would-be recognised bank may all be of the same height but their construction can apparently differ widely.

To qualify as a licensed deposit-taking institution, the applicant must not only conduct business in a prudent manner but also:

(a) maintain net assets sufficient to safeguard the interests of depositors;

(b) maintain adequate liquidity, having regard to the relationship between liquid assets and liabilities and also the times at which the liabilities fall due and assets mature;

(c) make adequate provision for bad and doubtful debts and obligations of a contingent nature.

THE SUPERVISION AND MONITORING PROPOSALS – THE POST-BANKING ACT POSITION

The new Act was brought into operation from October 1979. Since that time the Bank of England has been endeavouring to agree with the banking community on the general supervising principles to be agreed. The bank has published three consultative papers in this connection and is trying to maintain a traditionally participative and flexible approach to supervision. The Governor has gone out of his way to emphasise that these documents are consultative.

The three papers so far published include proposals on:

(1) *Capital Adequacy Ratios*

(2) *Exposure to Foreign Currency Risks*

(3) *Ideas on the Measurement and Monitoring of Liquidity*

(1) Capital Adequacy Ratios

The capital adequacy of a bank is measured by relating the capital base of the bank to the riskness of its assets. The objectives of capital ratios are viewed by the Bank as being necessary:

(a) To ensure that the capital position of an institution is regarded as acceptable by the depositors and the creditors.

(b) To test the adequacy of capital in relation to the risk of losses which may be sustained.

Two methods of assessing the adequacy of capital were outlined:

(i) *A "free resources" ratio* or (Gearing Ratio) broadly relates current liabilities to capital resources, excluding that part of capital which is devoted to financing infrastructure and other non-banking assets.

(ii) *a "risk asset" ratio* broadly relates the risks of losses which are inherent in the assets of the business to the capital which is available to finance such losses. The 1975 paper argued that this measure was more useful and in recent years the Bank has come to place increasing emphasis on it.

It is intended that the standard risk asset calculation will take into account three types of risk inherent in the assets themselves but that weightings should be applied to different assets reflecting the extent to which they are susceptible to these risks. The three types of risk are:

(a) *Credit risk* – the risk that claims on others may not be redeemable at the due date at their full book value;

(b) *Investment risk* – the risk that marketable claims on others, or directly held assets, may depreciate below their book value;

(c) *Forced sale risk* – the risk that actual and additional losses may be sustained because of the need to make untimely sales of assets which, depending on the narrowness of the market, may yield less than their quoted value.

Each category of asset currently identifiable from statistical returns has been reviewed and a factor representing a risk weight has been ascribed to it. These weights attempt to reflect the relative risk of loss arising from credit or investment and forced sale risks inherent in a particular class of asset. For this purpose commercial advances are taken as a benchmark to which a weight of unity is therefore ascribed. The risks attaching to other assets may be less or more than those attaching to commercial advances, e.g. the weight ascribed to market loans to listed banks is 0.2 and the weight attached to property is 2.0.

The risk asset ratio is calculated by multiplying each balance sheet asset by its weight to produce an adjusted total of risk assets and then establishing the proportion of the total represented by the capital base as modified by the items requiring a deduction. This calculation represents only the first step in the assessment of capital adequacy by this method. Final assessment will take into account the particular circumstances of each institution.

(2) Exposure to Foreign Currency Risks

The Consultative Paper – December 1980

The foreign currency paper followed from the abolition of exchange controls in 1979. Before that event, the Bank had through the exchange control mechanism a means to exercise some measure of prudential control and monitoring the banking system's exposure to exchange risks. Once that had gone, the Bank found it necessary to establish more explicit criteria appropriate to a world in which both the size of foreign currency business and the risks involved have increased greatly with the general floating of the leading currencies.

Following more than a year of discussions with banks over the early consultative documents which the banks thought too restrictive, the Bank of England has given ground to the banks over the extent to which they are allowed to speculate in foreign exchange dealing and a new agreed version has been published.

Banks as a matter of routine take positions in foreign currencies, risking their own cash, based on their judgements of exchange rate trends. At the end of any day's dealing a bank's exposure can vary greatly, depending on market conditions. The new guidelines relate maximum foreign currency exposure to a bank's capital base.

Banks will not now be expected to risk more than 10% of their capital base – measured after certain technical adjustments – in any one currency. The original suggestion was that the limit should be 3½%, which was criticised by some banks that had particularly large commitments in a single currency.

In addition, a bank's position at the end of the day in all currencies taken together should not be more than 15% of the adjusted capital base. The original proposal was 10%.

(3) Measuring and Monitoring of Liquidity

Banks need liquidity for three reasons:

(i) to meet day-to-day withdrawals. Note that this applies not just in the case of cash withdrawals but also settlement of the clearing. It is for this latter reason that the clearing banks maintain operational balances, "other balances" at the Bank of England over and above the ½% deposit which applies to all banks. The ½% deposit is not available for day-to-day use and is not, therefore, liquid.

(ii) To meet unforeseeable problems in financing known future commitments. So a bank which has known future commitments needs some liquidity in its existing assets in case it runs into difficulties in obtaining new finance to meet these future commitments.

(iii) In order to maintain confidence in the bank. If a bank was unexpectedly faced with large losses, occurring for whatever reason, it must be able to maintain the confidence of its depositors.

Banks can maintain an adequate level of liquidity in several ways:

(i) By maintaining a certain percentage of their assets in a liquid form, e.g. cash, Treasury bills or eligible bills.

(ii) By maintaining a diversified deposit base. In this regard the banks should ensure that their deposits could not be all withdrawn immediately, as, say, is the case with demand deposits.

(iii) By being able to raise extra deposits, if necessary, from elsewhere, e.g. the interbank market. In this case banks should recognise that there is the possibility of the market, as a whole, being short of cash. In addition they should ensure that their bank has a "good name" in the market.

(v) By ensuring that there is an adequate cash flow being generated from existing assets. So the bank should ensure that loans matured at fixed known future dates and that this was linked with known future liability obligations. Banks must allow, here, for potential shortfalls, should borrowers be unable to repay.

In 1981 the Bank of England issued a consultative document on liquidity with a view to establishing across-the-board criteria applicable to all banks. The document concentrated on a cash flow approach but issued guidelines only. All the aspects of providing liquidity mentioned above are taken into account.

In a paper issued on 20 July 1982 the Bank refined the criteria for liquidity adequacy. It did stress that responsibility for ensuring the liquidity of a bank rested with its own management. The Bank was not seeking to impose across-the-board liquidity-ratio norms. However, the Bank does require that it is fully satisfied that adequate management systems are implemented and it will monitor banks' liquidity. With these principles in mind the paper establishes a framework for measuring liquidity.

The measure described below is based on a cash flow approach, normally taking liabilities and assets in all currencies together. In this approach liabilities and assets are inserted into a "maturity ladder", with the net positions in each time period being accumulated. In the first maturity bands on the ladder this measure, by comparing sight and near sight liabilities with cash and assets capable of generating cash immediately, is similar to a customary liquid assets ratio. Marketable assets are placed at the start of the maturity ladder, rather than according to their maturity date, but account needs to be taken of limitations on their marketability and their susceptibility to price fluctuations. The measure is thus a series of accumulating net mismatch positions in successive time bands.

The measurement incorporates the following particular features:

(1) Liabilities

(i) Deposits of all types are included according to earliest maturity. The volatility of the deposit base is taken into account here.

(ii) The diversification of the deposit base is taken into account. So known firm commitments to make funds available on a particular date are included in the appropriate time band at their full value.

(2) Assets

(i) Assets are measured by reference to their maturity unless, as in the case of overdrafts, they are repayable on demand in practice only nominally.

(ii) Lending repayable on demand only nominally may yield some regular cash flow but this cannot be measured at all precisely. The Bank will wish to agree appropriate treatment with each bank.

(iii) The treatment of marketable assets take account of the extent to which they can be sold for cash quickly (or used as security for borrowing), and of any credit or investment risks which may make their potential value less predictable. It is important that the market for the asset should be sufficiently deep to ensure a stable demand for it. An important factor in this is the willingness of the central bank to use the asset in its normal market operations. These considerations are recognised in the measurement by applying varying discounts normally against the market value of marketable assets, all of which, as indicated earlier are included at the start of the maturity ladder.

APPENDIX 1

Table 2.8
Summary Capital Accounts and Financial Surplus or Deficit Analysis by Sector

£ million, seasonally adjusted

	Public sector[1]			*Financial companies and institutions*			*Industrial and commercial companies*		
	Saving[2]	*Capital transfers (net receipts)*	*Gross domestic capital formation*[3]	*Saving*[2]	*Capital transfers (net receipts)*	*Gross domestic capital formation*[3]	*Saving*[2]	*Capital transfers (net receipts)*	*Gross domestic capital formation*[3]
1979	3 337	- 264	11 448	4 391	-237	3 924	20 907	324	22 809
1980	2 704	-360	12 974	4 833	-302	5 087	17 102	387	16 916
1981	3 739	-226	12 068	5 273	-567	5 359	18 467	591	16 395
1982	6 145	-642	12 777	6 383	-439	5 759	17 987	584	16 102
1983	4 816	-1 188	14 203		-335			475	
1979 *1*	675	-66	2 687	1 030	-50	854	4 605	81	5 389
2	1 157	-89	2 700	1 048	-67	1 096	5 496	104	5 257
3	1 140	-57	3 080	1 238	-60	956	5 663	85	6 273
4	365	-52	2 981	1 075	-60	1 018	5 143	54	5 890
1980 *1*	1 341	-68	3 251	1 191	-65	1 204	5 635	62	5 275
2	532	-82	3 019	1 422	-83	1 218	4 798	80	4 982
3	117	-149	3 358	1 264	-81	1 305	3 467	115	3 437
4	714	-61	3 346	956	-73	1 360	3 202	130	3 222
1981 *1*	23	-107	3 201	1 202	-70	1 189	4 001	139	3 510
2	886	-115	3 079	1 177	-85	1 321	4 449	155	3 715
3	949	-9	2 842	1 257	-80	1 431	5 170	166	4 555
4	1 881	5	2 946	1 637	-332	1 418	4 847	131	4 615
1982 *1*	2 309	-163	3 174	1 183	-136	1 472	3 385	196	4 103
2	1 316	-33	3 042	1 625	-115	1 464	4 342	78	4 339
3	1 643	-143	3 224	1 798	-101	1 539	4 671	77	3 737
4	877	-303	3 337	1 777	-87	1 284	5 589	233	3 923
1983 *1*	1 187†	-286†	3 764	1 766	-86	1 530	5 413	226	4 533
2	1 513	-172	3 409	1 660	-107	1 456	5 326	91	4 282
3	1 193	-308	3 616	1 305	-91	1 393	7 116	73	4 560
4	923	-422	3 414		-51			85	

	Personal sector			Financial Surplus/Deficit[4]					
	Saving[2]	*Capital transfers (net receipts)*	*Gross domestic capital formation*[2]	*Public sector*	*Financial companies and institutions*	*Industrial and commercial companies*	*Personal sector*	*Overseas sector*[5]	*Residual error*[6]
1979	17 425	177	7 500	-8 375	+230	!1 578	10 102	553	-932
1980	23 403	275	7 602	-10 630	-556	573	16 076	-3 650	-1 813
1981	21 492	202	7 973	-8 555	-653	2 663	13 721	-7 272	96
1982	20 375	497	10 486	-7 274	185	2 469	10 386	-5 551	-215
1983		1 048		-10 575				-2 049	
1979 *1*	4 122	35	1 604	-2 078	126	-703	2 553	516	-414
2	3 202	52	1 843	-1 632	-115	343	1 411	-79	72
3	4 224	32	1 874	-1 997	222	-525	2 382	-124	42
4	5 877	58	2 179	-2 668	-3	-693	3 756	240	-632
1980 *1*	4 938	71	2 058	-1 978	-78	422	2 951	-179	-1 138
2	5 630	85	1 958	-2 569	121	-104	3 757	-100	-1 105
3	6 411	115	1 910	3 390	-122	145	4 616	-1 341	92
4	6 424	4	1 676	-2 693	-477	110	4 752	-2 030	338
1981 *1*	5 862	38	1 890	-3 285	-57	630	4 010	-2 698	1 400
2	5 020	45	1 773	-2 308	-229	889	3 292	-2 296	652
3	5 124	-77	2 161	-1 902	-254	781	2 886	-789	-722
4	5 486	196	2 149	-1 060	-113	363	3 533	-1 489	-1 234
1982 *1*	5 933	103	2 472	-1 028	-425	-522	3 564	-1 107	-482
2	5 377	70	2 585	-1 759	46	81	2 862	-1 027	-203
3	4 594	167	2 598	-1 724	158	1 011	2 163	-1 237	-371
4	4 471	157	2 831	-2 763	406	1 899	1 797	-2 180	841
1983 *1*	4 797	146	2 961	-2 863	150	1 106	1 982	-1 094	719
2	4 208	188	2 995	-2 068	97	1 135	1 401	37	-602
3	4 290	326	3 076	-2 731	-179	2 629	1 540	-653	-606
4		388		-2 913				-339	

[1] Excluding financial transaction in writing-off debt.
[2] Before providing for depreciation stock appreciation and addition to reserves.
[3] Comprises gross domestic fixed capital formation and increase in value of stocks and work in progress.
[4] This balance is equal to savings *plus* capital transfer *less* gross domestic fixed capital formation, *less* increase in value of stocks and work in progress.
[5] Equals, apart from the change in sign, the current balance of payments accounts, *plus* capital transfers.
[6] The residual error in the national income accounts.

Source: *Economic Trends* (March 1984)
Reproduced by kind permission of the Controller of her Majesty's Stationery Office.

Chapter 3

Money Markets

WHAT IS A MONEY MARKET?

The money market is a short-term debt market. An illustration of how the market functions gives some insight into how it acquired its name. As a debt market, the money market loans a specific amount of money for a specific period to a borrower who promises to pay a specified rate of interest. When the obligation matures, the entire principal amount is repaid to the lender, plus the interest involved (unless the borrower defaults). The obligation itself in this respect is no different from a bank deposit or an IOU. However, what differentiates this type of instrument from the simpler type of savings vehicles is its liquidity. The nomenclature of market suggests that these instruments may also be bought and sold in a secondary market after the date of issue (primary markets are ones in which *new* financial claims are issued, whereas a secondary market is one on which previously issued financial claims are traded). Thus, it may be said that debt with a short life, possessing a secondary market, is a highly liquid form of investment comparable to actual cash itself since most of it may be sold upon demand. Hence, the term "money market".

As debt markets, the primary function of the money markets is to redistribute funds from those economic units in society possessing a surplus to those in deficit. Business and government enterprises, net spenders by nature of their commercial and political mandates, borrow from the household sector and other sectors which are traditionally net savers. The money market is the place where the borrower and lender come together.

The London money market provides an efficient and competitive set of markets, through which banks, companies, local authorities, and indeed any entity with substantial resources or needs, may employ temporarily surplus funds or meet their short-term borrowing requirements.

The money markets are wholesale markets where professionals deal with each other in very large sums of money. This enables loans to be made and accepted on very "fine" terms.

THE LONDON MONEY MARKET

The London money market is one of the most sophisticated and the most active in the world for both sterling and foreign currency short-term money. Major borrowers in the market are the banks, the central government, local authorities and large corporations. Major lenders are the banks, financial institutions (domestic and overseas), corporations and, as a last resort, the Bank of England. The discount houses and moneybrokers play special roles as intermediaries and dealers in short-term money.

As already mentioned, the money markets are the mechanisms through which wholesale funds are channelled from lenders to borrowers. Most of the deals are not arranged directly between the participants but through the intermediary of brokers. Wholesale business involves the taking and giving of large deposits/loans (normally more than £50,000) and on which very competitive interest rates are paid and received.

Although there is not a rigid separation between them the money markets can be divided into:

(a) *The Discount Market* – predominantly a market on which lending is *secured*, i.e. backed by a financial asset and in which the Bank of England acts as *Lender of last resort*. This market is sometimes referred to as the "official" or "classical market".

(b) *The Parallel Market* – predominantly a market on which lending is *unsecured* and there is no Lender of Last Resort. This market can itself be further divided according to whether transactions are in *sterling* instruments or in *eurocurrencies*. This market is sometimes referred to as the "unofficial market".

We thus have the following simple division:

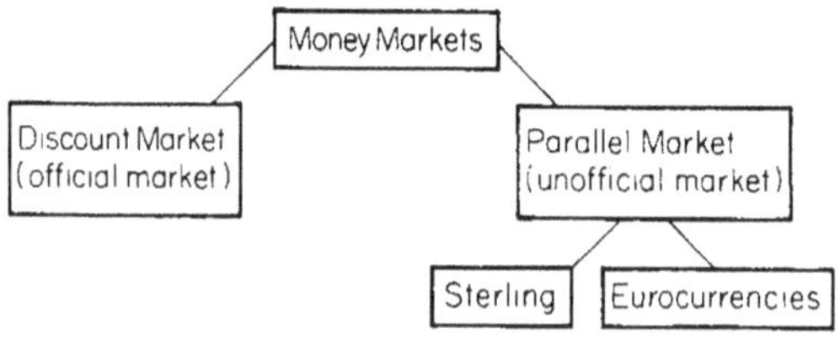

Fig. 3.1

Thus the money market consists of two parallel but interlinking markets:

(1) An *"official"* market characterised by the following features:

(a) it is made by the discount houses;

(b) it is a market in SECURED funds;

(c) all participants deal as principals;

(d) brokers or other middlemen play a relatively small role;

(e) there is the right of access to the Bank of England, but only for discount houses, subject to the availability of "eligible" assets.

(2) An "*unofficial*" market characterised by the following features:

(a) it is a market in UNSECURED funds;

(b) brokers are active as middlemen bringing borrowers and lenders together;

(c) the discount houses participate, especially as traders in certificates of deposit (CDs);

(d) there is no access to or participation by the Bank of England.

Transactions in this market are regarded as "unofficial" not in a pejorative sense, but because, being a market in certificates of deposit and unsecured funds, it is not directly underwritten by the Bank of England. In practice the discount market enables the parallel market to function smoothly, taking up the net shortage or surplus of funds.

THE DISCOUNT MARKET

INTRODUCTION

This market dates back at least 150 years but over the years the nature of its business has changed. Originally small country banks used the London market to discount bills because they lacked sufficient funds to discount all the bills presented to them by customers. With the growth of London as an international finance centre, the London discount market was increasingly used for discounting commercial bills. During the slump of the 1930s, the main business became discounting Treasury bills. The commercial bill was described by the Radcliffe Report, published in 1959 as having only "vestigial" importance to the discount houses. Subsequently the importance of Treasury bill business has declined and that of discounting commercial bills increased. Significantly the market has also become interested in certificates of deposit, and short-term government stock.

FUNCTIONS OF THE DISCOUNT HOUSES

Despite numerous changes over the past 20 years the nine discount houses (see Chapter 2 for membership details) still constitute the core of money market arrangements in London. They form the London Discount Market Association and they have accounts with the Bank of England which give them access to the Bank of England as lender of last resort to the banking system.

Discount houses have four principal economic functions:

(1) Since they finance their books by borrowing at call or short notice from banks and others, they add to the supply of highly liquid assets available in the market. They thereby improve the efficiency of the monetary system.

(2) They "make markets" in a variety of short-term financial instruments by quoting prices at which they stand ready to deal thus contributing to the liquidity of these instruments.

(3) They finance the governments short debt requirements by agreeing to purchase all the Treasury bills issued.

(4) They are the institutions through which the Bank of England conducts its money market operations. The discount houses are the principal financial institutions which may approach the Bank for funds when they cannot obtain funds from any other source. Strictly speaking some other financial institutions can approach the bank but only the Discount Houses can deal on a last resort basis. Other financial institutions include stock jobbers, money brokers, clearing banks and members of the "lifeboat" operation.

Figure 3.2 in Appendix 1 indicates the changing structure of the discount market. Table 3.1 gives details of their assets and liabilities. Whereas in 1960 there were only three short-term instruments, now there are nine. Note that commercial bills are by far the most important asset traded followed by British Government securities and sterling CDs. Treasury bills have considerably decreased in importance. The functions of the discount houses are discussed in turn.

Providing a source for deploying liquid funds

The discount houses borrow at short-term mainly from the banks and invest mainly in short-term assets such as commercial bills and Treasury bills. Essentially what the discount houses borrow are the temporarily surplus funds of banks and similar institutions mostly operating in or through the City of London. These institutions must keep available liquid resources adequate to meet sudden demands for cash. At the same time, they cannot afford to keep their funds idle. This creates the need for both an investment outlet and a form of investment that is highly liquid. Call and overnight money which is "secured" is highly liquid. By secured is meant that collateral in the form of assets held by the discount houses is provided whenever call money is borrowed. In addition, there is a monetary ebb and flow – the available supply of money must be held somewhere in the system; if it has left the tills of one bank, it will generally be found in the hands of another. In other words, there is a revolving fund of money, which may be added to or subtracted from (e.g. by the authorities) from time to time, but which always remains substantial, though subject of course to important seasonal movements (e.g. at holiday times and at Christmas). By speeding up the deployment of surplus funds and/or relieving money market shortages the discount houses improve the efficiency of the monetary system.

Apart from the sums made available from time to time by the Bank of England (for a limited period and primarily by buying assets from the discount market), the main sources of liquidity are the London Clearing Banks and their subsidiaries, the Accepting Houses, the Overseas and Foreign Banks, and the Scottish Banks. In all, there are about 560 potential lenders to the London Discount Market (of which about 400 are banks). Of the total number (say) 300 to 350 are active lenders, of which (say) 250 institutions (or more) would be in the monetary sector. Increasingly moneys come from large companies and abroad.

The resources of the market are then invested in commercial and other sterling bills; Treasury bills; local authority bills; other public sector debt; certificates of deposit; inter-bank money; and British Government stocks (mostly from one to five years) plus a number of "other currency assets". The most important single item is commercial and other sterling bills (excluding local authority and other public sector).

Market makers for a variety of short-term financial instruments

The discount market acts as market makers for:

(a) Treasury bills;
(b) Commercial bills – (eligible and ineligible bank bills, trade bills and foreign currency bills);
(c) Certificates of deposit.

Treasury Bills

The Bank of England issues 91-day Treasury bills on behalf of the British government in order to provide the government with its required short-term funds and as a means of influencing liquidity and interest rates in the money market.

The bills are fully guaranteed as to principal and interest by the government and backed by the Consolidated Fund of the United Kingdom. In the primary market, bills are issued at a discount determined by weekly tender. Each Friday the amount of bills to be issued the following Friday is announced by the Bank of England. Any institution or individual, either resident or non-resident, may subscribe, but through the intermediary of a London bank, discount house or moneybroker.

Tenders must be in minimum denomination of £50,000 or above in multiples of £5,000. They must state the price offered expressed as a net amount per cent. For example, £97.50 for every £100 represents an annualised rate of interest of 10%. Since Treasury bills are made available on every day of the week of each tender period, the applicant must also state the date on which he wishes to take up the bills. Such bills run for 91 days from the date stated at the option of the tenderer. Tenders must be received by the Bank of England before 1 p.m. on Friday and the Bank then makes a preliminary announcement of the minimum accepted price and the number of bills to be allotted at that price. Precise results are announced at 3 p.m. when the number of tenders received, the amount allotted and at what price, the average tender price and the amount of bills to be offered at the next weekly tender are given. Tenders received at above the minimum accepted tender price are allotted in full. Tenders received at the minimum accepted price are allotted proportionately and those received at below the minimum price are unallotted.

Payment in full of amounts due in respect of accepted tenders must be made to the Bank of England not later than 1.30 p.m. on the day on which the relevant bills are to be dated. Payment must be in cash, draft or cheque drawn on the Bank of England.

The whole amount of each weekly issue is underwritten by the 9 London discount houses which ensures that all Treasury bills on offer will be covered. By controlling the minimum price it is prepared to accept, the Bank of England can influence rates of interest in the money market and signal changes in monetary policy. More important for monetary control, however, in recent years have been the bank bill dealing rates.

Commercial Bills

The discount houses have been instrumental in fostering the use of commercial bills as a means of providing finance for industry. As already mentioned just over 20 years ago the Radcliffe Report described the use of bills as "vestigial". Now they are employed widely as an effective and cheap form of finance.

The legal definition of a bill of exchange is:

(a) an unconditional order in writing;

(b) addressed by the seller or exporter – the person who draws the bill (the drawer);

(c) to another, normally either the buyer or importer;

(d) signed by the person giving it (the drawer);

(e) requiring the person to whom it is addressed (the drawee, who when he signs becomes the acceptor);

(f) to pay;

(g) on demand or at a fixed or determinable future time;

(h) a sum certain in money;

(i) to, or to the order of, a specified person or to bearer (the payee).

Today, the bill is one of the most convenient methods of borrowing available to industry. Its liquidity also makes it an attractive asset for banking and non-banking institutions to buy as a short-term investment. During the 1970s there was a continued growth in the use of commercial bills for these reasons. Another factor behind their growth was the banks' need to find alternative methods of meeting their customers' borrowing requirements without increasing their Interest Bearing Eligible Liabilities (IBELs) during the time of the "corset" (described in detail in Chapter 7). If a bank's IBELs rose into the penalty zone, the bank risked being forced to place Supplementary Special Deposits with the Bank of England – a grave penalty, as these deposits did not earn interest. The commercial bill of exchange provided one method of circumnavigating this problem. The role of these bills has recently been further enhanced under the Bank of England's new system of monetary control which has meant a broadening of the market.

How does a commercial bill work? In the following simplified example, ABC Printing Company Ltd., purchases large quantities of paper from XYZ Paper Company Ltd., on a monthly account. Therefore XYZ Ltd. must wait one month for full cash payment. However, should XYZ Ltd. want immediate payment so that the funds can be invested elsewhere, the company can draw up a bill of exchange. The bill will contain a multitude of information (listed above), including the name of the drawer (XYZ Ltd.), the drawee (ABC Ltd.), the amount, date payable, etc. The bill is then sent to ABC Ltd. who signify their agreement to the order of the drawer to pay, by accepting it. In some circumstances a bank can be asked to accept a bill on behalf of the drawee, in which case the accepting bank will be the acceptor. The customary form of acceptance is to write the name and address of the paying bank and place the acceptor's signature on the bill.

For accepting the bill, the bank will receive a commission as it has thereby accepted the responsibility of full payment of the bill on its maturity date, on behalf of its client. The bill is now a banker's acceptance, the benefits of which will be noted later. The cost of this commission will depend on the state and credit worthiness of ABC Ltd. and the face value of the bill, but is normally between 1–1½% of the value. The bill is now a "two named" bill with the names of the acceptor and the drawer on them as opposed to a "one name" Treasury bill and as such is returned to the drawer (XYZ Ltd.). As payee (i.e. to whom the bill is payable), the bill should be endorsed by an authorised signatory of the company.

By endorsing the bill it can now be offered for sale to a discount house, whose business it is to purchase commercial bills. Normally companies have organised facilities for this purpose with one or more discount houses. The purchase price for the bill will be the face value less the "discount" which is dependent upon a number of factors:

(1) the level of interest rates
(2) the state of the money markets: are there surpluses or shortages?
(3) the standing of acceptor: if the acceptor's name means that the bill can be rediscounted at the Bank of England (i.e. it is an eligible bank), the price

the bill will command will be higher than an ineligible bank acceptance or trade customer acceptance

(4) the length of time: if the bill has 91 days to run the price will be lower than if it has only seven days to run. This is connected with the level of interest rates

(5) the demand and supply of such bills.

Therefore XYZ Ltd. receive a price for their bill dependent upon the various factors stated above. Although this is a very simple example, it provides the reader with a basic understanding of the operations that take place in the primary market.

Commercial bills are time drafts drawn on one company or trader by another to finance the import or export or inland sale of goods or to finance stocks. Because they finance actual transactions in goods, the bills are self-liquidating in that proceeds are generated by the sale of goods. The amounts for which such bills are issued vary: they may be for amounts as small as a few thousand pounds but sizes of £250,000 or more are the norm and £1,000,000 usually the largest size of bill issued. Bills may be issued for periods of one to six months, though three month bills are the most common.

Although drawn on one company by another, the bills are payable to the bearer and thus are readily negotiable in the secondary market. This market is very active in most types of commercial bills and maintained by the clearing banks, merchant banks and discount houses. There are four types of commercial bills traded in the UK money market. These are eligible and ineligible bank bills, trade bills and foreign currency bills.

Commercial bills are issued at a discount to the par value of the bill and quoted on a yield basis. Eligible bank bills are the most secure and most marketable and thus yield the lowest, while conversely trade bills have the lowest security and the highest yield.

Bank Bills

Bank bills are commercial bills that have been accepted by a bank. This involves the bank in accepting full liability to pay the face value of a bill on maturity through the drawing up of an acceptance credit that confirms that the terms on which bills drawn on a particular company will be honoured.

Eligible bank bills are those that have been accepted by one of a list of banks agreed by the Bank of England. Eligible bank bills are so called because, having been accepted by the requisite institutions, they are then eligible for rediscounting at the Bank of England.

Ineligible bank bills are those which, although they have been accepted by a bank, have not been accepted by one included on the Bank of England's approved list. Yields on ineligible bank bills are consequently slightly higher than for eligible bank bills of comparable terms.

Trade Bills

Trade bills carry two names only. They are not accepted by a bank, but accepted directly by a company or trader who is effectively the issuer of the bill and is party to the specific trade transaction that is stated on the face of the bill. At maturity the bill may be presented by the holder to the acceptor's bank which should also be stated on the face of the bill. The acceptor should make available to his bank the funds necessary to honour the bill, but if he has not done so then the holder has recourse to the drawer of the bill whose name is also on its face.

The rate of discount, and thus yield, attaching to a particular trade bill depends on the financial status of the acceptor by a bank. However, trade bills are considered less secure than bank bills and not only yield more but are less readily negotiable in the secondary market. Only the highest quality trade bills are held by discount houses although such trade bills as sold by the discount houses to their customers are normally accepted as the liability of the discount house.

Foreign Currency Bills

These are issued under the same terms as bank bills or trade bills but are denominated in a foreign currency. Normally they finance the import or export of goods between, usually, UK exporters and foreign importers. By their nature of being non-sterling bills, no foreign currency bills may be eligible bank bills and they may not qualify for sale to the Bank of England. The most common currency for such bills is US dollars, which enjoy an active market in London. Bills denominated in other currencies generally do not have active secondary markets. The rate of discount attaching to foreign currency bills depends on the credit rating of the parties whose signatures are on the face of the bill and whether the bill has been accepted by a bank. At maturity, the bills are payable in London by the transfer of funds from the country of the currency in which the bills are denominated.

Certificates of Deposit (CDs)

The discount houses also act as market-makers in the CD market holding a portfolio of CDs for this purpose. Indeed their willingness to act as market-makers was crucial to the development of the sterling CD market. The first sterling certificates of deposit were introduced in 1968. A certificate of deposit is a negotiable instrument certifying that a sum of money has been deposited with the bank issuing the certificate, at a fixed or floating rate of interest, and that on the stated maturity date the deposit will be repaid with interest by the issuing bank. CDs may be issued for periods of from three months to five years and in multiples of £10,000 from a minimum of £50,000 up to £500,000 for any one certificate, although issues of £1 million have been made. Certificates are issued at par on an interest to maturity basis, as opposed to being issued on a discount basis as in the case of Treasury, commercial or local authority bills.

Table 3.1
Discount Market
Amount outstanding at end of period

Discount Market
Amount outstanding at end of period — *£ million*

Liabilities: borrowed funds

	Sterling							Other currencies			
	Total	of which: Call and overnight	Other	Bank of England	Other UK monetary sector	Other UK	Overseas	Total	UK monetary sector	Other UK	Overseas
1983											
May 18	5,680	5,272	408	-	5,178	499	3	137	109	22	6
Jun 15	6,031	5,535	496	50	5,373	595	13	142	107	25	10
Jul 20	5,366	4,857	509	-	4,822	538	6	86	59	20	7
Aug 17	5,434	4,968	466	-	4,787	624	23	104	59	23	22
Sep 21	5,047	4,488	559	102	4,375	555	15	79	57	12	10
Oct 19	6,046	5,547	499	-	5,256	752	38	135	111	15	9
Nov 16	5,960	5,424	536	-	5,168	771	21	165	142	13	10
Dec 14	6,667	6,132	535	55	5,838	738	36	71	49	14	8
1984											
Jan 18	5,661	5,113	548	64	4,634	952	11	53	24	18	11
Feb 15	5,822	5,354	468	33	4,958	826	5	85	43	26	16
Mar 21	6,493	5,888	605	88	5,397	987	21	172	117	37	18
Apr 18	6,730	6,204	526	102	5,571	1,040	17	235	167	39	29
May 16	5,927†	5,439†	488	67	4,755	1,078†	27†	169	89	63	17
Jun 20	6,308	5,736	572†	-	5,334†	962	12	154†	69†	64†	21†

Assets

Sterling

	Total	Cash ratio deposits with the Bank of England	UK and NI Treasury bills	Other bills: UK local authority	Other bills: Other public sector	Other bills: Other bills	Funds lent: UK monetary sector	Funds lent: Certificates of deposit	Funds lent: UK local authorities	Funds lent: Other UK*	Funds lent: Overseas
1983											
May 18	5,924	2	114	146	4	2,999	30	1,996	143	31	-
Jun 15	6,274	2	116	232	-	3,269	20	1,792	139	88	-

Jul 20	5,559	2	21	13	2	2,875	71	1,796	140	155	-
Aug 17	5,634	2	122	35	3	2,805	139	1,701	140	165	-
Sep 21	5,278	2	22	110	6	2,207	215	1,590	144	266	-
Oct 19	6,238	2	123	116	45	3,156	68	1,634	142	275	-
Nov 16	6,178	3	118	76	46	2,892	53	1,788	144	332	-
Dec 14	6,860	3	31	161	45	3,371	96	2,044	149	359	-
1984											
Jan 18	5,868	3	64	79	45	2,809	91	1,716	143	338	-
Feb 15	6,038	3	76	63	31	2,337	123	2,180	157	374	-
Mar 21	6,681	3	118	53	7	2,410	231	2,417	164	372	-
Apr 18	6,990	3	50	58	8	3,000	72	2,529	162	419	-
May 16	6,212	4	22	25	13	2,543	523	2,038	172	317	19
Jun 20	6,556†	4†	39†	150†	10†	2,743†	241†	2,123†	179†	391†	-

Assets (continued)

	Sterling (continued)					*Other currencies*			
	Investments								
	British government stocks	*UK local authority securities*	*Other*	*Other sterling assets*	*Total*	*Certificates of deposit*	*Bills*	*Other*	*Total assets or liabilities*
1983									
May 18	237	159	38	25	139	104	18	17	6,063
Jun 15	401	152	37	26	141	122	14	5	6,415
Jul 20	266	152	39	27	84	50	20	14	5,643
Aug 17	306	136	39	41	103	79	18	6	5,737
Sep 21	505	130	40	41	78	55	16	7	5,356
Oct 19	468	121	48	40	146	121	18	7	6,384
Nov 16	514	134	44	34	182	154	16	12	6,360
Dec 14	364	154	46	37	93	70	13	10	6,953
1984									
Jan 18	312	151	55	62	72	49	16	7	5,940
Feb 15	412	143	77	62	102	58	41	3	6,140
Mar 21	594	158	89	65	187	118	58	11	6,868
Apr 18	353	149	119	68	241	169	63	9	7,231
May 16	239	136	114	47	167	117	31	19	6,379
Jun 20	366†	144†	119†	47†	153†	112†	12†	29†	6,709†

*** Including, with effect from 15 June 1983, holdings of sterling certificates of deposit issued by building societies.**
Source: Bank of England, *Quarterly Bulletin* (June 1984).
Reproduced by kind permission of the Bank of England.

The role of the discount market with respect to CDs can be summarised as follows:

(1) The discount market buys a considerable quantity of CDs in the primary market (i.e. direct from issuing banks). These can be used as security for loans (money at call) and also provide a means of taking a view as to future interest rates.

(2) The discount market buys and sells secondary CDs and in fact largely constitutes the secondary CD market.

(3) The discount market deals in secondary US dollar CDs to use as security for sterling loans thus providing a means of arbitrage between sterling and eurodollar interest rates.

In addition the discount houses participate in the interbank market and other short-term loan markets. Gilt-edged stocks of between one and five years to maturity and local authority bonds also form significant elements in their portfolios. Foreign currency assets consist mainly of dollar CDs and foreign currency bills.

The Discount Houses and the Bank of England

The discount houses, as the principal market-makers in bills, underwrite the whole of the Treasury bill tender (i.e. are prepared to purchase all the bills on offer). Between 1971 and 1981 the Bank of England generally set the amount of bills on offer each week in excess of the Government's need for funds so that there would be a shortage of cash in the market. The cash balances held by the commercial banks at the Bank of England thus provided the "fulcrum" for the Bank of England's open market operations. When Treasury bills were sold, either to the banking system or the non-bank public, the commercial banks' balances at the Bank of England were run down to pay for the bills. In these circumstances the banks would withdraw their "money at call" from the discount houses. If on any day funds were withdrawn from a discount house to such an extent that it was unable to balance its books the Bank of England was able to provide funds as "lender of last resort", but at a penal rate of its own choosing.

Using this mechanism the Bank of England was able to influence the level of interest rates when it judged necessary. For instance, by consistently keeping money short in the market through open-market operations the Bank of England could force the discount houses to borrow at minimum lending rate (MLR) (bank rate before October 1972). This raised the overall cost of money borrowed by the houses who would then lower the price which they bid for Treasury bills (at the tender), in order to increase the yield of the bill. Treasury bills sold by tender do not attract a stated rate of interest but instead prospective purchasers bid for a quantity of bills at a discount (i.e. a price below the redemption price).

Thus by lowering their tender price the discount houses seek to buy Treasury bills at a higher yield to restore their profit margins. This increase in Treasury bill yields then has an upward effect on other rates of interest in the money markets.

As from 20 August 1981, MLR was suspended in an attempt by the Bank of England to allow market forces more sway in determining interest rates.* Under the new system then introduced, short rates, defined later, are to be kept by the authorities within a range – the so-called "unpublished band"; longer rates are to be allowed to fluctuate more freely. "Decisions as to the band will be taken in accord with the same range of considerations as would have determined decisions about MLR, so that the new arrangements imply a change in techniques, rather than in the objectives of monetary policy"†. This meant scrapping the old structure of Treasury bill dealing rates whereby the Bank of England were not only ready to lend overnight at MLR (which had now been suspended), but also to buy Treasury bills of different maturities at predetermined levels. The announcement of bill dealing rates a week ahead was one of the first things to go. The next stage – in terms of day-to-day operations – was the decision in November 1980 to shift the emphasis from lending directly to open market operations especially by dealing in bills. In practice, this meant primarily eligible bank bills, i.e. bankers' acceptances issued by accepting houses, the clearing banks, some commonwealth banks, and (from August 1981) certain foreign banks. Actually, there was no deliberate decision to shift from Treasury bills to bank bills, although there was a decision to increase the eligible bank bill market. It was really an accidental by-product of a sharp increase in the size of operations needed to balance the banking system's cash and a decline in the stock of Treasury bills available in the market to meet it‡. When there is a shortage of credit and discount houses are obliged to sell bills to the Bank of England they are now required to name a price. If the Bank of England does not like the price, it may turn them down. The Bank of England still sets the rates, but it is the market that proposes them.

What the Bank of England is now trying to do is to:

> "smooth out day-to-day shortages or surpluses of cash by means of open-market operations, rather than by direct lending to the discount market. In dealing with shortages, the Bank has usually either bought bills outright or, if the shortage was to be followed before long by a day of prospective surplus, it has bought bills for resale on that day. When the market has been in surplus, the Bank has sought to sell Treasury bills set to mature on a day of prospective shortage. Where large transactions could be estimated in advance – notably oil tax payments or calls on part-paid gilt-edged stocks already sold – operations have been framed accordingly . . . All these operations were conducted within the context of a general objective for very short-term interest rates. Where the Bank dealt in longer-term bills, it did so to change market's cash position on the day of the transaction

*Although it was brought back for one day (14 January 1985) when the sterling exchange rate was under considerable pressure.

†See Bank of England, *Quarterly Bulletin* (September 1981), p. 312.

‡See Bank of England, *Quarterly Bulletin* (June 1982), p. 181.

and hence to influence short-term interest rates. The Bank did not aim to affect rates on longer-term bills themselves but, rather, operated at appropriate market rates to avoid giving a signal which could otherwise have had undue influence on the market."*

Foreign banks have been allowed to join the club of eligible acceptors, provided they fulfil certain requirements; this has had the effect of greatly enlarging the bill market, making it easier for the Bank of England to supply liquidity through the purchase of bills and to influence the inter-bank market.

Under the new arrangements†, the Bank of England maintains running forecasts of the cash position in the money market. It does this daily for several weeks ahead and also on a weekly or monthly basis over a longer horizon. It always did do this but now the daily forecasts are published.

So the Bank of England will attempt to forecast the cash position in the money market, both daily and over longer time periods.

"In effect, these forecasts estimate the likely level of the London clearing banks' operational balances at the Bank, after taking into account all transactions between the Bank (on its own behalf or for customers such as the Government) and the banking system (acting for all other sectors), but before any new official money market intervention by the Bank. By relating these projected balances to the aggregate of the targets which the individual clearing banks view at the start of business each day as the central objective for their closing balances, the Bank produces forecast of expected surpluses or shortages in the money market."‡

Needless to say, there is inevitably considerable uncertainty in these forecasts. On the basis of the information available, the Bank of England then makes known to the market simultaneously (by an announcement on a screen which will be transmitted to each of the relevant dealing rooms) its estimate of the day's position. This goes out at about 9.45 a.m.

An example of how the surplus or shortage is arrived is provided in this simple example of a day's estimated position and the precise mechanics are illustrated in Table 3.2.

	Sterling millions £M
Increase (+) or decrease (−) in the target operating balances with the Bank held by the clearing banks by the end of the day.	+50
Estimate of net Exchequer transaction (if positive this reflects the fact that government payments exceed government receipts and thereby put money into the market – if negative this reflects the fact that payments to the Exchequer in tax, gilts, National Savings, etc. exceed government receipts and thereby take money away from the market).	−200
Local Authority and commercial bills maturing in official hands i.e. had been bought by the Bank of England and had to be now repaid.	−75

*Bank of England, *Quarterly Bulletin* (September 1981), p. 333.
†See the excellent article in Bank of England, *Quarterly Bulletin* (March 1982): "The Role of the Bank of England in the Money Market", pp. 86ff.
‡*Ibid.* p. 90.

	Sterling millions £M
Repayment of late assistance, i.e. the Bank had provided late assistance and needed to be repaid.	−60
Take up of new Treasury bills by the market (negative) less maturing of existing bills held by the market institutions.	−30
Increase (−) or decrease (+) in the note issue. (An increase is negative because there is a corresponding decrease in bankers' deposits as banks pay for the notes: a decrease is positive because there is a corresponding increase in bankers' deposits as banks return notes.)	−60
Total morning estimate of market shortage	£M −375

Before lunch the Bank of England normally acts – if at all – only to relieve a shortage and, at this stage, its dealings with the discount houses are confined to operations in bills. The Bank, operating through its brokers (Seccombe, Marshall and Campion) informs the houses that "it will consider buying bills – there is usually no distinction at this point between Treasury, local authority, and eligible banks bills – in some or all of certain maturity bands".* There are four such bands – Band 1: 1–14 days (to which the Bank of England interest in "very short rates" would generally relate); Band 2: 15–33 days; Band 3: 34–63 days; and Band 4: 64–91 days. All periods are defined in terms of the remaining, not the original tenor of the bills. If possible, the Bank of England will prefer to operate in Bands 1 and 2, but when money is very short the Bank of England has to go into Bands 3 and 4, even though the Bank is normally reluctant to go out to the longer end. The Bank would not usually purchase bills with more than three months remaining to maturity. On this basis, each discount house:

> "May then offer quantities of the bills to the Bank, specifying a discount rate for each combination of instrument and band which it offers – or, if it so wishes, different rates for separate amounts within each combination. The Bank decides which offers to accept . . . Sometimes the amount bought may fall well short of the Bank's estimate of the shortage. This may be because the Bank considers some or all of the rates offered to be unacceptably low, more commonly, it may reflect a rather modest amount of offerings . . . ; alternatively, the Bank may have other reasons . . . ; and may therefore restrict its operations at this session."

An alternative technique in providing the houses with money is for the bank to invite them to enter into a sale and repurchase agreement in bills (a Repo), when the Bank will specify a terminal date (or dates) for the repurchase by the discount houses and the rate of discount used to calculate the proceeds of the bills. The houses then bid a rate of interest that they will pay to the Bank on the proceeds for the specified period. This rate the Bank may or may not accept. When the Repo is "unwound" the houses repay the proceeds to the Bank by repurchasing the bills. The rate of interest on the proceeds is the cost to the houses of their money. In effect, the operation is a secured loan for a fixed period. This technique may be chosen to enable the market position on future days to be smoothed out, e.g. a day of expected surplus could be offset by

**Ibid.* p. 92.

Table 3.2
Influences on the cash position of the Money Market

£ billions: *not seasonally adjusted*
Increase in the market's cash +

Banking months	*Dec. 83–Feb. 84*	*Mar. 84–May 84*	*June 83–May 84*
Factors affecting the market's cash position			
CGBR (+)	+0.4	+4.3	+12.3
Net sales of central government debt[2](–)	-2.7	-2.6	-13.7
of which:			
Gilt-edged	*-2.4*	*-1.7*	*-10.9*
National savings	*-0.9*	*-0.9*	*-3.2*
CTDs	*+0.6*	*-0.1*	*+0.4*
Currency circulation increase –)	-0.1	-0.3	-0.7
Other	-0.4	-0.5	-0.8
Total (A)	**-2.8**	**+0.8**	**-2.8**
Official offsetting operations			
Net increase (+) in Bank's holdings of commercial bills[3]	+2.6	-1.0	+2.5
Net increase (–) in Treasury bills in market	+0.1	-0.1	-0.1
Other	+0.2	+0.2	+0.4
Total (B)	**+2.8**	**-0.9**	**+2.9**
Change in bankers' balances at the Bank (A+B)	+0.1	-0.1	+0.1

[1] Components may not add up to totals because of rounding.
[2] Other than Treasury bills.
[3] By the Issue and Banking Departments of the Bank of England.
Source: Bank of England, *Quarterly Bulletin* (June 1984).
Reproduced by kind permission of the Bank of England.

choosing it as a repurchase date. They may be used on days of large shortage when houses are unable to sell sufficient "outrights" to "take out" the shortage. On some days, the Bank may be prepared to "repo" bills, which because they are not within 90 days of maturity would be ineligible for outright purchase. Again, "repos" may be used when the market is particularly reluctant to sell bills of certain maturities to the Bank, because of interest rate expectations.

The bank will vary its money market tactics during the day depending on new information as to shortages/surpluses and to changes in its operating stance. The attitude of the Bank has been succinctly summarised.

> "Because the authorities generally wish to allow market forces the fullest possible scope to influence longer-term interest rates, the Bank prefers, other things being equal, to confine its market operations to paper of as short a maturity as is feasible. This may often mean dealing only in bands 1 and 2, but there are many instances where operations in longer-term paper may be appropriate – for example if the pattern of future shortages

and surpluses in the market indicates that it is desirable to operate over a longer span, or if short-dated paper is scarce in the market, perhaps because of recent official purchases. Even so, the Bank may choose to avoid dealing in longer-term paper in the face of such a scarcity by conducting short-dated purchase and resale deals, thereby mobilising longer paper while dealing only at short-rates."

If temporarily there are inadequate funds in the market due to money leaving the commercial banking system and passing into the hands of the authorities (as a result of tax payments, gilt-edged purchases by the public from the Government broker, increases in the note issue, payments of oil royalties, foreign exchange settlements, etc.), the Bank of England will either lend on a short-term basis, or buy some of the assets held by the discount houses, or it may be that these are held by the clearing banks, and if so they can then make the relevant moneys available to the discount market. Alternatively, if there is a surplus of money in the market, the Bank of England will sell Treasury bills/commercial bills to the discount market (or to the banks) in order to "mop up" the excess. These are in the character of "smoothing out" operations.

The discount houses act as a "buffer" between the Bank of England and the banks. The Bank of England does not normally lend money direct to the banks. Although with Treasury bills and Local Authority bills as collateral it will "relieve" a money market shortage if necessary by giving direct assistance to the banks. Normally the Bank of England will lend to, or buy/sell bills to the discount market.

THE PARALLEL MARKETS

THE INTER-BANK MARKET

The largest of the sterling parallel markets is in inter-bank deposits. Dealings on this market between banks are on an unsecured basis and are ordinarily in amounts of £¼–½ million and £1 million or more. Money may be lent on an overnight basis, at call, or for a fixed term. The bulk of the transactions are for periods of under three months. Ultimate liquidity rests with the discount market, to which the Bank of England acts in turn as lender of last resort.

Since the sterling inter-bank market is the key link between all the other sectors of the London money market it is hardly surprising that the operators in this market consist of an amalgam comprising almost every branch of finance in the city. The main lenders of funds are the merchant banks (or accepting houses), the overseas and foreign banks in London, the clearing banks and their subsidiaries, central banks and "supra-national" institutions. Many non-bank lenders with surplus funds are also involved including pension funds, large commercial and industrial companies, insurance companies, finance companies, savings banks and the discount houses. In addition, acting as intermediaries, are the six main sterling money-brokers: Butler Till, Martins, Kirkland-Whittaker, Marshalls, Fulton Packshaw and

Astley-Pearce, and some 14 members of the Foreign Exchange and Currency Deposit Brokers' Association (FECDBA).

The banks deal in this market with a view to making a profit in the following ways:

(a) to finance loans made to their customers at a higher rate, and for general working capital;

(b) to utilise deposits taken from their commercial customers;

(c) to take "views" as to the future movement of interest rates, and less generally to borrow for short periods and lend for longer periods;

(d) to balance out the fluctuations in their books caused by customers' transactions, so that even the shortest-term resources of the banks are earning their keep.

The vast majority of dealings, where the initial deposit is for a period longer than three months, are now done by means of the issue of a Certificate of Deposit. Only the authorised banks in London (not including the discount houses) may issue CDs, although not all banks do so. (Specific permission from the Bank of England is required before CDs can be issued.) The banks that do issue CDs are known collectively as "the primary market".

As already discussed the CD is a negotiable instrument which evidences the fact that a certain principal capital sum (minimum £50,000) has been deposited with the issuing bank at a certain rate ("the coupon"), and that the deposit will mature and be repaid by the bank together with interest at a certain future date, not less than three months from the date of issue. Interest is, however, paid annually for CDs which are for more than one year. CDs might therefore almost be regarded as very high denomination interest-bearing private bank notes.

The advantage to the depositor of having a CD rather than simply depositing his money is that he is able, if he so wishes, to resell the CD, usually to another bank or to a discount house before the actual maturity of the deposit, thus gaining flexibility and a degree of liquidity which would not otherwise be available.

Those banks and discount houses who are prepared to buy CDs from the original depositor are known collectively as "the secondary market". Many banks operate in both the primary market, as issuers, and in the secondary market, as dealers.

THE LOCAL AUTHORITY MARKET

Local authorities issue a number of different types of securities; specifically, bills or promissory notes, bonds, variable rate bonds and stocks. The money so raised is used to supplement money raised through rates and to finance public works, local amenities and welfare institutions.

The local authorities raise finance via the money markets, in a variety of ways.

Short-term Local Authority Deposits

These are at call, on an overnight basis, at two days' or seven days' notice or at fixed periods of up to 364 days.

Local Authority Bills

Local authority bills are also known as local government promissory notes, corporation bills, money bills or revenue bills, although they are all the same type of security.

They are similar to Treasury bills, except that they are drawn on and guaranteed by one of over 500 local authorities rather than by the central government. Most bills are issued for 91 days, though some may be issued for 182 days. New issues are made on an irregular basis and require the prior approval of the Bank of England.

Once this has been granted, the local authority announces the amount of bills it is offering for sale and invites tender from the public to be made through the local authority's appointed bank. The major proportion of bills are subscribed for by the London clearing banks and the discount houses. The latter, along with the money-brokers, also maintain a secondary market in the bills. Once the subscription is closed, bills are allotted in the same manner as Treasury bills. Individuals and companies may also subscribe either directly or through a bank, discount house or money broker.

Normally, bills are issued in denominations of £5000, £10,000, £25,000, £50,000 and £100,000. They are bearer securities and enjoy an active secondary market. Although still considered highly secure, they do not have the benefit of a central government guarantee and thus yield slightly more than Treasury bills. They are popularly held by banks and discount houses because the bills are eligible for rediscounting at the Bank of England.

Local Authority Bonds (LABs)

Local authority negotiable bonds are usually yearling bonds, having a maturity of one year and six days, though some are issued with lives of up to five years. New issues are managed and underwritten by a merchant bank, discount house or stockbroker who arrange sales direct to clients although the bonds are also quoted on the stock exchange. Terms of a new issue require the prior authority of the Bank of England which also accepts responsibility for regulating the queue of borrowers. New issues are made every Tuesday by any of over 500 local authorities.

Local authority bonds are registered securities which usually carry a fixed rate of interest payable semi-annually net of tax. They may, however, sometimes be issued with variable coupons which are rebased semi-annually and calculated according to six months LIBOR (defined on pp. 99–100) plus an agreed margin. A fairly good secondary market exists in these bonds, made by the merchant banks, discount houses and moneybrokers. The financial institutions such as building societies as well as industrial and commercial companies are significant investors, but many tend to hold the bonds to maturity.

THE INTER-COMPANY MARKET

This market developed in the late 1960s to by-pass the ceiling imposed on bank lending at the time. Rather than depositing with a bank, a company with surplus funds was able to lend its funds directly to another company, often with a bank acting as agent.

FINANCE HOUSE MARKET

Deposits are made with finance houses on an overnight basis and for periods of three and six months. Finance houses were discussed on pp. 47–48.

THE EUROCURRENCY MARKETS

London is the world's leading Eurocurrency centre and the many domestic and foreign banks based in London make a market in international bonds and notes and accept deposits in any convertible currencies. Indeed the eurocurrency business transacted in London outweighs the sterling business done there by something like three times. Interest rates are determined purely by international supply and demand and are not regulated by any single government or monetary authority. Chapter 11 describes the operations of the eurocurrency market in detail.

Eurodollar Certificates of Deposit

Eurodollar CDs are issued by British, American and foreign banks based in London. Maturities range from between one month to five years with interest paid gross and free of withholding tax at maturity or annually if the CD life is greater than one year. Issue sizes are smaller than for sterling CDs. The minimum denomination is US$ 25,000 and thereafter in multiples of US$ 1000. CDs of US$ 1 million or more are, however, the most marketable. As with sterling CDs, eurodollar CDs are bearer certificates, fully negotiable in the secondary market which is maintained by London-based banks and discount houses. The secondary market is extremely active, particularly in CDs which have between one and twelve months' remaining maturity.

The volume of the market is substantial. The amount of Eurodollar CDs oustanding by the mid-1980s was approximately US$ 90 billion and turnover exceeds even that of the Eurobond secondary market. As with sterling CDs, Eurodollar CDs are quoted on a yield to maturity basis and available yields may often be at a premium to comparative yields obtainable on US domestic instruments. Typically, yields are 3% higher than for comparable domestic US dollar CDs (due to reserve requirements and Federal Deposit Insurance Corporation premiums). Yields and liquidity of particular CDs depend to some extent on the name of the issuing bank, since CDs are unsecured against specific assets of the issuer. CDs of the largest London clearing banks, American banks and major international banks therefore obtain the best prices in secondary trading.

SDR CDs

Since the beginning of 1981, when the SDR (special drawing right) was simplified to a basket of five currencies, a number of international banks in London have begun to make a market in SDR denominated deposits and CDs. (SDRs are discussed further in Chapter 10.) The interest rate is calculated as a weighted average of the Eurocurrency interest rates of the five component currencies. Payment may be made in any convertible currency, at the option of the lender, though dollars are the most usual form of payment. The exchange rate of the SDR relative to other convertible currencies is also calculated as a weighted average of its components. The interest and exchange value of an SDR deposit or CD is consequently less volatile than a single currency and provides the investor with a more stable return on funds.

MONEY MARKETS AND THE FINANCIAL PRESS

An excellent understanding of the money markets is gained by examination of the financial press money market coverage. Consider the 17 column table of the money market rates which appears regularly in the *Financial Times* (Table 3.3). Highly active markets exist for the major Eurocurrencies, namely US dollars, Deutschmarks, Swiss francs, Dutch guilders, French francs, Belgian francs, Japanese yen, Canadian dollars, Italian lire and Asian dollars. The market for Eurocurrencies has often been referred to as the Eurodollar market because US dollars account for by far the largest single currency traded, representing approximately two-thirds of the total market. Chapter 11 discusses these markets in more detail.

Deposits in any of these currencies may be made for the same terms as are available for sterling call and time deposits; that is, money may be placed as short as overnight or as long as 12 months. Interest obtainable depends on demand and supply in the international market and fluctuates from day to day. Rates are to some extent influenced by rates prevailing in the domestic money market of a particular currency, the volume of foreign exchange transactions in that currency and, in particular, intervention by central banks to support or sell a currency.

The interest rates quoted for Eurocurrency deposits, both in London and other financial centres, are usually the London inter-bank Eurocurrency lending rates – known as LIBOR (London inter-bank offer rate). The structure of

Table 3.3
London Money Rates

London Money Rates								*Discount Houses Deposit and Bill Rates*		
Sept. 14 1984	*Sterling Certificate of deposit*	*Interbank*	*Local Authority deposits*	*Company Deposits*	*Market Deposits*	*Treasury (Buy)*	*Treasury (Sell)*	*Eligible Bank (Buy)*	*Eligible Bank (Sell)*	*Fine Trade (Buy)*
Overnight	—	10 1/2–12	10 5/8–10 7/8	10 1/2–11 1/4	9–10 3/4	—	—	—	—	—
2 days notice	—	—	10 3/4–10 7/8	—	—	—	—	—	—	—
7 days or	—	—	—	—	—	—	—	—	—	—
7 days notice	—	10 3/4–11	10 3/4–10 7/8	10 7/8–11 1/8	10 1/2–10 3/4	—	—	—	—	—
One month	10 7/8–10 13/16	10 13/16–10 7/8	10 13/16	11	10 1/2	10 13/32–10 7/16	10 3/8	10 13/32	10 3/8	11 1/32
Two months	10 23/32–10 5/8	10 11/16–10 13/16	10 11/16	10 7/8	10 1/8	10 1/4–10 9/32	10 7/32	10 1/4	10 7/32–10 1/4	10 7/8
Three months	10 5/8–10 1/2	10 11/16–10 13/16	10 11/16	10 1/8	10 1/8	10 1/32–10 5/32	9 7/8	10 1/32–10 1/16	10	10 7/16
Six months	10 7/16–10 5/16	10 5/8–10 3/4	10 11/16	—	—	—	—	9 29/32	9 25/32	10 19/32
Nine months	10 7/16–10 5/16	10 5/8–10 3/4	—	—	—	—	—	—	—	—
One year	10 7/16–10 11/32	10 5/8–10 3/4	10 3/4	—	—	—	—	—	—	—
—										
—										
—										
—										

	Local Auth. negotiable bonds	Local Authority Deposits	Finance House Deposits	$ Cert of Deposits	SDR Linked Deposits	ECU Linked Deposits
One month	$11\frac{1}{8}$–11	—	$10\frac{7}{8}$	11.4–11.5	$9\frac{11}{16}$–$9\frac{15}{16}$	$9\frac{1}{4}$–$9\frac{7}{16}$
Two months	$11\frac{1}{8}$–11	—	$10\frac{3}{4}$	11.4–11.5	$9\frac{3}{4}$–10	$9\frac{1}{2}$–$9\frac{11}{16}$
Three months	$11\frac{1}{8}$–11	—	$10\frac{3}{4}$	11.4–11.5	$9\frac{15}{16}$–$10\frac{1}{16}$	$9\frac{5}{8}$–$9\frac{13}{16}$
Six months	$10\frac{3}{4}$–$10\frac{1}{2}$	—	$10\frac{5}{8}$	11.5–11.6	10–$10\frac{1}{4}$	$10\frac{3}{16}$–$10\frac{3}{8}$
Nine months	$11\frac{1}{16}$–$10\frac{13}{16}$	—	$10\frac{3}{4}$	11.8–12.0	—	—
One year	11–$10\frac{3}{4}$	—	$10\frac{3}{4}$	11.9–12.1	$10\frac{5}{16}$–$10\frac{9}{16}$	$10\frac{5}{16}$–$10\frac{1}{2}$
Two years	—	$11\frac{1}{4}$	—	—	—	—
Three years	—	$11\frac{1}{2}$	—	—	—	—
Four years	—	$11\frac{3}{4}$	—	—	—	—
Five years	—	$11\frac{7}{8}$	—	—	—	—

ECGD Fixed Rate Export Finance Scheme IV: Average Rate of Interest period August 8 to September 4, 1984 (inclusive): 10.806 per cent. Local authorities and finance houses seven days' notice, others seven days' fixed. Finance Houses Base Rate (published by the Finance Houses Association): $11\frac{1}{2}$ per cent from September 1, 1984. London and Scottish Clearing Bank Rates for lending $10\frac{1}{2}$ per cent. London Deposit Rates for sums at seven days' notice $7\frac{1}{4}$–$7\frac{1}{2}$ per cent. Treasury Bills: Average tender rates of discount 9.9324 per cent. Certificates of Tax Deposit (Series 6): Deposit £100,000 and over held under one month 11 per cent; one-three months 11 per cent; three-six months 11 per cent; six-nine months 11 per cent; nine-12 months 11 per cent. Under £100,000 $10\frac{1}{4}$ per cent from September 12. Deposits held under Series 6 $10\frac{3}{4}$ per cent. The rates for all deposits withdrawn for cash 7 per cent.

Source: *Financial Times* 17 September, 1984.

Eurocurrency interest rates is related to, but independent of, the domestic markets.

Table 3.3 lists the major London money markets and the interest rates received and charged.

Col. 1 lists 11 lending periods from overnight to two years. The line "7 days" means a fixed term of a week and is followed by the more flexible "7 days' notice" which has special appeal to local authorities, finance houses, and companies.

Col. 2 Sterling certificates of deposit. A company with spare cash could put it on fixed-term deposit with a bank, but by buying certificates of deposit it acquires bearer promissory notes which can be offered in the money market if need be. The figures in this column are the annual rates of interest which will accrue to the holder of such certificates.

Col. 3 Inter-bank. In this market banks of all kinds – clearing, merchant, etc. – offer money to one another on deposit at interest rates shown for the various periods.

Col. 4 and 13 Local Authority deposits. This column shows the rates at which borrowings are made in the market by the hundreds of borough, district and country councils up and down the country. The councils would deal either through their own banks or through brokers in the market.

Col. 5 Company deposits. These are the rates at which leading commercial companies may borrow without security. Normally they refer to companies among the 150 largest in the country. Rates paid by others vary widely with their credit standing. It is possible for them to borrow money in the market by offering a bank guarantee of repayment, but this business is excluded from the range of quotations given.

Col. 6 Market Deposits. These are the rates of interest offered by discount houses for funds borrowed against security in the form of gilt-edged stock, Treasury bills, commercial bills, or local authority loan certificates, to finance their holdings of these investments.

Cols. 7 and 8 Treasury bills. This column shows the discount which dealers are asking when buying Treasury bills and selling Treasury bills issued earlier. These are certificates of debt owed by the Exchequer, issued by tender each week. Each bill is for at least £5,000 and the minimum tender is £50,000.

Cols 9 and 10 Eligible bank bills. This column shows the rates applicable to bills that have been accepted by a bank that is on the Bank of England's list of recognised banks whose bills are eligible for discount at the Bank of England. Three criteria are used by the Bank of England to judge whether a bank should be allowed to join the list, these being:

(a) whether the applicant has and maintains a broadly based and substantial acceptance business in the United Kingdom;

(b) whether its acceptances, at present, command the finest rates in the market for eligible bills;

(c) whether, in the case of foreign-owned banks, British banks enjoy reciprocal opportunities in the foreign owners' domestic market.

Col. 11 Fine trade bills. Normal rates of discount at which discount houses will buy bills of high standard which have not been accepted by a bank. The rates for other classes of unaccepted bills vary widely according to the credit standing of the names on the bill, and could be substantially higher than those shown in the table.

Col. 12 Local Authority negotiable bonds. These are the rates of interest at which discount houses, stock brokers and others have loaned money to local authorities in return for bonds (fixed-term interest-bearing loans) for one year or more. Partly expired bonds with less than a year to maturity are dealt in a secondary market at rates shown for such periods.

Col. 14 Finance house deposits. This column shows the rates of interest which finance houses will pay for deposits offered in the market. The rates quoted are for houses of the highest standing; many other houses of good credit standing are excluded from the quotations, and the rates they offer could be higher. Among finance houses generally there is a wide range of borrowing rates, but day-to-day quotations usually give an indication of general movement.

Col. 15 Dollar certificates of deposit. This column shows the rates of interest on certificates of deposit denominated in dollars.

Col. 16 SDR linked deposits. This column shows the rates of interest on deposits/loans denominated in special drawing rights. SDRs are discussed further in Chapter 10.

Col. 17 ECU linked deposits. This column shows the rates of interest on deposits/loans denominated in European Currency Units. ECUs are discussed further in Chapter 9.

As can be seen from a glance at this Table the interest rates vary between different markets and between different time periods. Examination of the *Financial Times*' money markets section over time would reveal that these rates are subject to continuous fluctuation. The reason why interest rates do vary is discussed in detail in Chapter 5. However some examination of the rates is useful.

What can be learnt here? First, overnight rates are very volatile (see the spread on inter-bank deposits). Secondly, the rate on secured deposits (e.g. with the discount houses) being less risky has lower rates. Similarly risky deposits, e.g. with the finance houses, have higher rates.

One interest rate of particular relevance to the clearing banks is the London inter-bank offered rate. This rate (LIBOR) is the market rate which the banks will have to pay in order to obtain marginal funds in the inter-bank market.

Since a substantial proportion of the term lending of the banks is financed by wholesale funds obtained through the inter-bank market (again this is discussed in detail in Chapter 5). LIBOR rather than the base rate is used as the basis for setting interest rates on certain types of bank lending. Margins over LIBOR will be fixed according to the quality of the borrower. Using LIBOR as the basis for setting interest rates on term lending is of benefit to the banks since it gives them the opportunity to match their lending on the basis of similar rates as well as similar term with the wholesale deposits they obtain through the inter-bank market. Again LIBOR is regularly reported in the *Financial Times* (Table 3.4).

Table 3.4
FT London Interbank Fixing

London Interbank Fixing (11.00 a.m. September 14) **3 months U.S. dollars**	
bid $11\frac{11}{16}$	offer $11\frac{13}{16}$
6 months U.S. dollars	
bid $11\frac{7}{8}$	offer 12

The fixing rates are the arithmetic means, rounded to the nearest one sixteenth, of the bid and offered rates for $10m quoted by the market to five reference banks at 11 a.m. each working day. The banks are National Westminster Bank, Bank of Tokyo, Deutsche Bank, Banque Nationale de Paris and Morgan Guaranty Trust.

Source: *Financial Times*, 17 September, 1984.

In addition to the sterling markets the money markets also include the Eurocurrency markets. A Eurocurrency (discussed in detail in Chapter 11) is essentially held outside its country of origin. The term Euro- has no geographical significance (a US dollar held in Asia can be described as a Eurodollar, though the term Asian-dollar has also been coined). This is a foreign exchange market in which currencies are lent, not bought. Again these are reported in the *Financial Times*.

Of the various forms of Euro business, the *Financial Times* covers mainly dealings in straight, unsecured deposits, though certain rates for London US dollar certificates of deposit (similar to sterling certificates) are also included.

The Euro-deposit market is international in character, but largely centred on London. The US dollar is the main currency handled, but as already mentioned there are also dealings in Deutschmarks, Swiss francs and other currencies.

In Table 3.5 the quotations indicate the extremes of borrowing and lending interest rates quoted. The rates are generally inter-bank quotations towards the close of business each day, and may be nominal – since there are not always active dealings in all the periods listed, while quotations may vary from one bank to another, and may be only tentative.

Table 3.5
Euro-Currency Interest Rates (Market closing rates)

Sept. 14	*Sterling*	*U.S. Dollar*	*Canadian Dollar*	*Dutch Guilder*	*Swiss Franc*	*D-mark*	*French Franc*	*Italian Lira*	*Belgian Conv.*	*Franc Fin.*	*Yen*	*Danish Krone*
Short term	$10\frac{5}{8}-10\frac{7}{8}$	$11\frac{5}{16}-11\frac{7}{16}$	$10\frac{3}{4}-11\frac{1}{4}$	$6\frac{1}{16}-6\frac{3}{16}$	$2\frac{1}{8}-2\frac{1}{4}$	$5\frac{3}{8}-5\frac{1}{2}$	$11\frac{1}{8}-11\frac{3}{8}$	$14\frac{1}{2}-15\frac{1}{2}$	$10\frac{7}{8}-11\frac{3}{8}$	$11-11\frac{1}{4}$	$6\frac{3}{8}-6\frac{5}{16}$	$11\frac{9}{16}-12\frac{1}{16}$
7 days' notice	$10\frac{5}{8}-10\frac{7}{8}$	$11\frac{3}{8}-11\frac{1}{2}$	$11\frac{1}{8}-12\frac{1}{2}$	$6\frac{1}{16}-6\frac{3}{16}$	$2\frac{1}{8}-2\frac{3}{8}$	$5\frac{3}{8}-5\frac{1}{2}$	$11-11\frac{1}{8}$	$15-16$	$10\frac{7}{8}-11\frac{3}{8}$	$11-11\frac{1}{4}$	$6\frac{3}{16}-6\frac{5}{16}$	$11\frac{3}{4}-12\frac{1}{4}$
Month	$10\frac{5}{8}-10\frac{7}{8}$	$11\frac{1}{2}-11\frac{5}{8}$	$11\frac{11}{16}-11\frac{7}{8}$	$6\frac{1}{16}-6\frac{3}{16}$	$4\frac{1}{8}-4\frac{1}{4}$	$5\frac{7}{16}-5\frac{9}{16}$	$11-11\frac{1}{8}$	$15-15\frac{1}{2}$	$10\frac{3}{4}-11\frac{1}{4}$	$10\frac{7}{8}-11\frac{1}{8}$	$6\frac{3}{8}-6\frac{1}{2}$	$11\frac{3}{8}-11\frac{7}{8}$
Three months	$10\frac{11}{16}-10\frac{13}{16}$	$11\frac{5}{8}-11\frac{7}{8}$	$11\frac{7}{8}-12\frac{1}{16}$	$6\frac{1}{4}-6\frac{3}{8}$	$5\frac{1}{16}-5\frac{13}{16}$	$5\frac{9}{16}-5\frac{11}{16}$	$11\frac{3}{8}-11\frac{1}{2}$	$15-15\frac{1}{2}$	$10\frac{3}{4}-11\frac{1}{4}$	$10\frac{7}{8}-11\frac{1}{8}$	$6\frac{5}{16}-6\frac{7}{16}$	$11\frac{1}{4}-11\frac{3}{4}$
Six months	$10\frac{11}{16}-10\frac{13}{16}$	$11\frac{13}{16}-11\frac{15}{16}$	$12\frac{1}{8}-12\frac{5}{16}$	$6\frac{9}{16}-6\frac{11}{16}$	$5\frac{1}{8}-5\frac{1}{4}$	$5\frac{15}{16}-6\frac{1}{16}$	$11\frac{13}{16}-11\frac{15}{16}$	$15\frac{3}{8}-15\frac{3}{4}$	$10\frac{3}{4}-11\frac{1}{4}$	$10\frac{7}{8}-11\frac{1}{8}$	$6\frac{5}{16}-6\frac{7}{16}$	$11\frac{3}{8}-11\frac{7}{8}$
One year	$10\frac{11}{16}-10\frac{13}{16}$	$12\frac{3}{16}-12\frac{5}{16}$	$12\frac{3}{8}-12\frac{9}{16}$	$6\frac{11}{16}-6\frac{13}{16}$	$5\frac{1}{8}-5\frac{1}{4}$	$6\frac{1}{8}-6\frac{1}{4}$	$12\frac{9}{16}-12\frac{11}{16}$	$15\frac{1}{2}-16$	$11\frac{1}{4}-11\frac{3}{4}$	$11-11\frac{1}{4}$	$6\frac{1}{2}-6\frac{5}{8}$	$11\frac{1}{2}-12$

Asian $ (closing rates in Singapore); Short-term $11\frac{7}{16}-11\frac{9}{16}$ per cent; seven days $11\frac{1}{2}-11\frac{5}{8}$ per cent; one months $11\frac{9}{16}-11\frac{11}{16}$ per cent; three months $11\frac{11}{16}-11\frac{13}{16}$ per cent; six months $11\frac{15}{16}-12\frac{1}{16}$ per cent; one year $12\frac{1}{8}-12\frac{1}{4}$ per cent. Long-term Eurodollars; two years $12\frac{3}{4}-13$ per cent; three years $17\frac{7}{8}-13\frac{1}{8}$ per cent; four years $13-13\frac{1}{4}$ per cent; five years $13\frac{1}{8}-13\frac{3}{8}$ per cent nominal rates. Short-term rates are call for US dollars and Japanese yen; others two days notice.

Source: *Financial Times*, 17 September 1984.

The minimum amount to which these rates would apply might be about US$ 250,000 (or the currency equivalent) but there is no fixed rule.

All the rates are drawn from London sources, including the sterling rates. By definition there can be no Euro-sterling dealings in London but the international character of the market make such quotations available. The Eurosterling market is centred in Paris.

APPENDIX 1

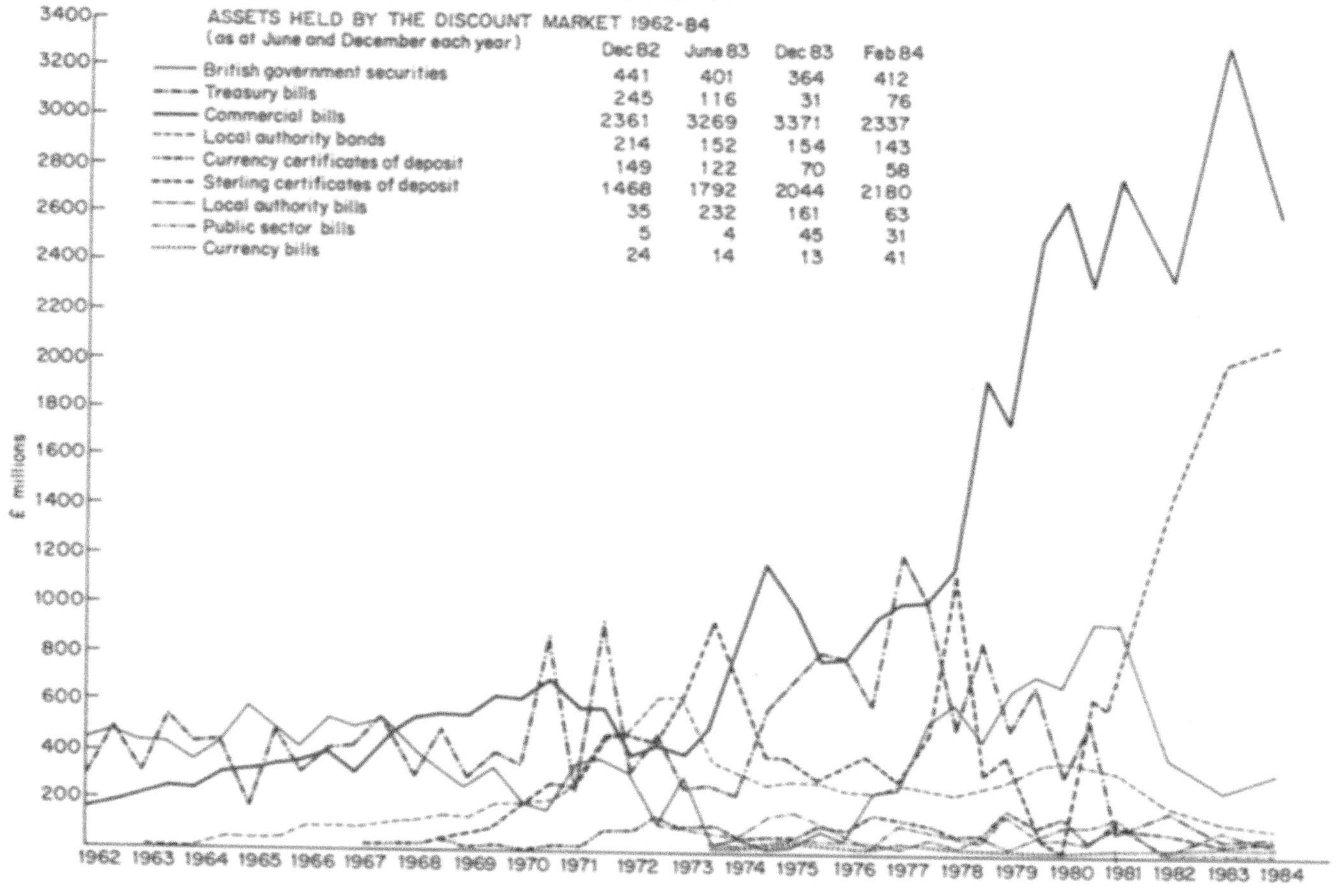

Fig. 3.2

Source: Bank of England, Quarterly Bulletin (June 1984)
Reproduced by kind permission of the Bank of England.

Chapter 4

The Money Supply

This chapter describes the precise mechanics of monetary creation and illustrates how the authorities can control (or at least attempt to control) the growth of the money supply. Chapter 7 develops this latter problem in more detail.

INTRODUCTION

Money is created in three ways:* by printing bank notes and coins, by cheques drawn on the Bank of England and issued by the government in payment for goods and services, and by banks providing overdraft facilities which are then used to buy assets and/or repay debts. Naturally money is destroyed by either reversing these expansionary forces or by somehow neutralising them.

Apart from notes and coin being issued, money is created when the banking system increases its lending. There are two essentially different forms that this money creation can take – discretionary, when the monetary sector lends to the private sector and overseas, and automatic when it lends to the government. (By guaranteeing to underwrite the Treasury bill tender each week the discount market, which is part of the monetary sector, assures the government of an automatic source of residual finance.)

To a very small extent new deposits are created when notes are deposited at the banks rather than remaining in circulation. *The greater part of the new deposits are, however, created at the initiative of the banks themselves.* This occurs whenever a bank makes a loan or overdraft. These may be made to the public or the private sector.

(i) *The public sector*. Loans to government, whether in the form of purchases of government securities or Treasury bills or in advances to the discount houses for the financing of Treasury bills, will all result in the creation of

* These points are well developed by T. Congdon, *Monetary Control in Britain* (Macmillan).

fresh deposits immediately the proceeds are spent: e.g. government funds raised in this way may be used to pay a civil engineer for road construction work. They then appear as an addition to his bank account.

(ii) *The private sector.* Similarly, advances to private customers or purchases of commercial bills result in an expansion of deposits when the loan is actually written up in the balance sheet. Remember that when a bank lends money, new deposits (the money supply) are created.

It will be noted that in neither case do the banks hand out notes over the counter. If they purchase bills or securities they do so with a cheque drawn upon themselves. If they grant an overdraft, the borrower uses his cheque-book to make payments from an account which now shows a debit balance. The extent to which banks can increase the money supply can be explained by an understanding of the bank credit multiplier.

THE BANK CREDIT MULTIPLIER

Until comparatively recently, it was customary to assume that the supply of money in the economy was exogenously determined, i.e. fixed by a central authority. Developments in monetary theory, along the lines of Keynesian multiplier analysis, however, suggest that such a view is over-simplistic and the actual supply of money in the economy is determined by the decisions of three economic agents, namely:

(i) The Central Bank – as an agent of the Government, with the overall responsibility for controlling the Supply of Money in the economy;

(ii) The commercial Banks – which exercise some control over their deposit liabilities via their portfolio behaviour; and

(iii) The non-bank public (e.g. individuals, pension funds, companies) – which decide how much currency (i.e. notes and coins) to hold as compared with its holdings bank deposits.

It is useful to begin an analysis of the determinants of the money supply by examining the role of commercial banks in the money supply creation process under a fractional reserve banking system (i.e. a system where the bank does not hold all the deposits it receives in a liquid form).

Consider a simplified economy described by the following assumptions:

(1) The banking sector consists of a single bank;

(2) The non-bank public's financial assets are zero and the public's demand for cash is *fixed*;

(3) The banking sector's assets consist of *cash* and *loans*;

(a) Loans earn interest whereas cash does not;

(b) The bank maintains a minimum cash to deposit ratio (reserve ratio) of 10% to meet its liquidity requirements;

(4) The supply of cash in the economy is determined by the central bank.

Assume initially that deposit liabilities of the banking sector of £100 m are matched by £10 m of cash and £90 m of loans, giving a cash-ratio of 10% as follows:

Initial Equilibrium
Balance Sheet 1

Liabilities	(£m)	Assets	(£m)		
Deposits	100	Cash	10	*Cash ratio:*	10%
		Loans	90		
	100		100		

Now suppose that the public acquire £10 m of cash through *open market purchase* of government securities by the central bank (the means by which open market operations work is discussed later). What will be the effects of such an injection of cash into the system?

Since we have assumed (above) that the public's demand for cash is *fixed* they will deposit the £10 m of cash with the banking sector. After receiving the cash as deposit, the balance sheet position of the banking sector becomes:

Balance Sheet 2

Liabilities	(£m)	Assets	(£m)		
Deposits	110	Cash	20	*Cash ratio:*	18.2%
		Loans	90		
	110		110		

Now at 18.2% the banking sector's cash ratio is higher than the required minimum of 10% and this is unprofitable because while loans earn interest, cash yields nothing. The bank will, therefore, take steps to increase their loans by £9 m.

After portfolio adjustment, the balance sheet position of the banking sector becomes:

Balance Sheet 3

Liabilities	(£m)	Assets	(£m)		
Deposits	110	Cash	11	*Cash ratio:*	10%
		Loans	99		
	110		110		

The banking sector is now in equilibrium but the public are not since they hold £9 m "excess" cash (after borrowing £9 m from the banking sector). The public get rid of this excess cash by depositing it with the banking sector and so increase bank deposits to £119 m as shown in Balance Sheet 4.

Balance Sheet 4

Liabilities	(£m)	Assets	(£m)		
Deposits	119	Cash Loans	20 99	*Cash ratio:*	16.8%
	119		119		

Once again, in Balance Sheet 4, cash ratio of 16.8% is higher than the minimum required ratio of 10%. The bank will, therefore, take steps to reduce the cash ratio to 10% and increase loans further in order to earn interest.

This process will continue until both the public and the banking sector reach equilibrium. Such a situation will occur when bank deposits are £200 m, the banking sector's required holding of cash amounts to £20 m and loans are £180 m as shown in Balance Sheet 5 below:

Balance Sheet 5

Liabilities	(£m)	Assets	(£m)		
Deposits	200	Cash Loans	20 180	*Cash ratio:*	10%
	200		200		

Summary

To sum up, a £10 m cash injection into the economy by the Central Bank has enabled the banking sector (largely supported by the non-bank public) to "create" deposits.

Since the supply of money is defined as currency in circulation + bank deposits, the banking sector has increased the supply of money in the economy.

More importantly, the preceding analysis of the deposit multiplier confirms the view that the supply of money in the economy depends on (1) central bank policy; (2) the actions of commercial banks and (3) the decisions of the non-bank public with respect to cash and deposits.

The credit multiplier operates not only in a positive (expansionary) sense but also in a negative (contractionary) sense. In the elementary example given above, if the banks lost by withdrawals £X of cash, then deposits would have to contract by £X × 10 unless of course the banks could obtain additional cash from somewhere else. Deposits can be contracted by either recalling loans or by not reviewing them as they mature.

If the commercial banks were to acquire liquid assets above what was needed for either prudential or legal reserves they could expand (in this example) their lending (and thereby the money supply) by a multiple of 10. Alternatively if the banks lost reserve assets then they would have to contract deposits, again by the same multiple.

We can summarise the quantitative side of credit creation of banks by writing the credit multiplier as:

$$\text{Change in Deposits (D)} = \frac{\text{Change in Cash (C)}}{\text{Cash Ratio (Cr)}} \quad \text{i.e.} \quad \Delta D = \Delta C.\ \frac{1}{Cr}$$

The smaller the cash ratio the bigger the size of deposits that a given amount of cash will be able to support (and vice versa). So the change in deposits will be a multiple of the change in the level of cash held by the bank, the size of the multiplier depending on the size of the cash ratio. In the example above the increase in deposits will be $10 \times 1/0.1 = £100$. Thus given information on the change in cash and the cash ratios one can calculate the increase in the money supply. There are several points here that need further discussion and clarification. Firstly we need to make the analysis more realistic and secondly some deficiencies in the simple model need to be brought in.

CAN THE BANKS MANUFACTURE MONEY INDEFINITELY?

The simple answer is no: There are several reasons for this.

(1) Government controls on bank lending.

(2) Leakages of funds. These occur where the proceeds of bank loans are not redeposited with the banks or when banks are unable to use extra deposits to lend to their customers. This arises when:

(a) recipients of bank loans decide to hold cash, government securities or overseas deposits rather than bank deposits;

(b) the banks buy government securities with funds deposited with them. This may reflect a legal requirement, e.g. monetary reserve ratios or a prudential need to provide liquidity to meet the possibility of withdrawals of deposits.

(3) Insufficient demand for bank loans.

(4) The capital base of the banks may be insufficient to support the risks associated with extra bank lending.

(5) Excess reserves may be held.

(1) The Existence of Government Controls on Bank Lending

From time to time governments have placed controls on bank lending (i.e. the growth of banks assets). Direct controls were a popular tool of policy in the 1960s. Indirect controls have also been used. For example the Supplementary Special Deposits Scheme (discussed in detail in Chapter 7) effectively penalised banks whose balance sheets grew above a specified rate. The SSDS scheme was, however, on bank liabilities not on assets. Reserve requirements and special deposits (a kind of variable reserve requirement) may also restrict bank lending by effectively raising leakages (discussed below).

(2) Leakages

The money multiplier operates by bank loans being redeposited with banks who then loan out the funds starting the whole process off again. Leakages drain funds out of this circle and limit its scope. There are several ways in which this happens.

(i) The Demand to Hold Cash

If upon receiving a bank loan an individual decides to increase his holdings of cash then the redeposit process is slowed down and the bank credit multiplication falls accordingly. As incomes rise so does the demand for notes and coins so the system has a built in tendency to reduce the extent of credit creation.

In addition some of the recipients of the payments made by the borrowers may not hold bank accounts. This may appear to be a trivial point but in the United Kingdom some 40% of the labour force does not possess a bank account.

(ii) Cash Could Flow Out of the Monetary Sector into Other Financial Institutions

There are other institutions within the monetary sector whose liabilities are not considered money. Funds deposited with these institutions would not raise the monetary stock.

Remember from Chapter 2 that the monetary sector is defined as those financial institutions holding accounts with the Bank of England (i.e. bankers' deposits or as they are sometimes called, bankers' balances). Due to competition within the financial system fund flows are very sensitive to interest rate differentials. An example of this could be the movement of funds by customers from their seven day bank deposits into a share account with a building society. Such accounts offer the investor the advantages of a seven day deposit with a bank – very liquid and very safe, with the additional benefit, usually, of a higher rate of interest.

If funds flow from the monetary sector to other financial institutions (OFIs) then again the scope for redepositing and thereby the extent of credit creation is again reduced. Naturally this assumes that the OFI does not deposit the funds with a bank, although in practice most of them do.

(iii) Cash Could Flow Out to Non-residents

If a bank loan is spent on imports the funds may not be redeposited with UK banks. Even if the non-resident does deposit the funds with a UK bank his holding will not be included in UK measures of the money supply. (These exclude non-resident holdings of sterling deposits.)

(iv) Bank Purchase of Gilts Sold by the Government

If banks purchased gilts sold by the Bank of England their funds would not be available for on-lending to their customers. Note however that if the gilt is sold by the general public what happens is that the customers bank deposit rises and the bank's holdings of gilts also rises so that the bank assets and liabilities have risen. Thus banks can purchase gilts from their customers without suffering a loss of cash or bankers' balances.

(3) Is There a Demand for Bank Loans?

Thirdly, credit creation is just like the tango – it needs two to do it! If a bank has some excess cash reserves then it needs to find customers that are willing to borrow money before the bank can expand its deposits. The willingness of customers to borrow cannot be taken for granted as it will depend on the interest rates charged and the conditions attached to the loan.

(4) Bank Lending Policy

Part of the art of banking is to make a judgement about the risk of a potential loan. This is particularly important as advances are the major asset item in the bank's balance sheet. In a recession the banks may be reluctant to expand their bank loans as naturally the risk of default is higher. Consequently even though there is a demand for bank loans the banks may be unwilling to satisfy it.

(5) Excess Reserves

In addition banks may hold excess reserves, i.e. reserves in excess of what they would normally hold for liquidity purposes and which they are statutorily obliged to hold. This could be because they fear that the economic situation is worsening and they may be subject to excessive cash withdrawals thereby threatening the solvency of the bank. Alternatively it could be to provide the bank with excess cash that it could use for any unexpected profitable loan or investment opportunity that may arise: again the existence of excess reserves, held for whatever reason, would reduce the extent of credit creation following the injection of new cash into the banking system.

So, in conclusion, the mechanistic credit-creation approach via the bank credit multiplier must be cautiously interpreted.

THE MAJOR INFLUENCES ON UK MONEY SUPPLY CHANGES

In the United Kingdom there are targets for two monetary aggregates (M_0 and £M_3)*. To understand monetary control it is instructional to examine the factors affecting movements in sterling M_3 in terms of the following accounting identity:

Change in £M_3 = Public sector borrowing requirement − Debt sales to the non-bank public + Sterling bank lending to the private and overseas sectors.

± External factors

− Increase in banks' non-deposit liabilities.

Thus monetary growth can stem from three separate influences:

- The public sector
- The private sector
- The external sector

These will be considered in turn. Finally we will discuss the last mentioned determinant, i.e. the increase in banks' non-deposit liabilities.

THE PUBLIC SECTOR

The public sector borrowing requirement (PSBR) can have a key role in the money supply process depending upon how it is financed. Its importance in the Medium Term Financial Strategy is discussed later in the chapter. But first of all what is the PSBR, why is it important and what are its major components?

To balance the books any excess of government expenditure over revenue must be covered by borrowing almost as soon as it occurs. This excess is termed the public sector borrowing requirement (PSBR).

The public sector consists of central and local government together with the public corporations (mainly nationalised industries). Total expenditure includes not only expenditure on goods and services but also all current grants to firms and persons, interest payments on government debt, and financing of losses of nationalised industries. Similarly total revenue refers to taxes, repayment of grants, interest received, profits made by nationalised industries and other public corporations, and proceeds from the sales of public sector assets.

The borrowing requirement of the whole public sector is important because government financial control extends over the whole sector, both through public expenditure programmes and, on the financing side, through the

*Before March 1984, M_1, £M_3 and PSL_2 were targeted.

central government's borrowing to meet not only its own needs but also a large part of those of the rest of the public sector. In return for access to funds through the central government, the rest of the public sector makes any temporary surpluses available to reduce the sector's overall borrowing requirement by investing them in public sector debt rather than in other assets.

The PSBR financing must come from the other financial sectors, namely:

(a) the non-bank private sector;
(b) the monetary sector;
(c) the overseas sector.

The reason for distinguishing between (a) and (b) is that it makes a tremendous difference to the expansion of the money supply if the government borrows from the monetary sector rather than from the non-bank sector (see below). First of all let us examine what the implications for the money supply of government expenditure exceeding government revenues. Assume civil servants are writing out cheques for more than the value of the cheques coming in (from say taxation). Thus the banking system will be receiving more cheques against the Exchequer than in its favour with the result that their working balances at the Bank of England (bankers' balances) will be increasing. The banks, having no reason to hold excess bankers' balances, will then transfer this excess cash into the money markets thereby bringing down interest rates and increasing the demand for funds. Alternatively the banks could extinguish their excess bankers' balances by increasing their lending and, as you will remember as bank loans expand, so do bank deposits (i.e. the money supply). Consequently excess government expenditure over receipts without any other action by the authorities will result in the money supply increasing. This process ceases at a new higher level of bank assets and bank liabilities (the money supply). Thus fiscal expansion has monetary implications illustrating that monetary policy and fiscal policy are not, as many textbooks suggest, independent of each other.

The PSBR can be financed in four main ways:

(1) the increase in notes and coin taken up by the public;

(2) borrowing from the non-bank public in the UK, excluding (1) above;

(3) borrowing sterling from the UK monetary sector;

(4) borrowing foreign currency from overseas, either directly or through the UK banks (discussed in the section: The External Sector).

(1) Increase in Notes and Coins Taken Up by the Public

The first source, increase in notes and coin in circulation, adds directly to the money supply. It represents a form of interest-free borrowing by the Government arising from the general public's increasing need for cash to finance day-to-day transactions as prices and output rises.

When the public requires notes it takes them from banks by drawing down deposits; the banks in turn replenish their holdings by drawing notes from the Banking Department where they maintain balances; and the Banking Department acquires notes from the Issue Department by giving up some of its government securities. The provision of notes in accordance with the public's requirements is automatic. It is a relatively stable component of any money supply increase and is not of very great importance.

To repeat, as both the Issue Department of the Bank of England and the Royal Mint are included in the public sector, the issue of notes and coin contributes to the monetary financing of the PSBR. In practice the Bank of England passively adjusts the note issue to the public's demand for notes through the banks. The excess of central government disbursements over receipts (of, say, 100) in itself adds 100 to bankers' balances. If the public demands 100 cash from the banks this is provided to the banks by the Bank of England. The increase in bankers' balances resulting from the central government's deficit is subsequently offset as the Bank of England makes debits in exchange for cash. The net result is zero change in bankers' balances, and a rise of 100 in the note issue which finances the central government's deficit.

(2) PSBR Financing by Borrowing from the Non-bank Private Sector

The non-bank private sector is that section of the financial system which does not possess an account with the Bank of England (unlike the monetary sector holding bankers' balances). What official financial instruments can the non-bank private sector invest in? These include:

(i) British Government securities (gilts)
(ii) National savings
(iii) Certificates of tax deposit

(i) Purchases of Gilts

Assume that the government is running a financial deficit which it is financing by selling gilt-edged stock to the non-bank public (say to a pension fund). When a pension fund invests in a new issue of government stock it writes out a cheque to the Bank of England and liquidates a bank deposit. The civil servant's cheque (mentioned earlier) increases the money supply and the pension fund's cheque reduces it; if the two cheques are the same size the money supply is unchanged. Thus when the PSBR is matched by an equal quantity of debt sales to the non-bank public there is no net effect on the money supply.

(ii) National Savings

National savings encompass a wide variety of investments; their common attributes are that they are not negotiable and that there is an upper limit on the amount that can be invested by a single individual. The upper limit restricts interest in national savings to the personal sector. They take several forms, all of which are well-known – index-linked savings certificates, premium bonds, National Savings Bank deposits, Trustee Savings Bank deposit and contractual investment through Save As You Earn.

Borrowing of this kind involves a reduction in the general public's bank deposits and offsets the funds initially received as a consequence of the excess of public sector expenditure over receipts. For this reason the government generally tries to finance a major part of its deficit in this way.

(iii) Certificates of Tax Deposits (CTDs)

Towards the end of 1978 CTDs were also activated as a significant instrument for financing the PSBR. A CTD is an acknowledgement by the Inland Revenue that money has been placed with it as an advance payment of a tax liability. The minimum purchase of a CTD is £5,000 so the opportunities for usage are greatest for companies with corporation tax liabilities.

CTDs earn interest until being applied to payment of corporation tax, petroleum revenue tax and so on. Because they cannot be redeemed against PAYE liabilities they are mainly taken up by companies. The main purpose why the government issues them is to smooth the seasonal inflows of corporate tax receipts rather than raise funds towards the borrowing requirement, but the stock outstanding has risen somewhat in recent years.

(3) PSBR Financing by Borrowing from the UK Monetary Sector

In order to appreciate the importance of the monetary sector supplying the finance for the PSBR it is useful to repeat some basic ideas about money supply creation.

The simplest case of money creation is that in an economy where currency issued by the monetary authorities, the government, is the only form of money.

In this simple economy, the most obvious way for the government to put the money into circulation would be to spend it. Clearly, in this case, the money supply would rise, i.e. the act of spending by the government would create money. In the widest sense of "spending", this is the only way in which money can be put into circulation. However, some forms of "spending" are not included in the official definition of government spending. For example, the government could pay off some of its debts, which would include repurchasing gilts and other securities it had previously sold. This form of spending is called an "open-market operation". To summarise, in this simple economy any government spending (including the purchase of assets) would necessarily create money, i.e. increase the money supply, as would any repurchase of government obligations (bonds, etc.).

Similarly, any action by the government which led private individuals to incur and settle a debt to the government would destroy money, and thereby reduce the money supply. This could be by taxation, by the sale of assets e.g. the British Telecom issue or by the sale of government securities. So by netting out these transactions, as discussed earlier, we can see that money is created by the public sector borrowing requirement (PSBR), i.e. government spending and purchase of assets less taxation and sales of assets, and that money can be destroyed by government sales of securities, i.e. by private sector lending to the public sector. (A negative PSBR will reduce the money supply and net repayments by the government to the public sector will increase the money supply.) These transactions are the only ways by which money can be created in this simple economy.

The process described above is applicable in any economy but needs to be expanded to include a description of the creation of bank deposits, the other form of money in most communities. Bank deposits are an asset to their holders but are also, by definition, a liability of the banks. There are two forms of bank asset which need to be included:

(a) bank lending to the (non-bank) private sector; and
(b) bank lending to the public sector.

The case of bank lending to the private sector is straightforward. The bank exchanges a claim on itself for a claim on the borrower. In the simplest case, the bank credits the individual or corporate borrower's account with the amount of the loan. This is the act of money creation, the decision by the bank to lend money, i.e. to simultaneously increase its assets and liabilities. This is what is meant by the statement, as we discussed earlier, "every loan creates a deposit".

The case of bank lending to the public sector is somewhat more complicated. The government can automatically borrow from banks to finance its spending without any transaction between the banks and the government. This latter is sometimes called "residual finance" and involves the following process. (Case 1) The government needs to pay someone, e.g. a student grant or a teacher's salary. (It might pay them in currency in the simpler example). It sends the individual a claim on the government for, say, £100. This usually takes the form of a cheque. The individual pays this into his/her bank account. At this point £100 of money has been created. The bank has accepted an obligation of £100 in the form of a bank deposit, thus the money supply has risen. In exchange the bank has acquired £100 claim on the government its assets have risen by £100 in the form of lending to the public sector (i.e. bankers' balances have risen by £100).

Case I

Assets	Liabilities
Bankers' Balances + £100	+ £100
£100	£100

Thus the public *sector has* borrowed £100 from the banking sector by this indirect method, i.e. it now owes the banks £100 more than it did before. It is crucial to the process of money creation that this, the direct impact of public spending on the money supply, is independent of how the banks hold their claim on the government. There are three possibilities:

(a) simply hold the government cheque – somewhat unlikely as there is no point in holding an asset which yields no return;

(b) buy a treasury bill;

(c) buy a government bond (gilt-edged stock).

The *important* point here is that it does not matter what the bank does, the money supply (i.e. the bank deposit) has still gone up. If the bank holds the government cheque the bank deposit still exists. If the bank buys a Treasury bill or a government bond its claim on the public sector stays the same, i.e. *bankers' balances fall* and *Treasury bill* or *gilt holdings rise*. (Case II)

Case II

Assets	Liabilities
Bankers' Balances + £100 Bankers' Balances − £100 Holdings of Gilts/Treasury Bills + £100	+ £100
£100	£100

Initially, as the cheque is credited to the bank, then its bankers' balances rise. Remember this leads to an expansion of the money supply. Let us examine the three alternatives. First, if the bank simply holds the cheque, then bankers' balances have risen. If now the bank purchases a Treasury bill or a gilt then there is a corresponding offset in bankers' balances, i.e. the initial increase is watched by a corresponding decrease. However, this is a rearrangement of the banks' assets – the bank deposit, i.e. the money supply still remains the same.

Thus if the banks purchase *government bonds* (or treasury bills) the initial rise in bankers' balances due to the disbursements of the central government is reversed, but the net rise in bank deposits is sustained as no bank deposit is extinguished in the process. The same applies in the case of banks absorbing notes and coin which form the assets counterpart of the increase in bank deposits induced by the central government's net expenditure.

If, however, the treasury bill or the gilt was purchased by the non-bank sector, e.g. a pension fund, then a different story emerges. When *the pension fund pays for the government stock by writing a cheque on its account, this means that its bank deposits fall and thereby, inter alia, does the money supply*. It is for this reason that the monetary authorities place such a heavy emphasis on selling government stocks and Treasury bills to the non-bank private sector. (Table 4.1 summarises the monetary consequences of alternative means of financing the PSBR.)

The concept of residual finance is guaranteed by the agreement with the Bank of England whereby the discount houses "cover the tender" of Treasury bills, on the explicit understanding that the finance required, to the extent that it is not obtainable from elsewhere, will be forthcoming from the Bank of England. Thus the banking sector meets the government's residual borrowing requirements automatically every week. The monetary sector is always prepared to hold the residue of the sterling national debt, namely that part of the sterling debt of the central government and public corporations which nobody else chooses to hold.

The Bank of England is not anxious that the banks acquire more Treasury bills as this, as already explained, does not extinguish bank deposits. The extent to which residual finance is provided by the banks can be reduced by reducing the PSBR or by the government borrowing more from the non-banks.

Any attempt to increase borrowing from non-banks was, until recently, complicated by the nature of the government's operations in the gilt markets. An example will make this clear. If the demand for gilts by the private sector fell, prices of gilts would tend to weaken. In order to prevent this the Bank of England, in the 1960s and early 1970s pursued a policy known as "leaning into the wind". Under this policy the Bank would, whenever there was excessive selling of gilts, be an active buyer of gilts. Although this strengthened gilts prices it raised the money supply. The Bank believed that attempting to force extra gilts on to the market when willing buyers were scarce would be destabilising and ultimately damage the attractiveness of gilts to investors. With time the Bank has become more aggressive in marketing gilts. The practice of buying back stock was stopped in the early 1970s and tenders for new issues were introduced in the late 1970s.

Table 4.1

Monetary Consequences of Alternative Means of Financing the PSBR

Government action	*Effect on bank deposits*	*Effect on bankers' balances*	*Ultimate effect on the money supply*
1. Writes a cheque - takes no other action	Rise Zero	Rise	Rise
2. Writes a cheque - sells gilts to the non-bank public	Rise Falls	Rise Falls	Remains the same
3. Writes a cheque - sells gilts to the monetary sector	Rise Zero	Rise Falls	Rises

THE PRIVATE SECTOR

The private contribution to monetary growth is sterling bank lending to the private sector and overseas. Its most familiar form in Britain is the overdraft, an agreed line of credit, taken up by a customer through his current account, but which a bank can recall on demand. How does a new act of bank lending increase the money supply? A brief description of the process will illustrate the point.

Suppose that individual A wants to borrow more from his bank (Bank 1) and that his bank manager gives him permission. An identical sum is credited to individual A's current account. The loan is an advance by the bank and forms part of its assets. As current accounts are bank deposits, the money supply has increased. The genesis of new bank deposits as we discussed earlier is as simple as that.

THE EXTERNAL SECTOR

Before describing the impact of the external sector on the monetary system, it is necessary to describe the mechanism by which foreign exchange is taken into or paid out of the official reserves.

The Exchange Equalisation Account (EEA) was set up by the Finance Act 1932, to provide a fund which could be used, under the control of the Treasury, for the purchase and sale of gold and foreign currencies in order to prevent excessive fluctuations, from day to day, in the exchange value of sterling. After the war the Finance Act 1964 extended the purpose for which the Account might be used to include "the conservation or disposition in the national interest of the means of making payments abroad". The Account is today the custodian of the country's reserves of gold and foreign currencies.

The EEA draws on its foreign currency reserves buying up sterling when it wishes to support the exchange rate and builds up its holdings of foreign currency by selling sterling when it wishes to hold the exchange rate down. The EEA also exchanges foreign currency for sterling for the government – e.g. to pay for the British army on the Rhine.

The EEA does not hold any sterling assets and balances its sterling position every day with the Exchequer. When it is increasing foreign currency reserves its requirement for sterling is passed on to the central government who must borrow to finance. When the reserves are falling the EEA provides sterling to the Exchequer and the government's need for finance is correspondingly reduced.

There are two ways in which the overseas sector can change the money supply. The first stems from the fact that governments normally purchase and sell foreign currency in order to manage the exchange rate, and to provide citizens with foreign currency to purchase goods, take holidays abroad, etc. Any such acquisition (or sale) will have similar effects on the money supply as when the government buys or sells any other assets. Thus the sale of foreign currency to a domestic resident (to, say, enable him to take a foreign holiday) will have similar direct impact on the money supply as the payment of taxes or the sale of government bonds (i.e. the money supply decreases).

The crucial point is that an acquisition or a sale of a foreign asset must be financed. If the government has acquired or supplied sterling then there is a clear impact on the domestic money supply. If the government has supplied sterling the money supply rises; if the government is receiving sterling, the money supply goes down. However, if the government can acquire sterling needed to purchase foreign currency assets from the private non-bank sector, then there is likely to be no net effect: the sterling that is obtained from the private sector is returned to it.

There is also an overseas impact which works through the banking system. The UK includes only resident sterling deposits in the money supply. Hence, if a deposit is transferred from a non-resident to a resident this will increase the money supply and the transfer of a deposit from a UK citizen to a non-resident will reduce the money supply. Such transactions are likely to occur in the course of international trade; one transfers a deposit to a non-resident by writing a cheque in his favour to pay for an import. Thus transactions between residents and non-residents which are settled by means of cheques drawn on UK banks will affect the money supply.

In addition it is useful to consider the case whereby the UK private sector is in balance of payments deficit even though the overall balance of payments is zero. When the private sector is running a balance of payments surplus it is receiving sterling from non-residents. If this is placed on deposit with a bank the money supply goes up. The reverse is true when the private sector is in deficit with its new transactions with non-residents. It may be that the non-resident supplies the sterling by reducing his sterling deposits with a UK bank. This would mean that *total* sterling deposits would be unchanged – but £M_3 (and all the other UK money supply definitions) include only residents deposits. The impact of external flows upon the money supply depends on the system of exchange rate management being implemented. These can be either fixed rates or some variants of floating rates.

Fixed exchange rates The monetary implications of external flows can often be broadly determined by considering whether the underlying transactions reflect, or are associated with, an excess demand for money on the part of UK residents. Assume that the growth in the demand for money is faster than the growth in the supply of money. Thus individuals are frustrated by not being able to get hold of as much cash as they need. They will react to this by selling overseas assets or by increasing their net sales of goods to foreigners and converting their foreign currency receipts into sterling. The commitment to a fixed exchange rate means that the authorities must supply this demand for sterling, and add the foreign exchange thereby acquired to the official reserves. In the process, their own total need for sterling finance will be increased. Unless successful offsetting action can be taken at the same time – for example by raising sales of public sector debt to non-banks – the end result will be an increase in the domestic money supply, which will accommodate the underlying growth in money demand.

However, it may be the case than an inflow takes the form of a rise in sterling bank deposits of overseas residents (private or official). The banks buy foreign currency from a non-resident, crediting his sterling account. The foreign currency is in turn sold to the EEA in exchange for sterling claims on the Government. However, this time there is no increase in sterling M_3 as non-residents' sterling deposits are not included in sterling M_3.

Freely floating exchange rates. Under this system the authorities will broadly aim not to add to or draw upon the official reserves in response to market pressures. Instead the foreign exchange rate will increase if there are capital inflows and/or a current account surplus and will fall if there are capital outflows and/or a current account deficit. Since the authorities are not buying or selling sterling, the net inflow, ultimately, must be zero. Capital inflows must be offset by a current account deficit or other capital outflows. In this way the money supply is largely insulated from external influences. But this insulation is not complete. An example will illustrate this point.

Assume that there was an increase in the demand for sterling which in turn led to a sterling appreciation. This could in turn reduce the demand for money as sterling holders then feared a sterling depreciation. Since the abolition of UK exchange controls, domestic residents as well as non-residents are free to switch between foreign currency and sterling assets; they, as well as non-residents, may therefore respond to a rise in the exchange rate by holding more foreign currency assets, and running down their domestic sterling bank deposits. As they do so, sterling M_3 (which includes sterling bank deposits) will be directly reduced. In the longer term, a higher exchange rate will help in a number of ways to hold down domestic prices and nominal incomes (and hence the demand for money) – most obviously by reducing the cost of imports, and by putting pressure on domestic producers to price competitively.

Details of the external and foreign currency counterparts are given in Appendix 1.

Since August 1981 banks in the UK have been required to adhere to a bankers' balances ratio (see Chap. 2). This involves no change in the effect EEA transactions have upon the Exchequer's financing. A balance of payments surplus causes the government's need for sterling finance to rise and the government is forced to issue more debt. If there is no rise in the demand for public sector debt from UK non-banks or from non-residents (e.g. the surplus is on current account), the supply of Treasury bills is increased and there is a greater volume of residual financing through the banking sector. The initial rise in bankers' balances due to EEA intervention is offset as the banking sector purchases Treasury bills. But under the pre-1981 regime Treasury bills were reserve assets and hence the initial rise in the reserve assets ratio was sustained.

The effect of external transactions on sterling M_3 is no different under the new institutional arrangement. An external surplus still raises the government's domestic borrowing requirement and forces the government to issue more debt. Also, as before, the supply of Treasury bills to the banking sector is

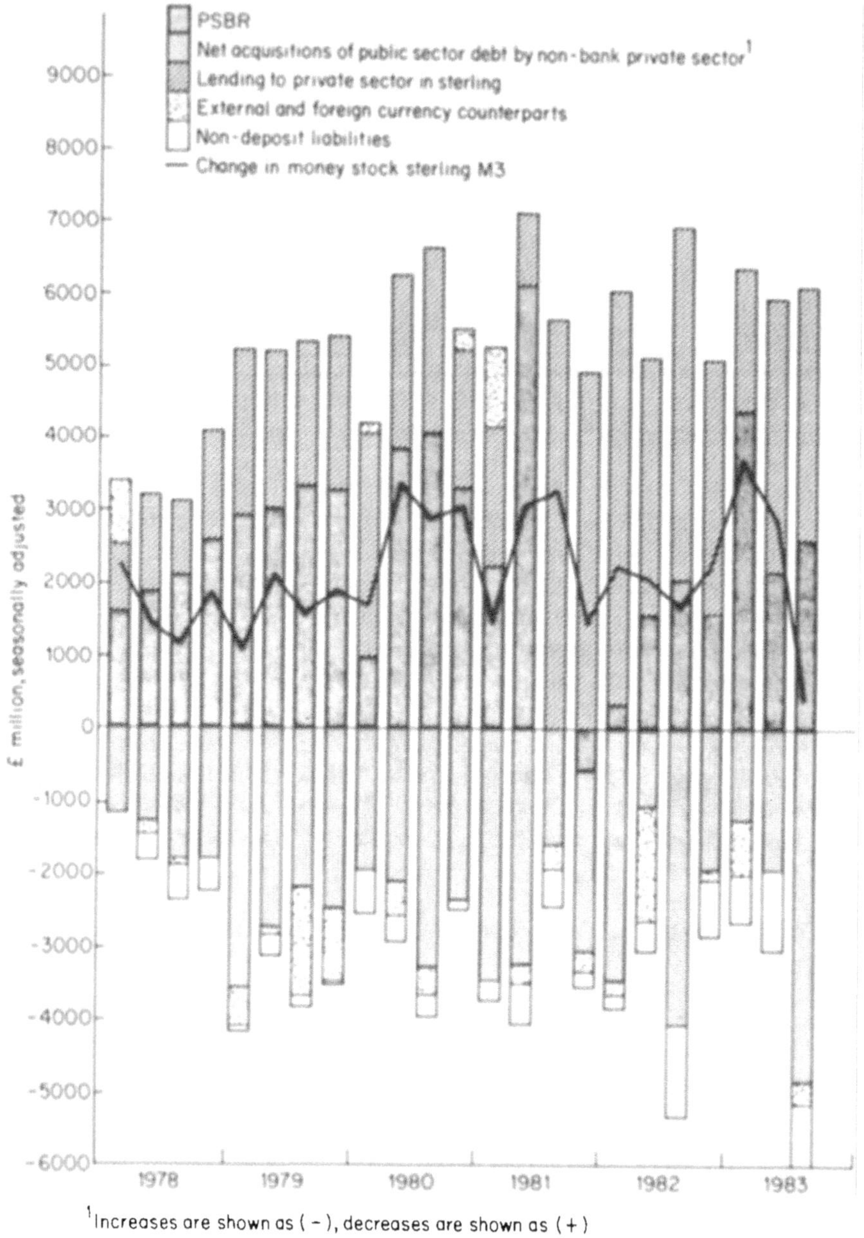

Fig. 4.1 Counterparts to changes in money stock
Source: *Economic Trends* March 1984
Reproduced by kind permission of the Controller of Her Majesty's Stationery Office.

increased if there is no net increase in demand for public sector debt by UK non-banks or non-residents.The difference is that Treasury bills are no longer "reserve assets". Thus the initial effect on bankers' balances is reversed when the banking sector purchases Treasury bills, and this now offsets the initial rise in the banks' reserve ratio as only bankers' balances are now included.

The link between balance of payments financing, external finance of the PSBR and sterling M_3 in 1982 are illustrated in Appendix 2.

COMMERCIAL BANKS NON-DEPOSIT LIABILITIES

Banks' liabilities are of two kinds – to their shareholders, i.e. their issued capital and reserves, and to their depositors. As with any balance sheet, liabilities and assets must always be equal. Thus any increase in assets, debts owed by other persons and institutions to the banks will always be matched by increases in liabilities. However, banks' liabilities to depositors are of a very unique nature in that they constitute the money supply. If a bank lends out money or purchases public sector debt both the assets and the liabilities of the banking system increase.

However only bank deposits are in the money supply and thus any increase in liabilities accruing to shareholders or reserves must be deducted.

Banks' non-deposit liabilities can increase in two main ways. First banks can make new issues of equity capital (shares) in order to raise their capital base. Secondly banks, for prudential purposes, can retain part of their profits and build up their reserves. In both cases these must be deducted from the banks' total liabilities in order to correctly estimate monetary growth.

THE MAJOR FACTORS INFLUENCING RECENT MONETARY GROWTH

The predominant influence on the growth of the monetary aggregates varies from one period to another. At times it is the size and financing of the PSBR: at times the level of bank lending. At other times it may depend on external flows. The monetary effects of external flows depend to a large extent on the nature of the Government's policy towards the exchange rate. Figure 4.1 and Table 4.2 summarise the counterparts of monetary growth between 1979 and 1984.

MONETARY CONTROL IMPLICATIONS

Given our understanding of the major determinants of money supply growth it is instructive to discuss how the authorities can use this information in their desire to control the money supply. We will discuss the exact mechanics of monetary control in Chapter 7.

Table 4.2
Public Sector Borrowing Requirement, and other Counterparts to Changes in Sterling M_3
Domestic and external counterparts

£ millions

	Domestic counterparts						*External and foreign currency counterparts*	*Net non-deposit liabilities (increase-)*	*Change in sterling M_3 (columns 6+7+8)*
	Public sector borrowing requirement (surplus-)		*Purchases(-) of public sector debt by UK private sector (other than banks)*		*Sterling lending to UK private sector (a)*	*Sub-total of columns 1-5*			
	Central government borrowing requirement	*Other public sector contribution*	*Other public sector debt*	*Central government debt*					
	1	2	3	4	5	6	7	8	9
Unadjusted									
Financial years									
1979/80	+8,211	+1,718	-945	-8,208	+9,330	+10,106	-2,464	-1,199	-6,443
1980/81	+12,851	+333	+608	-11,473	-9,248	+11,567	+596	-1,470	+10,693
1981/82	+7,695	+1,090	+405	-11,673	+14,928	+12,445	-895	-1,742	+9,808
1982/3	+12,653	-3,479	+265	-8,554	+14,360	+15,245	-2,757	-2,380	+10,108
Quarters									
1981 1st qtr	-127	-101	+391	-3,715	+2,250	-1,302	+1,137	-638	-803
2nd "	+7,501	+268	+45	-3,773	-1,010	+5,051	-418	-318	+4,315
3rd "	+2,240	+31	+119	-1,344	+2,939	+3,985	-344	-990	+2,651
4th "	+617	+294	+236	-3,226	+5,206	+3,127	-114	+203	+3,216
1982 1st qtr	-2,663	+497	+5	-3,330	+5,773	+282	-19	-637	-374
2nd "	+3,098	-237	-25	-1,302	+3,566	+5,100	-1,731	-170	+3,199
3rd "	+2,497	-822	+11	-3,986	+5,349	+3,049	-391	-1,261	+1,397
4th "	+4,874	-1,802	+397	-2,307	+2,869	+4,031	-179	-90	+3,762
1983 1st qtr	+2,184	-618	-118	-959	+2,576	+3,065	-456	-859	+1,750
2nd "	+5,450	-1,646	+209	-2,403	+3,187	+4,797	+47	-900	+3,944
3rd "	+3,388	-175	+219	-4,672	+3,680	+2,440	-401	-1,503	+536
4th "	+3,433	-343	+249	-3,204	+3,408	+3,543	+238	-434	+3,347
Month ended									
1984 Jan. 18	+157	-433		-1,138	+1,254	-160	+1,334	-554	+620
Feb. 15	+1,864	+14		-1,305	+1,032	+1,605	-577	-1,044	-16

Relationship between columns: 1+2-3-4+5=6; 6+7+8=9.

Source: *Financial Statistics* (March 1984).

To repeat, the changes in the money supply ($£M_3$) can be analysed as follows:

Change in $£M_3$ =	Public Sector Borrowing Requirement	– debt sales to non bank public	+ sterling bank lending to private and overseas sectors.	+ external flows (in (+) or out (–))	– Increase in banks non-deposit liabilities
	(1)	(2)	(3)	(4)	(5)

Because the PSBR, gilt sales and external flows can be identified respectively with fiscal policy, debt management and exchange rate policies, the above framework shows the interrelationship of the various arms of economic policy:

(1) is reduced by fiscal contraction (reducing government spending and/or increased taxation);

(2) is increased by high interest rates. If the whole of the public sector deficit and the refinancing of maturing national debt is covered by sales of gilts or short-term securities to the non-bank public there is no addition to the money supply from this source. Hence the enthusiasm of the monetary authorities to maximise sales to the non-banks. When any part of the borrowing requirement is financed by the sale of the Treasury bills or gilts to the banks then there is pressure for the money supply to increase.

(3) could be reduced by action which reduced the growth of bank lending either by directives on banking lending or by high interest rates, simply lowering the demand for bank loans. Remember bank loans create bank deposits (the major component of the money supply). In practice bank lending, as discussed below, has not been reduced by high interest rates.

(4) If the exchange rate mainly reflects market forces (that is, if there is no, or little intervention by the authorities to alter the exchange rate, or to maintain a fixed rate) then the direct effects of external flows on the money supply are likely to be small. (The price of the pound will change to equate supply and demand for pounds so that flows in = flows out.) With a fixed exchange rate, inflows lead to pressure for the money supply to increase and outflows for pressure for the money supply to decrease.

(5) is not amenable to official control.

In practice, in order to forecast future monetary developments forecasts of these major components have to be made. The monetary authorities will undertake the forecasts primarily with the intention of discovering the required net purchase of public sector debt by domestic non-banks. In this way the government becomes aware of how much debt they need to sell to the non-bank public. If this looks excessive in relation to current expected demand the authorities will take measures to:

(a) reduce the PSBR; and/or
(b) reduce bank lending in sterling; and/or
(c) increase sales of debt to non-banks by, for example, raising interest rates.

External finance and the increase in banks' non-deposit liabilities are not considered very amenable to monetary control.

RECENT DEVELOPMENTS

An official document *Monetary Control* issued in 1980 and discussed further in Chapter 7 noted that the two major monetary control mechanisms were to be reducing the PSBR and use of interest rate adjustments. Direct controls on bank lending have been plagued with problems (again see Chapter 7). However there are problems associated with the two chosen monetary control mechanisms.

Reducing the PSBR – Deficiencies as a Monetary Control Mechanism

A part of the Government's declared medium-term financial strategy is to reduce the PSBR as a means of contributing to control of the money supply. Unfortunately the PSBR is not always an appropriate mechanism for monetary control.

The PSBR is a financial balance of a heterogeneous set of income and expenditure components, in fact the balance of all public sector income and expenditure. It includes, for instance, public corporations' investment expenditure. If British Steel were denationalised the PSBR would immediately decline but the new owners of British Steel still need to borrow to finance steel-making activities. Consequently as the PSBR fell sterling bank lending would increase. Nothing of immediate substance in the financial system would have changed. Although the government would have contributed to its PSBR target, there would have been no change in the overall financing requirements in the economy. It might be noted in this context that the public sector has invariably maintained a current surplus and that the financial deficit which often exists results from an excess of public sector investment over saving. Real assets have been acquired and it is not unreasonable to borrow to fund the build-up of assets which yield an economic and social rate of return over time. There is an element of perversity in attempting to lower the PSBR by reducing real investment in the public sector which adds to unemployment and hence to an offsetting rise in the PSBR on current account. At the very least productive investment should be excluded from any PSBR target.

Above all, the size of the PSBR is not itself solely a reflection of government policy as its size (via automatic expenditure and revenue adjustments as unemployment rises/falls) is heavily determined by movements in the economy.

Two examples will make this clear:

(1) An extra 100,000 unemployed cost the treasury about £438 m in 1981–82, according to an estimate made by the Manpower Services Commission in late 1981. This includes the cost of paying unemployment and supplementary benefits; the loss of income tax and national insurance contribu-

tions; and the lower receipts from indirect taxation because the unemployed spend less than those in work.

(2) An extra percentage point on interest rates adds an estimated £200 m to the government's annual bill for debt interest.

The Treasury reckons that if GDP falls 1% short of forecast as a result of lower consumer spending, the PSBR that year will be £800 m larger than expected.

To the extent that a cut in government expenditure or rise in taxation deflates the economy the saving on the PSBR is markedly less than that implied by the policy adjustment itself. Policy induced fiscal adjustments can be an expensive way of reducing the PSBR. This latter problem has resulted in the introduction of a cyclically adjusted PSBR.

In addition the PSBR is the small difference between two large numbers. In 1981–82 public expenditure and revenues were each budgeted at more than £115 bn. If spending turned out to be just 2% more than predicted and revenues 2% less (not a particularly large error), the PSBR would be about 50% larger than forecast.

Finally the whole issue of public sector borrowing has been distorted by inflation. Public sector borrowing as a percentage of GDP in 1984 was only around a third of its level in the mid 1970s.

Interest Rate Adjustment-deficiencies as a Monetary Control Mechanism

The major UK monetary control mechanism, at least in the short run, is the adjustment of interest rates. The practice of the monetary authorities in the UK has been to manipulate interest rates to influence the money supply through the effect upon the non-bank demand for public sector debt and the private sector's demand for bank credit. In particular, raising interest rates, it was hoped, would increase gilt sales to non-banks and make bank loans too expensive and thereby reduce the demand for them. But there are problems here, too:*

(1) The demand for credit seems not to be very sensitive to interest rate movements. Indeed, as the recession, induced in part by high interest rates continues, companies are forced to increase their borrowing simply to repay the higher cost of their debts. This is referred to as "distress borrowing."

(2) As already mentioned, high interest rates designed to secure monetary control, add substantially to the PSBR.

(3) High interest rates induce a high proportion of corporate funding to be made through the banking system (which adds to the money supply) rather than through, for instance, the debenture market which does not. This is because debentures are fixed interest securities and when interest rates are high the idea of issuing debentures by borrowers is very unat-

* These points are more fully developed by D. T. Llewellyn, *The Framework of UK Monetary Policy* (Heinemann Educational Books, 1982).

tractive. If interest rates fall, e.g. because of low inflation, debenture borrowers must continue to pay the same interest charges. This could result in a crippling burden. It is generally recognised that the debenture market can only provide new finance in significant amounts when long-term interest rates are in single figures.

CAN THE AUTHORITIES CONTROL THE MONEY SUPPLY?*

Abstracting from the question of whether it is desirable to control the money supply due to, for example, variability in the velocity of circulation, it is necessary to ask the question whether the authorities CAN control the money supply. There are five basic conditions which, if met, ensure a precise control of the money supply:

(1) Mandatory reserve asset requirements are applied.

(2) The public sector is able to and does control the supply of these reserve assets. These reserve assets are often known as the monetary base (the monetary base is discussed in detail in Chapter 7).

(3) Only the banks hold them.

(4) The ratio of bank reserves to the denominator, for example eligible liabilities is constant or predictable.

(5) Either the bank's reserve ratio is related to the total volume of bank deposits or there is a constant relationship between the money supply and the magnitude to which the reserve ratio applies (eligible liabilities) in the UK.

None of these conditions is satisfied under current institutional arrangements. Taking them one by one:

(i) The UK does not have mandatory reserve asset requirements. The 12½% reserve requirement on banks was abolished in 1981 and although there are some requirements for banks to hold balances at the Bank of England (as discussed in Chapter 2) these are just ½% of their eligible liabilities and are not intended to be reserve assets. Indeed since these deposits (known as "bankers' balances") do not earn interest many commentators see them simply as a tax imposed by the Bank of England on banks in return for the supervisory and liquidity services that it provides.

(ii) The Bank of England faces several constraints and conflicts of objectives which can limit its capability of controlling the monetary base. Two particular conflicts discussed further in Chapter 7 severely constrain the operation of monetary policy: that between exchange rate and monetary objectives, and that between monetary and interest rate objectives.

*Many of the ideas and terms in this section are drawn from *The Framework of Monetary Policy* (Heinemann 1982) by Professor D. Llewellyn to whom grateful acknowledgement is made.

The constraints on the conduct of policy becomes acute if "targets" are set for the exchange rate, monetary growth and interest rates. Thus, monetary control is difficult to secure when the exchange rate is fixed as the central bank is forced to create or extinguish the monetary base as the domestic counterpart to its foreign exchange market intervention.

The second dilemma relates to the compatibility of monetary and interest rate objectives. For a given government borrowing requirement there is a choice between monetary financing (through the central bank or banking system) and non-monetary financing (non-bank private sector). As illustrated in Chapter 1 if the policy target relates to the rate of growth of the money supply, the course of interest rates will be determined by the necessity to sell the requisite volume of government debt to secure the monetary target at the given level of the government's deficit. Alternatively, if an interest rate objective is set this determines the volume of government debt sales and the money supply becomes residual. In effect, the monetary authorities cannot simultaneously target for both the money supply and the course of interest rates; a choice has to be made as to which is to be market or demand determined.

In addition, banks hold notes and coins for normal banking purposes and these are part of the monetary base. It would be absurd for the authorities to limit the supply of these both for practical reasons and because it could even lead to bankruptcy and a banking collapse.

(iii) The public holds notes and coins. Their holdings of them vary in line with changing interest rates and overall economic conditions.

(iv) As banks often hold excess reserves this introduces a degree of sogginess into the system. There is thus no precise link between bank deposits and bank lending.

(v) The reserve ratio may not be related specifically to the bank deposit component of the money supply. In the UK regulations have tended to relate to eligible liabilities and while this magnitude is highly correlated with the bank deposit component of £M_3 the relationship is not constant.

A more fundamental criticism of monetary base controls is that they may involve liability management by the banks and disintermediation (see Chapter 7). As a result, the money supply may be controlled but its value as an economic indicator is reduced.

APPENDIX 1

Table 4.3
External and Foreign Currency Counterparts Relationship with the Balance of Payments

£ million

	External transactions										Domestic foreign currency transactions		
	External and foreign currency counter-parts	Non-bank private sector capital account: Balance of payments current balance	Total	Overseas investment in UK	UK private investment overseas	Import credit	Export credit	Other identified trans-actions	Balance of payments balancing item	Public sector financial trans-actions with overseas contribu-ting to the PSBR	Bank lending in foreign currency to private sector	Public and private sector foreign currency deposits with monetary sector	Residual
	1	2	3	4	5	6	7	8	9	10	11	12	13
1979	-3,083	-553	-2,970	3,246	-6,056	136	-538	242	428	228	902	-802	-316
1980	-422	3,635	-3,532	4,455	-7,112	-419	-28	-428	-988	189	1,278	-1,427	423
1981	308	7,251	-6,348	3,074	-8,889	116	-234	-415	-745	407	2,792	-2,206	-843
1982	-2,298	5,774	-6,034	2,707	-8,828	-130	310	-93	-3,702	657†	1,733	-1,121	395†
1983	-463	2,924	-3,791	4,551	-8,371	-14	1	42	123	-534	1,354	-2,162	1,623
1979/80	-2,417	119	-2,857	4,275	-6,515	165	-488	-294	542	199	1,046	-1,269	-197
1980/81	658	6,549	-4,512	3,497	-7,689	-453	19	114	-840	330	1,469	-2,422	84
1981/82	-834	5,826	-4,994	3,936	-8,688	155	9	-406	-3,293	235†	2,784	-959	-433†
1982/83	-2,773	5,652	-6,102	2,293	-8,832	-118	105	450	-2,870	84	882	-901	482
1983/84	129†	2,146	-4,157	4,644	-8,279	7	—	-529	551	-94	2,698	-2,975	1,960
1979 1	-587	-883	-1,258	302	-1,487	-40	-134	101	1,107	2	314	130	1
2	-267	-138	185	1,185	-1,036	95	-197	138	158	-93	479	-671	-187
3	-1,300	568	-1,339	885	-1,917	89	144	-540	-394	-44	7	251	-349
4	-929	-100	-558	874	-1,616	-8	-351	543	-443	363	102	-512	219

1980	1	79	-211	-1,145	1,331	-1,946	-11	-84	-435	1,221	-27	458	-337	120
	2	-552	-123	-1,016	850	-1,819	-20	25	-52	-2	41	905	-362	5
	3	-288	1,553	-397	991	-1,410	-206	119	109	-1,466	41	136	-181	26
	4	339	2,416	-974	1,283	-1,937	-182	-88	-50	-741	134	-221	-547	272
1981	1	1,159	2,703	-2,125	373	-2,523	-45	-37	107	1,369	114	649	-1,332	-219
	2	-377	1,788	-1,543	1,212	-2,165	12	10	-612	48	219	-14	-753	-122
	3	-337	837	-1,021	737	-1,856	232	45	-179	-382	2	1,190	-1,065	102
	4	-137	1,923	-1,659	752	-2,345	-83	-252	269	-1,780	72	967	944	-604
1982	1	17	1,278	-771	1,235	-2,322	-6	206	116	-1,179	-58†	641	-85	191†
	2	-1,778	423	-1,212	745	-1,946	-28	72	-55	-1,273	157	378	-442	191
	3	-300	1,263	-1,682	381	-2,069	-4	2	8	-10	139	155	-502	337
	4	-237	2,810	2,369	346	-2,491	-92	30	-162	-1,240	419	559	-92	-324
1983	1	-458	1,156	-839	821	-2,326	6	1	659	-347	-631	-210	135	278
	2	81	-467	62	1,001	-2,032	-5	—	198	-143	69	542	-75	93
	3	-383	932	-478	1,412	1,876	-43	—	29	-1,974	31	1,191	-556	471
	4	297	1,303	-2,536	417	-2,137	28	—	-844	2,587	-3	-169	-1,666	781
1984	1	134†	378	-1,205	914	-2,234	27	—	88	81	-191	1,134	-678	615

Relationship between columns: 1=2+3+9+10+11+12+13; 3=4 to 8.

Source: *Financial Statistics* (July 1984).

APPENDIX 2

Table 4.4

Links between Balance of Payments Financing, External Finance of the PSBR and Sterling M_3: 1982

£M_3 change	7,984

Monetary sector

Change in liabilities			Change in assets
Sterling deposits by:			
–UK public sector	456		
–UK private sector	7,063		
–Overseas	4,477		Sterling lending to:
		–2,272	–UK public sector
		12,843	–UK private sector
		4,116	–Overseas
Foreign currency deposits by:			
–UK sectors	1,113		Foreign currency lending to:
–Overseas			
–To finance PSBR			
–CG and ECS[1]	–70	–52	–UK public sector
–non-ECS[2,3]	18		
–Other[3]	19,942	1,733	–UK private sector
		18,789	–Overseas
Non-deposit liabilities (net)	2,158		
	35,157	35,157	

Financing the PSBR

465	Notes and coin in circulation with the public
5,803	Other sales of debt to non-bank private sector
–2,272	Borrowing in sterling from banks
	External finance:
52	–foreign currency from banks*
1,504	–direct external finance*
5,448	PSBR

Financing the balance of payments	
Official financing*	1,284
Investment and other capital transactions (including balancing item)	
–Financing the PSBR*[3]	168
–Other[3]	–6,830
Current balance (deficit + ve)	–5,378

[1] Foreign currency loans to central government, to local authorities and to public corporations through the exchange cover scheme.
[2] Foreign currency loans to public sector outside exchange cover scheme.
[3] Not shown in tables – calculated by remainder.
* Components of external financing of the PSBR (£1,452m).

Figures, in £ million, relate to 1982 (January 1984 issue of *Financial Statistics*).
Sources: tables 2.6, 6.1, 10.1, 11.2, 11.3.

Chapter 5

Interest Rates

INTRODUCTION

Decisions as to whether to spend or not to spend, whether to borrow (or lend) now or to postpone borrowing (or lending) for six or nine months, whether to buy securities today or hold cash for the present, whether borrowing or lending should be short-term or long-term are all decisions influenced by current and expected *interest rates*. But what are the factors affecting interest rates and what, in particular causes the monetary sector (in particular banks) to raise or lower their key interest rate (known as base rate)? These are all questions which are discussed in this chapter. Initially we discuss interest rates as if there were only one single interest rate. The discussion is then broadened out to discuss the whole range of interest rates, known as the term structure of interest rates. Appendix 1 illustrates the price and yield relationship already discussed in earlier chapters.

FUNCTIONS OF INTEREST RATES

Interest rates serve a number of significant functions. First, they provide investors with a guide for allocating funds among investment opportunities. As funds are directed into projects that have higher expected rates of return (risk and other factors taken into account), the funds are optimally allocated from the viewpoint of both consumer and investor, since highest returns prevail where effective consumer demand is strongest. Unless an investment opportunity promises a return high enough to pay the market rate of interest, it does not justify the required capital outlay. The money market, by channelling funds into projects that have an expected return in excess of the interest rate, provides a valuable service to investors, borrowers, and society as a whole.

The interest rate also provides a measure of the relative advantage of current consumption compared to saving. By adjusting the available market rate for expected inflation and taxes, an individual can determine the real amount of additional future consumption that can be obtained by postponing current assumption.

Similarly, interest rates help businessmen decide among alternative production methods. Suppose a product can be made either solely with labour or with a combination of labour and machinery. By calculating the capital cost of the machine (the interest rate times the amount invested in the machine), the expected labour-plus-capital cost can be compared with the labour-alone cost to determine the less expensive means of production.

DETERMINATION OF INTEREST RATES, DEMAND AND SUPPLY OF FUNDS

Interest rates are prices. Unlike other prices they are usually expressed as percentages of the amount borrowed or lent. But, like other prices, they are determined by supply and demand. In a monetary economy (where money is the medium of exchange) interest rates depend on the supply of and the demand for loanable funds. The sources of the supply of funds are savings, reductions in the demand for money and increases in the supply of money. The sources of the demand for funds are investment demands, consumption demands (for spending on consumer goods) and increases in the demand for money.

THE SUPPLY OF FUNDS

Saving, which is the main source of supply of loanable funds, arises in all sectors of the economy and may take many forms. Personal saving, i.e. the excess of personal income over consumption spending, may consist, *inter alia*, of contributions to pension funds, the repayment of mortgage loans, deposits with building societies or banks, or the purchase of securities. Business saving comprises retained profits and, most important, depreciation charges. What is not reinvested in the business is usually held in a liquid form or used to reduce bank loans. The government too may contribute to saving in the economy by raising more in taxes than it needs for its own current expenditure; any surplus goes to offset part of the public sector's own investment.

It is important to distinguish between the potential and the actual supply of loanable funds. The reason for this is that households and businesses having savings may not be actually willing to make these funds available to borrowers. Money, remember, is a store of value. Households and businesses may not want to offer either their current savings or any of their accumulated savings to borrowers. On the contrary they may choose to add a portion of their current savings to their accumulated savings balances.

Having made choices as to how to divide their incomes and receipts between spending and saving, households and businesses must then decide the specific form in which to hold their savings. The basic choice is between money in the form of either idle cash or bank accounts on the one hand, and securities of some sort on the other. Idle cash and bank accounts are highly liquid assets; securities acquired from borrowers are somewhat less liquid but generally yield a better rate of return. That part of savings (current or accumulated) which households and businesses want to hold as securities flows into the money market as the supply of loanable funds. That part which households and businesses want to hold as cash obviously does not. This division depends upon the liquidity preferences of households and businesses. More specifically, there are three main reasons (stressed by Keynesians) why households and businesses prefer to hold cash rather than securities:

(1) There is a transaction motive for holding money rather than securities. Households and businesses both need a stock of cash on hand to make ordinary day-to-day purchases. Households, for example, usually receive a sizeable chunk of income every week, or every month. Disbursements, on the other hand, occur more or less evenly over time. This means that households have an average money balance of some size bridging the gap between paydays. And it is simply more convenient to have one's assets in their most liquid form, that is, as idle cash balances or bank accounts, than in the form of securities. Furthermore, there are costs – brokerage fees – in transferring cash into securities and back again.

(2) There is a precautionary motive for holding money. Households and businesses may hold cash balances to meet any rainy-day contingencies which might arise. Particularly relevant are those risks which one cannot protect oneself against by purchasing insurance policies – prolonged illness, unemployment, and so forth.

(3) There is a speculative motive for holding money. At any point in time, there is a certain rate of interest which households and businesses as potential suppliers of loanable funds consider to be about "normal". If the rate of interest is currently low, that is, "below normal", households and businesses may withhold a part of their savings which would otherwise flow into the money market as a part of the supply of loanable funds. They hold more money and fewer securities than they normally would. Why? Because they expect that the current below-normal interest rate will probably rise in the future. Conversely, if the current interest rate is unusually high, that is, "above normal", households and businesses will choose to hold less money and more securities to take advantage of high current interest rates as opposed to the lower normal rate expected to prevail again in the future.

The supply of loanable funds is critically influenced by the level of interest rates i.e. higher and higher interest (real) rates will induce households and businesses (but obviously not necessarily governments) to be less liquid. At relatively high interest rates, households and firms will prefer to hold their assets in the form of interest-bearing securities rather than as non-interest bearing current accounts and idle cash balances.

The supply of loanable funds depends on:

(i) *The rate of interest.* A high rate of interest encourages lending – the supply of lendable funds increases.

(ii) *The amount of savings.* Some countries such as Japan and Germany are very thrifty. This increases the amount of funds available for borrowers.

(iii) *A surplus on the Budget.* (negative PSBR). Occasionally the government spends less than its revenue. In these conditions the government has a surplus that it can lend to the private sector.

(iv) *International factors* (discussed below). When foreigners buy UK assets they are lending to British residents. Low interest rates overseas encourage funds to flow into Britain increasing the supply of funds available to UK borrowers (and vice versa).

The supply curve for loanable funds is upward sloping, i.e. higher interest rates increase the supply available, and vice versa.

THE DEMAND FOR FUNDS

Now let us turn to the demand for funds. Again this can be by private individuals, companies or governments. Private individuals borrow in order to increase their current level of consumption either for housing, cars, holidays or whatever. Companies borrow to pay for factories, plant and equipment. Finally Governments borrow to pay for current and capital spending (e.g. on schools, roads etc. which they cannot finance from taxation).

The demand for borrowed funds depends on:

(i) *The rate of interest.* When it becomes more expensive to borrow (i.e. when the interest rate rises) demand falls.

(ii) *The level of income.* The higher the level of income, the more individuals and businesses will want to borrow. For example, if investment rises firms will in general require outside finance. Similarly, consumers borrow money to buy washing machines etc. More generally when incomes rise individuals increase borrowing for all purposes (houses, cars, etc) and firms need more working capital.

(iii) *The PSBR.* In most countries governments are major borrowers of funds. The PSBR as discussed earlier measures the total funds that they borrow. This is also known as the fiscal deficit or Budget Deficit (Total government expenditure minus tax revenue).

(iv) *International factors.* When investors wish to buy assets abroad they will frequently borrow the necessary funds at home. High interest rates abroad increase the demand for borrowed funds at home.

The demand curve for loanable funds is clearly downward-sloping, i.e. lower interest rates raise the demand for funds. Businessmen will find it profitable to purchase larger amounts of capital goods when the price of loanable funds declines. Similarly, lower interest rates may encourage some increases in consumer and governmental borrowing. (In practice it is "real" interest rates which are relevant. These are discussed in a later section.)

INTEREST RATE DETERMINATION

In equilibrium the interaction between the demand for loanable funds and the supply of loanable funds will determine the interest rate.

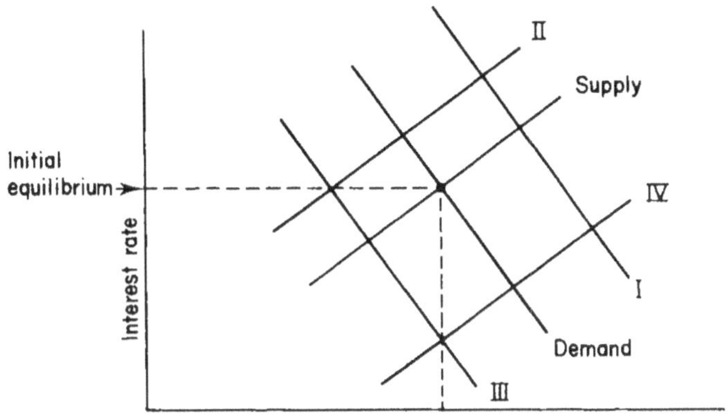

Fig. 5.1

Elementary economic analysis tells us that if the demand rises (I) or the supply falls (II) then the interest rate rises. Similarly if the demand falls (III) or if the supply rises (IV) then interest rates will fall.

The effect on the interest rate of any shift in demand or supply will depend on the elasticities of both lines.

Following a change in demand the less elastic (more elastic) is the supply curve the greater (less) will be the change in interest rates. Following a change in supply the less elastic (more elastic) is the demand curve the greater (less) will be the effect on interest rates.

How can changes in the supply of funds and demand for funds change interest rates? If there is more saving (relative to demand) by businessmen and consumers this will bring down interest rates. What happens if there is an increase in the supply of money? This adds to the savings in the capital market. To see how this can occur suppose that instead of raising new funds through the stock market companies borrow from their banks, and the banks increase the supply of money (remember bank loans create bank deposits which are in themselves the most important component of the money supply). Because companies are borrowing from the banks this will increase security prices (due to a lower demand) and the rate of interest on securities will fall correspondingly as companies can now raise funds more cheaply.

INTERNATIONAL FACTORS AFFECTING INTEREST RATES

Given the importance of international factors in affecting interest rates it is worth explaining, in some detail, the mechanics whereby overseas interest rates affect United Kingdom interest rates. The speed of the impact of international factors depends on official exchange rate policy.

If a country has a fixed exchange rate (i.e. the government is committed to official intervention in order to keep the rate fixed) and the currency is weak, i.e. it is being heavily sold on the foreign exchange market, the government may be induced to raise official interest rates. The objective is to make it more attractive for overseas holders of the currency to hold it and to make it less attractive for domestic holders to transfer it overseas. If a country has a fixed and strong exchange rate there may be pressure for the authorities to lower the exchange rate. As funds flow into the currency the authorities, being forced to increase the domestic money supply to keep the exchange rate fixed will, in an attempt to reduce the inflows, reduce domestic interest rates.

Under floating exchange rates the effects of capital flows on interest rates occur very quickly. With a weak currency investors will speedily reduce their holdings thereby driving up interest rates, e.g. by selling bonds. (The link between bond prices and interest rates is outlined in Appendix 1). Similarly investors will be keen to acquire liabilities in that currency since, if the exchange rate change occurs and is larger than the extra borrowing cost the investor can repay (say his bank loan) and make a profit. The combination of a decrease in the supply of loanable funds and an increase in the demand for loanable funds drives up interest rates.

With a strong currency and a floating exchange rate, the opposite happens. In an attempt to benefit from an appreciation investors will increase their assets in that currency, e.g. by buying bonds which in turn drives down interest rates. Similarly, borrowers fearing the effect of the appreciation will reduce their liabilities in that currency. The combination of an increase in the supply of loanable funds and a decrease in the demand for loanable funds drives down interest rates.

The effect of international factors also depends on the size of the home economy and how developed the domestic financial system is. For a small economy a given foreign inflow of funds is likely to represent a relatively high proportion of the total capital market. The impact is likely to be bigger therefore in a country with limited facilities for foreign investors e.g. because the capital market is undeveloped or exchange controls are in operation.

For an economy such as UK which is relatively small, has no exchange controls and a highly developed capital market international factors can be very important.

THE TERM STRUCTURE OF INTEREST RATES

Now let us drop the assumption about a single rate of interest and consider why is it that rates of interest or yields on different financial instruments vary. Why do some borrowers pay more than others? Why are the yields on long dated securities different from those on short-dated ones? Why do interest rates on different currency denominated assets vary? It is to these questions that we now turn.

In answering these questions it is useful initially to compare investments which have one common feature enabling us to isolate other factors affecting their yields. We will discuss the interest rate on government debt as government debt has the specific characteristic of being free of default risk, unlike private sector debt, as the government can always print money or raise taxation to repay any future debt obligations. The relationship between yields on different maturities of the same type of security is called the term structure of interest rates (from term to maturity).

If we plot on a graph the relationship between the yields on different maturities of government debt (the vertical axis) and the date of maturity (or, equivalently, the number of years to maturity) on the horizontal axis and draw a line through these points we can derive a relationship known as the yield curve. The yield curve portrays the term structure of interest rates at a point in time, i.e. it shows how the yields to maturity vary with the maturity of the debt instrument on a given date.

The four most common shapes are illustrated in Fig. 5.2. An "ascending" yield curve shows interest rates increasing as the maturity increases; a "descending" yield curve shows interest rates declining as the maturity increases; a "flat" yield curve shows interest rates relatively constant across securities of different maturities; a "humped" yield curve shows interest rates at first increasing as maturity increases and then declining as maturity increases.

Considerable effort has been devoted to determining the forces behind the shape of the yield curve. Despite extensive empirical and theoretical work in this area, however, no definite conclusions have been drawn, and three theories compete for explaining the term structure of interest rates the expectations theory, the liquidity premium theory, and the segmented market theory.

The expectations theory. The expectations theory views the term structure of interest rates as determined by expectations of future interest rate movements. The market participants are assumed to buy and sell securities with the objective of maximising profits with available funds. In addition, the expectations theory assumes that market participants have no preference between holding a long-term security or a series of short-term securities. They are only concerned with maximising profit. This necessarily implies that transactions costs of shifting between short- and long-term securities are not relevant.

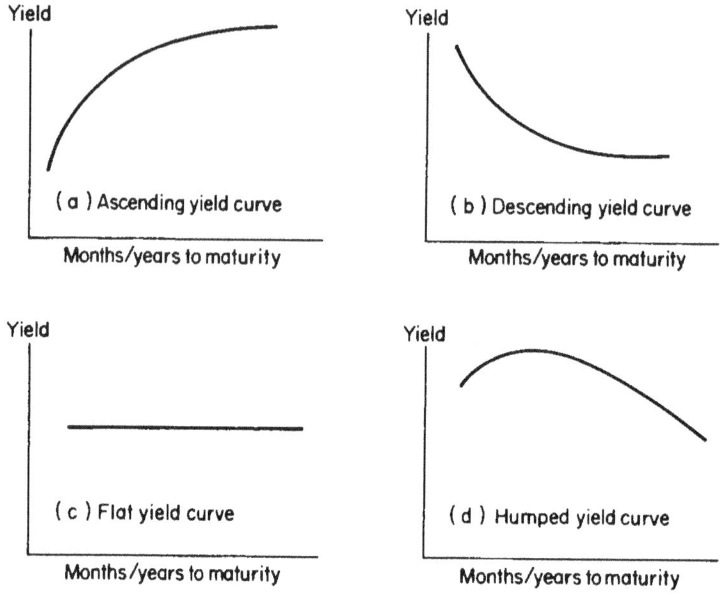

Fig. 5.2

The expectations theory is based on the view that the long-term rate of interest is equal to the average of the current short-term rate of interest plus the short-term rates of interest that market participants expect to prevail over the maturity of the long-term security. For example, the interest rate on a ten year bond should equal the sum of the current short-term rate (rate on a one-year bond) plus the short-term rates of interest anticipated to prevail over the long-term debt divided by the maturity of the long-term debt. To illustrate, assume that two types of bond are available to market participants: a one-year bond and a two-year bond. Market participants have funds available to use over a two-year period and desire to allocate those funds in such a manner as to maximise profits. If the current rate of interest on the one-year bond is 5% and market participants expect interest rates on a one-year bond for the second year to be 10%, the actual rate of interest on the two-year bond is approximately 7½%. The long-term rate (two-year bond rate) is the average of the current short-term rate and the expected short-term rates over the maturity of the long-term bond, i.e.

$$\frac{1.05 + 1.10}{2} = 1.075 \tag{1}$$

The important point emphasised in the expectations theory is that the market participants have definite expectations about the short-term rate in the second year at the beginning of the first year; however, this does not imply that the expectations have to be realised.

According to expression (1), the long-term rates should be 1.075 or 7½%. Why must this be? If market participants really anticipate a 10% short-term rate on one-year loans in the second year and the current short-term rate is 5%, then the long-term or two-year rate must be 7½%. If it were higher, say, at 8%, then the market participants could earn more profit by holding the two-year obligation instead of buying two one-year obligations in consecutive years. The increased relative attractiveness of long-term over short-term obligations would increase demand and thereby increase long-term prices and lower long-term interest rates until they were approximately 7½%. If long-term rates were lower than 7½% holders of two-year bonds would attempt to sell such bonds and buy one-year bonds (driving bond prices down and bond yields up to 7½%. These actions drive rates up and down until investors are neutral as to one-year bonds and two-year bonds.

The shape of the yield curve depends on the short-term rates of interest expected to prevail over the life of the long-term obligation. If market participants expect short-term interest rates to increase, the yield curve will be of the ascending type. Each long-term rate equals the current short-term rate plus the expected short-term rates over the life of the long-term maturity, and, because longer-term bonds will have a greater number of expected short-term interest rates included in their average, long-term interest rates will be higher than short-term interest rates.

Likewise, if market participants expect short-term interest rates to decline in the future, the yield curve will of the descending type. These two relationships are summarised in Table 5.1. If no changes in short-term interest rates are anticipated, the yield curve will be flat. A humped yield curve can be generated by the expectations theory if market participants expect interest rates to first increase then fall.

Table 5.1
The Effect of Expectations on the Yield Curve

	Expectation of rising interest rates	*Effect on yield curve*	*Expectation of falling interest rates*	*Effect on yield curve*
Lender	Lends short causing short-rate to fall	Rises	Lends long causing long rates to fall	Falls
Borrow	Borrows long causing long rates to rise		Borrows short causing short rates to rise	

The liquidity premium theory. The liquidity premium theory is based on the expectations theory but rejects the assumption that market participants are indifferent to short-term versus long-term obligations.

The normal situation is that long-term securities bear higher rates of interest than short-term, because of the bias of borrowers towards long-term liabilities and of lenders towards short-term ones (borrowers prefer to make known future commitments whereas lenders are normally keen on liquidity). The higher rates of interest on long-term securities are needed to persuade either lenders or borrowers to depart from their preferred maturities and to provide a margin out of which those financial intermediaries which help to bridge the gap through maturity transformation (defined in Chapter 2) are able to cover their costs. The differences in interest rates which are needed for this purpose are known as liquidity premia, and these may be expected to rise with the term of the security. According to the liquidity premium theory, the long-term rate is equal to the mean of the current short-term rate, the expected short-term rates, and a liquidity premium.

All four shapes of the yield curve are consistent with the liquidity premium theory. However, because the liquidity premium added to the long-term rate is positive, the upward-sloping yield curve is the most common shape predicted by this theory. Even if no changes in short-term rates are anticipated, the yield curve will still be upward sloping, because the liquidity premium is positive; that is, long-term rates of interest will exceed short-term rates of interest by the amount of the liquidity premium. A descending yield curve could arise if market participants' expected short-term rates to decline significantly below long-term rates so as to more than offset the liquidity premium.

The segmented market theory. This approach differs sharply from the expectations and liquidity premium theories. It regards the short- and long-term rates of interest as being determined in relatively separate markets. These markets are separated for institutional reasons. For example, many purchasers of securities have specific needs in mind usually related to the nature of their liabilities, e.g. pension funds and thus restrict their purchases to segments of the maturity spectrum. Many sellers of securities also have specific maturity objectives, usually related to the nature of their assets. Given the institutional factors that determine the segment of the maturity spectrum in which buyers and sellers of securities will operate, we then have restrictions on the degree of substitutability among securities of differing maturities.

According to the segmented market theory the term structure is determined by the relative supply and demand functions in each segment of the maturity spectrum. The theory is consistent with any particular shape of the yield curve.

Which Theory is Right?

In the last decade and a half, a great deal of empirical evidence has been published on the term structure of interest rates. Although some of the simpler versions have been rejected, there is still considerable controversy over which theory best explains the term structure. The basic problem is that *all these theories*, especially in their more expanded form, can account for any particular shape of the yield curve. Thus, economists have found that the same set of data on interest rates can be consistent with several theories of the term structure. Unfortunately, this is a common problem in the empirical testing of theoretical models.

Although there is still controversy over which theory is correct, there is widespread acceptance of the role of expectations of interest rate movements as being an important component to any interpretation of the term structure. The problem has been in determining how these expectations are formed by market participants and how these expectations shape the term structure.

Two other factors affecting interest rates are the risk of default and inflation to which we now turn.

DEFAULT RISK

The risk that a borrower may default on his debt affects the rate of interest he must pay for a loan, which includes a "loading" for risk. In many instances lenders distinguish a relatively small number of risk categories, and put potential borrowers into the category which they think appropriate. The loading in the interest rate the borrower is charged reflects the risk of loss for that category. Sometimes this classification is carried out on a formal basis – for example, in the USA there are bond-rating services, which classify companies into risk categories. Banks draw a distinction between "blue chip" companies and those to which they attribute a higher risk. Instalment loans from banks generally incorporate a lower risk-loading than similar loans from finance houses, because the risk of default is generally lower for the customers of the former. Commercial bills which have been accepted, i.e. guaranteed, by a bank yield less than trade bills which have no similar guarantee.

In Figure 5.3 we see the relationship between the default risk of a loan and the interest rate charged. The greater the risk the greater the return demanded and vice versa. The line representing risk/return relationship, of course, does not intersect at the origin because lenders must be paid something for the use of their money even on a riskless investment.

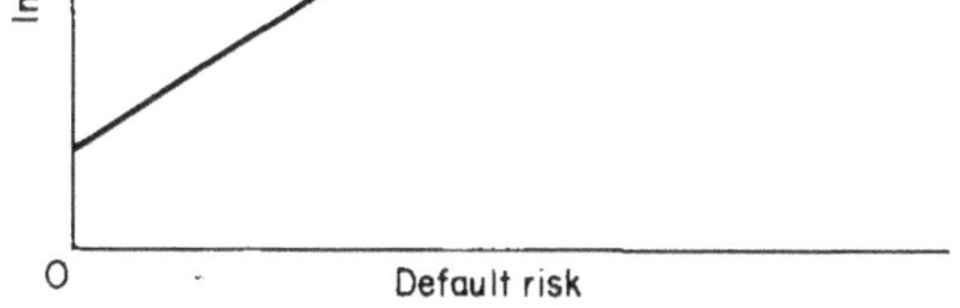

Fig. 5.3

THE ROLE OF INFLATION

Inflation has a powerful influence on interest rates. It affects the willingness of borrowers and lenders to enter into loan agreements. For this reason it is expectations about inflation rather than actual inflation that is relevant. Lenders will demand a higher nominal return if they expect inflation to erode the purchasing power of their interest receipts and principal. Borrowers, for their part, will tend to acquiesce to these demands if they – also expecting inflation – anticipate that their incomes will be rising enough in money terms to afford the higher interest charges. This suggests a natural tendency for interest rates to move in line with inflation.

It is important when discussing inflation to distinguish between nominal (or market) interest rates and real interest rates. Nominal rates are rates expressed in money terms. For example, if interest paid per annum on a loan of £100 is £10, the rate of interest would be 10%. Real rates of interest are the rates of interest adjusted for the expected rate of inflation. The real rate is therefore a measure of the increase in real wealth expressed in terms of the investor or lender. For example if the nominal rate of interest is 10% and the expected annual rate of inflation is 6%, the real rate of interest is the interest earned after allowing for the increase needed just to keep pace with inflation. The real rate of interest can be measured by subtracting the expected rate of inflation from the nominal interest rate. In the earlier example this would be 10% – 6% = 4%.

We find, therefore, that in times of inflation, creditors demand that an inflationary premium be added to the nominal interest rate for lending money. Debtors are willing to pay the inflationary premium because they know that they will be able to pay back their debts in money which is worth less in terms of purchasing power. Debtors can pay back in "cheap" money if there has been inflation during the time the loan was outstanding.

INDEXATION – IS IT DESIRABLE?

The British government is slowly moving towards indexation of its debt instruments. By indexation is meant that to the capital value an allowance for inflation is added upon repayment of the capital. The value of the principal on repayment is thereby related to the movement in the retail price index over the life of the stock. Indexed linked gilt edged stocks were first introduced in March 1981. Their arrival was preceded by controversy about the merits or otherwise of these types of stocks.

Some have argued that indexation "institutionalises" inflation: the more people whose financial assets are protected against inflation the more the government's incentive and ability to contain inflationary stocks is reduced. Furthermore, it is claimed that indexed gilts will be an expensive form of borrowing if inflation is high, and a profligate Government could thereby store up problems for future generations.

Against this, others point to the apparent illogicality of a Government committed to a sustained reduction of inflation continuing to issue high coupon long-dated gilts, which could prove very expensive in real terms, and maintain that indexation will, by reducing uncertainty about future real returns, allow lower interest rates in the economy generally. Far from encouraging a Government to spent, the argument goes indexed borrowing imposes discipline, in that it becomes less easy for a Government to inflate as a way of resolving immediate difficulties.

After careful analysis of the economic case, and the implications for other borrowers, the UK Government decided that it would, on balance, be right to issue indexed gilts, for two principal reasons:

(1) There should be improvements in monetary control. The possession of a new debt instrument of this kind gives the Bank of England additional flexibility in its debt marketing operations. Both conventional fixed-interest and indexed gilts will remain on offer, and this enables the Bank of England to match more closely the preferences of investors. Indexed gilts will be saleable at times of uncertainty about inflation without the need to raise nominal interest rates. This reduces the Government's vulnerability to surges of growth in sterling M_3.

(2) With conventional gilts substantial risks are incurred by both investors and the Exchequer, owing to uncertainty about future rates of inflation. An indexed gilt eliminates these risks. Moreover, investors should be prepared to accept a lower real rate of interest in return for insurance against inflation. This factor in itself can be expected to reduce the overall cost of servicing government debt.

For these reasons, and because of the positive impact on expectations – only a Government committed to a sustained reduction in inflation would wish to issue them. The introduction of indexed gilts could allow the Government to achieve a given monetary target with interest rates at somewhat lower levels than would otherwise be necessary, reducing the cost of conventional funding and having beneficial effects throughout the economy.

THE DETERMINATION OF RETAIL BANKS' BASE RATE

A bank's base rate is the published rate to which much of its lending and some part of its deposits are linked. Since it influences the price the bank charges for funds it obviously reflects the cost of those funds to the bank. Factors influencing base rate movements are (i) competition for deposits (from say building societies); (ii) the demand for loans and (iii) the cost of providing banking services. The rates actually charged on lending depend, apart from the above factors, upon the nature and status of the borrower and may range from base rate + 1% (for borrowers of the highest standing) to, say, base rate + 10% or more (for risky borrowers.)

The determinants of base rate have changed since August 1981. Prior to this date the key factor affecting interest rates was the Bank of England's Minimum Lending Rate which in turn was influenced by monetary growth and/or exchange rate considerations. When MLR changed, so, too, almost invariably did bank base rates. However, although commercial interest rates followed the lead of MLR, this was not so much a result of official "direction", but more because the Bank of England was able to enforce the desired level of short-term interest rates by its operations in the money markets. Because the banking system could always be short – or made short – of "cash" (specifically the balances the clearing banks maintain at the Bank of England) then the Bank in turn could dictate the interest rate at which it would supply cash in order to relieve this cash shortage, if necessary at MLR itself. The provision of this so called "lender of last resort" finance at a rate of interest centering on MLR ensured that MLR had more than just "psychological" significance, important though the latter undoubtedly was as a guide to official thinking. Even so, direct lending to the banking system at MLR (via the discount houses) was used only sparingly and was confined to very short periods – a week or less. Of greater operational significance in enforcing its desired level of short-term interest rates was the Bank of England's practice of quoting the price at which it would buy or sell Treasury and other eligible bills; and these were consistent with – i.e. somewhat below – the prevailing Minimum Lending Rate. Money market rates were therefore principally determined from day to day by the Bank of England, and speculation that MLR would be changed could be countered, if necessary, by the Bank reaffirming its bill dealing rates. Bank base rates, then, followed money market rates; and money market rates were controlled by the Bank of England; although the level at which these rates were pitched had naturally to take factors such as money supply or exchange rate pressures into account.

Towards the end of 1980 the Bank initiated changes in its methods of intervention in the money market in order to allow "market forces a greater role in determining the structure of short-term interest rates, and permit greater flexibility". In particular, the Bank's stated aim now is to keep very short-term interest rates (and the 7-day rate has become the key rate in this respect) within an unpublished band. The Bank no longer attempts to "peg" longer, e.g. 3-month rates. And consistent with the latter development, the Bank has abandoned completely the practice of quoting prices at which it will buy and sell bills and instead now responds to offers of bills. These developments are discussed in more detail in Chapter 7 and have already been discussed in Chapter 3.

Base rates must undoubtedly reflect conditions in the money market as is evident from Figure 5.4. But this statement is incomplete. Banks do not alter base rate from week to week*, so any base rate decision will be influenced by a view of how long current market conditons – the level of money rates – will prevail and the likely direction of the next change. Because of this, the banks

*Although Barclays Bank did announce that with effect from March 6 1984 that their base rate was to be within ¼% of 3 month inter-bank rate. They did stress, however, that this was to be a guideline and not a fixed rule.

Fig. 5.4 Short-term Money Rates
Source: Bank of England, Quarterly Bulletin
Reproduced by kind permission of the Bank of England.

will take into account what they perceive to be the underlying trend of both financial and general economic conditions – including the authorities' attitude to exchange rate and money supply pressures. Base rate decisions cannot depart far from commercial criteria – the cost of the banks' funds and the pressure of competition in financial markets.

The clearing banks' traditional deposit base – savings and cheque accounts – has diminished as a proportion of total deposits in recent years. Competition, particularly from the building societies but also from National Savings, has increased the dependence of the clearing banks upon the wholesale markets.

Indeed Barclays bank chairman stated in his statement in the 1983 Report and Accounts that in 1950, when he joined the bank current accounts (i.e. interest free) provided 75% of Barclays funds. In March 1984 the amount for cheque and deposit accounts together was 49% – with the remainder raised at rates linked to market rates.

The reason why wholesale rates are crucial to the clearing banks base rate determination is that they represent the banks' marginal costs of funds. In this context the cost of longer term money is most important. The three months rate is particularly significant; it is fairly stable and corresponds to standard money market maturities. However, shorter-term rates, from overnight to seven-day, are also relevant, for if they are too high in relation to base rate large corporate customers may borrow on overdraft and lend back to a bank through the wholesale market at the higher rate. So once money market rates get more than 1% above base rates (base rates plus 1% being the rate that a prime customer could borrow at) it becomes possible for customers to borrow from the bank and re-deposit at a profit. This is known as round tripping.

So it is in the wholesale money market that individual institutions adjust their liquidity position by lending or borrowing surplus funds. The position of the market as a whole is largely dependent on transactions between the monetary authorities and the private sector. Customers' tax payments or purchases of government securities, for example, can result in the banking system as a whole being potentially short of its first line of liquidity – its balances with the Bank of England.

Control of money market rates gives the Bank of England control of bank base rates because the clearers, as already indicated, cannot afford to let base rates get too far out of line with market rates. If they get too high, then borrowers will tend to transfer to market-related borrowing which may mean that the clearers lose not only money, but also lose customers to other banks (notably the foreign banks). If base rates get too low in relation to market rates, the borrowers will switch to overdraft borrowing, forcing the clearers to pay higher money market rates to fund the loans.

The only factor in the market of sufficient size to be able to influence the net supply of funds is the Bank of England. By selling assets (Treasury Bills, bank bills, gilts, foreign exchange) the Bank can make the market short of cash and hence force rates up. Similarly, purchases of assets can bring rates down. Every day, the imbalance of flows into and out of the Exchequer (whose account is at the Bank) affords an opportunity to exercise this power. The rates at which the Bank relieves a shortage or absorbs a surplus of cash (its dealing rates) have an enormous influence on money market rates.

Strictly speaking, imbalances in the flow of cash determine interest rates only at the very short end of the market, and indeed overnight rates fluctuate far more than any other sort of rate. But the influence of the Bank extends along the whole maturity spectrum, not only because the Bank can (and does) deal in longer-term bills, but more importantly because the predominant influence on longer-term money market rates is market expectations of future short rates. (In line with the expectational theory of interest rates discussed earlier.) Since the Bank (and hence ultimately the Government) determines short rates, the market's expectations of future rates are primarily determined by its view of Government policy.

So Bank of England intervention rates only influence bank base rate decisions to the extent that they change expectations about future short-term rates (especially three month rate).

On top of the wholesale market rate the banks, since they are obliged by the monetary authorities to hold ½% of their eligible liabilities in the form of cash at the Bank of England and 5% in the form of money at call to the discount houses, need to add a small percentage to their cost of funds.

APPENDIX 1

PRICE AND YIELD – A KEY RELATIONSHIP

The inverse relationship between price and yield is important in understanding how the financial system works. When interest rates rise, the market price of outstanding fixed-income securities, such as bonds and gilts, declines. When interest rates fall, the market price of fixed-income securities increases.

Holders of fixed-income securities, then, experience price depreciation on their portfolios during periods of rising interest rates. On the other hand, those who defer the purchase of fixed-income securities during a period of falling interest rates will later pay higher prices. The following example illustrates this inverse relationship.

Assume that a £1,000 bond has a fixed coupon interest rate of 8% and a maturity date of, to make the arithmetic easy, perpetuity. The bond pays £80 in interest per year, and the face value, or principal amount, is of £1,000.

If, some time later, similar bonds of comparable maturity are paying £90 in interest a year, bond dealers will continue to buy and sell the 8 percent issue, but they will lower its price until it also yields 9%. The principle behind this is that no one would buy a bond with an 8% yield when he could buy one of the same quality with a 9% yield.

At what price will the 8 percent coupon bond yield a 9 percent current return? By using the formula for current yield.

$$\text{current yield} = \frac{\text{annual interest payment}}{\text{prevailing market price}}$$

and transposing it

$$\text{prevailing market price} = \frac{\text{annual interest payment}}{\text{current yield}}$$

the price can be determined

$$\frac{£80}{.09} = £888.88$$

At a price of £888.88, the 8% coupon bond will yield 9%. Since the bond is selling for less than £1,000, i.e. less than par value, it is said to be priced at a discount.

What if market interest rates fall and new bonds are being sold with 7% coupons? Again, the 8% coupon bond must be brought into line with similar securities. In this case, the 8 percent bond will be "bid up" to yield 7%.

$$\frac{£80}{.07} = £1,142.86$$

Since the bond is selling for more than par, i.e. £1,142.86, it is said to be priced at a premium.

While the current yield formula is helpful in illustrating the relationship between yields and prices for fixed-income securities, the yield to maturity method is more accurate and a more commonly used pricing technique. Calculations for yield to maturity will not be further discussed here – except to say that tables are available for each coupon rate, yield and maturity which translate bond prices into approximate yield equivalents. These take account of the tendency of bond prices to move towards the price at which they are redeemed as they come close to maturity. As the earlier mentioned relationship is such a key factor to understand it is worthwhile giving another example. Given a coupon of say £50 one would pay no more for a bond than what one could get by putting that sum of money to work earning the going rate of interest. Or, if P is the price of the bond and r is the going rate of interest (e.g. 5% or .05), then one would pay no more than $P \times r = £50$. Since everyone knows about this bond, competition among potential buyers would force the price up to the level where $P \times r = £50$. Anything less and everyone would try to buy it, driving its price up. Anything more and no one would be interested, driving its price down. Hence in equilibrium the price of the perpetuity equals £50/r. More generally, if P is the price and C is the coupon, then the price is given by $P = C/r$.

Instead of talking about the supply of and demand for credit or loanable funds determining the rate of interest, we could talk about the same thing in terms of the demand for securities and the supply of securities determining the price of securities (see Figure 5.5). To supply credit (lend) is equivalent to demanding financial assets (securities) – financial institutions lend, for example, by purchasing financial assets. To demand credit (borrow) is the same as supplying securities – business firms borrow by selling their bonds or other IOUs. At a price of £833 (which corresponds, let us say, to 6 percent yield, assuming a 5% coupon on a £1,000 bond), relative eagerness to buy securities – or lend – would drive the price of securities up, and it would drive the rate of interest down. And at a price of £1,250, corresponding to a 4% yield, relative eagerness to sell securities – to borrow – would drive the price of securities down, and would drive the rate of interest up.

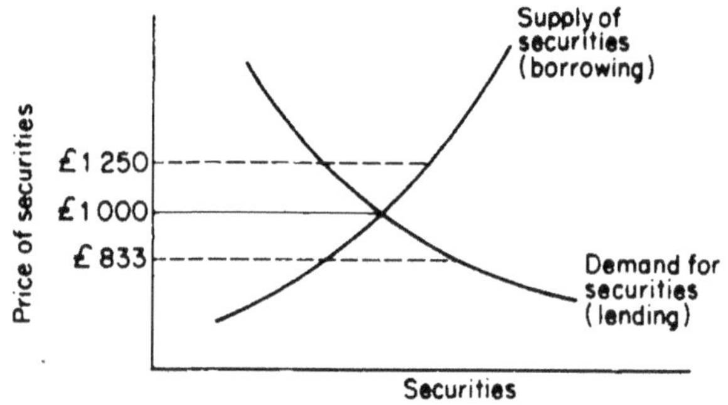

Fig. 5.5

As can be seen from the diagram: if C = £50 and r = 5%, then P = £1,000. If r falls to 4%, then P = £1,250. If r rises to 6%, then P falls to £833. This inverse relationship between the price of a bond and the going rate of interest holds for any type of bond.

Chapter 6

Aspects of Monetary Theory

Monetary theory is concerned mainly with the macro-economic effects of changes in the money supply. Will a reduction in money supply growth cut inflation? Can monetary policy be used to pull an economy out of a recession? Are money supply targets a good idea? These are some of the questions that we will be considering in this chapter.

Not all economists agree on the correct answers to these questions. Many of the differences arise from alternative views about what determines the *demand for money* and what happens when the demand and supply of money are not equal. The two principal schools of thought are:

(a) the monetarists;
(b) the Keynesians

The great battles between these two schools were fought in the 1950s and 1960s and their differences have been reduced to questions of emphasis. More recently, a group known as the "new classicists" have emerged which disagrees with both monetarist and Keynesian views of the economy and we will briefly examine their arguments. We will also discuss an area that is frequently ignored in discussion of monetary theory but is an important part of understanding of monetary policy: the role of the exchange rate (this is discussed further in Chapters 8 and 9).

MONETARISTS AND THE QUANTITY THEORY OF MONEY

Milton Friedman is the most famous monetarist but in fact his ideas can be traced back to another American economist, Irving Fisher, who developed the *quantity theory of money* (discussed in Chapter 1) at the beginning of the century. This dominated thinking about the determination of inflation until the 1940s when the ideas of Keynes became generally accepted. Milton

Friedman revived the quantity theory in the 1950s and the views of modern monetarists can be seen clearly in terms of the classical quantity theory.

The basis of the quantity theory is the *equation of exchange* also known as the quantity or Fisher equation which states that:

The quantity of money in circulation (M) × the velocity of money (V) = the price level (P) × the number of transactions (T),

i.e. $MV \equiv PT$

Velocity is not the complicated concept that it might appear; it is simply a measure of the number of times on average that the money stock changes hand over a given period. The above equation does not, as yet, say anything about how the economy works. This is because it must always hold – it is, in fact, an accounting identity (this is signified by the convention of using "≡" rather than "="). Since M is the amount of money in circulation and V is the number of times it changes hands in transactions, MV must be the total value of transactions that takes place. But this is precisely what is given by the product of the average price of each transaction and the number of such transactions.

It may seem that an identity is a very powerful relationship in economics. After all, if it always holds it should be a reliable theory, much better than most economic theories. But the problem with identities is that they have no predictive power. Suppose for example that we want to predict the effect of a rise in the money supply (M). The equation tells us that the following are possibilities:

(a) V falls, with P and T unchanged;
(b) P rises, with V and T unchanged;
(c) T rises, with V and P unchanged.

But these are not the only possibilities. The adjustment to a rise in M could take the form of movements in V, P and T. Indeed, P could fall if V falls and/or T rises sufficiently. Similarly, T could fall if P rose sufficiently and/or V fell. Clearly the equation of exchange cannot predict the effect of changes in M on the economy.

To make the theory operational we must make *assumptions*. These may be wrong – in which case our equation will cease to be valid – but it will enable us to make predictions about how the economy works. The quantity theorists and monetarists assume:

(a) M can be controlled by the government and does not respond to movements in V, P or T;

(b) T can be taken as given and does not respond to movements in M, V or P. The rationale for this is that T is closely related to the pace of economic activity and output. The classical economists believed that full employment was the norm and the level of output (and hence T) were unaffected by monetary factors like M and P. The monetarists did not take quite such an extreme view. They allowed for movements in T (e.g. in a recession) but believed they were moderate and temporary. To the monetarists, the quantity theory was therefore a theory about the longer run;

(c) V is constant, i.e. the amount of money held is determined by prices and the level of transactions or output. The monetarists saw this as the key assumption and reinterpreted the quantity assumption that V was constant to mean that the demand for money was a stable function of prices, output and interest rates.

The effect of these assumptions on the predictive power of the quantity equation is dramatic. We rewrite the quantity equation with an "=" sign to indicate that it is no longer an identity.

M	×	V	=	P	×	T
↑		↑		↑		↑
determined by the government		constant (i.e. does not change when M, P or T change)		free to move		constant (i.e. does not change when M, V or P change)

When M changes we now have just one possibility: a change in P. Moreover, we can predict exactly the amount by which P moves given a change in M.

Inflation of 5% a year can occur only if M is increased year after year by 5%. It is not surprising therefore, that Milton Friedman should say "inflation is always and everywhere a monetary phenomenon". Moreover, since movements in M affect only P, the real economy, proxied by T is unaffected. This is called the "neutrality of money". If money is neutral, monetary policy has no role to play in managing the real economy.

AN EXTENSION OF THE QUANTITY EQUATION: THE CAMBRIDGE K

If we formalise the link between T, the volume of transactions and the level of output, Y by replacing it in the equation of exchange we get:

$$MV = PY$$

$$\text{i.e. } M = \frac{PY}{V}$$

Cambridge economists re-expressed the American quantity equation in this way and replaced 1/v by k, the so-called "Cambridge k"

$$\text{i.e. } M = kPY$$

Many economists preferred this formulation because it emphasised the key role played by the assumption of constant velocity and, because it suggested the possibility that P or Y responded to M (e.g. a reduction in M could either reduce P or induce a recession by lowering Y). The Cambridge economists believed that k could vary. In particular, they argued that it would respond to the rate of interest. As we shall see later in this chapter, this was a key element of Keynes attack on classical economics but the earlier Cambridge economists did not see the implications of their assumption.

MEASURING VELOCITY

Statisticians do not measure velocity directly by examining the turnover of money. Instead they measure it indirectly by using the assumptions underlying the Cambridge k. Published statistics on velocity define it as the money value of national output (i.e. PY) divided by the money stock. In the UK the annual velocity of £M3 was close to 3 at the end of 1984.

THE CLASSICAL DICHOTOMY AND THE NEUTRALITY OF MONEY

The quantity theorists viewed money as a medium of exchange held purely for transactions motives. The amount of money required to finance a given value, PT of transactions is determined by velocity. But they believed that velocity was a technological constant, influenced by structural factors (e.g. whether workers are paid weekly, whether credit cards are available, etc.) but not responsive to changes in M.

Therefore, when the money supply rises, individuals have no wish to hold it until prices or the volume of transactions has risen. But the volume of transactions is determined by output and the organisation of business (e.g. a large number of small businesses leads to more market transactions than a small number of integrated businesses). These factors are not affected by money. Prices therefore simply reflect the quantity of money. Inflation occurs only when the money supply is steadily rising. Without a rise in money, inflation is impossible. Indeed some economics textbooks written at the beginning of this century used to define inflation as a general increase in the money supply.

The quantity theorists were experts in price theory. They knew that the theory of supply and demand when extended to the whole economy determined only *relative* prices. In other words *real* factors (like supply and demand) determined things such as the price of apples relative to oranges or real wages (which is the price of labour relative to the price of goods) and so on. Real factors could not determine the *overall* price level. Indeed, if all prices doubled so that the price of apples relative to oranges, real wages and all other relative prices were unchanged, supply and demand would be unaffected. Provided, that is, that the money supply also doubled. Otherwise it would be impossible to finance the higher value of transactions and prices would be forced back down again.

The quantity theory completed the jigsaw puzzle for the classical economists. The overall price level and hence all money values were determined by the money supply. Real factors determined relative prices. This was known as the *classical dichotomy*. Since it implied that money did not affect output and other real factors it is also described as the proposition of the *neutrality of money*. Do not forget, however, that money was certainly not considered neutral as far as the overall price level.

THE MODERN QUANTITY THEORY: MONETARISM

The quantity theory of money was discredited by the evidence of the great depression in the 1920s and 1930s and the subsequent ascendency of Keynesian ideas. In the early 1950s Milton Friedman of Chicago University began to reformulate the quantity theory. Since then his ideas have become increasingly influential.

Friedman's basic advance was to concede many of the arguments of Keynes as descriptions of the short-run behaviour of the economy – albeit with reservations – whilst retaining the basic tenets of the quantity theory as longer-term propositions. Furthermore, over the years he has generally shortened his estimate of the longer term so that Keynesian effects are now limited to about 18 months.

Friedman and the monetarists retained the old quantity theory assumptions that:

(a) money was held for transactions purposes;

(b) velocity was constant in the longer run (or at any rate grew at a constant rate);

(c) output was unaffected by money in the long run.

But he conceded that:

(a) short-term movements in velocity were possible in response to fluctuations in the money supply;

(b) velocity also depended on interest rates (though he asserted that the sensitivity was not great);

(c) short-term movements in output could be produced by varying the money supply. Indeed, Friedman argued that changes in money had powerful, albeit temporary, effects on output.

The monetarist view of the world is perhaps easiest understood by explaining how they see the effect of a rise in the money supply (the transmission mechanism). Initially a rise in M is absorbed by a fall in V, i.e. the extra money supply is hoarded. Very quickly, however, economic agents begin to run down their excess money holdings. They do this partly by increasing spending, partly by buying financial assets (such as stocks and shares) and partly by buying up physical assets (e.g. houses and oil paintings). This bids up the stock market and reduces interest rates, stimulating investment (see Chapter 5 for an explanation of the relationship between changing asset prices and interest rates). Through these diverse mechanisms the rise in money feeds through to an increase in the pace of economic activity. Whilst a fall in V takes up all the slack initially, T soon begins to increase.

However, whilst an individual can reduce his holding of money (by exchanging it for goods and services) this is not the case for the economy at large.

The effect of the increase in aggregate spending is to set prices rising. Firms initially respond to higher demand by producing more and widening mark-ups (which raises prices immediately). Extra output requires more workers and the associated tightening of the labour market pushes up wages which raises costs and feeds through into higher prices. As prices rise the demand for money is increased and the excess money holdings that began the whole process are eroded. When prices have risen by the same proportion as the rise in the money supply, excess money balances have disappeared and V and T return to their normal level.

The monetarists therefore believe that changes in M have temporary effects on output and permanent effects on prices.

COST PUSH VERSUS DEMAND PULL

Monetarists believe that inflation is essentially determined by an excess of demand in the economy, i.e. inflation is demand-led. By contrast, many economists particularly Keynesians believe that inflation is often determined by costs, i.e. *cost push* rather than *demand pull*. Cost push theories of inflation gained prominence during the last war and have radically different policy prescriptions for tackling inflation. Cost push theorists believe that inflation can be tackled directly by controlling wages (e.g. by an incomes policy) by reducing taxes like VAT which directly affect prices or by keeping up the exchange rate. To them reducing demand is a terribly weak method of cutting inflation. To demand pull theorists it is the only way. Monetarists take this further and say that demand will be automatically reduced by inflation unless the money supply is continually increased to meet rising demand for money.

Later in this chapter we will assess the evidence for these various theories but first we must discuss Keynesian views on money and inflation.

KEYNES, MONEY AND INFLATION

Keynes wrote at a time of deflation – falling prices – and mass unemployment and he died before he could fully develop his ideas. However, he had written about inflation and we can use the ideas developed by his followers which are described as Keynesian, as if they were Keynes' own.

Keynes' principal objections to the classical quantity theorists were:

(a) velocity is not constant, indeed he argued it is highly variable and responds to interest rates;

(b) there is no natural tendency for output to reach a full employment level and T may be depressed by a reduction in M for an extended period.

(c) as a result money is not neutral;

(d) in a recession, with low or negative inflation an increase in M may be totally ineffective in raising either T or P: velocity may adjust;

(e) money is held for a variety of motives (actually, three) and has three characteristics. It is not solely held for transactions purposes as the medium of exchange (as the monetarists believe).

His followers raised further objections. In particular they extended (a) by suggesting that money was difficult to define in practice. To many Keynesians, velocity is a "will o' the wisp".

Keynes' views about the role of money reflect to a large degree a distinctive view of the demand for money. He described the demand for money as a "liquidity preference". The alternative is to hold bonds. Money provides liquidity but no interest income. Bonds are illiquid but provide interest income. Interest rates are the mechanism by which the demand for money is brought into balance with supply.

Keynes identified three characteristics of money as being distinctive:

(a) it is the *medium of exchange*;

(b) it is the *unit of account*: prices, book-keeping, etc., are in pounds sterling, the denomination of money,

(c) it is a *store of value*: it can be used as a means of savings. Of course it is not unique in this regard.

These three properties give rise to three motives for holding money:

(a) *transactions demand*, as suggested by the quantity theorists.

(b) *precautionary demand*. This arises when individuals keep some cash available to take advantage of bargains either in the shops or in the stock market.

(c) *speculative demand*. This motive relates to special circumstances when there is a widespread fear that bond prices might collapse. This might happen when nominal interest rates are very low and are unlikely to fall further. Individuals rush to hold money for fear that holding bonds will be unprofitable.

Except when (c) applies there is a cost of holding money. More correctly, it is an opportunity cost: the return from holding bonds, i.e. the rate of interest. The higher the rate of interest the greater the cost of holding money (and vice versa).

Keynes' principal innovation was to suggest interest rates were determined by the supply and demand for money. When interest rates are high the cost of holding money is great (because the opportunity cost of not holding bonds is high). As result higher interest rates reduce the demand for money.

Higher prices or output in the economy increase the need for money balances on account of (a) and (b). If the supply of money is fixed by the government something would have to give. For the quantity theorists that something was the price level. Keynes introduced an alternative that broke the iron link between money and prices: interest rates. In Keynes' view individuals and firms switched between money and bonds, balancing the need for transactions and precautionary money balances against the cost of holding it (i.e. the interest foregone on the bonds).

Keynes believed that interest rates were the "price" that balanced the supply and demand for the stock of money. The classicists thought interest rates were determined by the supply and demand of the flow of savings.

We can display Keynes' view easily in a diagram.

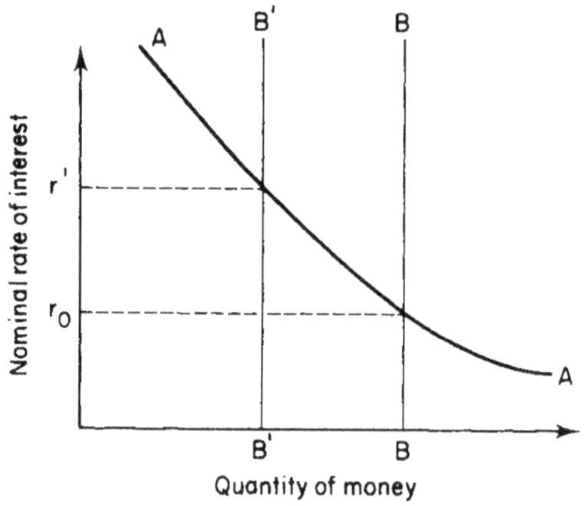

Fig. 6.1 Keynesian Demand for Money

AA shows the demand for money. It slopes downward to show that people hold more money when interest rates (and hence the opportunity cost of holding money) are low. BB is the fixed supply of money. The interest rate that will cause people to hold exactly that amount is r_0. At higher interest rates people will cut back their money holdings below BB and hold more bonds. The associated demand for bonds reduces interest rates back to r_0.

If the supply of money is reduced for instance to B′B′ there is a shortage of money. People sell bonds in an attempt to increase their money holdings. This depresses bond prices and thereby raises interest rates. When interest rates have risen to r′ the cost of holding money is sufficiently great to persuade people to reduce their holdings to B′B′.

The mechanism by which the demand and supply of money are equated is important not just because it explains how interest rates are determined. For Keynesians it is also the mechanism by which money affects prices and output in the economy as a whole. Because interest rates take over the role of prices in the quantity theory, money can affect prices and output only via interest rates. Interest rates constitute the transmission mechanism between money and prices and output.

For Keynesians the potency of monetary policy depends critically on;

(a) money having a big impact on interest rates;
(b) interest rates having a big impact on the economy.

(a) depends on the *interest elasticity* of the demand for money. If money is highly interest elastic a large change in money produces only a small change in interest rates. Variations in M have only minor effects on interest rates and hence the transmission mechanism is weak. If demand is inelastic, however, a change in the quantity of money has a large effect on interest rates. We can see this in Figure 6.2 below.

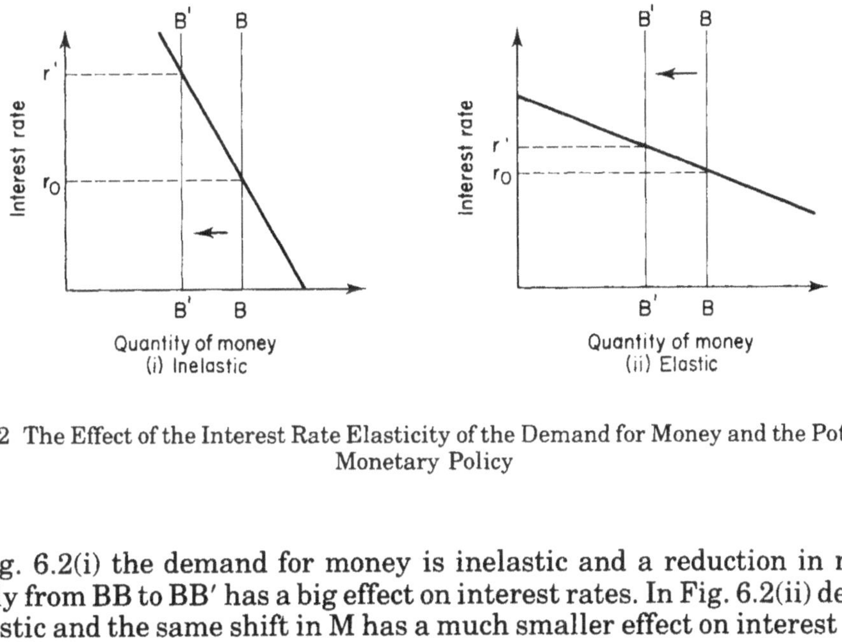

Fig. 6.2 The Effect of the Interest Rate Elasticity of the Demand for Money and the Potency of Monetary Policy

In Fig. 6.2(i) the demand for money is inelastic and a reduction in money supply from BB to BB′ has a big effect on interest rates. In Fig. 6.2(ii) demand is elastic and the same shift in M has a much smaller effect on interest rates.

Modern Keynesians typically argue that the demand for money is interest elastic. Keynes himself believed that the elasticity was very high when nominal interest rates were low. This is because he believed low interest rates led to fears that they would increase. If interest rates rise the market prices of bonds fall (as discussed in Chapter 5). If the fall is great enough the return on bonds could be negative and money would be a more profitable investment.

Since money would then provide liquidity and a higher return than bonds (albeit merely by avoiding capital losses) the demand for money would be very large. An increase in the money supply in these circumstances would not significantly reduce interest rates and, as a result, would not affect prices or output.

This puts the transmission mechanism from money to the economy into neutral. Keynes called it the *liquidity trap*. It was a major reason for his belief that expanding the money supply would not help to end the Great Depression in the 1930s.

The second link in the Keynesian chain from money to economic activity is the effect of interest rates on aggregate demand. Keynes emphasised the effect on investment. Companies invest to make profits. When interest rates rise the cost of finance goes up and the number of profitable projects declines. When interest rates go up, spending on investment declines. Other forms of spending that are typically financed by credit – spending on consumer durables, housebuilding and so on – are also likely to fall when interest rates rise. Most Keynesians however believe that the effect of interest rates on investment is weak. If an investment project is profitable, they argue, moderate variations in the cost of finance will not affect whether it goes ahead. They would stress the availability of credit rather than its cost as the key factor. The Keynesian view of money and its effect on economic activity is now complete. A cut in the money supply raises interest rates and this cuts aggregate demand. As a result there is downward pressure on output and prices. However, because (a) the demand for money is interest elastic and (b) changes in interest rates have only weak effects on aggregate demand, the effects of changes in the money supply are weak.

MACRO-ECONOMIC POLICY – IS IT NECESSARY?

So far we have pointed out the differences between the Keynesians and the monetarists in terms of how they view the transmission mechanism from money to prices and output. Another key difference is that monetarists believe that the economy has a natural tendency to move to a level of output consistent with full employment. Macro-economic policy does not have to concern itself with maintaining full employment, the forces of economic adjustment will get there on "autopilot". Of course, they do not believe that reducing inflation – the other traditional goal of macroeconomic policy – occurs automatically. Controlling the money supply is essential for that. But intervention to boost or stabilise output and employment is unnecessary. Keynesians vigorously deny this.

So what are these automatic forces that the monetarists believe will push the economy back to full employment? Basically, they boil down to demand and supply. Suppose there is unemployment. Translated into economic jargon, unemployment is an excess of labour supply (people who want to work at the going wage) over demand (the amount that firms want to employ at that wage). Excess supply of a commodity pushes down its price. Unemployment pushes down the price of labour, wages. This makes it more attractive to employ workers and demand for labour goes up. At a lower wage the supply of labour may fall. In these ways unemployment is reduced.

Similarly, a recession implies excess supply of goods, i.e. people do not wish to buy all that firms can produce. The result is a fall in the price level which encourages spending. It also reduces the transactions demand for money and individuals can spend the excess money (or buy bonds which reduces interest rates and thereby stimulates investment). The net effect is that aggregate demand rises. Eventually wages and prices will fall sufficiently to eliminate the recession.

Keynes believed that wage and price adjustments were weak and unreliable mechanisms for pulling the economy out of recession. Unemployment, he believed was due to deficient aggregate demand. Employment was too low because firms could not find buyers for their output – not because wages were too high. Cutting wages – the monetarists' remedy – might make matters worse by reducing workers' incomes and hence their spending. This would exacerbate the recession. Similarly, falling prices are hardly the way to assist industry in a recession when profits are under pressure. Keynes' remedy for curing recession was a direct injection of extra spending by increasing government spending. This would raise demand and boost output and employment. The economy could not be relied upon to generate the extra demand itself. Government intervention was necessary.

After several decades of debate this key distinction between the monetarists and Keynesians remains. Monetarists believe the private economy "works" so that government intervention is unnecessary. Keynesians take the opposite view.

THE NEW CLASSICISTS AND THE RATIONAL EXPECTATIONS SCHOOL

In the last 10 years a group of economists have challenged both the monetarists and the Keynesians. Monetarists, as we have seen, accept many Keynesian arguments as correct in the short run but deny them in the longer term. The new classicists deny Keynesianism has any validity even in the short run. They believe that the economy is always at the optimal maximum level of production and employment (optimal here simply means cannot be improved upon).

This may seem a curious viewpoint. Indeed given the history of recession and the current level of unemployment it may seem absurd. But the key element of their argument is straightforward: if the economy is not at any optimal position then a transaction would take place which would benefit both parties. If there are barriers to the transaction they should be removed. If not, transactions will take place until there are no further benefits to be reaped. The economy will then be at an optimal position.

Consider, for example, unemployment. If workers are genuinely unemployed they would accept work at a wage slightly below the current level. Employers would be happy to oblige because it would reduce their costs and so raise profits. The two parties (the employer and the previously unemployed worker) both gain so the transaction (the employment of the worker) takes place.

This is similar to the monetarists view in the previous section. The difference is that the new classicists see no reason for delay. Adjustment can take place immediately. There is no short run "window" in which government intervention can help.

The new classicists also believe that the price level adjusts quickly. Suppose for instance the money supply is increased. According to the monetarists the price level will rise eventually. Keynesians would also accept that some increase was likely and that it would take time. According to the new classicists, households, firms and workers will also realise this and their actions shorten the lag. If prices are expected to rise, shops which sell the same goods cheaper today will be giving up profits. Shoppers will be willing to pay higher prices today rather than wait because prices are going up. The price level moves immediately to the long-run level. Why? Because if it didn't there would be scope for profitable transactions.

This also works in reverse. In particular the rate of inflation can be cut "at a stroke" merely by announcing that the money supply growth is to be reduced. There is no cost to reducing inflation, no trade-off between output and inflation even in the short run.

Apart from the key assumption that gains from trade will always be exploited the new classicists made two other assumptions to produce their conclusion:

(a) individuals form expectations and act upon them;

(b) these expectations are "rational" i.e., they take account of all the available information including economic theory.

These are powerful assumptions. They have generated a vast amount of economic research. One of the results that has emerged is the distinction between anticipated and unanticipated changes in economic policy. If a change in the money supply is announced then it will immediately feed through into higher prices for the reasons set out above. But if people are aware of the change they can hardly react immediately. The new classicists argue that unexpected changes work through in much the same way as the monetarists describe.

The ability of macro-economic policy to raise output and employment is dramatically reduced if the new classicists are correct. Only by changing economic policy secretly can it be effective. And if policy can only work by "fooling" people into doing things they would not do otherwise, it is not at all clear that it can ever be a good thing.

THE PHILLIPS CURVE AND INFLATION

In the 1950s and 1960s there was broad agreement amongst macroeconomists along broadly Keynesian lines about how the economy worked. At the core of their thinking was the notion that there was a trade-off between the level of economic activity and inflation. Economic policymakers faced a choice:

(a) raise aggregate demand and this will boost output and lower unemployment but will lead to higher inflation or;

(b) cut aggregate demand to reduce inflation but pay the penalty in terms of higher unemployment.

Evidence to support this view came from the famous Phillips curve named after the engineer/economist who first presented the data (see Figure 6.3).

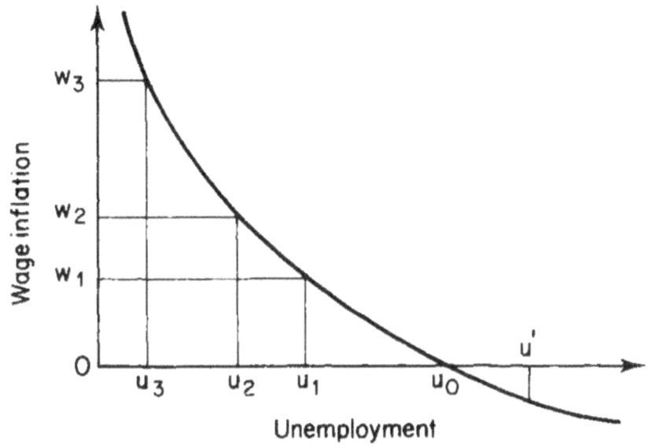

Fig. 6.3 Phillips Curve

At an unemployment level of u_1 wage inflation is w_1. If unemployment is lower at u_2 wage inflation rises to w_2. Because the line is not straight but curved inwards successive reductions in unemployment lead to progressively greater increases in wage inflation (note the jump from w_2 to w_3 when unemployment falls from the fairly low level u_2 to an even lower level u_3). Similarly, to reduce wage inflation to zero requires a high level of unemployment, u_0. Negative wage inflation (i.e. cuts in wages) require very high unemployment (u').

The Phillips curve can be translated into a relationship between price inflation and unemployment since wages form the greater part of business costs – by assuming a fixed profit mark-up we can replace wage inflation in Figure 6.3 by price inflation. After allowing for productivity growth (which means that some wage growth is possible without raising costs and hence prices) the trade-off applies in exactly the same way.

The Phillips curve says that inflation and unemployment vary inversely. But in the late 1960s and throughout the 1970s both inflation and unemployment rose together for the first time in history in the UK and throughout the developed world. Pundits coined a new word "stagflation" to describe the experience of high inflation coupled with low growth/high unemployment.

Obviously the Phillips curve trade-off had collapsed. Milton Friedman had the explanation. Recall in an earlier section that he accepted much of the Keynesian analysis as a description of the short run but rejected it as a long-run proposition. This is how he reconciled the experience of stagflation.

His argument was based on expectations. Consider a stable economy with unemployment of 500,000 and wage inflation of 5% p.a. Assume productivity growth is 2% p.a. This means that wage *costs* are going up at 3% p.a. (i.e. 5% less 2%) and, assuming a constant profit margin, price inflation will also be 3% p.a. Now suppose the government boosts aggregate demand and firms require extra workers – say 100,000 more. They will be forced to pay higher wages to attract workers – say wage inflation rises from 5% to 7%. With price inflation of 3% this represents an increase in real wages growth from 2% to 4% p.a. as well. However, with wages rising 2% p.a. faster in money terms firms will put up prices faster to maintain profits. Inflation will go up by 2% a year, to 5%.

Before Friedman and the post-1960s experience, this was where the analysis stopped: inflation was permanently higher, unemployment was permanently lower. Friedman, however, pointed out that workers and firms are concerned about *real* wages not money wages and the 2% rise in wage inflation in the above example was wiped out by higher inflation. Once workers realised that price inflation was eroding their real wage growth (i.e. once expected inflation rose) they would demand higher wage increases to compensate. Firms, also aware that inflation was faster, would be willing to grant the extra money wage increases.

But higher wage growth would raise inflation further. Even though workers and firms now expected inflation to go up the actual increase would be even greater.

The process continues with inflation continuously accelerating and just keeping ahead of expectations. Obviously this situation is unsustainable. Unemployment cannot be maintained at the lower level.

Friedman's argument leads to the following conclusion:

(a) at some level of unemployment real wage inflation will equal productivity growth and price inflation will be steady; this is called the "natural" rate of unemployment or NAIRU (non-accelerating inflation rate of unemployment);

(b) but inflation could be steady at 0%, 10%, 50% or any other rate;

(c) unemployment can be below the natural rate temporarily; the result will be permanently higher inflation. Similarly, a permanent reduction in inflation requires a temporary rise in unemployment;

(d) there is no long-run trade-off between unemployment and inflation.

This means that macro-economic policy cannot solve the problem of unemployment. For Friedman and many of his fellow-monetarists the solution lies in improving market efficiency to reduce the "natural" rate. Their policy prescriptions involve removing barriers to competition in the labour market – by limiting union power, reducing minimum wages (which are prevalent in the USA), cutting unemployment benefit, general reductions in wages, improving labour mobility, better information about job vacancies, retraining of redundant workers, etc. These are all micro-economic measures. Monetarists believe that unemployment cannot be reduced (except temporarily) by macro-economic measures to boost aggregate demand because the result is higher inflation.

THE MONETARISTS VERSUS THE KEYNESIAN DEBATE: ITS IMPLICATIONS FOR MONETARY TARGETS

The case for monetary targets (discussed further in Chapter 7) is based on a series of premises.

(1) Inflation is caused by money supply expansion and the only way to stop it is to reduce the growth in the money supply.

(2) There is a simple, stable and predictable relationship between the money supply and inflation.

(3) Governments have a tendency to pursue excessively expansionary policies (especially in the run up to elections) and need an external discipline.

(4) Monetary targets help to reduce inflation expectations and this cuts inflation faster and with a small cost in terms of recession.

Argument (1) simply means that money supply control is a *sine qua non* of an anti-inflation policy. The second argument suggests that a simple policy – such as that implied by monetary growth targets will suffice. Argument (3) suggests that announcing monetary targets will help to keep errant governments in line. Argument 4 is another argument for announcing targets, though this time it is the private sector whose behaviour is to be influenced.

Opponents of monetary targets object to all four of these premises, but their key objections relate to arguments (1) and (2). Keynesians, as you will recall, believe that inflation can be the result of a variety of influences – including cost pressures. They believe that whilst cutting money supply growth might cut inflation the cost in terms of unemployment is too heavy and prolonged. Direct action such as incomes policy is better. They also believe as we have already discussed that the link between money and prices is unstable because velocity is unpredictable and volatile. Money supply should not be rigidly fixed. Remember that Keynesians believe that monetary policy has its effects via interest rates. Therefore, they argue that the best policy is to control interest rates and let the money supply accommodate changes in money demand. This is called an *accommodating* monetary policy.

EXPERIENCE WITH MONETARY TARGETS

Almost all developed countries adopted monetary targets during the late 1970s and most still include control of the money supply as an objective. But the conviction with which these targets have been pursued has varied enormously. The two countries who have declared their monetarists intentions with greatest conviction are the UK and the USA. Their experience has not been entirely favourable towards the proponents of monetary targets. In particular, both countries have temporarily abandoned their monetary targets at different stages to allow the money supply to grow rapidly because they felt that velocity was changing. This happened in the UK in 1981 and in the USA in 1983. At the time many monetarists predicted that a surge in inflation would result but, in both cases, inflation fell. It is clear with hindsight that rigidly following monetary targets would have been wrong. But the real test will come over the next few years: once economies recover, will monetary targets prevent an upsurge in inflation that followed the two major world booms in the 1970s?

FISCAL POLICY

A detailed discussion of fiscal policy is not necessary but a brief outline is relevant to understanding economic policy.

Fiscal policy concerns the setting of tax rates, subsidies and government expenditure. In particular the fiscal deficit or budget deficit (also called the PSBR), is an important economic variable.

Fiscal policy affects aggregate demand either directly because government spending (e.g. on roadbuilding) is part of aggregate demand, or indirectly via taxes and subsidies which affect peoples' real incomes and hence their spending. You will not be surprised that Keynesians believe active changes in fiscal policies to influence aggregate demand are the key element of economic policy. Monetarists believe fiscal policy is at best impotent and at worst positively damaging if governments pull the wrong levers at the wrong time.

Fiscal policy also affects monetary variables in two ways:

(a) government borrowing from the banking system (as discussed in Chapter 4) is equivalent to printing money and this increases the money supply. This together with bank lending are the principle source of money supply expansion;

(b) when government borrowing increases the general level of interest rates rises, particularly if the government tries to borrow outside the banks (who tend to be passive lenders).

The UK government under Mrs Thatcher has stressed the importance of these links and sees reducing the PSBR as a key component of an anti-inflationary strategy.

THE ROLE OF THE EXCHANGE RATE

Exchange rates are relevant to monetary policy for two reasons:

(a) changes in the exchange rate affect economic variables including variables that monetary policy seeks to influence;

(b) the exchange rate is an important route through which monetary policy operates, i.e. it is part of the transmission process.

Exchange rates (as we discuss in more detail in Chapter 9) are the prices of national currencies determined, like other prices by demand and supply. Sterling's value against other currencies is determined by the demand and supply for sterling, i.e. the balance of payments (discussed further in Chapter 8). To understand this process we can split demand and supply into two components: the current account and the capital account. Demand for sterling arises from exports (because foreigners need to buy sterling to pay for British goods). Supply arises from imports. The current account is the net demand for sterling arising from international trade in goods and services. The capital account measures capital inflows (i.e. foreigners buying UK assets, e.g. equities) net of supply from capital outflows (Britons selling sterling to buy foreign assets).

Sterling appreciates in response to a rise in demand due to higher exports or capital inflows. High imports or capital outflows lead to a rise in supply and a depreciation of sterling.

Changes in sterling's value affect both aggregate demand and prices. For example a depreciation of sterling will make British goods cheaper relative to foreign goods and this boosts demand. This "competitiveness effect" has been very important in recent experience in the UK. In 1979 and 1980 sterling appreciated sharply and British industry suffered a severe recession. The price effect arises because an exchange rate depreciation raises import costs which feed through into higher prices.

Exchange rates need to be taken into account therefore in setting economic policy because of the impact on the authorities' ultimate objectives. They are also relevant because monetary policy effects exchange rates. In particular a restrictive monetary stance, by raising interest rates and reducing inflation expectations, attracts capital inflows and generates an exchange rate appreciation. This helps to reduce inflation via the price effect and means that monetary policy has a quicker effect on inflation. But the competitiveness effect means that it has quicker effect on output too. Indeed it is now generally accepted that exchange rates may overeact to major shifts in monetary policy so that, e.g. a cut in the money supply to reduce inflation could generate such a large exchange rate appreciation that it more than offsets the improvement to international competitiveness following a cut in inflation. This is known as "exchange rate overshooting" and is discussed in detail in Chapter 9.

The importance of the exchange rate to the economy has led many economists to suggest that it should be an explicit objective of policy. For instance, a counter-inflation policy could seek to push up the exchange rate. Alternatively, a depreciation could be induced to stimulate export industries.

The principal means by which the authorities can influence the exchange rate is by changing interest rates (which affect capital flows). The UK authorities and most other governments do take some account of the exchange rate in setting interest rates. In particular, interest rates are used to limit violent fluctuations in exchange rates which can be very disruptive. Before 1984 this was not the case in the USA but such was the overvaluation of the dollar from 1981 until early 1985 that it is now taken into account.

MONETARISTS AND KEYNESIAN VIEWS: SOME FURTHER CONSIDERATIONS

So far we have discussed the monetarists and Keynesian views on particular issues. In this section we pull together the issues to describe in turn and in brief the two schools of thought as a whole.

THE MONETARIST CLAIM REVISITED

The basic monetarist claim is that prices are determined by the supply of money. All that a government has to do, in order to control the level of price increase, is to obey a fixed monetary rule which would permit the money supply to increase by no more than the anticipated growth in output. Any departure from this rule, or any attempt to use other means, such as fiscal measures, to influence economic developments, will be self-defeating.

The basis for these claims as already discussed has been most fully advanced by Professor Milton Friedman in *A Monetary History of the United States, 1867–1960*, written in association with Anna Jacobson Schwartz. According to Friedman, the United States' experience over this period shows that (1) changes in the behaviour of the money stock have been closely associated with changes in economic activity, money incomes and prices; (2) the interrelation between monetary and economic change has been highly stable; and (3) monetary changes have often had an independent origin – they have not simply been a reflection of changes in economic activity.

These three propositions, stated somewhat rigorously; have become embodied in a body of doctrine which can be summarised as follows:

(1) Past rates of growth in the stock of money are the major determinants – indeed, virtually the only systematic non-random determinants – of the growth of GNP in terms of current prices. It follows from this that fiscal policies do not significantly affect GNP in money terms, though they may alter its composition and also affect interest rates, and that the overall impact on GNP in money terms of monetary and financial policies is for practical purposes summed up in the movements of a single variable, the stock of money. Consequently, monetary policy should be exclusively guided by this variable, without regard to interest rates, credit flows or other indicators.

(2) Nominal interest rates are geared to inflationary expectations and thus, with a time lag, to actual inflation. Although the immediate market impact of expansionary monetary policy may be to lower interest rates, it is fairly soon reversed when premiums for the resulting inflation are added to interest rates.

(3) The central bank can and should make the money stock grow at a steady rate equal to the rate of growth of potential GNP plus a target rate of inflation.

(4) There is no enduring trade-off between unemployment and inflation. There is, rather a unique natural rate of unemployment for each economy which allows for structural change and job search but which cannot be departed from in the long term. Government policy will produce ever-accelerating inflation if it persistently seeks a lower than natural rate of unemployment; if it seeks a higher rate, there will be an ever-accelerating deflation. The natural rate of unemployment cannot be identified except through practical experience; it is the rate which will emerge if the proper steady-growth monetary policy is pursued.

The attractive simplicity of this doctrine is easily recognised. The essence of the monetarist position is that increases in prices and wages can be held in check by nothing more complicated than the apparently simple device of controlling the amount of money in circulation. Ideally, a condition of nil inflation is achieved when the increase in the money supply equals the increase in the real output in the economy. Since both wage and price increases can only occur if extra money to finance them is made available, no increase will take place if no more money is provided. If attempts are made by firms or wage-earners to gain an advantage by putting up the cost of their goods and services on the one hand or labour rates on the other, a constant money supply will mean unsold goods and services for the firm and the loss of jobs for labour. Thus, as long as the government is prepared to control the money supply, everyone will see it as being in his interest to exercise restraint, and inflation will be reduced to whatever level is deemed to be acceptable.

THE KEYNESIAN CLAIM REVISITED

Now what of the Keynesian counter arguments? There are two of particular importance. Keynesians believe that wages are determined largely by prices and are not affected by the state of the job market, at least in the short run. They also are much more sceptical than monetarists about the ability of the government to control the rate at which the money supply grows.

In spite of a very large increase in unemployment in the past decade, Keynesians would argue, there has been precious little sign that wages respond to unemployment. Wages are highly influenced by trade unions, and large settlements in one part of the economy are copied across other sectors. Companies set prices not so much in response to changes in supply and demand, as in response to what is happening to their unit costs.

The most common causes of inflation are thus external shocks to the price structure – such as the rise in the world oil price in the early 1970s, or the increase in trade union militancy at the end of the 1960s. If the level of demand falls, that may actually contribute to inflation: it will raise companies' costs, because they will be able to sell fewer goods while carrying the same overheads. If companies do indeed aim for a fairly steady mark-up, they may even raise their prices rather than lower them.

Monetarists, in other words, emphasise the importance of the market, and of shifts in supply and demand, in setting prices. Keynesians emphasise the imperfections of the market in the complicated economy of the modern world, and think that supply and demand may adjust more freely than prices.

The point comes out more clearly when one looks at the Keynesian view of the monetarist cure for inflation. Keynesians usually argue that the cure for inflation lies in incomes policy – or more broadly, in reforming the structure of collective bargaining.

The monetarist cure for inflation, they argue, is simply a recipe for a slump. While an expansion of monetary growth may make faster inflation possible the effect of slower monetary growth will be on output. Workers will not accept a cut in their living standards, and companies will not reduce prices. The rate of unemployment will rise, and inflation will persist. Eventually, many Keynesians concede, the familiar technique of scaring workers into accepting lower pay increases may work. But it may involve a much higher rate of unemployment than the government's nerve will stand.

It may also involve higher interest rates than politicians are prepared to tolerate. In the Keynesian heyday, the main purpose of monetary policy was to keep interest rates as low as possible. But high interest rates are an inextricable part of monetary policy which is attempting to bring down the rate of inflation. Interest rates are the mechanism – they are the way in which the government attracts savings to pay for its borrowing, and the way in which companies are deterred from borrowing from the banks.

Indeed the monetarists' critics would claim that the rate of growth of the money supply was just as likely to be determined by the demand for money as by the direct attempts of the government to influence the supply. Companies faced with rising interest rates may be forced to increase their demand for bank borrowing in order to finance higher interest payments. Thus as interest rates rise the demand for bank lending may rise – the opposite view to that of the monetarists.

CLASSICISTS, MONETARISTS AND KEYNESIANS: WHO IS RIGHT?

We have discussed a wide range of issues in this chapter. The view of the classicists, monetarists and Keynesians on many of these issues are summarised in Table 6.1. Their disagreements can be traced to two basic differences of opinion:

(1) Does the Economy Move by Itself to Full Employment?

(a) Classical economists (and particularly their modern followers) believe that the economy moves quickly to full potential output with the minimum feasible level of unemployment.

(b) Monetarists believe this as a long-run proposition but accept that deficient demand can cause recessions and unemployment temporarily.

(c) Keynesians believe that the short run can last a very long time.

(2) The Role of Money

(a) Classicists see a simple, direct, mechanical link from money to prices.

(b) Monetarists allow some short-run slack but basically agree.

(c) Keynesians believe the link to be uncertain, unstable and unreliable.

The differences amount to statements about how the world works and can, in principle, be verified or rejected by examining the data. The evidence overall provides some support for all three schools but there are plenty of examples where the various theories have been contradicted. For example:

(a) It does seem to be the case that most major and sustained inflationary explosions have reflected money supply increases. However, substantial changes in inflation have taken place (e.g. in response to movements in oil prices) that were not obviously due to rises in the money supply.

(b) There is evidence of a stable link between money and prices operating over a lengthy period of time in the USA but the results are not clear cut for the UK. Moreover, financial innovation (such as the use of credit cards and interest payments on current accounts) threaten to disturb the link.

(c) The economic recessions of the 1970s suggest that the economy does not recover quickly. However, fiscal expansion has often led to higher inflation rather than faster economic recovery.

The key problem is that so much of macro-economic behaviour is not properly understood. In these circumstances unusual and extreme views can flourish. Economists need more time to reach agreement.

Table 6.1
Summary of Economists' Views on Money and the Economy

	Quantity Theorists	*Monetarists*	*Keynesian*	*New Classicists*
Transmission of Money to Prices and Output	Direct effect on Prices and Spending	Via interest rates, prices of stocks and shares, and directly on spending	Only via interest rates	Direct effects on prices. Output effects depend on changes in real interest rates and the extent to which money changes are not anticipated
Inflation	Always and everywhere a monetary phenomenon. Direct and quick link from M to P. Demand-led	Always and everywhere a monetary phenomenon. Lags from M to P long and may be variable. Demand-led.	Demand and cost factors relevant. Money supply could be important but not always. No simple relationship between M and P	Depends on M; especially on expected M
Shape of Phillips Curve	Not discussed	Downward sloped in short run, vertical in long run	Downward sloping	Vertical in long and short run when inflation anticipated
Cause of unemployment	Real wages too high	Short run; deficient demand. Long run; real wages too high/labour market uncompetitive	Deficient demand	Unemployment is voluntary, caused by workers searching for higher paid jobs
Demand for Money	Depends only on money expenditure (PT)	Stable function of small number of variables. P and Y are most important and interest rates weakly relevant	Complex relationship, difficult to pin down, possibly unstable. Highly responsive to interest rates (especially when interest rates are very low)	Essentially a stable function of a small number of variables. But structure depends on expectations and may change when economic policy changes

Effect of M on output	None	Powerful short run effect, no long run effect.	Powerful and enduring effect when M contracts sharply but may be impotent to bring economy out of recession	No effect if M is anticipated; otherwise temporary effect
Demand and supply of money equated by	Price Level	Interest rates and output initially but prices in the long run.	Interest rates initially. Output and possibly prices later.	Price level
Best way to control the economy	No macroeconomic policy necessary	Monetary targets are essential to control inflation. Fiscal policy has uncertain and weak effects so should be passive	Fiscal policy should be active to control output monetary policy should be accommodating. Incomes policy to control inflation	Set M to grow at desired rate of inflation. Do not use fiscal policy to control economy

M = money, P = price level, T = volume of transactions, Y = real output.

Chapter 7

Controlling the Money Supply

INTRODUCTION

The system of monetary control in the United Kingdom has, in the last 15 years, been subject to rapid and continuous change. In this Chapter we discuss the desirable features of monetary control, the links between instruments, intermediate indicators, targets and goals of monetary policy. We conclude by examining the extent to which monetary policy has been, and is, conducted in light of the efficiency criteria described below.

CRITERIA OF EFFICIENCY IN MONETARY CONTROL

Three particular criteria of efficiency in money supply control command widespread support.

(1) Predictability

A predictable system of monetary control is one in which the authorities know, with a high degree of probability, that by changing the level of a particular control variable, such as selling a certain amount of gilt-edged stock or calling for an increase in special deposits, they are able to change the growth in the money supply by a known amount.

(2) Minimum Distortion of Financial Markets

Distortions imply that resources are being misallocated and that the institutions which bear the brunt of regulation are effectively being subjected to a form of taxation. The consequences of these two developments is that they provide an incentive for institutions to devise ways to get around the distortions. This is socially wasteful in the sense that energy, effort and money is used up in this way instead of being used towards providing a more efficient monetary system.

(3) Market Forces Rather than Administrative Decisions Should be Used to Allocate Credit

The case for relying on markets (for example through purchases and sales of debt which in turn influence the growth of the money supply and interest rates) rather than administrative decisions (e.g. through reserve requirements, the imposition of ceilings on the growth of certain bank assets and liabilities, or ceilings on interest rate levels) in conducting monetary policy is that the use of the market mechanism allocates scarce resources more efficiently (via changes in relative prices). The advantages and disadvantages of using market forces rather than administrative decisions (sometimes known as "portfolio constraints" is discussed on pp. 195–198).

INSTRUMENTS, INTERMEDIATE INDICATORS, TARGETS AND GOALS OF MONETARY POLICY

A major purpose (goal) of monetary policy is often to regulate the volume of expenditure in the economy. However, the authorities do not have the power to control expenditure directly. What they can do is to try to regulate one or more monetary variables (known as targets) which in turn affect the desired goals of monetary policy, e.g. the money supply.

However again these targets may not be under the direct control of the authorities thereby necessitating the authorities to act on another monetary variable (called an intermediate indicator) which in turn affects the targets and ultimately the goals.

So, in between targets and instruments, we have intermediate indicators which provide us with an indicator of monetary policy in the economy, e.g. how restrictive or expansionary it has been. In order to influence the intermediate indicator variables, which in turn affect the targets and ultimately the goals of monetary policy, the government makes use of a series of monetary instruments. Instruments are set on the basis of the intermediate indicators which they then influence.

The full links between the instruments of policy and indicators are set out in Figure 7.1. The intermediate indicators are not directly controllable by the authorities for two reasons. There may be uncertainty over the exact links between instruments and intermediate indicators. This uncertainty can occur for two reasons. First, the actual structure of the economy may be unknown so that the authorities have no clear idea how a call for special deposits, for example, affects the goal variables. Secondly, the whole system may receive a shock. An example should make this clear. Suppose that the authorities in an attempt to reduce the money supply sell gilt-edged securities. However now, suppose the gilts are bought by non-residents who run down their sterling bank deposits to pay for them. Since these are excluded from the UK definitions of money supply the authorities would fail in their objectives. The aim of an intermediate indicator is to give a clear independent signal of the strength and direction of policy.

Intermediate indicators in turn affect a further set of variables for which targets can be set. These include the various monetary aggregates, bank credit and long-term rates of interest. Particular values for these variables are not desirable in their own right. However they are the targets of monetary policy which the authorities believe will facilitate the attainment of the ultimate macro-economic objectives (goals). The distinction between the targets of monetary policy and the goals of overall economic policy is therefore crucial.

Note that as we move from left to right in Figure 7.1 the direct influence of the monetary authorities becomes weaker. The central bank is completely in charge of its own instruments and may be able to exert close control on the

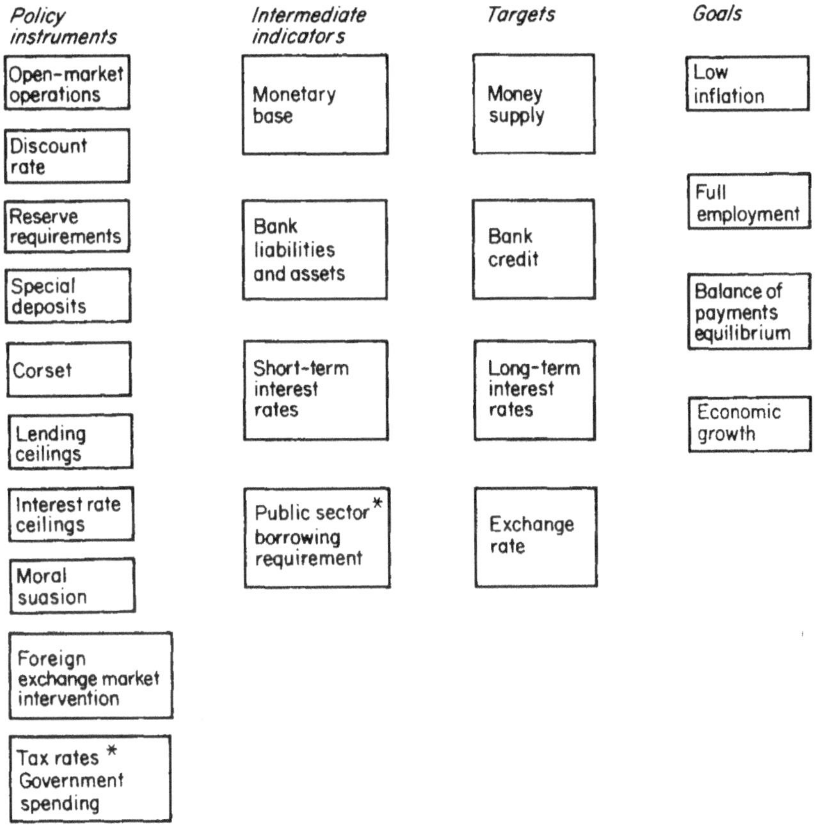

* Strictly speaking the PSBR is an element in fiscal policy. To the extent, however, that it has monetary consequences it is necessary to include it.

Fig. 7.1 The Instruments, intermediate indicators, targets and goals of monetary policy.

Source: G. E. J. Dennis, Monetary Economics (1981).
Reproduced by kind permission of Longman.

intermediate monetary indicators. However, it is more difficult for the central bank to control monetary targets, such as the money supply, since the growth of the money supply depends critically on the behaviour of the banks and their customers. The monetary authorities do not know for certain how much the banks will desire to lend and their customers to borrow at a given level of interest rates? And the link between the monetary target and the amount of expenditure (which in turn affects, say, inflation) depends on the behaviour of the general public – how much spending will take place with a given amount of money in the economy. The whole question of lags needs to be then brought in.

THE GOALS OF MONETARY POLICY

The goals of monetary policy have varied through time. At different time periods emphasis has been placed on one or more of the following goals:

(1) to maintain a high (and stable) level of employment;

(2) to secure continuous real economic growth;

(3) to keep inflation to a low level;

(4) to maintain a healthy balance of payments and manage the pound sterling on the foreign exchange markets. Before the system of "floating" currencies this meant keeping a stable value of the pound at a fixed exchange rate.

These goals can rarely be achieved simultaneously thereby forcing governments to choose which goals they assign the highest priority. For instance there are often conflicts between reducing inflation and achieving full employment. Similar conflicts arise between balance of payments equilibrium and full employment.

(1) The Level of Employment

Since the publication of the Beveridge Report in 1944 the majority of governments have been concerned to raise the level of employment. There are several reasons for this:

(1) Unemployed resources are wasted resources. Man-hours lost today can never be made up; they are lost forever.

(2) The cost to the government in terms of unemployment pay and lost income tax is high. Every newly-unemployed person means additional public sector borrowing of £5,000.

(3) Social costs. These are harder to calculate but real. They include the rise in physical and mental ill-health, increased vandalism, petty crime along with the sheer misery of doing nothing. In addition there is considerable social stigma attached to being unemployed.

(2) Economic Growth

By economic growth is meant a sustained increase in a nation's gross domestic product, especially in its real GDP per capita. Why do governments want the output of goods and services to grow?

(1) Because there is much unsatisfied need for both goods and services and because new needs are always arising.

(2) Faster growth creates a better climate for innovation and development.

(3) Greater productivity in producing goods means more resources available for services and for leisure.

(4) Growth in output of goods other countries want can provide the foreign currency for the goods and services we both need and wish to import from abroad.

(5) If we are to contribute to the economic welfare of the less-developed countries, we require the extra resources arising from faster growth.

(6) Economic growth makes it easier to redistribute wealth towards the less well off without actually reducing the wealth of the rich. This in turn can reduce tensions within society.

(3) Low Level of Inflation

Inflation is a general rise in the level of prices. Most governments are unconcerned with low rates of inflation – say, 2 to 3% – and only become alarmed when annual rates are relatively high. The key word of course is relative: many South American countries would regard 15% inflation as very low.

Governments become alarmed with high rates of inflation because:

(1) Those on fixed money incomes lose, in particular pensioners.

(2) In most cases inflations are neither steady nor predictable. Changes in the distribution of income and wealth are therefore arbitrary. The uncertainty associated with this is probably unpopular with both gainers and losers. Tensions between social classes also seem to increase.

(3) Attempts by governments to live with inflation, e.g. by indexation often result in the inflation accelerating, e.g. in response to increases in oil prices.

(4) The Government's own macro-economic control becomes more difficult. With unpredictable rates of inflation, company and consumer behaviour is more than usually difficult to forecast and the Government's own taxation and expenditure planning is disrupted.

(5) In an open economy such as the UK, inflation makes it more difficult to finance balance of payments deficits, because foreign lenders are uncertain about the future exchange rate (and in the extreme case are uncertain whether debts will ever be repaid).

(6) Inflation raises nominal interest rates and damages company cash flow. High nominal interest rates can stifle investment because the cost of servicing such loans is too onerous, particularly in the early years. This is known as the front end loading of profits.

(7) Adjusting to inflation requires considerable effort by consumers, workers and businessmen. This diverts scarce resources away from productive activities.

(8) It has an adverse effect on competitivity: Nations rarely have inflation rates which are exactly in line with their trading partners; sometimes they race ahead of the rest. This may not be important if the foreign trade sector is relatively small or if it is felt that the exchange rate can adjust to compensate for this. In the United Kingdom the foreign trade sector is large and in recent years the exchange rate has not moved fully to offset relative inflation rates.

(4) Balance of Payments Equilibrium

Nations strive towards balance of payments equilibrium as continuous balance of payments deficits cannot easily be maintained. A current account deficit normally means that a country is borrowing from abroad. A continuous deficit can only be sustained if lenders are willing to lend indefinitely. Obviously this will not be the case in practice and adjustment can involve a reduction in foreign trade. Foreign trade is important to the British economy. One third of all Britain's goods and services and one quarter of our manufactured output are exported; one half of our food is imported; over a quarter of all the manufactured goods we consume is imported. Why do governments want foreign trade?

(1) To finance the needs of a growing economy for the food stuffs and basic materials needed that we ourselves do not produce; to finance the semi-manufacturers and capital goods and the licences which will advance our technology; and to finance the consumer goods which increase the well-being of consumers and their freedom of choice.

(2) To provide jobs and increase employment in industries and services in those sectors which can serve markets abroad.

(3) To contribute to the development and industrialisation of the less developed countries.

THE TARGETS OF MONETARY POLICY

As already mentioned the need for targets arises as the government cannot directly influence its desired goals but can try to influence whatever in turn influences them. A basic requirement for any target variable is that the central bank has the ability to control it albeit indirectly reasonably well. To the extent that monetary policy is designed to control expenditure, the main criteria to use, in choosing between the different targets, is to decide which one is related most reliably (or predictably) to expenditure.

The monetary authorities can choose from four main targets of monetary policy. These are:

(1) The money supply;
(2) Bank credit;
(3) Long-term interest rates;
(4) The exchange rate.

These are discussed in turn.

(1) The Money Supply

Those economists ("monetarists") who believe that the central bank should control the stock of money see a fairly simple process (or transmission mechanism) through which increases in the money stock lead to higher expenditure. As we have already discussed in Chapters 1 and 6 monetarists suggest that when the money stock increases the immediate effect is that people will be holding more money, in relation to their holdings of other assets, than they wish to. Therefore, they will seek to lower their money holdings and increase their holdings of other assets. Some of the new money will be used to buy goods and services which increases expenditure directly. And some will be used to buy other financial assets, such as bonds. The increased demand for bonds will drive up the price of bonds, thus lowering the rate of interest on them. Lower interest rates will lead to an increase in investment (and perhaps other) expenditure. In recent years the United Kingdom has adopted "public" monetary targets. The rationale for the adoption of monetary targets embraces one or more of the following arguments:

(a) that is necessary to provide a framework of financial stability if broader macroeconomic policy goals are to be realised;

(b) that control of monetary aggregates plays an important part in economic management, particularly in controlling inflation – published targets help economic agents form expectations about future inflation. In this way targets help to reduce inflation directly;

(c) that targets give a clear indication of the thrust of monetary policy and provide checkpoints against which monetary developments may be monitored;

(d) that adoption of published targets imposes a necessary discipline on the governments' conduct of policy that, at times, might prove invaluable if basic economic objectives are to be secured rather than subordinated to short-run political expediency;

(e) the failure of attempts to "fine tune" the economy.

A possible disadvantage of publicly announcing targets is that it makes it more difficult to change policy. For example, if the central bank discovers that the relationship between money and expenditure has changed, it may be reluctant to change the target for the growth of the money stock after this has been publicly announced. But this would prevent the central bank from achieving the desired increase in expenditure. Also, a government might wish to change the target rate of growth of the money stock because of a change in economic circumstances, e.g. a recession. It might be that the monetary policy was successful in regulating the growth of expenditure, but because unemployment was higher than expected, the government might wish to increase the rate of monetary growth. This would obviously be more difficult once the target had been announced.

For the money stock to be a useful target for monetary policy it is essential for the demand for money to be related in a predictable way both to income and to interest rates, so that the central bank has a reasonably good idea of how much money the public will demand at given levels of income and interest rates. If the demand for money fluctuates wildly then so will the velocity of circulation of money and the link between money and income will be unreliable.

Other problems involved in using the money supply revolve around the choice of money aggregate, the sources of money supply growth and data collection problems. Controversy exists as to which of the seven major monetary aggregate M_0, M_1, M_2, £M_3, M_3, PSL_1 PSL_2 are most highly correlated with the ultimate objectives of monetary policy. Secondly, the money supply is particularly prone to exogenous (i.e. external to the system) influences, e.g. foreign currency inflows and outflows. Thirdly, some money supply data (in particular M_0) in contrast to interest rate data, are only available weekly. It is however only published monthly and tends to be very erratic. (See pp. 216–218 for discussion of the Medium Term Financial Strategy.) The behaviour of £M_3 compared with its target range is illustrated in Figure 7.2 below.

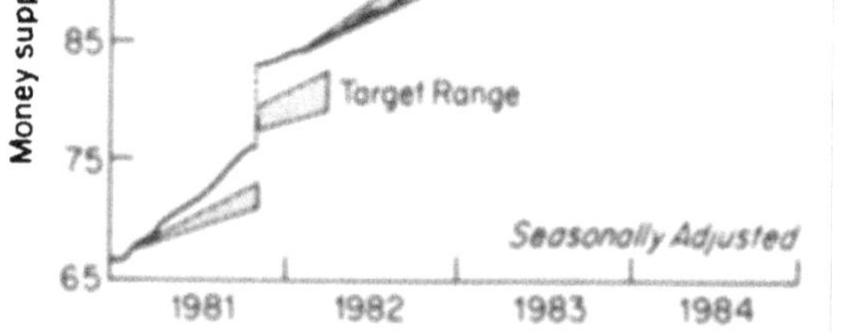

Fig. 7.2 Sterling M_3: Targets and Outcomes
Source: Bank of England, Quarterly Bulletin (March 1984)
Reproduced by kind permission of the Bank of England.

(2) Bank Credit

A rise in bank credit (or bank lending) is one of the ways in which the money supply may increase. But the money stock may also increase without an increase in bank lending – for example, if the banks buy securities previously held by the public who in turn bank the proceeds. And bank lending may increase without an increase in the money supply, for example, if banks increase their loans and at the same time sell securities to the public. There is, therefore, no reason why the money supply and bank lending should grow at the same rate.

Some economists believe that bank credit is a better target for monetary policy than the money supply. The idea behind this view is that households and firms rarely borrow money unless they wish to spend it and therefore an increase in credit should have a fairly predictable effect on expenditure. (The position is much the same when firms issue securities to finance their expenditure.) It is suggested that when the money supply increases with no increase in credit (for example, if banks buy existing securities from the public) then the effect on expenditure is much less certain; the public may simply be content to hold more of their savings in bank deposits, and less in form of securities.

(3) Long-term Interest Rates

A third possibility would be to treat the level of long term (i.e. on long-term government securities) interest rates in the economy as the target of monetary policy (more specifically the "real" rate of interest could be targeted). This would make sense if there were a reliable link between interest rates and expenditure so that the authorities knew reasonably well what level of expenditure would result from a given level of interest rates.

However there are problems with interest rate targets (some of which were discussed in Chapter 4). First, making the central bank announce an *interest rate target* for the year is tantamount to depriving it of control over the volume of money and credit. It would force the central bank to accommodate all changes in demands for money and credit in order to avoid upward (or downward) pressure on the interest rate. In an inflationary period, it would amount to giving up on efforts to control inflation should the chosen interest rate target have been wrong (for example, too low relative to inflationary expectations).

Secondly, and equally basic, setting an interest rate target assumes that the proper value for the rate can be known in advance, or at least known with more certainty than the growth in the money supply. Whether this is so depends on whether it is probable that the demand for goods and services, which depends in part on interest rates is sufficiently more stable or predictable than the demand for money in relation to the nation's ultimate economic objectives. If the demand for goods is sufficiently more predictable, then interest rates are a better target than money; otherwise, money is the better target.

In addition an expansionary monetary policy will initially cause interest rates to fall but as overall demand in the economy, including the demand for credit, picks up and inflationary expectations increase, interest rates will turn up and eventually move in the same direction as the money supply growth. In an environment in which volatile inflationary expectations affect the extent to which nominal market rates of interest in fact represent "real" rates, the relationship between market interest rates and spending is especially uncertain. Thus it seems that interest rates are a highly risky target.

Finally whilst it is generally accepted that interest rates have some influence on business investment and some other types of expenditure, few economists believe that interest rates are the major factor. Expectations as to future demand and profitability are generally believed to be more important.

(4) The Exchange Rate*

The exchange rate – that is, the price of domestic currency in terms of foreign currencies – has important effects on the economy. Although we discuss this in more detail in Chapter 9 two features are worth stressing here:

(1) If the exchange rate depreciates, exports become more competitive, imports less competitive and economic activity is stimulated; similarly if the exchange rate appreciates, economic activity is likely to be depressed.

(2) A change in the exchange rate affects the prices of imported goods in terms of domestic currency. If the exchange rate rises then the price of imported goods falls, and if the exchange rate falls the prices of imported goods rises. Therefore a rise in the exchange rate tends to reduce domestic inflation and a fall in the exchange rate tends to increase inflation.

Because of the importance of these effects few governments can afford to ignore what happens to the country's exchange rate. And it is possible for the monetary authorities to treat the exchange rate as the target for monetary policy. This policy is more likely to be pursued in small open economies – that is, in those economies in which international trade accounts for a relatively high proportion of economic activity – where wide swings in the exchange rate can cause considerable disturbance in the domestic economy.

The case for having the exchange rate as a target for monetary policy depends to a large extent on the sort of economic policies being pursued in other countries. A fixed exchange rate implies that, over time, the rate of inflation in the domestic economy will be similar to inflation abroad. If prices increase at a different rate then the competitiveness of domestically produced goods, in relation to foreign goods, will change, thus leading to pressure for a change in the exchange rate. Therefore if other countries pursue policies designed to control inflation, an exchange rate target will impose a similar discipline on

*Strictly speaking discussion about exchange rate movements should emphasise "real" exchange rates, i.e. nominal rates adjusted for inflation.

the domestic economy. But if inflationary policies are followed abroad, then an exchange rate target will lead to high inflation at home.

As a target the exchange rate suffers from many of the same deficiencies as interest rates. It exerts discipline by setting a "price" to be attained, but at the cost of control of the quantity of money and credit. The amount of money to be supplied would, as already mentioned, depend not simply on conditions in the home market, but also on policies and conditions in foreign countries. For example, inflationary policies abroad that were causing foreign currencies to tend to depreciate relative to the home currency would force similar policies at home if the announced parity in exchange rates were to be maintained.

EXCHANGE RATE TARGETS AND MONETARY TARGETS: THE NEED FOR CHOICE*

Basic macro-economic theory suggests that there are certain links between exchange rates and monetary growth which make it extremely difficult, if not impossible, to control over a long time period both the exchange rate and the money supply as independent targets. It is easy to see this by way of an example. Imagine a situation where the authorities announce a sharply reduced rate of monetary growth in order to bring down inflation and at the same time the country has a fixed exchange rate. The financial markets would in these circumstances probably adjust fairly rapidly to the prospect of lower price inflation which would make UK securities more attractive than before, relative to foreign securities. An inflow would therefore occur across the exchanges, and if this were met by official intervention to hold sterling steady, it would place upward pressure on the money supply. (The Exchange Equalisation Account would purchase foreign currency in exchange for sterling, thereby increasing the non-bank private sector's holdings of sterling and inflating the money supply.) In principle, the monetary consequences of such capital inflows could be mopped up by the sale of additional government debt to the private sector, a procedure which is known as "sterilising" the effect of inflows. Provided that sterilisation is possible for an indefinite period, then monetary and exchange rate targets might prove compatible. Unfortunately, however, prolonged sterilisation is extremely problematic, since it involves the sale of ever-increasing quantities of government debt to the private sector. This, in turn, will probably eventually require an increase in interest rates which might make the original problem – capital inflows across the exchanges – even worse. On the other hand, any attempt to maintain the exchange rate target by reducing interest rates, rather than by direct intervention in the foreign exchange markets, might hold sterling down but would probably place upward pressure on monetary expansion, thereby threatening the money supply target.

*Many of the ideas and terms in this section are drawn from articles in *The Economics Analyst* by David Morrison and Gavyn Davies of Simon and Coates to whom grateful acknowledgement is made.

It is possible that for a short period sterilisation techniques might make money and exchange rate targets compatible. However, in general it will not prove possible to run such targets in tandem. Maintaining an exchange rate target involves the authorities intervening in the foreign exchange markets to an extent which is determined by the whims of private sector capital flows. Since this intervention directly affects the domestic money supply (in the absence of complete sterilisation), it follows immediately that the money supply is at the mercy of speculative capital flows, and not directly under the control of the authorities. It will therefore not usually be possible for the government independently to control its own money supply under a regime of fixed exchange rates. (These ideas were discussed in Chapter 1 pp. 26–28.)

Under fixed exchange rates, the money supply therefore becomes an endogenous variable (i.e. is determined by relationships within the economy) rather than an exogenous variable subject to policy control. This is, in itself, an important result, but it also carries a further important implication. With a fixed exchange rate target, any individual country's inflation rate will over the long-term tend towards the world average. If inflation is above the world average, a balance of payments outflow will occur; this will reduce domestic monetary growth, and deflate the economy until inflation is back at the world average. Only if continuous sterilisation is possible – involving in this case infinite gains or losses to international reserves – can inflation rates differ for very long between economies which are linked together by fixed exchange rates.

If however, exchange rates are allowed to fluctuate freely, monetary policy regains its independence. An example will make this clear. Consider a country which wished independently to reduce its inflation rate relative to the world average. In the monetarist system, this can only be done by announcing money supply targets which are below the expected rate of growth of world money aggregates. The reduction in the relative rate of monetary expansion has two effects. First, it is argued, it reduces the rate of domestic price inflation: and secondly, it leads to an appreciation in the effective exchange rate. So in this case monetary policy does regain its independence.

In conclusion then, in the long run the authorities must choose between having a monetary target or having an exchange rate target. Both cannot be achieved simultaneously.

INTERMEDIATE INDICATORS OF MONETARY POLICY

Intermediate indicators are used to guide monetary policy to achieve its targets. Three indicators are available to the authorities:

(1) the monetary base;
(2) bank liabilities and assets;
(3) short term interest rates.

(1) The Monetary Base

The monetary base is defined as holdings of notes and coins and bankers balances at the Bank of England. Bankers' balances, as discussed in Chapter 4, are the reserves of the banking system upon which banks are able to create deposits. It follows that if the supply of the total monetary base is controlled, and if the proportion held by banks is constant, and if the banks' reserve ratio is stable, the money supply can also be precisely controlled. Clearly changes in the monetary base will not induce the predicted change in the money supply if these assumptions do not hold true.

Two variants of a monetary base control (MBC) system were suggested in the 1980 Green Paper. The authorities would either control the amount of base money in existence or use divergences of the base money figure from the desired trend as a trigger for a change in interest rates intended to correct the divergence. The first would limit the increase in the money supply – because the banks' balance sheets cannot exceed a multiple of the base – and the limit would then generate the interest rates necessary to bring the rate of growth of the money supply back towards the desired path. The second would either be discretionary or would be determined by a scale set in advance by the authorities. The Bank of England would no longer be able to provide unlimited support to the banking system as a matter of routine and interest rates would be set automatically at market-clearing levels.

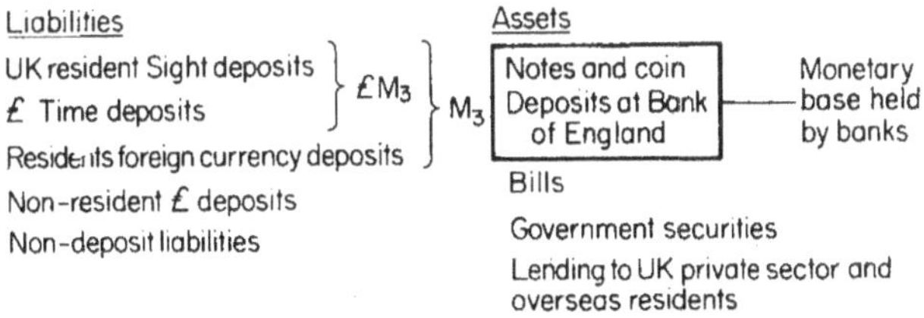

Fig. 7.3 UK Banks £ Balance Sheet

Under the first variant of monetary base control a definite quantity target would be set for total sales of public sector debt to the non banks. Remember that as the non bank sector purchases public sector debt then bankers' balances fall. In consequences banks, seeing bankers' balances fall below some critical level would be forced to take action involving the acquisition of more bankers' balances either by raising interest rates and/or selling off assets. If banks raised interest rates they would have to be raised to a level which would choke off borrowing and attract new deposits. Or they would have to sell off bills and/or government securities thereby driving down prices and again raising interest costs.

In this approach, interest rate adjustments are the equilibrating mechanism rather than an *instrument* of monetary control. It is no longer necessary for the authorities to estimate the required interest rate level for its monetary target. Thus, for example, if at current interest rates the demand for bank credit exceeds the volume possible given the monetary base level banks, competing to increase their share of the "fixed" volume of reserves, raise interest rates on deposits and hence loans. This competitive bidding continues until the demand for credit has been reduced to a level consistent with what the banks can satisfy at the given level of the monetary base. The banks in aggregate can increase their lending only to the extent to which they can collectively increase their share of the monetary base by inducing the public to switch from notes and coin to bank deposits.

Advocates of MBC see five main advantages to this procedure: (1) it offers the prospect of more precise monetary control as it directly restricts the "supply capacity" of the banking system, (2) interest rate adjustments are made more quickly and with more precision, (3) it removes the necessity of the Bank of England estimating the required interest rate level, (4) it enables the PSBR to be funded by short-term securities which will not soon become reserve assets if held by banks and (5) it "depoliticises" necessary interest rate adjustments.

The second variant is more mechanistic. Divergences would simply trigger interest rate changes until the excess monetary growth was eliminated. Strict adherence to monetary base control would result in considerable interest rate volatility. (See key issue in monetary theory in Chapter 1.)

(2) Bank Liabilities and Assets

The basic principle of using bank liabilities and/or assets as indicators of monetary control is that these give clear guidance as to the ease or stringency of monetary policy. Thus if bank liabilities and/or bank assets are expanding or contracting then the various monetary targets will be expanding or contracting. Perhaps the best example of an indicator in use in the UK is the monthly data on the liabilities and assets of the banking system. Appearing two weeks before full money supply figures, these data are used as an early indicator of the level of the money supply and therefore of the stance of monetary policy.

(3) Short-term Interest Rates

The major argument in favour of an interest rate target is that it is observable, with information on the level of interest rates being available very promptly. Therefore the lag between the need for policy action and the action occurring is potentially very short.

Some of the arguments against the use of long-term interest rates have already been discussed and apply also to short-term interest rates.

INSTRUMENTS OF MONETARY POLICY: MARKET FORCES VERSUS PORTFOLIO RESTRAINT

The traditional instruments for controlling the money supply can be divided into two broad groups – those relying on market forces to restrict credit and those relying on portfolio constraints on the monetary sector. Both are discussed in this section. In recent times the public sector borrowing requirement, although strictly speaking falling into the domain of fiscal policy, does have monetary implications and in consequence has been subject to official control. In consequence the PSBR is also discussed.

By market forces is meant the reliance on the price mechanism to alter interest rates. The idea is that if interest rates rise bank lending falls and the money supply falls and similarly if interest rates fall bank lending to the private sector rises and the money supply rises. If a system of market forces control is in operation the monetary authorities are expected to operate in financial markets to either restrict credit or make credit freely available thereby reducing or increasing the money supply. (Remember from Chapter 1 that if the monetary authorities want interest rates to fall they must increase the money supply and if they want interest rates to rise they must decrease the money supply.) Thus market forces operate by influencing the availability and rate of return on assets in a general way, thus affecting both the desire of the public to hold money balances and the willingness of banks to take deposits and lend. This method of control relies on the demand for credit being highly responsive to interest rate changes. Clearly, as is discussed below, the demand for credit may not be interest rate responsive.

Portfolio constraints place restrictions on a particular group of institutions (usually banks) limiting their freedom to acquire assets and liabilities. Banks may be prevented, by controls, from increasing their lending thereby preventing deposit creation taking place. Alternatively, again by controls, the taking of deposits could be made prohibitively expensive thereby preventing them from increasing their lending.

United Kingdom monetary policy has alternated between these two types of monetary instruments. Broadly speaking the control system is as classified in Table 7.1.

Table 7.1

Time Period	*Techniques*
Pre-1971	Portfolio constraints
1971-1973	Market forces
1973-1979	Partial portfolio constraint (moral Suasion plus the corset)
1976	Market forces (Monetary targets)
1978	Portfolio constraints (the corset)
1981-Present	Market forces

In order to appreciate the effects of different monetary instruments it is essential to discuss the advantages and disadvantages of the use of markets forces and portfolio constraints on the banks as means of monetary control. One must always bear in mind that no one system of monetary control is likely to be perfect and that the authorities should select the one that is least inefficient.

ADVANTAGES OF RELYING ON MARKET FORCES FOR MONETARY CONTROL

(1) Administratively simple. It avoids all the problems caused by having to define money or banks.

(2) Equitable. No one sector is penalised compared with another sector. In contrast portfolio constraints tend to penalise property companies and individual consumers.

(3) Allocative efficiency. Funds will flow from profitable to unprofitable sectors. The desirability of this, as every economics text book tells you, depends on the extent to which prices measure "desirability", i.e. there may be market failure or "externalities" to consider.

(4) Monetary control. A sufficiently high interest rate will cut the demand-for-bank credit and thus the money supply.

DISADVANTAGES OF RELYING ON MARKET FORCES FOR MONETARY CONTROL

(1) They may result in reduced monetary control for two reasons:

(i) If interest rates become variable this could lead to fluctuations in the prices of gilt-edged stocks thereby potentially reducing the non-bank private sector demand for them and thereby reducing monetary control. For many years prior to 1973 the Bank of England, with this consideration in mind, had sought to smooth out fluctuations in the prices of gilts – a policy known as "leaning into the wind".

The authorities have, in several places, and over many years, expressed the belief that, if they did not resist movements in the price of existing debt, investors ". . . would be seriously discouraged from investing their funds . . . the capacity of the market would be reduced, and with it the ability of the Government to borrow at long-term." (Treasury Evidence to the Radcliffe Committee, 1959.)

In other words, movements in interest rates induced by changes in supply of government borrowing or in the demand for it should be resisted lest they deter investors. In recent years this argument has been given less weight in official circles.

(ii) The demand for credit could shift in a perverse way. If the authorities squeeze the economy by raising interest rates then the corporate sector is faced with falling profits and rising stocks of goods. In these circumstances firms have no choice but to borrow from the banks. Thus at a time when there is a monetary squeeze the demand for sterling bank lending, and thereby the money supply, is increasing.

(2) Inappropriate interest rate indicator. The authorities in the early 1970s believed that monetary tightness as measured by nominal interest rates, was being achieved whereas in fact monetary ease when measured by real interest rates was actually what was occurring. Thus with rising inflation rates the real rates of interest are falling and if the rise in market rates does not fully reflect the rise in inflation rates there is still an incentive to borrow and the money supply continues rising. So in order to "clear" the market interest rates may have to rise very steeply.

(3) Political sensitivity. Politicians do not like to see interest rates rise: the house-buying lobby is powerful and likes cheap finance. In practice then the authorities will, by official controls tend to err on the side of optimism when trying to judge what should be done with interest rates. They are raised too slowly and too little, and lowered too soon.

(4) Certain sectors, in practice, however, are always penalised. In particular industry and housing are always penalised by high interest rates. The construction and housing industry are primarily financed by bank/building society loans and are immediately penalised as interest rates rise. In addition these industries are labour intensive and as they contract there is an immediate increase in the unemployment rate.

ADVANTAGES OF RELYING ON PORTFOLIO CONSTRAINTS FOR MONETARY CONTROL

(1) Monetary control may be achieved with a lower level of interest rates. As with any form of rationing, price is lower if markets do not clear by price because a lower price is fixed by the central authorities – in this case the central bank fixes interest rates at below market clearing levels. The resulting excess demand for credit is, supposedly, eliminated by official regulations. Thus if the controls were never evaded interest rates *could* be lower.

(2) Shorter time lags than relying on market forces. If market forces are slow acting then an asset or a liability ceiling could be effective for a short time before other policies take effect.

(3) The "needy" sectors of the economy can be aided. Thus if quantitative/qualitative guidelines are introduced then the authorities can compel banks to lend to, say, exporters and not to, say, property companies even if the latter are willing to pay higher interest rates and provide better collateral.

DISADVANTAGES OF RELYING ON PORTFOLIO CONSTRAINTS FOR MONETARY CONTROL

(1) They may be inequitable. As the banking system, which is subject to controls, is penalised there is an incentive for the development of alternative sources of finance. These may or may not involve the banking sector.

Any system of controls in which prices are fixed by the authorities inevitably creates the potential for a "black" or "parallel" market to develop. Thus if the price is fixed too low inevitably the demand for finance will be supplied from elsewhere. One sector which was penalised prior to 1971 and again after 1977 was property companies. As they could not obtain finance from the banks they turned from the banks to the insurance companies for their finance. The insurance companies, seeing large potential profits on lending to the property companies simply stopped lending to the government, i.e. they reduced their purchases of gilts and they replaced them with property loans. So the government found that the money supply was rising rapidly and simultaneously they were losing control over the financial system. In Figure 7.4, as the authorities have fixed interest rates below market rates (i.e. at r_1 instead of r_0), then the excess demand for credit will be supplied from outside the banking system. This process is known as "disintermediation".

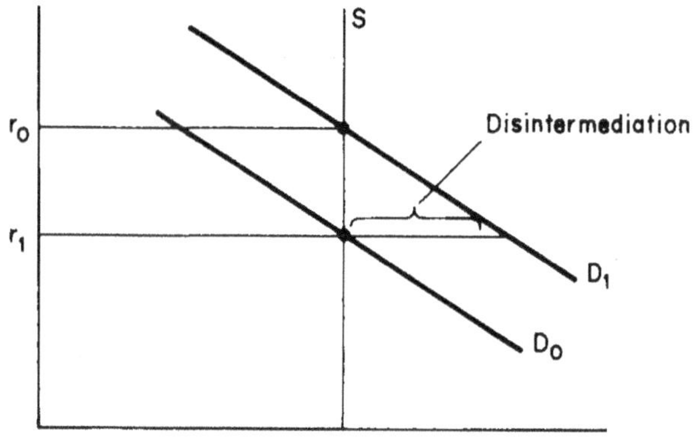

Fig. 7.4

An example of this was provided by the "corset" (pp. 204–205). When the corset was last placed in position, thereby limiting the banks' ability to acquire more liabilities in order to maintain their lending levels, credit demand did not disappear overnight. The commercial banks who could no longer sell CDs and acquire deposits for on-lending, met their clients' requirements by accepting bills and then selling them to the private sector (who bought them because CDs were scarce) and having been sold the clients now did not require finance. The buyers were mainly portfolio managers of large and liquid industrial concerns or of financial institutions such as insurance companies, those very people in fact who, before the introduction of the corset, would have bought the commercial banks' CDs and increased the latter's deposits. In other words, the non-bank private sector was now lending to the non-bank private sector; that is, companies and institutions who were flush with money were lending to companies and institutions who were short of money. One major problem here for the authorities was that official monetary aggregates become increasingly misleading. This problem emerged in the UK in August 1980. The money supply statistics for July showed a jump of 5%

because of the partial re-inclusion in the official statistics of certain transactions following the abolition of the IBELs ceiling. Official spokesmen expressed the view that all figures from August 1980 to April 1981 would be so heavily distorted by the control and its removal as to be seriously misleading. The problems for the rational conduct of monetary control are obvious.

Two other, less substantial methods of non-bank satisfaction of credit demand also came into use. One was the "local authority leak", whereby rates on local authority borrowings rose owing to the increasing refusal by banks to place funds, and attracted instead short-term investment by non-bank portfolio managers. The other was the "Eurosterling leak" under which offshore banks, whose deposits are not included within the count of the UK money stock, were able to provide finance for domestic UK credit seekers.

(2) They may cause allocative inefficiency to occur. There is no guarantee that the actual borrower from the point of view of the economy as a whole was the most desirable one. It may simply have been his turn in the queue. In addition, ceiling controls encouraged bankers to favour well established "safe" customers.

(3) They may reduce competition between banks. The most efficient banks are not able to compete in the most direct way, i.e. by changing the price (interest rate) it traded at. Thus inefficient banks could easily stay in business by undertaking the business that the efficient banks should have been doing.

The major monetary instruments can be subdivided along the following lines.

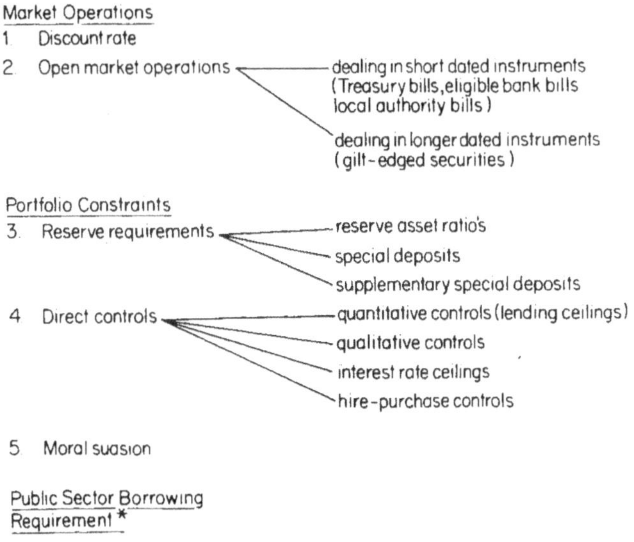

* Strictly speaking the PSBR is an element in fiscal policy. To the extent, however, that it has monetary consequences it is necessary to include it.

Fig. 7.5

MARKET OPERATIONS: THE TECHNIQUES

(1) Discount Rate Changes

Discussion of market operations is complicated by the fact that changes in the discount rate and open market operations are inextricably linked. However for the purpose of clarity we will attempt to disentangle them. The official discount rate, previously called "minimum lending rate" and before that the "bank rate", was officially abolished in 1981.* However a variant of it still exists and the effect it has on monetary conditions still needs to be described. Bank rate was defined by the Radcliffe Report as "the minimum rate at which the Bank of England stands ready to lend at last resort to a discount house which has the privilege of access to the Discount Office of the Bank either by re-discounting bills of approved quality or by lending against the security of such bills or short-dated Government securities."

Prior to November 1980 the authorities money market intervention could be summarised as follows: by the over issue of Treasury bills the Bank could create cash shortages in the money market which would subsequently be relieved by direct lending to the discount market (discount window lending) or by the purchase of bills at prices quoted by the authorities. In short, the authorities fixed the price at which they were prepared to provide funds to the market and this provided a clear signal as to what rates were deemed appropriate. These rates varied little from the prevailing minimum lending rate.

Only the discount houses had access to tender of last resort facilities at the Bank of England. In addition they act as intermediaries between the Bank and the banking system. Thus the discount house cash shortage was relieved by borrowing at MLR which was generally above the return on the discount houses asset portfolio.

The discount houses would respond to this by putting in lower bids at the Treasury bill tender (i.e. raising interest rates) and this in turn would trigger off higher interest rates on short-term deposits with local authorities, finance houses, and bank overdrafts. The process of money market arbitrage very quickly raises interest rates all round as arbitrageurs borrow from the cheaper sources and avoid the expensive sources. (Changes in these institutional details are discussed later.) Thus a rise in the discount rate combined with this continued cash squeeze forced up interest rates. This rise in interest rates was designed to reduce the demand for overdrafts (which remember feed into bank deposits and thus the money supply) and to also encourage saving at the expense of spending.

In addition to the above effect MLR changes also had a psychological significance. Thus announcements of the level of MLR had significant impacts upon the appropriate level of short term rates. It also signalled movements in the direction of monetary policy.

*Although it was brought back, for one day only, on 14 January 1985.

(2) Open Market Operations

(1) Dealing in Short-dated Securities

Open market operations consist of the buying and selling of short term government securities (Treasury bills, eligible bank bills and local authority bills) in the money market. The aim of these operations is to influence interest rates. Thus when the authorities seek a credit expansion the Bank of England will buy bills (eligible bank bills and Treasury bills) in the market. As the demand for bills rises interest rates fall. By the same token the Bank of England could bring about a credit squeeze by its open market operations. This would be done by selling Treasury bills or re-selling eligible bank bills. As there would be a decrease in the price of bills interest rates would increase. Both the credit expansion and the credit contraction are illustrated diagrammatically below (Figs 7.6 and 7.7).

Remember that as the price of bills rises the interest rate decreases. Similarly if the price of bills falls the interest rate rises. In the first case (credit expansion) the effect can be illustrated by an increase in the demand for bills.

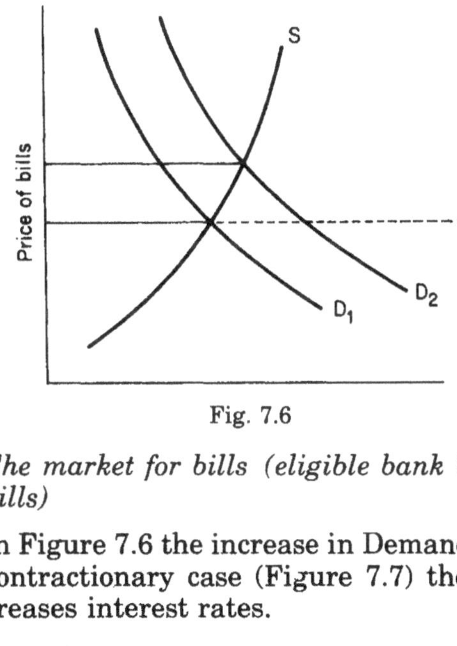

Fig. 7.6

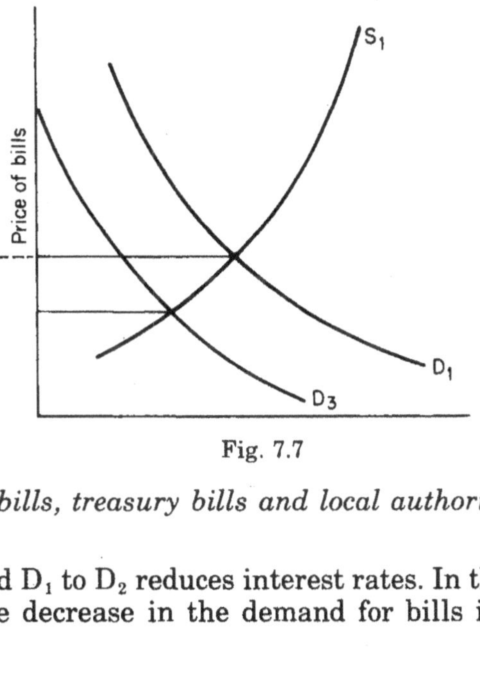

Fig. 7.7

The market for bills (eligible bank bills, treasury bills and local authority bills)

In Figure 7.6 the increase in Demand D_1 to D_2 reduces interest rates. In the contractionary case (Figure 7.7) the decrease in the demand for bills increases interest rates.

(2) Dealing in Longer Dated Securities

Open market operations are conducted by the authorities in order to fund their on-going fiscal needs, and to influence monetary conditions. The effect of government sales/purchases of gilts have a direct effect on monetary growth (see Table 7.2).

Table 7.2
The Effect of Open Market Operations on the Money Supply

Monetary action taken by the Bank of England	*Impact on liquidity*	*Effect on interest rates*	*Effect on the money supply*
Bank of England:			
Buys - Eligible bank bills - Treasury bills - Local authority bills - Gilt-edged stocks	Increase	Decrease	Rises
Sells - Treasury bills - Gilt-edged stocks *Resells* - Eligible bank bills - Local authority bills	Decrease	Increase	Falls

The Government broker (in practice the stockbroking firm Mullens) has the job of selling gilt-edged securities. One problem with selling a security with a fixed coupon is that if interest rates are rising the price of a fixed coupon stock automatically falls. Consequently the Government broker in these circumstances, finds it very difficult to attract buyers for the stock. The Government broker's response to this problem has varied. Three distinct types of tactics have been used.

In the period from 1945 up until 1958 and again from 1971 (with the reforms inaugurated by Competition and Credit Control) until 1975, his reaction to a falling market was simply to bide his time and wait for the market to recover. Between 1958 and 1970 he reacted to a falling market by coming in as a buyer, in the hope by thus making gilts more readily marketable in the eyes of the investor, he would in the long run attract more custom.

Under this policy, known as "leaning into the wind" gilt prices would rise or fall under market pressure, but never very quickly in either direction, thanks to the Government broker's transactions. This policy was deemed unsatisfactory as it placed severe limits on the Government's ability to sell gilts, and was modified in 1973.

Although the authorities felt able to leave the market without positive support when prices were weak, they did not actually force gilts on the market in these circumstances. Under monetary targetry this led to occasional "hiatuses" in gilt sales: low gilt sales would raise fears about a rising money supply and hence increased future interest rates (to curb it). This would reduce gilt sales further and the circle would continue. The authorities attempted to break out of this by sharply raising short-term interest rates (MLR up to 1981). The result was to sharply lower gilt prices creating the expectation that the next movement in prices would be downwards. Once gilt sales had been restarted MLR could be cut. This procedure was dubbed the "Grand Old

Duke of York" tactic. Since its heyday in 1979 it has gradually been replaced by a combination of increased flexibility and aggression on the part of the Bank of England and Government broker.

Overfunding

In order to mitigate the effect of rapidly rising bank lending to the private sector on the growth of sterling M_3, it has been necessary to sell large amounts of public sector debt to UK non-banks. It is helpful here to define the net funding position as net purchases of public sector debt by the UK non-bank private sector *less* the public sector borrowing requirement (PSBR). When this difference is positive, as was the case in 1977/78 and again in 1981/82, overfunding is said to have occurred.

Table 7.3
Sterling M_3 and Overfunding

Seasonally adjusted	*1977/78*	*1978/79*	*1979/80*	*1980/81*	*1981/82*
	Percentage increases at annual rates				
Target set for sterling M_3 (a)	9-13	8-12	7-11	7-11	6-10
	£ billions				
Actual growth in sterling M_3	6.2	5.3	6.4	10.7	10.0
Increase in bank lending to UK private sector	3.7	6.3	9.2	9.2	14.5
PSBR	5.5	9.3	10.5	13.1	8.6
UK non-bank residents' net purchases of public sector debt	6.9	8.4	9.1	11.0	11.1
Net funding (overfunding + underfunding -)	+1.4	-0.9	-1.4	-2.1	+2.5

Source: Bank of England, *Quarterly Bulletin*.
Reproduced by kind permission of the Bank of England.

The periods for which ranges were published often did not correspond exactly with financial years; for example, a range of 6–10% per annum was published in March 1981 for the period mid-February 1981 to mid-April 1982.

Interest rates, as a result of changes in the structure of credit, have now become such a blunt instrument that any given change in loan demand requires a much bigger adjustment of interest rates rather than used to be the case.

This has led the authorities to place much greater emphasis on *overfunding* – borrowing more than the actual budget deficit – to offset directly the impact of bank lending on the money supply.

So when the debt sales persistently outstrip the government's borrowing requirement (so-called "overfunding") the policy becomes a longer term way of reducing the money supply – by reducing the size of banks' balance sheets. People hold less of their wealth in bank deposits (the liabilities of the banks – in turn part of the money supply) and more in government debt. It used to be the case that this enabled the Government now holding this "surplus" cash to reduce their Treasury Bill Issue. However as this is now already low the Government (via the Bank of England) buys in commercial bills. In this way the Bank alleviates market shortages at the short end of the market. In effect the Bank of England is becoming a commercial bank.

The main objection to over-funding is that although it makes the money supply figures appear acceptable in the short run, there is a heavy long-term cost in the slow development of the corporate bond market. Long-term interest rates are higher than they need be and it is cheaper for companies to borrow short.

PORTFOLIO CONSTRAINTS: THE TECHNIQUES

(3) Reserve Asset Ratios

Reserve requirements force banks to hold, in specified assets, a certain proportion of either their assets or deposits or both. If a bank finds that it is nearing the minimum reserve assets ratio, it will either have to stop expanding its lending or increase its holdings of reserve assets (for example by selling off non-reserve assets such as gilts). In both cases this extinguishes bank deposits and therefore the money supply. If it stops lending new loans creating new deposits are not occurring. If it sells gilts these may be paid for by individuals writing cheques thereby extinguishing bank deposits.

Reserve assets typically earn interest below market rates. Thus reserve requirements lower the loanable funds available for profitable investment. This will result in an overall fall in the size of the balance sheet since the banks cannot make their liabilities (deposits) as attractive if they are obtaining less on their assets. Thus the imposition and increase in reserve requirements will impose contractionary pressure on the banking system.

If the relationship between supply growth as illustrated in Chapter 4 is

$$\Delta D = \Delta C \frac{1}{Cr}$$

then a clear relationship could exist between changing Cr (the reserve ratio) and the money supply. Namely:

RAISE RESERVE RATIO – CREDIT CREATION FALLS
LOWER RESERVE RATIO – CREDIT CREATION RISES

The preciseness of the control which can be achieved over the money supply, discussed in Chapter 4, by means of reserve ratios depends on two factors:

(a) the ability of the monetary authorities to control the total volume of reserve assets in the hands of the banking system; and

(b) the stability of the ratio of reserve assets to total deposits.

As a system of credit control reserve asset ratios in the United Kingdom have never been watertight. This has been particularly true as the total of reserve assets has never been fully under the control of the authorities. Experience of the past few years has shown that a shortage of reserve assets does not necessarily encourage banks to restrict the growth in their eligible liabilities, but to bid for funds in the interbank market to buy more reserve assets. This drives up interbank rates relative to rates for reserve assets (such as those on Treasury bills) and encourages the non-bank holders of reserve assets to switch them into bank deposits. A fall in non-bank private sector holdings of public sector debt and a rise in its holdings of bank deposits sometimes has the perverse initial effect of increasing £M_3, when the shortage of reserve assets is intended to reduce it. In addition, if banks do not raise their lending rates as quickly as their deposit rates in the wholesale market for bank deposits, "round-tripping" develops, which involves corporate borrowing from the banking system in order to lend back to the banking system at a turn, thereby increasing £M_3.

In addition banks could manufacture reserves with the discount houses within certain limits. Banks could also adjust their holdings of reserve assets by transactions with the private sector, buying or selling qualifying short-term government debt.

Reserve Requirements Have Not Been Used for Monetary Control

Despite the widespread belief, as expounded in numerous text books, monetary control via altering the reserve ratios and thereby, via the bank credit multiplier, controlling monetary growth, is not what the reserve ratio changes have been designed to achieve. The Radcliffe Report denied that the 8% cash ratio and the 30% later reduced to 28% liquidity ratio of the 1950s and 1960s were imposed to control the money supply.

In addition the Governor of the Bank made it plain that the 12½% reserve assets ratio introduced as part of CCC was not designed to direct monetary control. Instead its purpose was to influence interest rates.

> "It is not to be expected that the mechanism of minimum reserve ratio and Special Deposits can be used to achieve some precise multiple contraction or expansion of bank assets. Rather the intention is to use our control over liquidity, which these instruments will reinforce, to influence the structure of interest rates."

The same theme was repeated in the 1980 Green Paper on Monetary Control.

> "The Reserve Assets Ratio was never designed to serve as an officially controlled monetary base through which the pyramid of credit created by the banks might be directly limited. Instead in conjunction with Special deposits, the RAR, was regarded as an element in the control of short-term interest rates."

Thus in the UK RARs are for prudential purposes or are a minor weapon to influence interest rates.

As we discussed in Chapter 4 the authorities have taken the decision that the reserve asset requirement is to be abolished (other than the requirement that banks in the monetary sector should hold ½% of eligible liabilities with the Bank of England). As is explained in the Green Paper on monetary controls, "for the supervision of bank liquidity for prudential purposes, the Bank of England is instead proposing a system of liquid asset requirements based on the maturity structure of bank balance sheets." Thus the prudential and credit control purposes of official requirements for bank holdings of liquid assets have been disentangled.

Special Deposits

Because of the difficulty of controlling the volume of credit with any precision through open-market operations alone, the Bank of England has long considered how the mechanism could be modified in order to make it more effective. One suggestion, considered in the late fifties, was a variable liquidity ratio (i.e. one that could be changed as circumstances demanded) and in July 1958 a modified form of this idea – the special deposits scheme – was announced.

Special deposits are designed to reinforce control over liquidity. The Bank of England is empowered to call for special deposits from the clearing banks in proportion to each bank's own deposits. The Bank of England opens a special account for the monetary sector and it debits the monetary sector's account (i.e. bankers' balances) with the specified sum and at the same time it credits their special account with this same figure. These assets did not count as part of the clearing banks' liquidity ratios (and now do not count as part of the cash ratio). The Bank of England lend this money to the government and consequently the government does not need to borrow so much through the Treasury bill issue. The effects of special deposits is to transfer part of each bank's assets from the liquid to the non-liquid category. This mechanism works in reverse when Special Deposits are released. The clearing banks receive interest on these deposits approximately equal to the average Treasury bill rate for the preceding week.

Supplementary Special Deposits Scheme

One means by which banks can evade a cash shortage induced by the authorities is simply to borrow more, i.e. to increase their liabilities and place the proceeds in reserve assets. But this raises the money supply – precisely the opposite of the authorities' intentions. In order to prevent banks acting in this manner the authorities introduced in 1973 a non-market method of bank regulation entitled the "Supplementary Special Deposits Scheme". (It has introduced and abolished the SSDS three times and finally abolished it in 1980.) The scheme announced in 1973 established a special rate of growth for interest – bearing eligible liabilities for the period November 1973 to May 1974. The rate of growth chosen by the Bank of England was 8% and the deposit base selected was calculated as the average for each bank and finance house on the make-up days of the last three months of 1973. If a bank moderated its growth of interest bearing eligible liabilities (IBELs) to the 8%, then there would be no penalty. Growth in excess of 8%, however, would result in a sliding scale of supplementary deposits required by the Bank of England (see Table 7.4). These deposits did not bear interest, whereas the banks would, quite naturally, be paying interest to their depositors. The more the permitted IBEL growth was exceeded the greater were the penalties.

Table 7.4
The Supplementary Special Deposit Scheme

IBEL growth	*Supplementary Special Deposit Call*
8%	nil
9%	5% of excess deposits
10 - 11%	25% of excess deposits
over 11%	50% of excess deposits

The corset was put into effect on two subsequent occasions, November 1976 to August 1977 and June 1978 to July 1980. It was effectively a device which restricted the private bank's ability to bid competitively for certificates of deposit (CDs), and one of the reasons for which it was introduced initially was to prevent "round-tripping" within the banking system.

In general terms the "corset" had two major effects. First it led to a distortion of money market interest rates, lowering those in the private sector relative to the public sector, and so making public sector debt more attractive to hold. In this sense it was an alternative to raising interest rates through open market operations. Secondly, it led to increased disintermediation through the use of acceptance credit. If customers were unable to obtain bank loans, their bills could be accepted by the bank then sold to the non-bank investing public. In this case credit flows were distorted and money supply (£M_3) growth artificially held down. On each occasion on which the "corset" was introduced it had clear effects:

(1) In anticipation of the imposition of the "corset" banks increased their IBELS by issuing CDs – hence the ratio of IBELS to Sterling M_3 rose;

(2) The discount houses increased their holdings of CDs and financed them by borrowing call money from the banks;

(3) As a consequence the balance sheets of the banks and discount houses grew rapidly as they held each others newly issued liabilities;

(4) After the imposition of the "corset", the rate of growth of IBELS and CDs fell and the ratio of IBELS was more rapid than the decline in the growth of £M_3;

(5) The restriction on bank lending encouraged disintermediation – hence bank acceptances rose as did the discount holdings of bank bills.

In addition, the "corset" distorted the official money supply statistics and hence gave the appearance of the money stock being under control, even though in reality it was not.

(4) Direct Controls

Direct controls operate by placing limits on the banks' freedom to undertake certain activities. They are usually adopted because it is feared that other methods of influencing bank activity will not work sufficiently quickly or else will cause unacceptable consequences in other directions. For example market operations rely on increased interest rates reducing the demand for bank loans. However bank loans, for various reasons, may not be substantially influenced by higher interest rates. In addition politically influential groups (e.g. house buyers) may prevent market forces being introduced. Direct controls can be both quantitative and qualitative.

Quantitative and Qualitative Controls. Quantitative controls have been, periodically, imposed on bank lending. These controls usually involve the placing of a ceiling on lending by each bank. They have normally been accompanied by qualitative controls whereby the permitted lending ceiling was only to be reached by lending to certain, well specified categories, e.g. property companies were discriminated against in favour of loans to industry.

Qualitative and quantitative guidance certainly provided tight monetary control and helped the authorities to fund the PSBR. For if the growth of the bank advances to the private sector was limited the only outlet for the profitable deployment of bank deposits lay in lending to the government and other public sector bodies. But in such circumstances the banks were under no pressure to compete in efficiency, preferring rather to engage in what was to some extent conspicuous consumption by proliferating branch networks. There were no incentives for the banks to compete with each other, and control of advances meant that they tended to lose business to other financial intermediaries, like finance houses, hire-purchase companies, building societies and merchant banks.

Interest rate ceilings. Competition and Credit Control provided for the possibility of interest rate ceilings. The ceilings instrument has been used only once. For the period from September 1973 to February 1975 a ceiling on bank deposits of less than £10,000 was fixed at 9½%. This was designed to protect the building societies from the loss of small depositors to the banks. Naturally market forces are not being allowed to operate and the banks were discriminated against compared with the building societies.

Hire-purchase controls. HP controls work by altering either the size of down payments for goods and/or repayment period required from prospective purchasers. The advantage of HP controls is that they are a speedy and effective means of choking off demand in the short term. The disadvantage is that they penalise those sectors in which they are imposed and they are consequently inequitable.

(5) Moral Suasion

Moral suasion is the technique whereby the Bank of England suggests priorities for bank lending. Finance for exports tends to receive high priority closely followed by encouraging increased investment. Importing and private consumption tend to receive the lowest priority.

Moral suasion is normally employed when it is felt that the ordinary market mechanism does not, and can not, easily be made to take full account of the public interest. Thus the group willing to pay the highest interest rate may not be the group providing the most benefits to society, e.g. property speculators. Under these cases it may be advantageous to the economic welfare of the community if the banks can be induced to follow the wishes of the government.

The advantage of moral suasion over direct controls is that it is flexible. It does not involve legislation, imposition of rules, policing, etc. Any change in the situation which led to the operation of the agreed policy can quickly be met with an appropriate response; the agreed policy can be modified or scrapped altogether. Naturally any system of control which is not actively policed risks the problem that it may not be effective.

THE PUBLIC SECTOR BORROWING REQUIREMENT (PSBR)

In the Green Paper on monetary control (March 1980) the main monetary instruments are described as being "fiscal policy and interest rates"; the former being taxation and expenditure policies to alter the PSBR, the latter to influence, amongst other things, sales of public sector debt. Thus fiscal policy, it is accepted, has monetary implications. In other words the authorities cannot ignore the link between fiscal policy and monetary policy as any excess of government spending over receipts will have to be financed. This will have implications, for the monetary sector.

In recent years sales of gilts and other public debt to the non-bank private sector have meant that little finance has been provided by the banking system (remember that gilt sales to the banking system are quickly monetised). The authorities however argue that sales of gilts to the non-bank private sector have only been achieved by high interest rates which tend to reduce private sector spending at a time when it was desirable to maintain this thereby increasing employment levels. Thus, the authorities argue, if the PSBR was lower interest rates and the level of investment could be higher.

The PSBR can be altered by

(a) raising (lowering) taxation;

(b) reducing (increasing) expenditure on current goods and services;

(c) reducing (increasing) expenditure on transfer payments;

(d) selling (buying) assets. In the UK, these have included BP shares (1977 and 1979), council houses, Cable and Wireless 1983, Jaguar Cars Ltd 1984, Enterprise Oil, 1984 and British Telecom in 1984.

(e) cutting public sector lending to the private sector. Notably in the UK, this applies to local authority mortgages in 1975–78.

The major argument in favour of controlling the PSBR is that its effects neither depend on the correct definition of money nor on predicting the response of banks and the public to the change in interest rates. There are neither dangers of evasion nor of lack of knowledge of the response of bank lending to interest rate changes. If pursued with vigour the policy cannot fail to work. If the government can control its deficit then it will succeed in reducing monetary growth, albeit at possibly higher interest rates.

However, as we discussed in Chapter 4, there are several problems with the suggestion that a lower PSBR would reduce monetary growth. First, the PSBR is not a policy variable. With given tax scales and expenditure programmes, its size will vary with the level of activity and prices, as taxation receipts and social welfare spending change. A policy of fiscal restraint (cutting government spending programmes and raising tax rates) may not succeed in reducing the PSBR to the desired extent if in the process economic activity falls off and unemployment is increased. This reduction in income may in turn serve to reduce the money supply, either through the reduced demand for money or for bank advances, but it is an indirect method of controlling the money supply. In addition it is difficult to vary expenditure and taxation, especially in the short term. For example, income tax rates and the number of teachers employed cannot be varied as easily as interest rates. This is for both legal and practical reasons.

The effects that a lower level of economic activity has on lowering revenue and raising expenditure were well summarised by the February 1981 Treasury Economic Progress Report:

Expenditure rises due to:

"1) higher unemployment and supplementary benefit, because of higher unemployment;

2) higher payments out of the Redundancy Fund, because of higher redundancies;

3) a higher take-up of special employment measures, such as the short-time compensation scheme;

4) larger loans to nationalised industries and to state supported firms, because their internal finance – generated largely by sales revenue – is diminished by the fall in demand in the economy. If, however, these extra loans or grants are charged to the contingency reserve, then there need be no impact on the PSBR;

5) earlier deliveries by private firms carrying out government contracts as a result of the fall in orders from the private sector."

Receipts fall due to:

"1) lower receipts of income tax and national insurance contributions because fewer people are employed and less overtime is worked;

2) lower receipts from company taxes, because profits fall in a recession;

3) lower receipts from expenditure taxes, because of a lower volume of sales;

4) perhaps some delays in handing over tax due."

Finally interest rates may not be reduced merely by lowering the PSBR. There is not a fixed pool of loanable funds. A smaller PSBR reduces the demand for funds for government financing but if income is depressed, then savings and profits and so the supply of loanable funds may also be less.

LAGS

A lag, as the name suggests, is a delay – in this case a delay between one event, perhaps engineered by the authorities, and the desired response on the part of the rest of the community. It is, in fact, the lagged response of certain variables to a policy change that is one of the key reasons for the use of intermediate (indicator and target) variables at all. The lags involved in the effect of any policy can be divided into inside and outside lags. The inside or implementation lag is the delay that ensues between the need for a policy change occurring and the policy adjustment actually being made. This inside lag can itself be subdivided into a recognition lag, between the need arising and it being recognised, and an administrative lag i.e. between recognition and the policy change being made. The latter will be fairly short for monetary policy, as action can soon be taken to alter the scale of open market operations, change key interest rates or amend any other monetary instrument.

The outside lag is the time elapsing between the policy instrument being adjusted and the effect being felt on the goal variables. The outside lag can also be subdivided. It consists of the intermediate lag, between the adjustment of the policy instrument and its effect on the major target variable (e.g. the money supply) and the reaction lag between the change in the target variable and the effect on the goal variable itself. The existence of all these lags leads monetarists to advocate a policy of steady growth of the money supply.

THE EFFICIENCY OF MONETARY CONTROL

Remembering our three criteria of monetary efficiency, predictability, minimum distortion of financial markets, and reliance on market forces rather than portfolio constraints we can now judge the effect to which, in the pre August 1981 monetary system, they were achieved. We can then examine the Medium Term Financial Strategy.

Predictability

The authorities have difficulty in predicting both the demand for money, the size of the PSBR, the amount of gilt-edged sales to the non-bank private sector, the change in the volume of bank lending and external flows through the banking sector.

From the authorities point of view the case for choosing £M_3 as the monetary variable to be controlled is that monetary policy is then easily related to fiscal policy (through the size of the PSBR), to debt management policy (since interest rate levels can be seen to affect not only sales of public sector debt to the non-bank private sector but also the scale of bank lending), and to exchange rate policy (since this affects foreign currency assets and deposits). In the short term, however, it is debt management which bears the brunt of the adjustment to ensure control of the monetary aggregate. Suppose £M_3 is found to be rising too rapidly. The authorities are not able to influence the size of the PSBR in the short term, and the effects of exchange rate changes on currency flows are exceptionally difficult to determine even supposing that the exchange rate can be considered an exogenous policy instrument. The major instrument of policy must perforce be the level of interest rates.

However, our knowledge of the effects of interest rate changes on the demand for bank loans and gilt-edged sales and hence indirectly on the growth of M_3 is very imprecise.

Because of the authorities' inability to estimate with great precision the non-bank private sector's demand for gilts, the need to ensure that money supply growth is under control forces the authorities to take exaggerated action on the level of interest rates. For example, assume that £M_3 is growing too rapidly and that as a consequence the pound is weakening and interest rates begin to rise. For the authorities to bring £M_3 growth under control they must induce the non-bank private sector to purchase debt. If they raise interest rates by a small amount they are uncertain of the result. To be sure that they can sell sufficient debt they must ensure that rates are raised to such a level that they cannot but fall consequently and that, therefore, investors will buy. This interest rate "overkill" is precisely what happened in December 1976, February 1979, and January 1985.

The authorities start with some estimate of the public's demand for money and the way it is influenced by income and interest rates. Increases in income raise the demand for money while increases in interest rates reduce it. On the assumption that, in the short term at least, the level of income is given, the authorities seek to change the stock of money by changing interest rates. The process is shown in a simplified and static form in Figure 7.8, in which the demand for money relative to income is shown as a decreasing function of the rate of interest. If the authorities wished to obtain a money stock of M_0, they

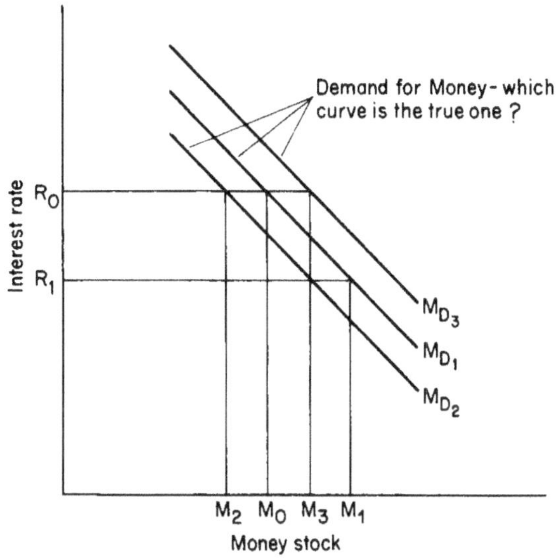

Fig. 7.8 Interest Rates and the Demand for Money
Source: M. K. Lewis, *Economics* (Autumn, 1981).

would attempt to move interest rates to R_0, while if they wished the money stock to increase to M_1, they would allow interest rates to fall to R_1.

But Llewellyn et al have shown that this procedure has been found to be uncertain in its operation for several reasons.* First, the demand for money (£M_3 is not stable). A stable function has eluded econometric testing. We do not have a stable demand for money function able to predict the interest rate level to secure a target demand for money. Secondly, the demand for bank credit appears not to be sensitive, at least in the short run, to interest rate movements in the range experienced over the past few years. This means, thirdly, that banks, in competing for funds to satisfy the insensitive demand for bank credit, raise their own interest rates in line with market rates with the result that the required interest rate differential is not secured simply by the Bank of England's money market operations. Instead, a competitive spiral of interest rates can emerge. Indeed, there are ways in which a policy-induced rise in interest rates can make it *more* difficult to secure the monetary target. First, "high" interest rates may encourage corporate borrowers to fund their financing requirements through the banking system (which raises the money supply) rather than through, for instance, the issue of debentures (which does not). The corporate debenture market has been weak for many years. Secondly, high interest rates may induce a capital inflow though the net monetary effect depends crucially upon where the funds are placed and upon the Bank of England's intervention tactics in the foreign exchange market. Thirdly, in the short run (and partly because of the endowment profits earned at high interest rates on banks' current account deposits) bank base rates may not rise fully in line with market rates. To the extent that this

* See D. T. Llewellyn, G. E. J. Dennis, M. J. B. Hall and J. G. Nellis, *The Framework of Monetary Policy* (Heinemann Educational Books, 1981).

induces "round-tripping" (drawing down advances to secure funds to invest in certificates of deposit $£M_3$ is raised. Fourthly, a rise in interest rates on public sector debt adds to the PSBR which may further hinder the attempt at monetary control. If the rise in interest rates itself induces expectations of further rises in interest rates there may also be a disequilibriating shift in the demand for money function. For these reasons the pre-August 1981 procedures for adjusting interest rates produced very uncertain and sometimes perverse effects upon the money supply.

As already discussed faced with these problems the authorities fell back on trying to predict – at a given level of interest rates (and exchange rates) – the growth of all those items in their own balance sheets, and in the balance sheet of the consolidated banking system.

The broadly defined money stock, $£M_3$, consists of notes and coin in the hands of the public, and current and deposit accounts at United Kingdom banks. The numerous balance sheet counterparts to these liabilities can be summarised into four aggregates – the public sector borrowing requirement, public sector debt taken up by the non-bank public, the volume of bank lending to the private sector and external flows to the private sector. The precise relationship between money supply ($£M_3$) growth, discussed in Chapter 4, and those assets which back the money supply can be written as follows:

Change in $£M_3$ = PSBR − Debt sales to the non-bank public + Sterling bank lending to the private and overseas sectors ± External factors − Increase in banks non-deposit liabilities

If the forecast for the growth of these items taken together implies excessive money supply growth, the authorities will have to take action by allowing either interest rates or foreign exchange rates to change. For example, assume that on the basis of such a forecast the authorities decide that $£M_3$ is growing too rapidly. If the cause of the rapid increase is an inflow of foreign currency they will have to allow the exchange rate to appreciate; if on the other hand it is an inability to sell gilt-edged stock to the non-bank private sector, they will have to raise interest rates and/or call for special deposits; while if it is a rapid and sustained rise in the volume of bank lending they can re-impose the "corset" or make its existing imposition more effective. Within this framework:

> "the essence of monetary management as I see it, is to act to offset divergencies from forecast in these sources of monetary expansion – difficult to predict and control – as soon as it becomes reasonably clear that inaction is likely to undermine achievement of the monetary target." (Governor of the Bank of England, Mais Lecture, 1978).

Minimum Distortion of Financial Markets

Two types of distortions in the pre-August 1981 monetary system can be highlighted. These relate to controls on bank lending and to the definition of reserve assets.

(1) Controls on Bank Lending

The deficiencies of these controls are best illustrated by examining the consequences of the introduction of the "corset". Although this was discussed on pp. 204–205 it is useful to repeat some of the shortcomings of the supplementary special deposits scheme. First the corset reduced the extent to which banks could compete amongst themselves for lending business. Secondly, it had the effect of diverting credit flows into uncontrolled channels. This meant that part of the monetary restraint achieved was purely cosmetic and that the usefulness of the money stock as an indicator of monetary conditions was undermined. This process, known as "disintermediation", took a variety of forms. One channel of disintermediation which was of major importance on the final occasion that the corset was used was the so-called "bill-leak". Under the bill-leak, instead of borrowing directly from the banks, companies would issue commercial bills which would then be "accepted" by the banks. (By accepting a bill a bank guarantees that the holder will be repaid when the bill matures and has the effect of making investors more willing to buy bills.) With bill finance the company receives the funds it needs, the supply of liquidity to the public increases in the form of additional holdings of commercial bills, and the net effect on the economy is much the same as if bank lending had increased. The scale of the bill-leak is illustrated by the fact that bank acceptances of commercial bills increased by around £1.7 billion, or by 43% in the second half of 1979. It was mainly because of the scope for this and other types of disintermediation that the corset was finally abandoned in June 1980. Also, however, the government had abolished exchange controls in 1979 and this meant that there was little point in continuing with the corset as borrowers were now free to seek funds abroad.

(2) Definition of Reserve Assets

To ensure that they can always meet withdrawals of deposits, banks hold reserves in the form of liquid assets of various kinds and combinations. In most countries the authorities reinforce the banks' own prudence in this matter and actually require them to hold liquid reserves in certain specified minimum quantities in relation to their deposits. This enables the authorities to control the overall level of bank deposits provided that the reserve assets which they require the banks to hold are such that the banks collectively can be made short of them (if, for example, the authorities wish to see the level of bank deposits lower) or can be stopped from adding to them (if for example, there is an upsurge in the public's desire to borrow from the banks which the authorities do not wish to see transformed into a higher level of bank deposits). This control mechanism requires that the system of reserve assets exclude the possibility that the banks, unbeknown to the authorities, may come into possession of additional supplies either of reserve assets or of other assets easily convertible into them.

To be precise, in order that a system of reserve asset control is efficient then two conditions have to hold. The Central Bank must be able to:

(a) impose on the banking system a ratio to be maintained;

(b) control the supply to the banking system of the reserve asset(s) which the banking system is required to hold to fulfil the ratio requirement.

The main criticism of the post October 1971 until August 1981 monetary control arrangements was that these requirements were not met. Under the CCC paper of October 1971 the definitions of eligible liabilities were:

sterling deposits minus any money at call lent to discount houses and also any funds lent to other banks in the inter-bank market.

There were three main ways in which the banks could avoid these reserve asset controls:

(1) The discount houses could sell gilt-edged securities with less than a year to maturity to the banks, which could count them as reserve assets, and buy from them gilt-edged securities with between one and five years to maturity, which the houses could do without hindrance from the maximum set by the authorities, in relation to the houses' capital, on their holdings of undefined (i.e. non-public sector) assets. The discount houses may well have been unwilling to lengthen their portfolio in this way, except at prices which make it expensive for the banks to acquire reserve assets through "swaps" of this kind.

   Should they have room, however, within the maximum applying to their "undefined assets", the discount houses might have been willing to buy additional commercial bills or certificates of deposit with additional money at call from banks; the latter would add to reserve assets.

(2) It is possible that the banks' customers borrow less on overdraft and more through the medium of commercial bills. Bills accepted by one bank can be discounted by another and included in its reserve assets. There was a limit of 2% of eligible liabilities on the extent to which commercial bills could count as reserve assets; so banks with that amount or more had no room for manoeuvre there. In any case it involved a cost in reduced earnings.

(3) Probably more important than either (1) or (2) is the fact that there was a substantial reservoir outside the banking sector of Treasury bills and of gilt-edged securities with less than a year to run, which could flow through the secondary markets into the portfolios of the banks and add to their reserve assets. At the end of September 1979, some £217 m Treasury bills were held by the UK non-bank private sector; no corresponding figures are publicly available for gilts with less than a year to run. A

switch of £50 m from non-bank to bank holdings could permit an expansion of eligible liabilities of up to £400 m or almost 0.8%.

These limitations on the authorities' ability to keep a taut control on the total of the banks' reserve assets have meant that one of the major weapons in their monetary armoury, the power to call on the banks for special deposits with the Bank of England (which do not count as reserve assets), was found to be of a correspondingly limited effectiveness. To be fair, however, the reserve asset ratio has not been regarded as a means or fulcrum for controlling the volume of bank deposits (despite the claims in numerous textbooks) still less as a means of inducing multiplier changes in the money supply (see Chapter 4).

The major operating fulcrum of the Bank of England has been, a development reinforced following the August 1981 measures, the bankers' balances ratio. Prior to August 1981 it was the practice of the Bank to issue more treasury bills each week than was necessary to finance the residual PSBR. This enabled the Bank to supply the required volume of cash to the banks at a rate of interest of its own choosing. For these reasons the weakness of monetary control deriving from the reserve assets structure was more apparent than real. The Bank of England has traditionally viewed monetary control as operating through the interest rate mechanism and it has been by operating on bankers' balances that the Bank has sought to influence interest rates. Neither the 1½% bankers' balances ratio nor the reserve assets ratio had been used to secure a lever to engineer a multiple change in bank deposits. Rather it has been predominantly the bankers' balances ratio that has been a fulcrum to engineer changes in bank liquidity and hence interest rate movements as a means of influencing the money supply via the demand for public sector debt and bank credit. The only time when the reserve asset ratio became an effective constraint was when the banks were short of reserve assets at a time when the corset constrained their liability management.

If the banking system is short of bankers' balances, the banks seek repayment of call money from the discount market. It is mainly the discount houses that subsequently sought money market assistance from the Bank of England which could be given either by loans at MLR (such direct assistance is given only to the discount houses) or by the Bank purchasing Treasury bills, local authority or commercial bills. To the extent that the rate charged by the Bank is penal, discount houses adjust their subsequent treasury bill tender price and are prepared to pay a higher rate for call money. Money market rates in general are likely to rise through a ripple effect. Alternatively, the Bank of England may ease liquidity conditions through transactions at its own initiative with banks via sale and repurchase agreements in government securities and via foreign currency swaps. This is done to ease upward pressure on liquidity when the bank provides bankers' balances in a way that does not reduce the banks' holdings of the assets.

Reliance on Market Forces

In the pre-August 1981 monetary system excessive reliance was placed on portfolio constraints on the banks. In particular special deposits and the corset were brought in, scrapped, and brought in again on numerous occasions. These were used as an alternative to open market operations. The disadvantages of these portfolio controls are illustrated on pp. 195–197. In practice the original role of special deposits as a constraint on bank advances was, throughout the 1960s, abandoned. Instead they were used to ameliorate the worse effects of the authorities "overkill" tactics in the gilt-edged market.

THE MEDIUM-TERM FINANCIAL STRATEGY

The incoming government in May 1979 confirmed its commitment to monetary targets and made the control of the money supply the central part of the strategy. In the first medium term financial strategy (MTFS) a path of progressive deceleration of the money supply to a rate of increase in the range of 4 to 8% in 1983/84 was set out (see Table 7.5). And it was stated that there would be no departure from the policy of progressively reducing the rate of monetary growth. In order to avoid an excessive reliance on interest rates, the PSBR was to be substantially reduced over the medium term. The intention was that this reduction in the PSBR would be achieved through cuts in public expenditure in volume terms.

The early years saw monetary growth well in excess of the target ranges – by some 9 percentage points in 1980/81 and 3½ percentage points in 1981/82 – and to a much greater extent than had occurred between 1976 and 1980 when the outcomes had more often than not been within, or even below, the target range (see Table 7.6). Moreover, the PSBR was substantially larger than projected for the fiscal year 1980/81, the outturn being equivalent to 5¾% of GDP compared with the planned 3¾%. The inflation rate nevertheless came down from over 20% at the beginning of the year to 12% by the start of the next year. Thus, the medium-term causal links between the PSBR, growth of sterling M_3 and the rate of inflation, which has been stressed as fundamental in the first MTFS in 1980, were not evident in the short term. A similar, though less marked pattern occurred in 1981/82 when the PSBR was roughly on track; sterling M_3 grew by 13½% compared with the 6 to 10% target range, yet the inflation rate declined by a further 2¼% points to 9½%. In the following two years, inflation fell to below 5%, indicating that the earlier surge in sterling M_3 did not appear to have strong lagged effects, as had sometimes been suggested.

With inflation falling fast and real GDP being depressed, these monetary increases – partly distorted by structural changes – implied a declining velocity of circulation (of sterling M_3) against a very constant upward trend over at least the six previous years. In effect, nominal income growth turned out to be lower than expected, despite monetary growth exceeding the target

Table 7.5
Key MTFS Indicators

Key MTFS Indicators

	1982–83	1983–84	1984–85	1985–86	1986–87	1987–88	£bn cash 1988–89
General government expenditure	132.4	139	146	152	157½	161½	166
General government receipts	122.1	128½	138½	146½	156½	164½	172
Annual fiscal adjustment*	—	—	—	2	4½	3½	3½
Cumulative fiscal adjustment*	—	—	—	—	2	6½	10
PSBR	9.2	10	7	7	7	7	7
as % of GDP	3.3	3¼	2¼	2	2	1¾	1¾
Money GDP at market prices	281	304	328	350	371	392	412
% increase	10.3	8.2	7.9	6.7	6.0	5.7	5.1

* Means lower taxes or higher expenditure than assumed in lines 1 and 2.
Constituent items may not sum to totals due to rounding or minor adjustments.

Table 7.6
Ranges for Monetary Growth

	Per cent change during year				
	1984-85	*1985-86*	*1986-87*	*1987-88*	*1988-89*
Narrow money—M0*	4-8	3-7	2-6	1-5	0-4
Broad money—£M3†	6-10	5-9	4-8	3-7	2-6

* Weekly averaged series.
† New definition: excluding public sector deposits.

Source Financial Statement

ranges. A variety of factors were mentioned at the time as being responsible for this unexpected change in velocity, including the following:

(a) a strong rise in personal savings, reflecting a large growth of disposable incomes and perhaps a rebuilding of the real value of financial assets, leading to a substantial rise in private sector net financial assets, thus affecting wider measures of the money supply;

(b) companies, suffering a profit squeeze, reacted by increasing bank borrowing as well as reducing stocks and employment;

(c) the removal of the "corset" in June 1980 affected sterling M_3 more than either the narrower measures of money (M_1 rose by only 11%) or the broader measures (PSL_2 rose by 15%); and

(d) the removal of exchange controls in October 1979 meant an increasing use of foreign currency deposits for transactions purposes.

In the March 1982 Budget, two important changes in the setting of the MTFS were introduced:

(i) The target for monetary growth in 1982/83 was set at 8–12% compared with a range of 5–9% indicated in the 1980 MTFS and repeated in 1981. The range for 1983/84 was increased and the MTFS was extended to 1984/85 (see Table 7.5). The possibility of clawing back earlier overshooting was no longer mentioned: base drift was accepted as was the increase in the target ranges.

(ii) The target range was now to apply to the growth of three principal monetary aggregates – M_1 and PSL_2 as well as sterling M_3 – and interpretation of monetary conditions was said explicitly to take account of the behaviour of the exchange rate.

In the 1984 budget public sector borrowing was expected to fall from 3¼% of the GDP in 1983–84 to 2¼% in 1984–85 and 1¾% by 1988–89. Sterling M_3 was expected to fall from a downward path of 6–10% in 1984–85 to 2–6%. The new target for M_0 is of a fall 4–8% in 1985 to 0–4% by 1988–89.

Chapter 8

International Trade and the Balance of Payments

INTRODUCTION

A glance at any financial newspaper reveals widespread discussion about world trading developments and about changes in a country's balance of payments. But why do countries trade and is it desirable that they do so? Again, what is the balance of payments and why is it important? And what is the structure of the United Kingdom's trade and balance of payments? This chapter provides answers to these questions.

WHY DO COUNTRIES TRADE?

Most international *trade* can be explained in terms of *four aspects*: cost of factors of production, technology, tastes, and incomes.

(1) Cost of factors of production

A country will tend to import products which require a relatively high input of those factors of production with which it is relatively poorly endowed. For example, the UK imports lamb and butter from New Zealand despite transport costs, because these products require much land relative to labour, and because New Zealand has an abundance of land relative to its labour force, when compared to the UK. The abundance of land will tend to make it relatively cheap, and this would give rise to relatively low costs for such products. Similarly, a country with little capital per man compared to other countries may tend to import products which are capital-intensive in production, again because the relative abundance of capital abroad may make such products relatively cheaper.

(2) Technology

Another reason may be technology: Britain imports, for example, television sets from Japan, some pharmaceutical products from Switzerland, and several types of aeroplane and computers from the United States. In each case, the exporting country generally has a relative technical lead in their manufacture; indeed, because of the heavy costs of small-scale production, patents, and other obstacles to the international transmission of knowledge, these commodities may not even be produced in Britain at all.

Both differences in costs of factors of production and technology will cause differences in product prices, but the crucial question is whether they generate different *relative* prices. In order to understand this point, it is necessary to distinguish between absolute and comparative advantage.

Adam Smith, in *The Wealth of Nations*, published in 1776, argued that if one of two countries could produce one product more efficiently and more cheaply and the other country could produce a second product more efficiently and more cheaply, then it would be natural for them to trade and both would benefit from doing so. Countries would gain from specialising in the production of, and the exporting of, the product in which they had an absolute advantage and importing other products in which they had an absolute disadvantage.

David Ricardo, in *Principles of Political Economy and Taxation* (published in 1821), took the argument a bit further. He showed that it was comparative, not absolute, advantage that mattered. Suppose, to take Ricardo's example that if no trade took place the production of a certain quantity of cloth and a certain quantity of wine in England and Portugal would require the following number of hours of labour:

	Cloth	*Wine*
England	100	120
Portugal	90	80

Portugal would have an absolute advantage in both wine and cloth since it could produce both more efficiently than England. However, Portugal would be relatively more efficient in wine which it could produce for two-thirds of the hours of labour required in England, while in cloth it would need nine-tenths of the hours required in England: so Portugal would have a comparative advantage in wine. England on the other hand would have a comparative advantage in cloth, which it could produce with 111% of the hours required in Portugal (100 ÷ 90), whereas it would need 150% of the time taken in Portugal to make wine (120 ÷ 80). Now countries could gain if each specialised in the product in which it had a comparative advantage and trade took place between them. England could specialise in making and exporting cloth and obtain wine more cheaply by importing it from Portugal, which in its turn would specialise in making wine and import cloth. If for example the international price ratio were 1 unit of cloth for 1 unit of wine, Portugal would be able to obtain a unit of cloth for 80 hours instead of 90 hours of labour, while England could get a unit of wine for 100 hours instead of 120 hours.

The principle of comparative advantage can now be seen to have a very specific implication: if planners are to decide which commodities Britain should export and import, they should ensure that the trading patterns corresponds with, and does not run counter to, the direction of trade one would predict if there were free competition in all markets.

The relative price of exports to imports is known as the terms of trade – the ratio of a price index of exports to a price index of imports. This therefore represents the import-purchasing power of a given volume of a country's exports. A rise in the terms of trade is known as an "improvement", and implies that fewer exports have to be sold to obtain the foreign currency necessary to purchase a given volume of imports. Less work is required, therefore, to obtain the imports, and this represents a rise in the standard of living. A fall in the terms of trade is known as a "worsening" and has the opposite implications.

Demand factors can also influence relative prices of products, and this leads us to the other two main influences on trade – tastes and income.

(3) Tastes

The third possible cause lies on the demand side. The size of British imports of tea, port, sherry, and champagne is partly explained by the lack of domestic production (for climatic reasons), but partly also because of a traditionally high level of consumption in comparison with many other European countries, reflecting different tastes.

In each example, the foreign country is a cheaper source of supply than Britain. By and large, the lower the level of foreign costs and prices, the greater the probability that a particular commodity will be imported, and – if it is already imported – the greater the volume of imports.

Even if costs were identical in two countries trade might take place as a result of differences in tastes. Thus, it might pay both Norway and Sweden to produce fish from the sea and meat from the land in about the same amounts. But if the Swedes have a relatively great fondness for meat and the Norwegians for fish, then a mutually profitable export of meat from Norway and fish from Sweden would take place. Both parties gain from this trade. The sum total of human happiness is increased, just as it is when Jack Spratt trades fat meat for his wife's lean.

(4) Income

In addition to these price and cost influences on imports, there is the powerful effect of changes in aggregate demand at home. In a boom, with incomes rising, the demand for most commodities rises. In the early stages many domestic producers can increase their own sales and output roughly in pace, so imports as a whole rise little faster than demand itself. In a few sectors, however, the boom may start to eat into stocks of materials, and attempts by producers to re-stock lead to sharp rises in imports. As the boom progresses, more and more bottlenecks appear: steel, bricks, machine tools, consumer durables all run short, as the limits of current domestic production are reached. Further rises in demand then begin to spill over almost entirely into imports. After the boom breaks, and demand starts to ebb away, the ratio of imports to national income stops rising and often starts to drop back.

What are the benefits and limitations of free trade?

If we are to search for the advantages of trade, we may consider the differences between a world with trade and one without it. First, consider the individual level. If there were no trade between individuals, each person would have to make himself self-sufficient; he would have to produce for himself all the food, clothing, shelter, medical services, entertainment and luxuries of life that he required. Living standards would be very low in a world of individual self-sufficiency. Trade between individuals allows each person to specialise in things he can do well, and buy from others the things he cannot easily produce for himself. Thus trade and specialisation are intimately connected. Without trade, everyone must be self-sufficient; with trade everyone can specialise.

The same principles apply to regions. Without interregional trade, each region would have to be self-sufficient. With such trade, plains regions can specialise in growing grain, mountain regions in mining and lumbering, and regions with abundant power sources in manufacturing; cool regions can produce wheat and other crops that thrive in such conditions, and tropical regions can produce bananas and coconuts. The living standards of the inhabitants of all regions can be made higher if the inhabitants of each specialise in producing the commodities in the production of which they have some natural or acquired advantage, and obtain other products by trade, than when each region is self-sufficient.

Through international trade a nation is able to obtain more goods with which to satisfy the needs and desires of its people (the ultimate end of economic activity) than if it were to produce all goods at home. This is the true gain from international trade; it is the fruit of international specialisation in accordance with comparative cost advantages. So international trade enables, under free competition, each country to combine its factors of production more effectively by specialising in the production of those goods that are best produced by using large amounts of its relatively abundant factors and small amounts of its relatively scarce factors.

So, the argument goes, if there is free trade in goods, then the more efficient industries in the world can expand their output. As the inefficient industries contract they release factors of production which may then be utilised by the efficient industries. Thus prices are kept in line with the costs of the efficient industries and consumers benefit from overall low prices. These gains to producers and consumers are at the basis of the arguments in favour of free trade. Any development, such as an ill-designed prohibitive tariff or quota, far from helping the protected industry, will instead reduce its growth by making imports more expensive and by making the whole world less productive through eliminating the efficiency inherent in the best pattern of specialisation and division of labour, would lower world economic welfare.

However, most contemporary economists are reluctant to support free trade without some reservations. Their qualifications of the free trade doctrine spring from two basic concerns: (i) the departure of real world markets from the conditions of free markets and (ii) the absence of any necessary correspondence between higher income and higher welfare at both national and international levels.

The (simple) theory of trade rests on the assumption of perfect competition – no monopoly or oligopoly, no product differentiation (i.e. advertising), no internal economies of scale, and no ignorance, uncertainty or risk. Furthermore the theory implicitly assumes that external economies and diseconomies (defined below) do not cause a divergence between private and social benefits and costs and that market prices truly indicate the full opportunity costs confronting a society. External economies exist when a firm (or industry) creates values for society that cannot be sold in the marketplace (such as training workers who subsequently leave the firm for other employment). This situation makes the private value (benefits) of the firm's output less than its social value. External diseconomies refer to social costs of production (such as pollution) that are not borne by the producer, making private costs less than social costs. In the case of external economies the firm is producing *too little* to maximise social value; in the case of external diseconomies, *too much*. Since all the above mentioned assumptions are only partially matched in actual markets, it follows that free trade will not necessarily bring a higher allocative efficiency to the national and world economy.

A second reason why most economists are often reluctant to offer unqualified support for free trade lies in the question of economic welfare. Even if efficiency were achieved in the allocation of national and world resources it would not necessarily follow that free trade would also optimise national and world welfare. By altering relative prices, free trade also alters income distribution among individuals and groups both within and between nations. It is not at all evident that what some groups gain from free trade outweighs what other groups, e.g. the unemployed, lose from free trade. This is one reason why governments often interfere with free trade in order to protect those sectors of society which would lose from it.

In addition some countries use strategic arguments for not advocating free trade, e.g. South Africa does not want to be dependent on imported oil and the UK Ministry of Defence prefers to buy British armaments.

HOW HAS WORLD TRADE EVOLVED?

In the period 1913–48 world production rose 2% p.a., world trade ½% p.a., in 1948–73 production rose 5% p.a., trade 7% p.a. Both faltered in the 1970s and came to a halt in the late 1970s and indeed have fallen since 1980. This latter development does not represent merely a slow down in output. It is not just the flat demand of a recession that is stopping some of the world's exporters increasing their sales as they used to; they also face new barriers against their exports, put up by governments, who increasingly treat foreign goods as a threat to employment levels.

Most governments know that their economies remain heavily dependent on exports. World trade is a large business – US$ 2.6 trillion in 1981, roughly 40% of it in manufactures. The importance of world trade was accepted in 1947 when 24 governments signed the General Agreement on Tariffs and Trade (GATT). There are now 88 signatories to GATT.

From the beginning GATT was a pledge not to return to the protective, high unemployment, days of the 1930s. It was not a free-trade charter in any textbook sense of free trade. It recognised that trade barriers would exist, but aimed to make them transparent (so that all would know what they were up against) and non-discriminatory. The central text of this latter view is in Article one of the GATT:

> ". . . any advantage, favour, privilege or immunity granted by any contracting party to any product originating in or destined for any other country shall be accorded immediately and unconditionally to the like product originating in or destined for the territories of all other contracting parties."

GATT also provided for trade barriers to be lowered – especially tariffs, the most obvious form of protectionism. They were also the most common, and the most negotiable: ideal candidates, in fact for the GATT treatment. So down they came. The United States levied tariffs averaging 26% in 1946; by 1948 they were down to 8%, and by 1987 they are due to be 5%.

These falls in tariffs were reflected in rising world trade (see Fig. 8.1). During the three decades since 1950, the value of world exports grew at an annual average of 12.3% in nominal terms and 6.7% in real terms, according to data contained in the *International Financial Statistics Supplement on Trade Statistics*. In the 1950s, the average annual increase in world trade export volume was 6.4% (7.1% in value), and in the 1960s, the average annual increase in export volume was 7.9% (9.4% in value). However, the close correlation between the changes in world export volume and value disappeared in the 1970s, when the annual increase in export value of 20.7% was more than three times the 5.5% increase in export volume. Thus, although approximately 90% of the increase in the value of world trade during the 1950s and 1960s represented volume growth, during the 1970s volume growth contributed less than 30% of the increase in world export value.

As already discussed the postwar expansion of world trade was facilitated by the steady liberalisation of trade and payments restrictions undertaken

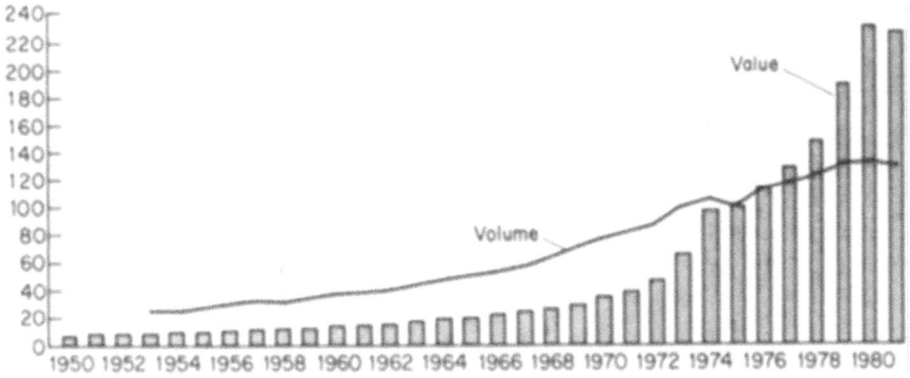

Fig. 8.1 Thirty-two Years of World Trade Developments

Source: IMF, *IFS Supplement on Trade Statistics*
(world exports indices: 1975 = 100)

under the auspices of the General Agreement on Tariffs and Trade (GATT) and, as will be seen later, by the International Monetary Fund (IMF). Although the liberalisation of payments systems in the industrial countries had been virtually completed by the middle to the late 1950s, trade liberalisation continued until the early 1970s.

The biggest impact on the growth and distribution of world trade since 1950 appears to have been the increasing problem of domestic inflation that emerged in the mid-1960s and culminated in the middle and late 1970s with rapid price increases. Until then, as already indicated, the growth of world trade had been mainly a result of rising volumes of trade flows. In the 1970s rapid inflation in the world economy, particularly after the oil-price increases of 1973 and 1974, affected the non-oil developing countries in the form of higher import prices. Modest increases in the volume of imports became associated with much larger increases in the value of imports, which, for many countries, were not matched by similar increases in export earnings. As a result, more and more countries recorded larger trade deficits.

As a direct result of the differing rates of growth for the three major areas of the world (defined below), the distribution of world trade among these areas has changed substantially. In addition, the decision of the members of the Organization of Petroleum Exporting Countries (OPEC) to triple posted prices of petroleum in late 1973 and the concomitant boom in the prices of primary products had a marked impact on the changes in the structure and growth of world trade.

The increases in the value and volume of world trade since the 1950s have been spread across all areas of the world, although there have been wide disparities among countries. Table 8.1 shows, for imports and exports separately, the magnitude of these changes for three major country groups, in terms of value, unit value, and volume. The three major groups are industrial countries, oil exporting countries and non-oil developing countries.

Trade of Industrial Countries

The 20 industrial countries as a group recorded an annual growth rate of 12.5% in export value and 7.2% in volume during the three decades from the 1950s to the 1970s, slightly greater than the world average. During the 1950s and 1960s, the industrial countries' growth rate was above that of both the oil-exporting countries and the non-oil developing countries. This pattern was reversed during the 1970s as large increases in oil prices and a simultaneous commodity boom, fuelled by rapid growth and inflation in the industrial countries, caused the export revenues of the non-industrial countries to rise to record levels.

Trade of Oil Exporting Countries

With both total exports and imports of less than US$5.0 billion in 1950, the oil exporting countries accounted for only 7.3% of world exports and 3.8% of world imports. These percentages remained at similar levels through 1972; however, following the threefold increase in posted prices of petroleum in late 1973, this group's share of world exports more than doubled to 15.3% in 1974 and, after a decline in 1975, remained in the 13–15% range for the rest of the decade. The large increases in export earnings were also reflected in the growth of the imports of the oil exporting countries; their share of world imports rose from 3.7% in 1973 to 4.1% in 1974, 6.3% in 1975, and 7.0% in 1980. In this regard, the oil exporting countries unlike the other developing countries, were not required to restrain imports to alleviate balance of payments deficits. The oil exporting countries as a group have always recorded trade surpluses, and the surpluses became larger following the oil price increases of 1973. By 1975, the trade surplus was US$60.3 billion (down from $87.1 billion in the previous year), and by 1980, after further large rises in the price of petroleum in late 1979 and early 1980, the surplus reached a record US$162.2 billion but has since fallen substantially. Most of this surplus was in trade with the industrial countries (US$111.7 billion), but a sizeable surplus with the non-oil developing countries was also recorded ($44.4 billion).

Trade of Non-oil Developing Countries

Following annual growth rates of 3.4% in the 1950s and 6.5% in the 1960s, the annual increase in export earnings of the non-oil developing countries accelerated in the 1970s to 21.0% a rate above that for the industrial countries. The annual increases of the group's imports were 5.7% in the 1950s, 7.2% in the 1960s, and 20.8% in the 1970s.

The rapid increase in the value of exports of the non-oil developing countries in the 1970s was partly attributable to a rise in export unit values (following the boom in commodity wholesale prices) and also to a sizeable increase in the volume of exports. In the first five years of the decade, approximately 30% of the average annual increase in export earnings resulted from increases in volume, but this share increased to more than 40% in the latter half of the decade. During this period, the annual increase in the export volume index of

Table 8.1
World Trade Summary
(compound annual rate of change; per cent)

	1950–55			1955–60			1960–65			1965–70			1970–75			1975–80			1976–81	
	Value	*Unit Value*	*Volume*	*Value*	*Unit Value*	*Volume*	*Value*	*Unit Value*	*Volume*	*Value*	*Unit Value*	*Volume*	*Value*	*Unit Value*	*Volume*	*Value*	*Unit Value*	*Volume*	*Value*	*Unit Value*	*Volume*
Exports																					
World	**8.1**	...	...	**6.2**	**0.4**	**5.8**	**7.8**	**0.9**	**6.8**	**11.1**	**1.9**	**9.1**	**23.1**	**16.5**	**5.6**	**18.4**	**12.3**	**5.4**	**14.9**	**11.7**	**2.9**
Industrial countries	10.0	2.7	7.1	7.5	0.7	6.7	8.4	0.9	7.4	11.9	2.0	9.6	20.9	14.1	5.9	16.8	9.9	6.3	14.0	8.8	4.8
Oil exporting countries	6.8	...	...	4.3	...	...	7.4	0.1	7.2	10.8	0.5	10.2	45.5	45.4	—	21.6	23.0	-1.2	15.0	24.1	-7.4
Non-oil developing countries	4.0	...	...	2.9	-1.5	4.5	5.4	1.2	4.1	7.8	1.7	5.9	20.6	13.1	6.6	21.4	10.9	9.4	18.3	8.3	9.3
Imports																					
World	**8.7**	**2.5**	**6.0**	**6.1**	**-0.6**	**6.8**	**7.9**	**0.5**	**7.4**	**11.0**	**1.5**	**9.4**	**22.4**	**16.5**	**5.0**	**18.6**	**12.1**	**5.8**	**15.5**	**11.3**	**3.8**
Industrial countries	9.2	2.5	6.5	6.7	-0.8	7.5	9.0	0.4	8.5	11.6	1.6	9.8	21.0	16.7	3.7	18.4	12.3	5.4	13.8	11.3	2.2
Oil exporting countries	11.1	...	...	6.7	...	...	3.1	1.0	2.1	9.3	2.0	7.2	39.9	14.3	22.4	21.2	10.4	9.8	20.5	9.1	10.4
Non-oil developing countries	6.9	...	...	4.5	0.6	3.8	5.5	1.0	4.4	9.0	0.6	8.3	23.3	16.5	5.9	18.3	12.0	5.6	19.5	12.1	6.6

Source: IMF, *IFS Supplement on Trade Statistics*

9.4% was substantially above the 6.3% increase of the industrial countries and the 1.2% decline of the oil exporting countries.

The Growth of Barter

The recession in developing countries, the oil glut and inefficiency in Eastern Europe are making money less important in international business as many countries are tending to revert to barter (more accurately referred to as countertrade).

According to some studies countertrade is estimated to have amounted to about 30% of world trade worth $592 bn in 1982, compared with some 2%, worth $18 bn, in 1976.

The developing world is responsible for the phenomenal growth of countertrade of the 1980s; some 40% of Third World trade is now said to take the form of countertrade. For developing countries, particularly rapidly industrialising and overborrowed nations such as Brazil, countertrade offers several potential benefits:

(1) It enables them to continue importing despite a lack of foreign exchange and without further harming the balance of payments. It can help soften the domestic impact of an International Monetary Fund austerity programme calling for drastic action to balance outgoings and receipts.

(2) By emphasising bilateral agreements, as opposed to multilateral free trade, and extracting concessions in return for the right to sell in a developing market, countertrade presents a chance for a developing country to regain access to a western market which might otherwise be closed off by protectionism.

(3) Under "compensation" arrangements, countries can acquire vital technology and plant in return for a proportion of their output.

The European Economic Community and its importance in world trade

The EEC is a common market, or customs union; it has eliminated internal customs duties, to enable manufacturers to treat the whole EEC as their domestic market, and has replaced individual national tariffs on imports from outside the community with a single system of tariffs at its outer frontier, known as the common external tariff (CET). Once imported, items that have paid duty at their point of entry into EEC territory are free to circulate within the community without further tariffs.

The EEC is the world's biggest trading block. It accounts for more than one third of world exports, considerably more than the United States and Japan put together. EEC economies are more dependent on trade for their livelihoods than the other economic powers. Exports are equal to 25% of EEC countries' gross domestic product (GDP) on average, compared with 8% for the United States and 12% for Japan. Just over half of EEC members' trade is with each other while another 20% is carried out between the Ten and their neighbours in the European free trade association (EFTA) – Sweden, Norway, Iceland, Switzerland, Portugal, Austria, and Finland.

In the European free trade association, tariffs between the members have been eliminated, so that EFTA goods can circulate freely, but each member imposes its own tariffs on imports from outside EFTA. In a free trade area, elaborate rules have to be concocted to stop imports entering the area through a low-tariff country and then circulating to the rest.

The EEC has been at the heart of many of the GATT negotiations. In 1958 the community's average common external tariff on industrial goods was 10%. By 1985 the community's average tariff was about 5% compared with 3% for Japan and 6% for the United States.

The EEC, under the pressure of recession, has started to lose its free-trade virtues. Increasingly, member states are throwing up new protectionist barriers against imports from each other – though they are not reimposing tariffs. Rather, they are introducing a variety of administrative and non-tariff barriers to block trade, from inside and out, such as:

(1) Costly and time-consuming frontier formalities. Dutch lorry drivers claim they have to get 300 rubber stamps on their customs and other papers to get a lorryload of Gouda cheese into France. France announced in October 1982 (a decision later rescinded) that all video cassette recorders must go to a tiny customs post at Poitiers in south west France, miles from the main ports for customs clearance. This post has just eight staff, and can delay imports for weeks, giving domestic producers a big advantage. For all French imports the customs papers must now be in the French language. The European commission reckons needless frontier red tape can add up to 10% to the cost of the goods being shipped.

(2) National regulations on health or safety standards. Some of these regulations, serving such praiseworthy ends as environmental protection, quality control, energy conservation or public health requirements are being forged into weapons of indirect protectionism.

(3) Disregard for community rules on state subsidies for industry. In a bid to save jobs (and so export unemployment), member states grant aids to whole industries or individual lame ducks which are illegal under EEC competition rules.

(4) Discrimination by national governments against foreign firms when awarding public contracts. Despite community rules, recently reinforced by a new GATT code, fewer than 1% of public contracts are placed outside their country of origin.

Infringements to community rules on the free circulation of goods among member states are counted by the hundred and no longer by the dozen. At the beginning of 1982, the commission was taking action against member states for a total of 140 confirmed infringements. The breakdown of cases was:

France	40	Holland	11
Italy	28	Britain	9
Germany	17	Ireland	7
Denmark	12	Luxembourg	5
Belgium	11		

WHAT IS THE BALANCE OF PAYMENTS AND WHY IS IT IMPORTANT?

INTRODUCTION

The reason for having balance of payments accounts is to identify and record transactions between residents of the United Kingdom and residents overseas (non-residents) in a way that is suitable for analysing the economic relations between the UK economy and the rest of the world. The transactions may involve a flow of real resources, that is, of goods, services or property income, between the United Kingdom and the rest of the world; a change in the United Kingdom's foreign assets or liabilities; or a transfer payment.

The Sign Convention

In interpreting the balance of payments accounts it is important to be aware of what is known as the "sign convention", i.e. whether items are credits or debits in the accounts. The basic principle is that transactions which result in there being a demand for sterling in the foreign exchange market (discussed in detail in Chapter 9) are listed as "credits" and transactions which result in there being sterling selling in the foreign exchange market are listed as "debits".

Exporting, falls in foreign assets owned by UK residents (explained below) or increases in the UK liabilities to non-residents are all credits. The process of exporting requires the buyers to pay in such a way that either he or the seller will buy sterling. An example of a fall in foreign assets held in the UK would be if there were sales of US Treasury bills for sterling. An example of an increase in UK liabilities to non-residents would be if there were purchases of gilts by non-residents, deposits by foreigners with UK banks or the takeover of a British company by foreigners. Similarly importing, increases of the UK's foreign assets or decreases in the UK liabilities to non-residents are debit entries.

The UK balance of payments accounts are a summary of all transactions between UK residents and non-residents over a given period. Each transaction, whether it be, for example, the sale of a good to a non-resident or the purchase of stocks and shares from a non-resident, involves both a credit and a debit to the UK. The balance of payments accounts is thus an amalgam of credits and debits, indicated by appropriate signs, which ensures that the total of the whole account is always zero for each period, provided all transactions are measured accurately (the reason for this caveat is explained below). The balance of payments always balances because at the end of the day the demand for sterling must equal the supply of sterling. In practice errors and omissions enter the recording process and in presenting the accounts a balancing item is included to compensate for this.

The whole account always sums to zero, but the sum of credits and debits will not necessarily net out to zero for each individual group within the accounts. The sum of transactions in each group produces a balance for that group, for example the sum of exports of goods (exports carry a positive sign) and the imports of goods (imports carry a negative sign) is the balance on visible trade, which naturally can overall be in balance, deficit or surplus.

A simple way to appreciate why total debits and credits must be equal is to realise that a country, like an individual, cannot buy goods and services worth more than what it sells unless it either:

(a) reduces its cash reserves (gold, foreign money and bank accounts abroad);
(b) earns profits from or sells off some of its investments;
(c) receives repayment of debt owed to it;
(d) borrows/ or receives credit;
(e) receives gifts.

Conversely, a country cannot sell more than it buys in goods-and-services transactions unless it engages in matching debit transactions by accumulating cash reserves, investing, lending, paying off debt or giving gifts.

To clinch an understanding of the balance of payments concept, it is worthwhile to draw the analogy between a country and a single family. Examples of *credits* in the family's balance of payments might be: (i) sales of goods, such as crops grown or goods produced by members of the family, (ii) provision of lodgings to tourists, (iii) work done by wage-earning members of the family, (iv) earning of interest and dividends on bank accounts and bonds and stocks, and earning of profit from a family-owned business, (v) receipt of gifts, perhaps from relatives or from public-relief authorities, (vi) new borrowing, including the obtaining of hire-purchase credit from sellers of goods, (vii) undoing loans and investments previously made, including, for example, selling stocks, cashing in savings bonds, spending wads of currency kept in the mattress, and drawing down bank accounts, and (viii) sale of gold coins from a collection. *Debits* might include: (i) purchase of groceries and other goods, (ii) travelling, staying in hotels, and eating in restaurants, (iii) buying medical and legal and repair services, (iv) incurring interest on money previously borrowed, (v) making gifts, (vi) repayment of borrowing, including payment of instalments on credit purchases, (vii) purchases of stocks and bonds and increases in bank accounts and hoards of currency, and (viii) purchase of gold coins. The family clearly cannot be spending more than it earns on current account (items (i) to (iv)) without at the same time receiving gifts, borrowing, drawing down bank accounts and hoards of cash, recovering loans or selling off investments or selling gold. Conversely, a family cannot be earning more than it spends on current account without lending, investing, making gifts, accumulating cash and bank accounts, or the like.

The necessary balance of debits and credits is a matter of sheer definitions and arithmetic and gives no guarantee of "equilibrium" in any reassuring sense of the word. Total debits would equal total credits even for a family or a country in terrible economic straits.

Thus, like a family, unless there is some transaction on the credit side a country would not be running the deficit in the first place. A country simply cannot be importing more goods and services than it can pay for in some way or other.

If debits and credits are equal one may wonder why the existence of a deficit creates a "problem". The problem occurs when the deficit is financed in a merely stopgap way, as by drawing down bank accounts abroad, selling off gold or investment assets, receiving stopgap loans from abroad, or receiving gifts granted by foreigners precisely in order to tide the country over the crisis. The worry is that such stopgaps cannot go on for ever: eventually, foreign banks accounts and gold and other saleable assets will be exhausted, and foreigners will become tired of making bad loans and unrequited gifts. The deficit country may suddenly be caught up by the unpleasant need to live within its income. A persistent current-account deficit may indicate the impending need for sudden unpleasant readjustments.

Even borrowing in a monthly non-stopgap way can involve difficulties. High interest costs may have to be made for foreign currency inflows. If borrowings are from the International Monetary Fund, discussed in the next Chapter, severe "austerity" conditions may be attached to the loans.

If a currency becomes so weak that it is not wanted by the residents of any other country (i.e. it becomes inconvertible) the residents of the country in question will find foreign trade extremely difficult to organise and in turn will lose many of the gains from trade discussed earlier.

THE STRUCTURE OF THE BALANCE OF PAYMENTS

At a high level of aggregation, the UK balance of payments can be arranged into four main groups. The first of these is called the *current account* and it covers exports and imports of goods and services, interest profits and dividends and current transfers. The balance on the current account has been described as "an indicator of whether the nation is paying its way". *Capital* transfers form the small second group of transactions. These comprise compensatory payments to holders of sterling under the Sterling Agreements introduced in 1968 and terminated in 1974. "Investment and other capital flows", the third group, covers such things as *official long-term* capital transactions, external lending or borrowing by UK banks, overseas investment and trade credit extended by exporters to foreigners buying British goods. The second and third groups make up what is known as the "capital account". The fourth group, *official financing* is the net transactions of the Bank of England in the foreign exchange market, i.e. changes in the UK official reserves of gold and foreign currency and other transactions concerned with their management through the Exchange Equalisation Account (EEA).

In the standard presentation of the balance of payments accounts, these four groups are listed in the above order and the balance for official financing, the dividing line across the accounts, is the aggregate balance for the first three groups. The fourth group, official financing, is sometimes said to be "below the line" and completes the accounts. The structure of the accounts may therefore be summarised in the form of a table:

Table 8.2

	Net credit or debit
Current account	A
Capital transfers	B
Investment and other capital flows*	C
Balance for official financing	A+B+C
Official financing	-(A+B+C)
Total	0

*In practice the balancing item (see above) is included here to compensate for the extent that the sum of the three autonomous groups as measured does not match the total of official financing transactions - which, as defined, is known exactly.

The reasoning behind the presentation of the accounts is that transactions in the first three groups, which are often designated "autonomous", contribute to the fourth group the balance for official financing which is financed by the items below the line.

When analysing the balance of payments it can be useful to make a distinction between autonomous and accommodating external transactions. Autonomous transactions are undertaken for private gain, e.g. as would occur with a capital inflow by private individuals wishing to benefit from higher interest rates. This can be contrasted with accommodating external transactions, transactions undertaken or induced specifically to finance a gap between autonomous credits or debits. This distinction is not altogether satisfactory as the government can, by manipulating UK interest rates, create an inflow of short-term capital to accommodate a given current account deficit even though, from the point of view of individuals or banks buying and selling the assets, the transactions are autonomous. However, as will be discussed later, the autonomous – accommodating distinction provides a useful starting point for discussing the concept of balance of payments "equilibrium".

The balance of payments can be said to be in equilibrium when, at the existing exchange rate, autonomous credits are equal to autonomous debits over a period of good and bad years, without involving:

(a) departures from full employment or price stability;

(b) departures from the desired rate of economic growth;

(c) adoption of tariffs or subsidies inconsistent with accepted international obligations.

We can now discuss the major constituent items in the balance of payments: the current account, the capital account and official financing.

THE CURRENT ACCOUNT

The two main divisions within the current account are visibles and invisibles. Visibles refer to goods, i.e. to all those things such as cars, coffee, coal, video recorders, that we can see when they cross international borders. Invisibles refer to cross frontier income flows which are related to underlying services. These can be for supplying some service, e.g. banking, tourism, insurance, interest profit and dividend payments. Interest may be paid or earned on past investments, e.g. a bank deposit. Profits may be earned if say a UK company has a subsidiary abroad and makes a profit. Dividends may be earned if a UK firm owns some shares in a foreign company and in turn this company pays out a dividend. Finally the invisible account includes transfer payments. These are payments where money is transferred without any underlying movement of goods or services, e.g. payments made abroad by foreigners working in the UK.

The visible balance is simply the difference between the value of exports and imports, a positive or negative sign indicating a net inflow or outflow of currency respectively. The difference between the value of exports and the value of imports is known as the balance of trade. The invisible account is described in detail in Appendix 1.

THE CAPITAL ACCOUNT

The current account quantifies how well a particular country performs in the buying and selling of goods and services with the rest of the world, whereas investment and other capital flows record capital transactions.

Before discussing individual items, it is useful to make some general comments about the types of flows in the capital account. First, there is the distinction between official and private transactions, the former being carried out by government or governmental agencies and the latter by the rest of the community. Secondly, most capital movements can be classified into those which are long-term and therefore more permanent in nature, and those which are short-term and more easily reversible. Long-term transactions are usually carried out after consideration of the general prospects for profitability in other countries, whereas short-term transactions are determined more by interest rate differentials or by the prospect of capital gains or losses from potential exchange rate movements. Finally, a distinction is often made between direct investment and portfolio investment, even though the former is generally long-term and the latter short-term in nature. Direct investment is typically associated with financial flows connected to capital formation overseas and/or financial flows between parent companies and overseas subsidiaries. Portfolio investment takes the form of the acquisition of stocks, shares or other overseas financial assets.

Appendix 2 gives a detailed breakdown of the components of the capital account.

OFFICIAL FINANCING

The composition of official financing shown in the balance of payments accounts in any period, summarises the way that the UK monetary authorities have reacted to the net demand for, or accommodated the net supply of, foreign currency at whatever exchange rate prevailed. The direct effects are drawings on or accruals to the official reserves; the other official financing transactions represent the effects of directly reconstituting or supporting the official reserves by borrowing or similar arrangements. Historically such arrangements have been with overseas monetary authorities (including the IMF) but in the 1970s HM Government borrowed on the euro-currency and New York securities markets and, since 1969, public corporations and local authorities have borrowed foreign currencies under the exchange cover scheme. Under this scheme, public bodies are able to borrow in foreign currencies from abroad with the guarantee of the Treasury that the foreign currency required for interest payments and capital repayments will be available at the same cost in sterling terms as at the time that the loan was raised. The public bodies require sterling to finance domestic projects and the foreign currency supplements the United Kingdom's official reserves.

The sources of official financing are threefold:

(1) net transactions with overseas monetary authorities;
(2) foreign currency borrowing;
(3) official reserves.

These are discussed in detail in Appendix 3.

Balancing Item

As we have stressed throughout this Chapter, because a flow in one direction (say an export of goods) must be offset by another (say, an inflow of foreign currency), with the conventional use of plus and minus signs, in principle, all entries should sum to zero. In practice, however, a balancing item is included to offset the sum of errors and omissions.

The balance of payments statistics for 1961 to 1983 are given in Table 8.3.

Table 8.3

Summary Balance of Payments[1]

£ million

	1961	*1962*	*1963*	*1964*	*1965*	*1966*	*1967*	*1968*	*1969*	*1970*	*1971*
CURRENT ACCOUNT											
Visible balance	-140	-100	-119	-543	-260	-108	-599	-712	-209	-34	+190
Invisibles											
Services balance	+21	+18	-31	-50	-36	+31	+168	+357	+422	+481	+625
Interest, profits and dividends balance	+254	+334	+398	+394	+435	+388	+378	+334	+498	+554	+502
Transfers balance	-88	-97	-123	-159	-169	-181	-216	-223	-206	-178	-193
Invisibles balance	+187	+255	+244	+185	+230	+238	+330	+468	+714	+857	+934
CURRENT BALANCE	+47	+155	+125	-358	-30	+130	-269	-244	+505	+823	+1 124
FINANCIAL ACCOUNT											
Investment and other capital transactions	-316	-3	-99	-311	-316	-579	-504	-755	-169	+549	+1 792
EEA loss on forward commitments	-	-	-	-	-	-	-105	-251	-	-	-
Allocation of SDRs	-	-	-	-	-	-	-	-	-	+171	+125
Gold subscription to IMF(-)	-	-	-	-	-	-44	-	-	-	-38	-
Official financing											
Net transactions with overseas monetary authorities[2]	+370	-375	+5	+573	+599	+625	+556	+1 296	-699	-1 295	-1 817
Foreign currency borrowing (net)	-	-	-	-	-	-	-	-	+56	-	+82
Official reserves (drawings on +/ additions to -)	-31	+183	+53	+122	-246	-34	+115	+114	-44	-125	-1 536
Balancing Item	-70	+40	-84	-26	-7	-98	+207	-160	+351	-85	+230

£ million

	1972	*1973*	*1974*	*1975*	*1976*	*1977*	*1978*	*1979*	*1980*	*1981*	*1982*	*1983*
CURRENT ACCOUNT												
Visible balance	-748	-2 586	-5 351	-3 333	-3 929	-2 284	-1 542	-3 449	+1 233	+3 008	+2 119	-500
Invisibles												
Services balance	+701	+786	+1 075	+1 515	+2 503	+3 338	+3 816	+4 071	+4 267	+4 249	+3 844	+4 389
Interest, profits and dividends balance	+538	+1 257	+1 415	+773	+1 365	+116	+661	+990	-186	+1 257	+1 577	+480
Transfers balance	-268	-436	-417	-468	-775	-1 116	-1 777	-2 265	-2 079	-1 967	-2 112	-2 320
Invisibles balance	+971	+1 607	+2 073	+1 820	+3 093	+2 338	+2 700	+2 796	+2 002	+3 539	+3 309	+2 549
CURRENT BALANCE	+223	-979	-3 278	-1 513	-836	+54	+1 158	-653	-3 235	+6 547	+5 428	+2 049
Capital transfers	-	-59	-75	-	-	-	-	-	-	-	-	-
FINANCIAL ACCOUNT												
Investment and other capital transactions	-673	+178	+1 602	+154	-2 975	+4 156	-4 263	+2 157	-1 887	-7 594	-2 851	-2 044
Allocation of SDRs(+)	+124	-	-	-	-	-	-	+195	+180	+158	-	-
Official financing												
Net transactions with overseas monetary authorities	+449	-	-	-	+984	+1 113	-1 016	-596	-140	-145	-163	-213
Foreign currency borrowing (net)	-	+999	+1 751	+810	+1 791	+1 114	-187	-250	-941	-1 587	+26	-
Official reserves (drawings on +/ addition to -)	+692	-228	-105	+655	+853	-9 588	+2 329	-1 059	-291	+2 419	+1 421	+603
Balancing Item	-815	+89	+105	-106	+183	+3 141	+1 979	+206	-156	+202	-3 861	-821

[1] Figures for earlier years are published in earlier editions of this publication and are given back to 1946 in *United Kingdom Balance of Payments 1971*, and also in *Economic Trends Annual Supplement* (1979) and later editions).

[2] Including transfers from dollar portfolio to reserves in 1966 and 1967.

Source UK Official balance of payments statistic 1984.

THE CHANGING NATURE OF UK TRADE AND PAYMENTS

The United Kingdom has a very open economy, so the development of trade flows is a very important aspect of economic performance and prospects. Over the period 1974 to 1980, exports of goods and services accounted for an average 29% of UK gross domestic product (GDP), the highest percentage for any of the major seven western economies. This percentage has increased significantly over the past 20 years – it was only around 20% in the early 1960s. Similar rises have occurred in most other developed countries, reflecting the growing importance of international trade in an increasingly interdependent world economy (see Table 8.4).

Table 8.4

How Exports have Grown (as a percentage of GDP in the main industrialised countries)

	1960-65	*Averages 1967-73*	*% 1974-80*
United Kingdom	20.2	22.5	28.8
France	13.8	15.8	21.2
Germany	18.2	21.1	25.9
Italy	14.8	17.8	25.1
United States	5.1	5.6	8.7
Canada	18.9	22.5	25.5
Japan	9.9	10.5	12.9

Source: OECD

Since 1970 there have been significant structural changes in the United Kingdom's visible trade, in terms of both composition and trading pattern. In particular, the development of the energy resources of the North Sea and membership of the European Economic Community (EEC) have had a major impact. Changes in the composition of visible trade have been most pronounced over recent years. Exports of crude oil and petroleum products have risen sharply, whilst the share of manufactured exports has fallen since 1975. Imports of manufactured goods, on the other hand, have become increasingly important, and by 1981 accounted for some 64% of total imports, compared with around 53% in 1975.

An analysis of the United Kingdom's major trading partners reveals a major shift in favour of Western Europe. Although membership of the EEC has accelerated this trend, such a movement had been evident before 1973. By 1980, Australia, South Africa and Canada no longer featured in the United Kingdom's top 10 trading partners, following a reorientation of trade in favour of the EEC and oil exporting countries. At the same time, there has been an increase in the concentration of UK trade. In 1970, the top ten export markets accounted for around 52% of total exports; 10 years later, the proportion had increased to just over 61%. Figures for UK imports reflect a similar pattern. Thus, not only has UK trade shifted towards Western Europe, and towards the EEC in particular, but it has also become increasingly concentrated in fewer markets (see Figure 8.2).

The changing composition of UK visible exports and imports is illustrated in Table 8.5. The fall of manufacturing exports and increase in manufactured imports between 1963 and 1982 is striking. Similarly the increase in food, drink, tobacco, basic materials and fuel exports and the decrease in the importance of these items as imports should also be noted.

Table 8.5
Changing Structure of UK Exports and Imports (as a percentage of total trade)

	Exports	*Imports*
Food, drink, tobacco basic material and fuels		
1963	12	47
1972	8	30
1982	23	25
Manufactures		
1963	62	27
1972	58	42
1982	51	52
Services		
1963	26	27
1972	31	26
1982	24	20

Source: Bank of England, *Quarterly Bulletin* (December 1983). Reproduced by kind permission of the Bank of England.

As can be seen from Table 8.3 and Figure 8.3 the UK has traditionally had an invisible balance surplus and visible balance deficit. Indeed since 1971, with the exceptions of the early 1980s, the UK has had a visible trade deficit.

The balance on invisibles has traditionally made a large positive contribution to the UK's balance of payments. Invisibles have been in surplus since 1948, while the balance of visible trade has been favourable in just a few years over this period – 1956, 1958, 1971, and the early 1980s. For the last four years the balance on invisibles has been around £2 b, with a £6 b surplus on private sector and public corporations' net earnings from services and interest, profits

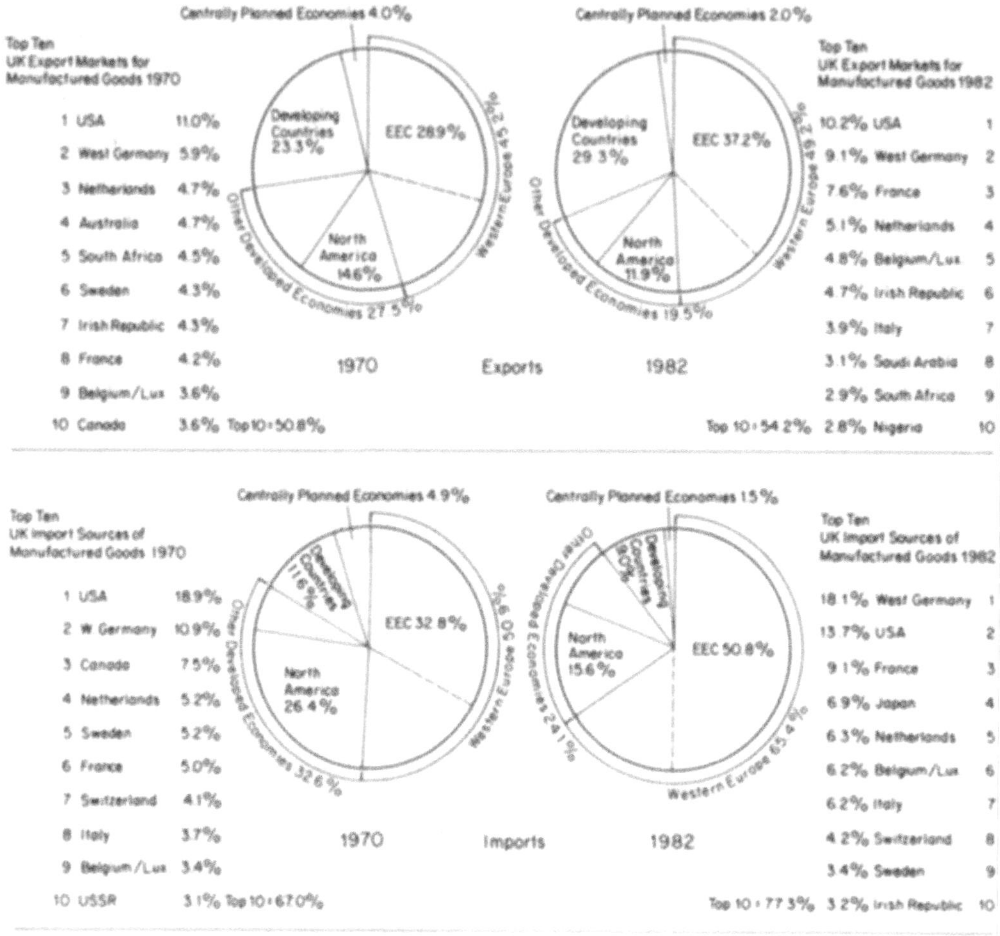

Fig. 8.2 Area Analysis of UK Trade in Manufactured Goods

Source: Overseas Trade Statistics of the United Kingdom

and dividends offset by a deficit of nearly £4 billion on general government transactions and private transfers.

NORTH SEA OIL: ITS CONTRIBUTION TO THE UK BALANCE OF PAYMENTS AND TO GNP

Oil's effect on the UK balance of payments comes through in several ways. Three are on the current account:

(1) Visible exports plus imports saved. Despite being a net exporter of oil, Britain imported nearly £5½ b of other countries' oil in 1983. Most oil is blended to produce petrol, diesel, etc. North Sea Oil is of a high quality, so it is mixed with lower-grade imports at domestic refineries, leaving a

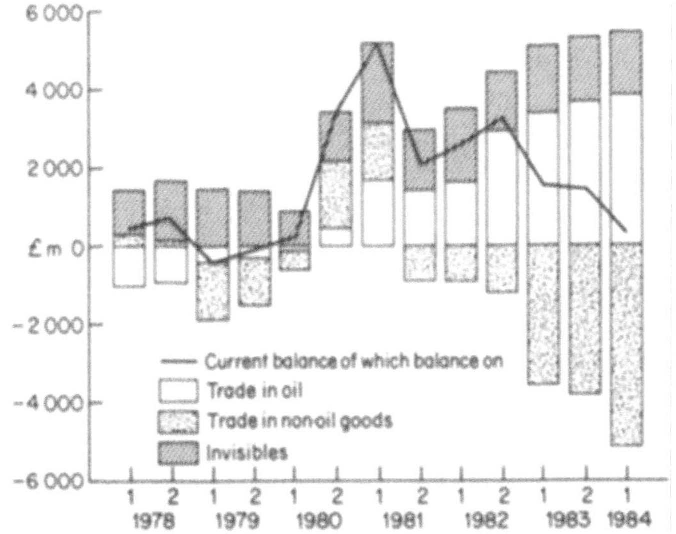

Fig. 8.3 Balance of Payment current accounts

Source: CSO
Reproduced by permission of Her Majesty's Stationery Office

large (and higher-priced) surplus to be exported. The current account "savings" are therefore quite complicated to pin down. For simplicity, they can be measured by the total value of oil and gas production (see Figure 8.4).

(2) Interest, profits and dividends going overseas. Foreign oil companies produce half of all the North Sea's oil, hold 57% of the exploration rights, and have invested about twice as much in oil and gas production as British companies have done. They are now taking out their rewards which count as a debit on invisible trade whether or not they are actually repatriated. If they retain their profits in Britain (e.g. for reinvestment), it shows up as a capital inflow. By 1985, the interest, profits and dividends due to foreign companies will be worth an estimated 16% of all oil and gas production.

(3) Capital inflows connected with the North Sea are treated as a credit on the capital account. They were heavy in the mid-1970s, the result of foreign companies bringing in capital to finance their operations and of British companies borrowing from abroad. Since then they have tapered off, though they are still positive.

Overall, the North Sea has given a large boost to the balance of payments (see Figure 8.4). On the current account, oil and gas production in 1980 was worth the equivalent of 10% of total exports of goods and services. The North Sea's net contribution in 1981 was about £10 billion, more than three times what it was in 1978. Since Britain ran a current account surplus of about £6 billion in

1981, the North Sea Oil benefit loomed large. However in later years interest, profits and dividends due abroad substantially increased.

One must however be careful in comparing these figures directly. Without the North Sea, the British economy would have behaved very differently; sterling's exchange rate would have been lower, and non-oil exports higher.

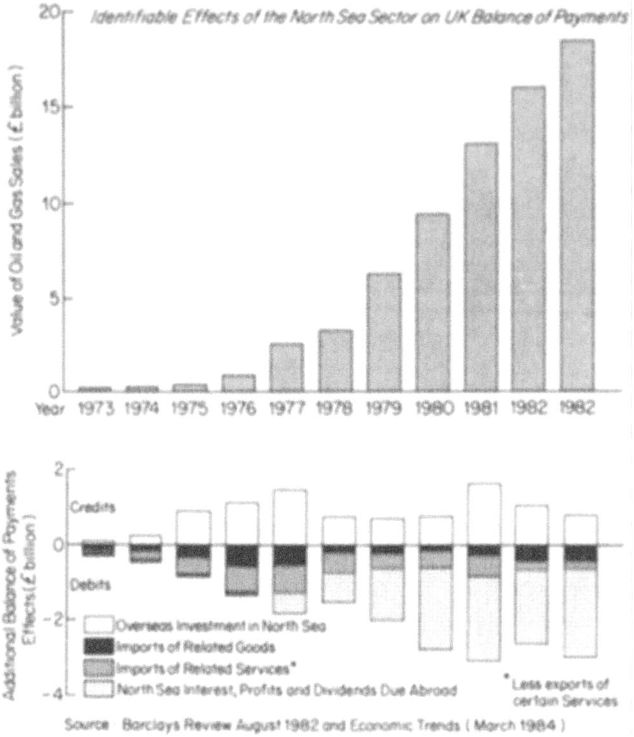

Fig. 8.4

Treasury estimates of the contribution of North Sea oil and gas to gross national product are set out in Table 8.6 below. The contribution is defined as the total sales value of oil and gas production and services rendered, less the goods and services bought by the North Sea sector, and interest profits and dividends due abroad.

The contribution of North Sea oil and gas is now estimated to have been about 5¼% in 1983 compared with 4¾% in 1982. The sector's contribution to GNP is projected to show a slight fall in 1984, partly because of a forecasted rise in total GNP and partly because real sterling oil prices are assumed to fall compared with their level in 1983. With oil production projected to peak between 1984 and 1988 the contribution of the sector to GNP is assumed to fall to about 4% by 1988.

Table 8.6
The Contribution of North Sea Oil and Gas to GNP: Estimates to 1988

£ billion, current prices

	1980	*1981*	*1982*	*1983*	*1984*	*1988*
Value of oil and gas sales	9.6	13.3	15.5	18.3	19.7	19.5
less goods and services purchased*	1.0	1.4	1.9	2.2	2.5	2.9
less IPD due abroad	2.2	2.4	2.6	3.0	3.2	2.7
GNP arising within sector	6.4	9.5	11.0	13.1	14.1	13.9
AS % of total GNP† in that year	3¼	4½	4¾	5¼	5	4

*Defined as operating plus exploration costs less employment incomes.
†The projection of the denominator - total GDP at factor cost - is based on GDP in money terms growing at the rates assumed in the MTFS.

Source: The Financial Statement and Budget Report (1984).

THE ADJUSTMENT PROBLEM

If all transactions have been recorded correctly, the over-all balance of payments must balance exactly. An excess of expenditure over income implies more foreign currency going abroad than is received from abroad. The extra foreign currency must either come from borrowing from the reserves, or both. Each of these generates a surplus which offsets the deficit generated by the excess expenditure.

However some form of adjustment will inevitably be required if a country persistently faces the problem of finding official finance, given that the official reserves are finite and borrowing may not be possible, may be expensive or involve onerous 'conditions' attached to the loans.

Adjustment can take place on either the current account the capital account or both. Adjustment policies can be either automatic or discretionary. The basic difference is that automatic adjustment comes about by itself as a result of prevailing economic forces, whereas discretionary adjustment requires policy actions to rectify the disequilibrium. Two groups of discretionary policies are possible; expenditure reducing policies and expenditure switching policies. These will all be discussed in turn.

(1) AUTOMATIC ADJUSTMENT

An optimistic school of thought maintains that balance of payments deficits are usually transient phenomena and that automatic forces are brought into play to reverse deficits or surpluses. Automatic adjustment may come about when, with imports being greater than exports, an economy suffers a fall in incomes and prices, imports (income related) fall and exports (price related) rise. In addition with a fall in the money supply associated with the outflow of domestic currency interest rates would rise, attracting capital inflows thereby improving the capital account, and reducing domestic spending and prices.

To be more precise there are three ways in which a balance of payments disequilibrium can be "cured" automatically. To correct a deficit (and conversely) a surplus each of these involves a fall in home money income in line with the fall in foreign money earnings (as exports fall). First there could be a fall without any decline in the physical volume of domestic production and employment if there was a fall in prices and wages at which goods and services were valued. This would stimulate exports and reduce imports. Secondly home income could fall through a shrinkage in the physical volume of goods and services produced with prices and wage rates unchanged. Again as fewer domestic goods are bought then domestic incomes fall thereby reducing the demand for foreign goods. Thirdly home income could fall if there was a decrease in the exchange rate making domestic goods more competitive abroad and foreign goods more expensive at home.

Which mechanism or combination of these mechanisms operates depends at least in part on the international financial arrangements amongst the various countries. Under a gold standard or fixed exchange rate standard requiring governments to fix their exchange rates the first and second mechanisms operate together. The gold standard was a particular form of fixed exchange rates within which the price of gold was fixed in terms of domestic currency, and therefore the exchange rate was determined for all countries adhering to this standard by the ratios of gold prices specified in domestic currencies. Since the exchange rate was fixed, a balance of payments surplus would be met by inflows of international specie (gold). This approach, known as the price-specie flow mechanism, was discussed in the eighteenth century by David Hume. With the domestic money supply based on gold, the inflow of gold induced by a balance of payments surplus would cause in its turn an expansion of the domestic money supply. In line with the traditional quantity theory discussed in Chapter 1 it was believed that this would drive up the domestic price level. If the rate of increase of the domestic price level was faster than the rate at which the rest of the world price level was increasing, then imports would expand and exports contract until such time as the balance of payments surplus was eliminated. Conversely, a balance of payments deficit would entail an outflow of gold, which would result in a decrease in the domestic money supply and the domestic price level; and the falling prices would be expected to improve the balance of payments. Thus the important prediction of this approach was that there was an automatic adjustment mechanism which would lead to the correction of balance of payments disequilibria. Naturally the extent to which automatic adjustment occurred would depend on the extent to which there was this degree of wage and price flexibility.

If the countries had flexible exchange rates the third mechanism would operate. The mechanism and limitations of relying on exchange rate changes to automatically cure balance of payments problems are discussed further on pages 246 *et seq*.

(2) DISCRETIONARY ADJUSTMENT

Proponents of the need for discretionary adjustment (i.e. government induced adjustment) maintain that automatic adjustments, if they occur, operate with a long time lag during which time the country risks losing its entire foreign exchange reserves and/or paying unacceptable costs of foreign borrowings and that therefore governments need to take action to ensure that the appropriate adjustments occur.

The two major types of discretionary adjustment policies are known as "*expenditure-reducing*" and "*expenditure-switching*". The former policy is based on the observation that the level of imports is related to domestic national income. Fiscal and monetary policies designed to reduce domestic demand (and thereby incomes) should improve the current account by reducing the volume of imports. Exports should not be affected as much because they are related more to overseas demand.

Expenditure-reducing policies include cuts in government expenditure, increases in taxation, and changes in monetary variables such as interest rates and the money supply.

The policy of expenditure-reducing is often referred to as deflation. Deflation affects expenditure and production by reducing the money supply, forcing money incomes and possibly prices down, and making new expenditure, particularly on investment less attractive. Expenditure on foreign goods is reduced along with expenditure on domestic goods.

The problem with deflation is that it imposes *high adjustment costs* of having an external disequilibrium (i.e. balance of payments deficits). Prices respond only slowly to a lower level of demand because of rigidities in the goods and labour markets: deflationary policies therefore impose a high cost in terms of foregone output and high unemployment in the period of adjustment. In addition, if investment is curtailed because of the fall in demand, this may impair the efficiency of industry and hence its future capacity to compete in world markets. Finally there are the social costs of high unemployment. It is for this reason that expenditure switching policies are frequently advocated.

Expenditure-switching policies are policies which induce a switch of expenditure towards home-produced and away from foreign produced goods. Two types of expenditure-switching policies can be distinguished. One is devaluation, which by making the country's goods relatively cheap compared with foreign goods will tend to switch both domestic and foreign expenditure towards domestically-produced goods. The other is by the introduction of protectionist measures. These are usually designed to reduce imports and can take various forms. They include tariffs, quotas, "voluntary" restraint, orderly marketing arrangements, administrative delays, government purchasing schemes and subsidies, etc. They are discussed further on pp. 251–255.

(1) Devaluation

Devaluation is defined as a reduction of the value of the domestic currency (say the pound sterling) relative to foreign currencies. The objective of devaluation is to lower the foreign selling price of exports and to raise the domestic buying price of imports. The foreign selling price of a commodity is its domestic price multiplied by the exchange rate. The domestic buying price of an import is the overseas price multiplied by the exchange rate.

A devaluation means that it requires less of the foreign currency to buy the home currency. So the foreign selling price can then be lowered which may well increase the volume of exports. Similarly a devaluation of the home currency means that it now requires more domestic currency to buy the same amount of foreign currency. This means that the domestic buying price of an import would rise which in turn may lower the volume of imports. This will become clearer with a numerical example. It is convenient to illustrate the effect of devaluation by using the sterling exchange rate with the dollar, but the same effects hold for other major currencies.

On 18 November 1967 the UK devalued the pound sterling from US$2.80 = £1 to US$2.40 = £1. What does this devaluation mean in terms of export prices and profitability and of import prices? A UK exporter who sold goods for US$280 in the USA before devaluation received £100 for them. After devaluation three options are open to him:

(1) Continue to sell the goods in the USA for US$280; then he will receive not £100 but £116.66 and thus have a really big increase in profit per unit.
(2) Sell the goods for US$240, when he will receive £100 as before but can expect an increase in his total sales because his foreign selling price is now one-seventh (14.3%) less than before. The size of the increase in demand and sales depends on the response of demand (the elasticity), but unless this is zero, there will be some increase in sales.
(3) Sell the goods at an intermediate price between US$280 and US$240, in which case his profit per unit will rise (but not as much as in the first instance) and his sales increase (but not as much as in the second instance). Thus devaluation makes exporting easier and more profitable.

The purpose of a devaluation is to enable a country to earn more foreign currency on exports and spend less foreign currency on imports. Devaluation encourages exports because exports have become cheaper or exporting has become more profitable or a combination of the two; this applies to both visible and invisible exports.

On the import side the effect of a devaluation is to raise import prices in terms of the domestic currency (the domestic buying price). An import from the USA priced at US$280 which cost £100 before devaluation costs £116.66 afterwards, a rise of nearly 17%. This higher price is designed to discourage imports and encourage the substitution of home-produced goods, which are now relatively cheaper, for imports. This reasoning applies also to invisible imports; thus, for example, devaluation not only encourages foreigners to take holidays in the devaluing country because these are cheaper, it also encourages nationals to holiday at home because domestic holidays have become cheaper relative to holidays abroad.

A Caveat

It should be stressed that one of the purposes of devaluation is to make exporting more profitable. It does not follow that if a firm retains its pre-devaluation price in terms of foreign currencies (i.e. puts up prices in terms of its own currency), this is necessarily contrary to the purposes of devaluation. For example, the additional profit margin might be more effectively used for a sales campaign than by offering lower prices; if demand is unresponsive to price, i.e. inelastic, more foreign currency would be earned by retaining the previous price in terms of foreign currency than by lowering it. Earnings of foreign currencies are only increased from lower export prices if sales expand more than proportionately to the reduction in price (i.e. if the price elasticity of demand is greater than one and supply is elastic – this is discussed further below).

The Importance of the Marshall-Lerner Conditions

The increase in demand for a country's goods, due to an improvement in its international price competitiveness, is predicted and measured by the price elasticity of its exports and imports. From these elasticities economists calculate the effect of a change in competitiveness on the balance of trade, and also try to predict its effect on domestic output and employment. These elasticities do not directly measure the improvement in the balance of trade or current payments, as they only relate to the volume of trade.

The rise in import prices relative to export prices, which a fall in an exchange rate produces, worsens the terms of trade (the ratio of export prices to import prices). However devaluation will alter the volumes of production as competitiveness is altered. The question which needs to be answered is: following a devaluation, will the positive volume effects offset this worsening in the terms of trade? The rule derived to answer this question is known as the Marshall-Lerner condition. The Marshall-Lerner condition states that, under certain assumptions, devaluation will improve the balance of trade of a country and appreciation will worsen it if the sum of the price elasticities of demand for a country's exports and of the price elasticities of demand for imports are greater than one.

In order to see why this is the case let us examine different assumptions about price elasticities. Discussion of the Marshall-Lerner conditions may be undertaken in terms of the currency of the devaluing country or in terms of the currency of the other country, but not in terms of both currencies. This Section will examine the consequences of a sterling devaluation. Throughout the Section we will assume that following a sterling devaluation export prices remain unchanged in sterling terms and import prices remain unchanged in dollar terms, i.e. foreign export prices and home import prices move fully in line with the devaluation.

In Table 8.7 the United States elasticity of demand for UK exports is assumed to be 2 and the United Kingdom's elasticity of demand for US imports is assumed to be 1½, so that the sum of elasticities of demand is 3½. (Strictly speaking price elasticities should be negative.) A 10% sterling devaluation is assumed. The price of UK exports in terms of sterling, as assumed, remains unchanged. However the dollar price of UK exports is reduced 10% by devaluation. A 10% fall in price induces a 20% increase in quantity demanded when the elasticity of demand is 2.

Table 8.7

Elasticity of demand of exports = 2 Sum = 3½
Elasticity of demand for imports = 1½
10% sterling devaluation

$$\text{Elasticity} = \frac{\text{Percentage change in export volume}}{\text{Percentage change in export price}} = \text{elasticity of demand for exports} = \frac{20\%}{10\%} = 2$$

$$\text{elasticity of demand for imports} = \frac{\text{Percentage change in import volume}}{\text{Percentage change in import price}} = \frac{15}{10} = 1\tfrac{1}{2}$$

	Change in Sterling Price	*Change in Quantity*	*Yields*
Row 1	...	+20%	+20% receipts
Row 2	+10%	-15%	-5% expenditure
		Net *improvement*	25%

In row 1 the sterling price of exports is shown unchanged and quantity is shown to rise by 20%, so that receipts in sterling rise by approximately 20%. The price of UK imports in sterling terms rises by 10% as a result of devaluation. Given the elasticity of demand for imports of 1½, quantity demanded falls by 15%. A 10% rise in price combined with a 15% fall in quantity leads to an approximately 5% fall in expenditure. The 20% increase in receipts combined with a 5% fall in expenditure leads to a reduced deficit and an improvement in the balance of Trade. So if the sum of the elasticities is greater than 1 the trade balance is improved by devaluation.

In Table 8.8 it is assumed that each elasticity of demand is ½ so that the sum of the elasticities of demand equals 1. Again a 10% sterling devaluation is assumed. The change in sterling receipts from exports is shown in row 1; devaluation (again as assumed) does not affect the sterling price of exports, but as a result of devaluation, the price of UK exports is 10% cheaper in dollars. With an elasticity of demand for exports of ½, quantity will increase by 5% upon a 10% fall in price. Thus sterling receipts for exports will increase by approximately 5%. Whether the balance of trade is improved by devaluation also depends on what happens to sterling expenditures on imports. The

Table 8.8

Each elasticity of demand = ½, sum = 1
10% devaluation of sterling

$$\text{Elasticity} = \frac{5\%}{10\%} = \frac{1}{2}$$

	Change in Sterling Price	*Change in Quantity*	*Yields*
Row 1	...	+5%	+5% receipts
Row 2	+10%	-5%	+5% expenditure
		Net change	0

devaluation makes the sterling price of all imports rise by 10%. Given the elasticity of demand for imports of ½, this increase of 10% in price brings a fall of 5% in quantity demanded. Expenditure on imports rises by approximately 5%. Devaluation brought about an equal increase in export receipts and import expenditure. Thus if the sum of the elasticities of demand is equal to 1, the trade balance will be unaffected by devaluation.

When the sum of elasticities of demand is greater than 1, devaluation improves the balance of trade; when it is equal to 1, devaluation does not affect the trade balance. The consequences of devaluation when the sum of the elasticities of demand is less than 1 must by now be considered.

Again assume the sterling price of exports is unaffected by devaluation, as shown in row 1 of Table 8.9, but the dollar price of UK exports is 10% cheaper. The fall in price of 10% will induce an increase in quantity of 2½%, with an elasticity of demand for exports of ¼. With the sterling price unchanged and quantity increased by 2½% receipts in sterling terms increased by approximately 2½%. Devaluation increases the sterling price of imports by 10%. Given the elasticity of demand for imports of ¼, the 10% increase in price results in a fall in the quantity of imports of 2½%. A 10% increase in price combined with a 2½% fall in quantity yields a 7½% increase in expenditure on imports. Receipts from exports increased by 2½%; expenditure on imports by 7½%. Devaluation, with the sum of elasticities of demand less than 1, results in expenditures increasing by more than receipts, thereby making the trade balance worse.

Table 8.9

Each elasticity of demand = ¼, sum = ½
10% devaluation of sterling

$$\text{Elasticity} = \frac{2.5\%}{10\%} = \frac{1}{4}$$

	Change in Sterling Price	*Change in Quantity*	*Yields*
Row 1	...	+2.5%	+2.5% receipts
Row 2	+10%	-2.5%	+7.5% expenditure
		Net *increase* in expenditure	5.0%

The elasticities approach to analysing balance of payments adjustment is however subject to some major flaws. The first major flaw in this analysis is that domestic wage earners are unlikely to accept readily a reduction in their real incomes at the same time as a redistribution of domestic incomes towards profits is taking place. Hence it can be difficult to control internal costs, so that the benefit of the devaluation is quickly eroded. Trade unions may demand higher wages to offset rising import costs in turn forcing the manufacturer to raise his foreign selling price and placing him at a competitive disadvantage.

The second main flaw in the elementary analysis of how devaluation is expected to work is that clear-cut advantages are presumed to appear automatically across most of industry, shifting demand towards the devaluing country's goods. That view is based upon two false assumptions – firstly that non-price factors are unimportant and secondly that small scale firms dominate production. By non-price factors is meant that factors other than price may be all-important in influencing sales so that even if the product is cheaper there will not be an increased market for it. Non-price factors are considerations such as after-sales service, reliability, delivery times, etc.

The second false assumption is that small firms dominate production. In fact some 60% of world trade takes place between the subsidiaries of multinational companies. Their decisions as to where to sell products may be unresponsive to the potential benefits of devaluation and will reflect broader corporate considerations. So international firms in important export sectors tend to divide up their international markets between different subsidiaries and to avoid large scale direct competition between subsidiaries in different foreign markets. For this reason the increased export competitiveness, which would be possible for a national firm decreasing its prices in line with a national devaluation, may be ruled out by a multinational company for those markets in which it has other subsidiaries with which the increased exports would compete.

This is quite apart from the fact that multinational companies tend to operate in oligopolistic markets in which a few companies influence the prices on a world of regional scale. For various reasons these companies tend to earn "super-normal" profits of a kind which allows them considerable room for manoeuvre if either their costs rise or their prices fall in relation to other currencies, following a devaluation. In general, they make considerable efforts to avoid a price war with their principal regional or world competitors which may leave them all worse off in the longer run. Consequently multinational companies may tend not to reduce export prices by the full extent of a devaluation.

A third flaw in the analysis entails a consideration of what is known as the J-curve. The J-curve is caused by prices changing more rapidly than traded volumes can change. A country's import bill in terms of its own currency is, as already discussed, increased overnight by a devaluation of its currency. The revenue from its exports is initially unchanged. Its trade balance initially

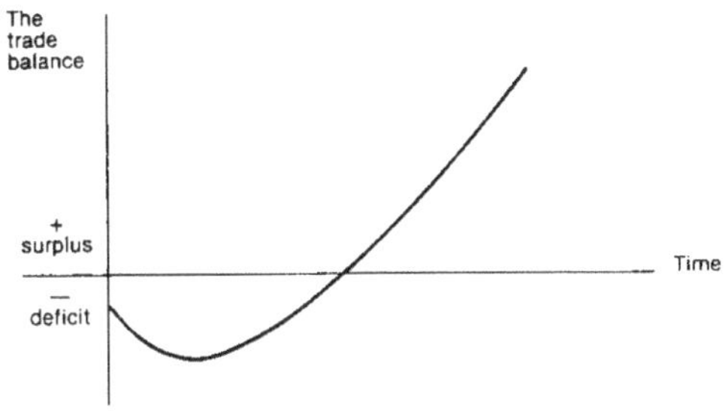

Fig. 8.5 The J-Curve

gets worse at a stroke. But then the theory goes higher priced imports are progressively replaced by cheaper home-produced substitutes. Exports expand because they are cheaper in foreign currency terms on overseas markets. The trade balance gradually improves.

Thus the J-curve is a way of describing the phenomenon whereby imports are less price-elastic than exports (which is the case for most industrial countries) causing the effect of devaluation on prices to be unfavourable. However, with high price elasticities increased volumes of exports in due course occur, overcoming the adverse price effect. Hence both the dip and the rising right side of the J. For the various reasons mentioned above, in particular with relation to export volumes, the trade balance however may not improve even some time after a devaluation.

The existence of the J-curve is actually a reflection of the fact that there are lags in the trade elasticities so that the Marshall-Lerner conditions are not initially satisfied.

(2) Protectionist Measures

There are a variety of means by which one country may limit or prohibit the inflow of foreign produced goods into the domestic economy: such policies go under the collective name of "protectionism". When adopting such a strategy, the government is employing tools which either make it more difficult, or more expensive, or impossible, for the purchase of imported goods. The most widely known of import controls are "Tariffs" and "Quotas".

Tariffs are a tax on foreign produced goods. Levied at varying percentages they result in the sellers of the imported commodities having to raise their domestic purchase price. The impact on domestic consumers and on their demand for imports then has two facets. Firstly, there is the income effect. The higher post-tariff price of imports effectively cuts the real income of consumers, and their demand for imports falls. Secondly, there is the substitution effect. With imports higher in price after the imposition of the tariff, consumers may deem it rational to switch to cheaper, home-produced alternatives. This will stimulate demand, production and employment domestically at the expense of the country producing the imports. Unlike devaluation tariffs do not involve a terms of trade loss.

Quotas are quantitative restrictions on imports. By stating a limit on the volume of categories of goods which may be imported within a given period (usually a year) the government exerts a direct control on the flow of imports and the level of import expenditure. This direct rationing of imports contrasts with the tariff system which is dependent upon the mechanics of the price system and the rationality of consumer choice. At its most extreme, a quota of zero may be imposed on categories of goods or upon the goods made within a specific country. This is termed an embargo, and is usually applied only under specific political (as opposed to economic) circumstances. A recent example was the embargo on trade imposed by many Western economies against Iran in 1980.

Other types of protectionism some of which were discussed earlier in this Chapter include:

Health and safety standards, demanded for imported goods. By imposing strict safety standards on certain goods (in the name of consumer wellbeing) imports would be curbed by the inability of foreign producers to meet the required specifications. With large-scale production methods, the necessary changes may only be effected over the long run. It is only when the final goods meet the stipulated health and safety standards that import licences are granted for the overseas produce. The limited penetration of British-made cars into the Japanese market has been ascribed to such safety and health standard protectionism, applied by the Japanese government.

Exchange controls. Imports must eventually be paid for in the currency of the producer country (e.g. Datsuns paid for in Yen). Placing limits on the amounts of domestic currency which may be exchanged for foreign currencies; or even denying convertibility between domestic and certain foreign currencies, will lead to a cut in import levels.

Government subsidies to domestic industry may be viewed as an indirect form of protectionism when such subsidies are paid to import competing firms. Such subsidies will facilitate a cut in the final price of the domestically produced goods, allowing them to undercut the imported goods.

Informal agreements between importing and exporting countries. The most notorious example of these is the agreement between Japan and Britain on the export of Japanese cars to the British Isles. By negotiation a level of 10–11% of the British market was assigned to Japanese-produced cars for the period 1976 to 1980.

ARE IMPORT CONTROLS DESIRABLE?

THE ARGUMENTS AGAINST

First import controls *undermine free trade* and reduce the living standards of those within the trading community. Just as Adam Smith stated in the eighteenth century and David Ricardo in the nineteenth, so twentieth century economists, as discussed earlier in this Chapter (pp. 222–223), stress that free trade enables consumers throughout the world to make purchases of goods from the lowest priced and most efficient producers. If low price imports undercut domestic producers the consumer benefits through an increase in real income. The resources employed by the relatively inefficient industries can be diverted into more productive areas. The logic is simple: free trade maximises consumer welfare by enabling production and sales of each good to be undertaken by the most efficient producer in the global economy. By contrast, if import controls are adopted consumers may be diverted from making purchases from the most efficient producers (remember the provisos mentioned earlier).

Secondly, it is argued that import controls may *induce retaliation* by other countries who experience a cut in their exports. As retaliation follows protectionism, the export sector in each trading country contracts. The burden is borne by the consumers who pay for the protectionist policies via higher prices and cuts in real income. Any gain one country can achieve from import controls will only last the time it takes other countries to take retaliatory action.

Thirdly, import controls are deemed to be *unfair*, or non-neutral, in their impact on consumers in the importing country. Since different individuals allocate varying proportions of their income to import expenditure, any controls will fall most heavily on those with the greatest propensity to import.

Fourthly, the belief that *import controls will stimulate domestic production and employment may be misguided*. If domestic citizens are forced to buy fewer foreign goods they may buy domestic goods which may otherwise have been exported. Only if the restricted imports are replaced by an increase in production of domestic substitutes can import controls work.

A final argument against import controls applies specifically to the circumstances of Britain. The United Kingdom's *dependence on trade* (discussed on pp. 238–240) makes policies which threaten UK exports (like import controls and retaliation) inadvisable. Moreover, it is argued that controls, like tariffs, tend to have little impact upon UK import demand. This is because British demand for imports is price inelastic i.e. price changes, like those induced by tariffs, do not affect demand greatly. The reason for this is that many of the United Kingdom's imports are "essentials" like fuel and food-stuffs. If tariffs are to be used by Britain, they would have to be applied selectively, to goods with a high price elasticity of demand (like consumer durables) to be effective.

THE ARGUMENTS IN FAVOUR

Those who argue in favour of import controls usually state that, in specific circumstances, they are preferential to free trade. This would particularly be the case if the latter leads to a rapid rise in domestic unemployment and mass closure of firms. The arguments in favour of import controls fall into five categories.

First, the *temporary transformation argument*: this approach states that as an economy will go through periods of adjustment in its structure of production and that during such times protectionism is needed to facilitate a smooth transition. Thus an infant industry, just established in the domestic economy, may require protection from existing foreign competition. The latter might already be benefiting from economies of scale, low-cost production and expertise and would stifle the emergent domestic industry (with initial high costs and technical inexperience) unless it were protected by import controls.

Similarly contracting industries (such as shipbuilding and textiles in Britain) may require time to adjust to the changing economic environment. Labour would have to be reskilled and capital stocks redeployed. During this time import controls can be used to allow the transition period to be as smooth as possible. Limitations on imports would help to avoid high unemployment and regional depression.

Secondly, the *anti-dumping argument*: this states that in certain circumstances free trade leaves domestic industry open to unfair competition from overseas. This occurs when overseas commodities are sold or "dumped" in a country at below cost price. The motivation behind such dumping varies: some countries short of hard currencies (like dollars) may dump goods to obtain foreign exchange. This has been the case with East European countries. Alternatively, dumping may be a means of establishing a sellers' monopoly in the importing country by undercutting and eliminating domestic competition. Once established the good can then be raised in price to recoup earlier losses. Dumping may also be used to get rid of excess production – like agricultural surpluses – or to facilitate market penetration in overseas countries. Accusations of dumping have been applied most frequently to Japanese goods in the past decade. For instance the closure of Thorn Electrical (colour TV tubes) in Skelmersdale in 1976 was ascribed to the dumping of TV tubes in Britain by the Japanese. Under such circumstances the effects of import controls may be deemed to be more acceptable than free trade.

Thirdly, the *Balance of Payments argument:* countries with a deficit on their international payments can reduce it by using curbs to cut import expenditure. This policy was used by the Labour Government in 1965, when an import surcharge was imposed. It was introduced as an alternative to fiscal and monetary deflation.

Fourthly, the *Terms of Trade argument:* the terms of trade is the ratio between exported and imported goods' pre-tariff price levels. If tariffs are imposed upon imported goods, the overseas producer may feel it necessary to cut the price of the goods (reducing the post-tariff price to the pre-tariff price) in order to maintain its share in the domestic market. The terms of trade now move in favour of the country imposing the tariffs: they can now buy more imports (at the lower prices) for a given level of exports.

Fifthly, the *"cheap labour" argument:* import controls can be used to circumvent competition from imports produced by cheap labour overseas and thus sold at prices below those of domestic goods. Competition under such circumstances is deemed "unfair" due to the foreign producers' access to a cheap resource.

In conclusion, the case for import controls largely rests on the assertion that, particularly at times of change in the structure of the domestic economy, higher import prices and lower real incomes are preferential to mass unemployment and industrial decline.

APPENDIX 1

THE INVISIBLES ACCOUNT

The invisibles accounts are subdivided initially as to the sector which receives or makes payment, i.e. either the general government sector or the private sector and public corporations. The accounts can then be further subdivided into services, interest profits and dividends (IPD) and transfers. For each sector the various sub-components are described.

General Government

This section consists of:

(1) all credit and debit transactions in services between the UK government, including its employees stationed abroad, and overseas residents;

(2) the value of all purchases of goods from non-UK sources by UK government installations abroad.

Credits

European Community institutions. These services comprise receipts by the UK government for its activities as an agency for the collection of contributions to the European Community budget.

US forces' expenditure. These are receipts by the UK government for the United States forces stationed in the United Kingdom for supplies and services.

Other military receipts by UK government. This item includes:

(i) receipts from offshore sales of goods to the United States government;

(ii) contributions from overseas governments towards common defence projects;

(iii) contributions from other NATO countries, from March 1972, towards the cost to the United Kingdom of military facilities in Malta;

(iv) the value of goods held abroad and then handed over to overseas countries by the UK forces;

(v) the value of services provided in the United Kingdom and elsewhere to overseas residents by the services departments, for example military training schemes.

Other receipts. These are the value of services which the government provides to overseas residents under its economic aid programmes and which are then offset under economic grants, plus miscellaneous receipts by the UK government from overseas countries.

Debits

Military expenditure. The items included are:

(i) wage and salary payments to locally engaged staff of UK military bases abroad;

(ii) contributions towards common defence projects;

(iii) local drawings of pay by UK forces;

(iv) local purchases of food, equipment, fuel and services;

(v) total cost of the use by the United Kingdom of military facilities in Malta from 1972–78.

Administrative, diplomatic, etc., expenditure. The operating costs of UK embassies, High Commission offices, consulates, British Council and Commonwealth War Graves Commission account for most of the expenditure under this heading. The wages and salaries of locally engaged staff and the local salary drawings of UK diplomatic and other non-military personnel stationed overseas are also included.

Private Sector and Public Corporation

Sea Transport

Credits consist of the following earnings by UK operators: freight on UK exports, freight on cross-trades (i.e. trade between countries other than the United Kingdom), passenger fare receipts from, and on-board spending by, overseas residents and receipts from the chartering of ships to non-residents.

Conversely *debits* comprise UK operators' disbursements abroad, plus payments by UK residents to overseas operators for time and voyage charters, freight on UK imports, and passenger fares.

Civil Aviation

Credits include receipts by the British airlines from overseas residents for passenger fares, for the carriage of UK exports, freight on cross-trades, mail and charter hire, together with disbursements in the United Kingdom by overseas airlines.

Debits include expenditure abroad by British airlines on airport charges, crews' expenses, charter payments, etc., together with payments to overseas airlines by UK residents for passenger fares, freight on UK imports and the carriage of mail.

Travel

This covers personal expenditure by UK residents in overseas countries and by overseas residents in the United Kingdom.

Financial Services

Items recorded under this heading are the earnings, net of expenses, of financial and allied institutions for services, including brokerage, merchanting, arbitrage, banking charges and commissions, underwriting of capital issues, risk underwriting, and other insurance.

Other Services

This, statistically very large component, consists of:

(a) agent's commissions;
(b) overseas receipts and expenditure from telecommunications and postal services;
(c) film and television payments and receipts;
(d) royalties, licence fees;
(e) expenditure by overseas students;
(f) consulting earnings, etc.

Interest, Profits and Dividends (IPD)

Interest, profits and dividends (IPD) are the returns on the credit side on overseas investments, banking flows, and foreign investment in the United Kingdom. In 1983 they accounted for around 33% of invisible earnings. These current account flows are directly related to entries in the capital account. For example, where a UK subsidiary overseas makes a profit which is reinvested in that subsidiary, the profit will be recorded as an IPD earning while the investment is recorded as a capital outflow which increases the value of the UK's external assets. When the profit is not reinvested overseas, the balance of payments benefit will usually be received in the form of a dividend paid to the UK company by the overseas subsidiary. Interest on borrowing and lending abroad by UK banks in foreign currency is recorded net (interest received less interest paid) to reflect the close link between banks' borrowing and lending.

All interest flows between UK residents and non-residents are included in IPD. These include payments and receipts of interest by UK banks; interest payments by the public sector on that part of its debt held by overseas residents; interest receipts by the public sector on its loans abroad and on holdings of foreign currency assets; interest payments by companies on their overseas borrowing whether to overseas banks, etc. or to affiliates or parents abroad; interest receipts by companies in the United Kingdom from overseas affiliates or parents; and interest receipts by private UK residents on bank deposits overseas.

Profits and dividends include the earnings of overseas affiliates of UK-registered companies and the payments of profits and dividends abroad by UK-based affiliates of foreign-based companies.

Transfers

As we have already explained the basic principle of balance of payments accounting is that there is an interchange of goods, services and financial items of equal value. Thus the grand total of such transactions might be expected to be zero. In practice, however, there are examples of imbalance where one of the parties in the transaction does not expect, or receive, anything in return, i.e. has no quid pro quo. The object of the transfers entries is to provide the notional counterparts of such free gifts in order to bring the overall accounts to a balance.

General government transfers comprise grants to overseas countries, subscriptions and contributions to international organisations, other transfer payments by the UK government to overseas residents and similar receipts from overseas by the United Kingdom government.

General government credits include receipts from the EEC organisations including the agricultural fund, the social fund, the regional development fund and budget refunds. General government debits include bilateral aid, subscriptions and contributions to international organisations, military grants, pensions and benefits. As the UK has a substantial debit on transfers (see Table 8.3) it is worthwhile detailing the main items.

Bilateral aid. This heading covers:

(1) Project grants: Cash grants to developing countries for the establishment or expansion of production and infrastructure facilities.

(2) Non-project grants: Cash grants to developing countries for use in financing imports and budgetary support including the value of goods and services provided without charge by the UK government, e.g. as food aid or disaster relief.

(3) Technical co-operation: This represents the value of the provision of "know-how" to developing countries either as the provision of qualified manpower or facilities for the training of nationals of these countries.

Subscriptions and Contributions to International Organisations

This heading covers:

(1) Contributions to institutions of the European Community, including levy payments made by the steel industry under EC regulations.

(2) Contributions to international organisations for multilateral economic assistance to the developing countries and other international projects.

(3) Subscriptions to meet the United Kingdom's part of the administrative expenses of (a) the United Nations and other international bodies and (b) international military agencies (SEATO, CENTO, etc).

Military grants. These consist of cash grants for military purposes and goods and services of a military nature provided, without charge, to overseas countries and international organisations by the UK government.

Pensions and benefits. These include national insurance pensions and benefits and war pensions paid to overseas residents by UK government departments.

Private transfers comprise gifts of goods sent by parcel post, payments by UK residents to their dependants overseas, transfers of sums by missionary societies, relief organisations and other charitable institutions.

APPENDIX 2

THE CAPITAL ACCOUNT

The components of the capital account, as can be seen from Table 8.10, can be broken down as follows:

Overseas investment in UK public sector consists of net transactions by overseas residents (other than overseas monetary authorities) in UK government and government guaranteed stocks; dated British government foreign currency bonds which were offered in April 1977 to overseas official holders of sterling, local authorities' securities and mortgages; and public corporations' and local authorities' net issues abroad.

Overseas investment in UK private sector covers: direct investment by overseas non-oil companies in their affiliates, including the re-investment of unremitted profits and all other types of financial flows between affiliated companies; changes in overseas residents' holdings of UK company securities, including any issued abroad; investment by overseas oil companies, broadly comparable with direct investment.

UK private investment overseas covers: direct investment by UK non-oil companies and a number of public corporations in their overseas branches, subsidiaries or associates, and includes the re-investment of unremitted profits and all other types of financial flows between affiliated companies; UK portfolio investment in overseas government, municipal and company securities, including issues of such securities bought or sold on the London market by UK residents; UK oil companies' investment abroad.

Official long-term capital consists of inter-government loans and other official long-term capital (net). Inter-government loans cover drawings and repayments of loans between the UK government and overseas governments.

Table 8.10

Analysis of Capital Transactions

£ million

	1972	*1973*	*1974*	*1975*	*1976*	*1977*	*1978*	*1979*	*1980*	*1981*	*1982*
CURRENT BALANCE	+223	-979	-3 278	-1 513	-836	+54	+1 158	-653	+3 235	+6 547	+5 428
CAPITAL TRANSFERS	-	-59	-75	-	-	-	-	-	-	-	-
INVESTMENT AND OTHER CAPITAL TRANSACTIONS											
Overseas investment in United Kingdom											
Direct[2]	+408	+734	+354	+615	+799	+1 325	+1 261	+1 793	+2 573	+902	+1 154
Investment by oil companies	+78	+382	+924	+883	+819	+1 131	+666	+1 215	+1 714	+1 882	+1 770
Portfolio	+290	+386	+323	-4	+438	+1 853	-85	+1 253	+853	+508	+415
of which, British government stocks	+108	+42	+105	-13	+116	+979	-3	+929	+571	+201	+495
Miscellaneous investment	-4	-5	+103	+20	+35	+89	+35	+75	+100	+70	+120
Total overseas investment in UK	+772	+1 497	+2 204	+1 514	+2 091	+4 399	+1 877	+4 336	+5 240	+3 362	+3 459
UK private investment overseas											
Direct[2]	-737	-1 621	-1 575	-1 171	-2 145	-1 885	-2 710	-2 777	-3 430	-5 103	-2 638
Investment by oil companies and miscellaneous investment	-61	-415	-298	-137	-214	-461	-821	-2 858	-1 566	-1 418	-1 960
Portfolio	-604	+276	+725	-59	+90	+12	-1 073	-909	-3 150	-4 150	-6 170
Total UK private investment overseas	-1 402	-1 760	-1 148	-1 367	-2 269	-2 334	-4 604	-6 544	-8 146	-10 671	-10 768
Official long-term capital	-254	-255	-287	-291	-161	-303	-336	-401	-91	-336	-337
Import credit	+198	+349	+88	+59	+111	+280	+292	+64	-254	+122	-224
Export credit	-409	-552	-810	-577	-1 103	-635	-922	-856	-902	-969	-1 165
Foreign currency borrowing or lending abroad by UK banks	+471	+535	-295	+253	-106	+364	-433	+1 623	+2 054	+1 462	+1 173

Exchange reserves in sterling:											
British government stocks	+65	+74	-124	+7	+12	+6	-113	+247	+945	+267	-32
Banking and money market liabilities etc.	+222	+87	+1 534	-622	-1 413	-16	-	+509	+317	-118	+140
Other external banking and money market liabilities in sterling	-91	-7	+148	+549	+256	+1 481	+293	+2 580	+2 558	+2 607	+4 164
External sterling lending by UK banks[3]	-241	+35	+53	+96	-350	+58	-504	+205	-2 500	-2 934	-3 243
Other external borrowing or lending											
UK public sector[4]	+7	+19	+72	+56	+27	+750	+22	-7	-173	-18	-105
UK private sector	+139	+320	+279	+260	+94	+63	+84	+467	-692	-449	+537
Other transactions	-150	-164	-112	+217	-164	+53	+81	-66	-243	+101	+250
Total investment and other capital transactions	-673	+178	+1 602	+154	-2 975	+4 166	-4 263	+2 157	-1 887	-7 594	-7 851
Allocation of SDRs	+124	-	-	-	-	-	-	+195	+180	+158	-

1 Assets: increase-/decrease+. Liabilities: increase+/decrease-
2 Overseas direct investment in the UK excludes the transactions of oil companies. UK direct investment overseas excludes the transactions of oil companies but includes investment by a number of public corporations.
3 Excluding credit for UK exports.
4 Excluding official financing.

Source: UK official balance of payments statistics 1983.

Other official long-term capital covers all long-term capital transactions with overseas residents by the central government.

With the distinctions mentioned on pp. 234–235 in mind we can now examine the types of flows included in the capital account, using the UK balance of payments records as an illustration. Table 8.10 shows that *long-term capital* flows are carried out at an official and private level, as is indicated by the entries overseas investment in the UK, official long-term capital, and UK private investment overseas just discussed. When a UK firm builds a factory overseas there is a capital outflow (−), but when interest, profits, and dividends arise from such investments there is an inflow of currency (+) in the invisibles section of the current account.

Import and Export Credit

When overseas residents delay payment for UK exports, then the value of those exports in a stated period of time will exceed the money payments received by the amount of export credit. Similarly, import credit arises when UK residents do not pay for the goods and services received from abroad during the period in question (i.e. credit is granted to UK importers).

Foreign currency borrowing or lending abroad by UK banks comprises external borrowing and lending denominated in foreign currencies by UK resident banks. It covers the financing of UK banks' net foreign currency business with UK residents plus any switching by the banks between foreign currencies and sterling.

Exchange reserves in sterling provides a broad measure of the changes in sterling reserves of overseas countries and international organisations (other than the International Monetary Fund) as reported by the UK monetary sector.

Other external banking and money market liabilities in sterling consist of the changes in UK external banking and money market liabilities in sterling to overseas residents other than central monetary institutions and international organisations.

External sterling lending by UK banks consists of sterling advances and overdrafts (net of repayments) provided to non-residents; also sterling commercial bills and acceptances, other than bills connected with UK export credit.

Other external borrowing or lending comprises borrowing or lending abroad, net of repayments, by UK residents other than UK banks. From 1982 onwards it includes transactions by financial institutions previously included with UK banks but which did not become part of the UK monetary sector. It covers transactions with overseas banks, EC institutions, unrelated companies and some persons abroad.

Other transactions consist of official short-term transactions not included elsewhere; and other commercial short-term transactions.

The entries overseas currency borrowing by UK banks, exchange reserves in sterling, and other external banking and money-market liabilities in sterling are all short-term flows and the last two items come under the general heading of "sterling balances".

APPENDIX 3

OFFICIAL FINANCING

As discussed on p. 235 and detailed in Table 8.11 the sources of official financing are threefold:

(1) Net transactions with overseas monetary authorities.
(2) Foreign currency borrowing.
(3) Official reserves.

Net transactions with overseas monetary authorities can be either with the IMF or 'Other'.

(1) Net Transactions with Overseas Monetary Authorities – IMF

These include drawings and repurchases by the United Kingdom, and drawings and repurchases in sterling by other countries which affect the UK's repurchase obligations to the IMF. From July 1972 any drawing or repurchase in sterling by another country which affects the UK's reserve position in the Fund results in a change in the published total of UK official reserves and is accordingly shown in the balance of payments accounts as a drawing on or addition to official reserves. Any transaction by the United Kingdom, which affects the United Kingdom's reserve position in the Fund, merely alters the composition rather than the level of the reserves.

Net Transactions with Overseas Monetary Authorities – Other

This item covers net borrowing from Switzerland, with a sterling counterpart, in parallel with drawings from the IMF under the "general arrangements to borrow", and other net borrowing from monetary authorities in the form of assistance with a sterling counterpart; net borrowing from other monetary authorities in the form of foreign currency deposits; amounts swapped forward into later months with overseas monetary authorities in 1971 and 1972; and net borrowing from The Group of Ten countries, Switzerland and the BIS under the US$5.3 billion facility in 1976.

Foreign currency borrowing can be by either the Government or by public bodies which are protected from the exchange risk by the exchange cover scheme.

(2) Foreign Currency Borrowing by HM Government

These are primarily drawings on two eurodollar facilities, of US$2500 million and US$1500 million respectively, arranged by the Bank of England with UK clearing banks and their associates on behalf of HM Government, and repaid during 1980 and 1981. The transactions are allocated to the debtor (HM Government) rather than the transactor (the clearing banks). Also included is an issue of US$350 million of HM Government 7 and 15 year bonds made in New York in April 1978.

Foreign Currency Borrowing (Net) by Public Bodies under Exchange Cover Scheme

This is all borrowing by UK public corporations, local authorities and other public bodies under the 1969 and subsequent exchange cover schemes. These borrowings (net of repayments) are in the form of issues abroad, borrowing from banks, etc. overseas (in recent years, largely the European Investment Bank and European Coal and Steel Community) and borrowing through UK banks; they are included in official financing because they are regarded as primarily motivated by considerations of reserve management, the foreign currency generated being added to the official reserves (see Table 8.12).

(3) Official Reserves

The official reserves comprise gold, convertible currencies and special drawing rights held in the exchange equalisation account, together with the United Kingdom reserve position in the International Monetary Fund (IMF). Currencies may be held in the form of financial instruments. In calculating the levels, non-dollar components are translated to dollars as follows:

Gold is valued at US$42.2222 per fine ounce up to end-March 1979; thereafter at 75% of the average of the London fixing prices for the 3 months up to end-March or (from end-March 1980) at 75% of the final fixing price on the last working day in March, whichever is the lower.

Special drawing rights are valued at SDR1 = $1.20635 up to end-March 1979; thereafter at the average of the exchange rates in the 3 months to end-March or (from end-March 1980) at their actual dollar values on the last working day in March, whichever is the lower.

From July 1979, reserve holdings include European Currency Units acquired from swaps with the European Monetary Co-operation Fund.

Table 8.11
Official Financing

Summary of Official Financing [1]	*1972*	*1973*	*1974*	*1975*	*1976*	*1977*	*1978*	*1979*	*1980*	*1981*	*1982*
											£ million
Net transactions with overseas monetary authorities											
International Monetary Fund[2]											
UK drawings	-	-	-	-	+1 018	+1 525	-	-	-	-	-
UK repurchases	-313	-	-	-	-	-412	-948	-596	-140	-145	-163
Other net drawings	-102	-	-	-	-	-	-68	-	-	-	-
Total	-415	-	-	-	+1 018	+1 113	-1 016	-596	-140	-145	-163
Other monetary authorities											
Foreign currency deposits	-	-	-	-	-20	-	-	-	-	-	-
Other	+864	-	-	-	-14	-	-	-	-	-	-
Total	+864	-	-	-	-34	-	-	-	-	-	-
Foreign currency borrowing (net):											
by HM Government	-	-	+644	+423	-	+871	+191	-	-629	-1 234	-
by public bodies under exchange cover scheme[3]	-	+999	+1 107	+387	+1 791	+243	-378	-250	-312	-353	+26
Drawings on (+)/additions to (-) official reserves	+692	-228	-105	+655	+853	-9 588	+2 329	-1 059	-291	+2 419	+1 421
Total Official Financing	+1 141	+771	+1 646	+1 465	+3 628	-7 361	+1 126	-1 905	-1 372	+687	+1 284

1 Valued in sterling at current market rates of exchange.
2 From July 1972, excludes transactions which affect the United Kingdom's reserve position in the Fund (thereafter part of official reserves - see notes). UK drawings on the oil facility are included.
3 See detail in Table 10.2.

Source: UK official balance of payments statistics 1983.

Table 8.12

Foreign Currency Borrowing by HM Government and by Public Bodies under the Exchange Cover Scheme

£ million

	1972	1973	1974	1975	1976	1977	1978	1979	1980	1981	1982
HM GOVERNMENT BORROWING (NET)											
Through UK banks	-	-	+506	+314	+28	+729	+22	-	-543	-1 002	-
From banks, etc. overseas	-	-	+138	+109	-28	+142	-22	-	-86	-232	-
Issues abroad	-	-	-	-	-	-	+191	-	-	-	-
Total	-	-	+644	+423	-	+871	+191	-	-629	-1 234	-
BORROWING BY PUBLIC BODIES UNDER THE EXCHANGE COVER SCHEME (NET):											
Through UK banks:											
Public corporations	-	+736	+325	-1	+424	-41	-290	-406	-154	+133	-70
Local authorities	-	+88	+270	-21	-24	-1	-149	-208	-25	+1	-
Net issues abroad											
Public corporations	-	+28	+250	+166	+581	+45	-126	+109	-233	-377	-84
Local authorities	-	+96	+25	+25	-1	+1	-4	-59	-64	-38	-2
From banks, etc. overseas											
Public corporations	-	+43	+210	+227	+811	+219	+185	+275	+85	-126	+72
Local authorities	-	+8	+27	-9	-	+20	+6	+20	+35	+33	+60
Northern Ireland Central Government	-	-	-	-	-	-	-	-	-	-	-
British Nuclear Fuels Ltd	-	-	-	-	-	-	-	-	-	-	-
Total	-	+999	+1 107	+387	+1 791	+243	-378	-250	-312	-353	+26
of which:-											
Borrowing	-	+1 007	+1 107	+393	+1 889	+296	+672	+1 045	+582	+447	+353
Repayments	-	-8	-	-6	-98	-53	-1 050	-1 295	-894	-800	-327

Source: UK official balance of payments statistics 1983.

Chapter 9

The Foreign Exchange Market*

INTRODUCTION

The foreign exchange market is the organisational framework within which individuals, banks, firms and governments buy and sell foreign currencies. Foreign exchange means different things to different groups in society. To individuals foreign exchange is what is needed for spending on holiday. Foreign exchange transactions also occur when international trade and investment take place. Foreign exchange transactions, large or small, are alike in that each is simply an exchange of one country's money for another's. A foreign exchange rate is simply the price of one country's money in terms of another's. There is another common feature. Individuals and companies normally do not buy and sell foreign currencies for their own sake, but do so in order to pay for something else, e.g. a product, a service, or a financial asset. In that sense, foreign exchange transactions are fundamentally a part of the payments mechanism and consequently it is to the commercial banks that individuals and companies have turned to convert foreign exchange into domestic currency and vice-versa. The commercial banks are the natural channel for this business, and many of them operate in the foreign exchange market not only on behalf of their customers, but also on their own account.

It is useful to examine diagrammatically the foreign exchange market. The supply of domestic currency (sterling) on to the foreign exchange market could arise out of the need for UK residents to purchase goods imported (say from the United States) and thereby necessitating a demand for dollars. So the supply of sterling is equivalent to the demand for dollars. The demand for domestic currency (sterling) could arise from the need for non-UK residents (say Americans) to pay for United Kingdom goods and so they in turn convert

*A more advanced treatment of the foreign exchange market can be found in B. Kettell and S. Bell, *Foreign Exchange Handbook* (Graham and Trotman, 1983).

US dollars into UK pounds. So the demand for sterling is equivalent to the supply of dollars.

Figure 9.1. shows the foreign exchange market in a simplified two nation world. The intersection of the US market demand curve for pounds ($D_£$) and the US market supply curve for pounds ($S_£$) determines the equilibrium exchange rate of $1.30 = £1 and the equilibrium quantity of pounds demanded and supplied per year of £6 billion. $D_£$ is negatively sloped because at lower R's England becomes a cheaper and more attractive place in which to buy and invest and so US residents demand a greater quantity of pounds. So as the price of pounds falls (rises) it takes fewer (more) dollars to buy the same amount of pounds. On the other hand, $S_£$ is usually sloped upwards because as the price of pounds rises (falls) sellers of pounds receive more (less) dollars for the same amount of pounds.

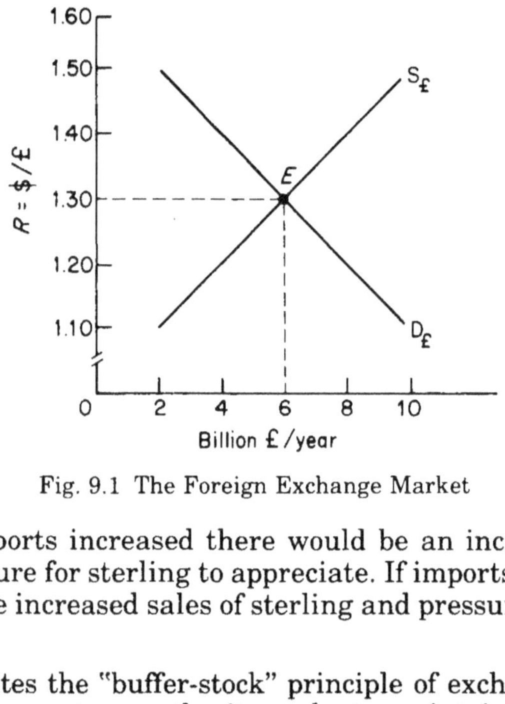

Fig. 9.1 The Foreign Exchange Market

If sales of UK exports increased there would be an increased demand for sterling and pressure for sterling to appreciate. If imports increased into the UK there would be increased sales of sterling and pressure for the exchange rate to fall.

Figure 9.2 illustrates the "buffer-stock" principle of exchange rate management. The central monetary authority seeks to maintain the spot exchange rate at a certain level (pm in Figure 9.2) or at least within a certain range of values or "band" by intervention buying or selling of foreign exchange. If there are market pressures for the rate to rise above (below) the pegged level then the authorities must seek to resist these forces by supplying (demanding) additional sterling on to the market to buy up foreign exchange.

In Figure 9.2 an upward shift in the demand schedule for sterling would, in the absence of intervention, push the price of sterling up to Pe. However, the provision of the necessary additional sterling (Q2 − Q1) by the authorities to buy up the excess dollars at pm thereby satisfying the demand for sterling, will prevent any alteration in the exchange rate.

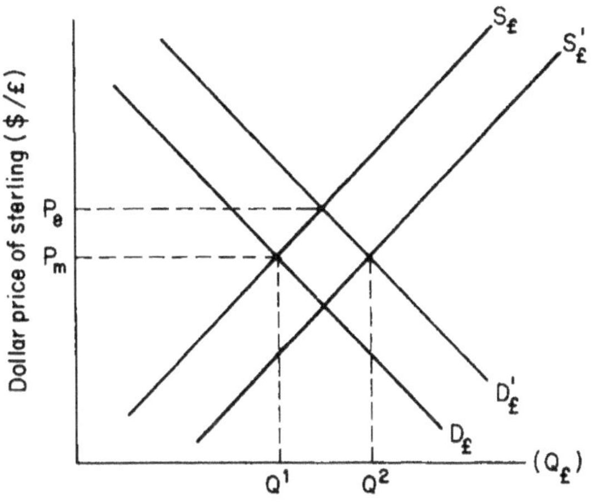

Fig. 9.2 Managed Exchange Rate

EXCHANGE RATE REGIMES

During the twentieth century the world economy has been characterised by alternating periods of fixed and fluctuating exchange rates.

As shown in Table 9.1, the 1930s, 1950s and 1970s and early 1980s were, by and large, periods of exchange rate flexibility, whereas the 1940s and 1960s were characterised by greater rigidity.

Four main types of exchange rate regime can be distinguished, all of which have operated in one form or another. Proposals for alternative exchange-rate regimes fall within one or other of the four main categories of regime distinguished, though some schemes comprise features of more than one of the main types. The four main types of regime that we shall discuss briefly are as follows:

(1) rigidly fixed exchange rates, epitomised by the gold standard;

(2) flexible rates, of which we will discuss three variants:

   (a) the adjustable peg or par-value system, which was the system which governed international monetary relations between 1944 and the early 1970s, and was sometimes referred to as the gold exchange standard. A par-value system, known originally as the "snake" and later developed into the European Monetary System was established in 1979;

   (b) a wider bands system.

   (c) a crawling peg system.

(3) managed exchange rate flexibility;

(4) freely floating rates.

Table 9.1
International Attitudes to Exchange Rate Variations and Capital Movements in the Last Half Century

	Flexibility	*Rigidity*
1930s	- Gold parities abandoned - Fluctuating exchange rates	
1940s		- Wartime controls - Reaction to post-war inflation - Bretton Woods
1950s	- Trade liberalisation and freeing of markets - Relaxation of monetary regulations - Currency adjustment process loosely applied	
1960s		- Controls on capital flows - US balance of payments strains - inadequate adjustment mechanisms
1970s	- Smithsonian agreement - "Managed" floating exchange rates - Extreme currency volatility	
1973–1985	- Dollar flexibility - Yen/Sterling/Swiss franc flexibility	- European Snake 1979- EMS

(1) The Gold Standard*

The international monetary system which was generally adopted among major industrialised countries before the First World War is referred to as "the Gold Standard". On a full gold standard the money of the country concerned, be it dollars, pounds, francs or whatever, consists of a fixed weight of gold of a definite fineness; the price of gold is fixed by law; and there is complete freedom to buy or to sell gold, to import it or to export it. When Great Britain was on the gold standard before the First World War the Bank of England was legally obliged to buy gold at £3 17s. 9d. and to sell gold at £3 17s. 10½d. per standard ounce.

A gold standard really performs two functions, to a certain extent separate and distinct. These functions are both internal and external to the economy. On the full gold standard, gold coins are in circulation and on demand bank notes can be exchanged for gold. This means that an adequate reserve of gold must be kept by the central bank to meet the demand. In Great Britain the Bank Charter Act of 1844 permitted a small fiduciary note issue (i.e. the notes were not backed by gold), but the rest of the note issue required a full gold backing. The amount of the note issue in the country then depended on its stock

*The gold standard is discussed in more detail in B. Kettell, *Gold* (Graham and Trotman, 1982).

of gold. If the stock increased the quantity of currency could be expanded; if it declined the amount of currency had to be reduced. On the gold standard the volume of currency is then directly and rigidly controlled; the volume of bank deposits is dependent on the amount of cash held by the commercial banks, and so this kind of money also is indirectly controlled. The gold standard's internal function is to control growth of the domestic money supply. Thus if the fiduciary issue (if there is any) is fixed, the volume of a country's currency depends on its stock of gold and so it is impossible for an over issue of bank notes to occur thereby ruling out the possibility of inflation or hyperinflation.

In the international field the gold standard provides stability of exchange rates between different currencies, for the exchange rate cannot fluctuate beyond the limits of the gold points (discussed below). In addition in international dealings the gold standard provides, assuming a country keeps to the rules, an automatic solution to its balance of payments adjustment problem. Certain preconditions, as already mentioned, are necessary for the successful operation of a gold standard. First, since in theory gold would be the only form of internationally acceptable money, domestic monies must be freely convertible into gold in order to permit international trade. Second, individuals must have complete freedom to import and export gold. Third, central banks must stand ready to buy and sell unlimited amounts of their own currency at a fixed gold price. Finally, each country's gold stock has to form the reserve base of its domestic money stock, thereby ensuring that domestic financial policies are dependent on any gold inflows and outflows.

Each country in the system would have a fixed gold price for its currency. Exchange rates between different currencies would therefore be automatically determined. If for example, the Bank of England fixed the price of £1 at 112.982 grains of pure gold, whilst the US authorities set $1 = 23.2 grains, then the sterling-dollar exchange rate would be £1 = $4.87 (i.e. 112.982/23.2). This would be known as the mint par rate. On either side of this value would be a gold import point and a gold export point. The gold import point is the exchange rate above which gold flows into a country and the gold export point is the exchange rate below which gold flows out of a country. The precise locations of these points would be determined by the cost of shipping and insuring gold bullion. Suppose the costs of shipping and insuring gold were 1%, i.e. 1 cent per dollar, then the gold import point would be $4.92, the gold export point $4.82. The sterling-dollar exchange rate would be kept strictly within these limits by the profit seeking activities of arbitrageurs. At any rate below $4.82 gold flows out and at any rate above $4.92 gold flows in. An example will help to illustrate how this would be accomplished.

Assume for instance that an excess supply of sterling temporarily pushes the exchange rate to $4.70 in London. Under such circumstances, it would profit an American arbitrageur to convert $4.70 into £1, use the £1 to purchase 112.982 grains of gold from the Bank of England, then resell the gold to the US treasury at the fixed price $1 = 23.2 grains. For his 112.982 grains, the arbitrageur would therefore receive $4.87, which yields him a net profit of 12 cents on the transaction (17 cents less 5 cents costs incurred in transporting the gold from London to New York). The incentive for arbitrageurs to shift gold from London to New York remains as long as the transport costs involved are less than the price differential between the two markets. The increased demand for sterling forces up the sterling/dollar exchange rate until sterling reaches $4.82. At this stage the incentive to shift funds from the United States to England is removed ($4.87 minus 5 cents gives $4.82.) Similarly $4.87 plus 5 cents gives a rate of $4.92 at which level gold imports would be unprofitable.

Thus the authorities do not intervene in the foreign exchange market, they merely stand ready to buy and sell domestic money at a fixed gold price; it is the profit-seeking activities of gold arbitrageurs which maintains the exchange rate between the gold import and export points. Since a single gold reserve had to serve both internal and external needs, the export or import of gold to meet the needs of the balance of payments will affect the internal situation. An export of gold reduces the gold basis for the internal currency, the volume of which, by the rules of the gold standard, must then be reduced. To accomplish this, the banking system must adopt a policy of deflation. The central bank discount rate will be raised, and by open-market operations the central bank will reduce the cash reserves of the commercial banks, which in their turn, in order to maintain their cash ratio, will reduce deposits by restricting their loans. As a result internal prices, including wages, should fall. This will make foreign goods relatively dearer, and so imports will be checked, while the export of home-produced goods will be stimulated because they will now be cheaper in world markets. In this way an adverse balance of payments will be rectified.

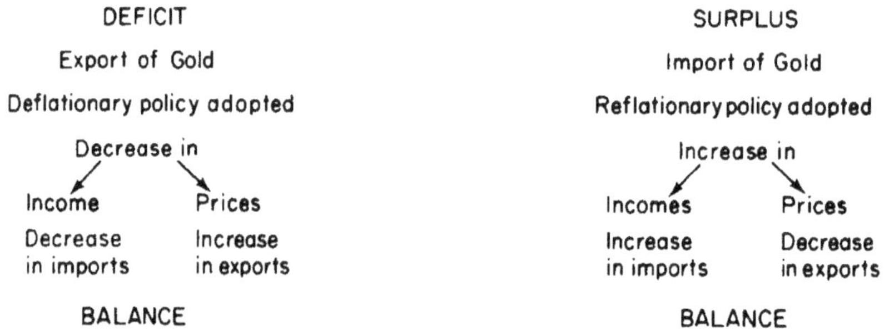

Fig. 9.3 Balance of Payment adjustment under the gold standard

If, on the other hand, a country on the gold standard has a favourable balance of payments it will receive gold. This will increase the cash basis for the internal currency, and the banking system should then adopt a policy of credit expansion. As inflation occurs the demand for imports will increase and exports, now being dearer, will be discouraged. In this way a favourable balance of payments will tend to disappear. Figure 9.3 illustrates the self-regulating character of the gold standard, a deficit or surplus in the balance of payments being corrected "automatically".

During the First World War all countries left the gold standard, and many of the main belligerent countries had substantial inflation. There was a general attempt to restore the old system after the war – the British government in particular maintained strong deflationary policies during the early 1920s in order to be able to return sterling to its pre-war parity with gold, under the impression that such a move would restore not only the prosperity of the world economy but the financial supremacy of London as well. However, the world slump which originated in the US in 1929 led to the collapse of the restored gold standard and initiated a period characterised by the breakdown of international cooperation, increasing protection, bilateral trading arrangements and a series of competitive depreciations by the major countries in an attempt to reduce unemployment at each other's expense.

(2) Flexible Rates

The Adjustable Peg or Par-value System

It was against this background that the major Allied powers met at Bretton Woods (in New Hampshire in the United States) in 1943 and 1944 to construct an international monetary system for the post-war period. The negotiations were complex but certain principles were generally accepted by the countries attending the conference; the desirability of internationally agreed fixed exchange rates and the need for a means of increasing the world stock of gold and foreign exchange reserves so that countries would not be forced to meet short-run balance of payments deficits or surpluses by disrupting their domestic economies. The agreement at Bretton Woods in 1944 re-established fixed (but adjustable) exchange rates between currencies in the form of so-called "par values" defined in terms of gold. Countries were obliged to intervene in the foreign exchange market to maintain the exchange rate within 1% either side of its par value.

The system evolved was a gold exchange standard in which domestic currencies were not convertible into gold as under a gold standard, but in which the monetary authorities undertook to buy and sell the currency of another country which was itself operating a gold exchange standard, i.e. the United States.

Under the Bretton Woods system national currencies were convertible into the dollar, and the dollar itself was convertible into gold at $35 per ounce. In effect the dollar replaced gold as the reserve asset of the international monetary system.

In theory balance of payments adjustment under a gold exchange system is supposed to work in the same way as under the gold standard, with deficit countries allowing prices to fall and interest rates to rise, while surplus countries allowing prices to rise, and interest rates to fall. In the Articles of Agreement of the Bretton Woods system, however, it was clearly recognised that internal price flexibility could not be relied on and that if provisions were not made it would be income and employment that would bear the brunt of adjustment, as in the inter-war years. Two provisions were made to safeguard full employment. First, a country in temporary disequilibrium could borrow from the IMF to tide it over its difficulties without having to pursue internal adjustment policies which threatened employment. The mechanics of borrowing are discussed in detail in Chapter 10. Secondly, provision was made for exchange rate adjustment – in practice this was rarely used.

The general reluctance to change exchange rates was attributable to several factors. There was a general fear that devaluation might preserve or even exacerbate inflation, and not merely correct its effects on the balance of payments. Memories of the interwar years were important. Surplus countries' governments were wary of the deleterious consequences of revaluation or appreciation on profits and employment in industries producing tradable goods. In Britain's case, opposition to devaluation in the 1960s was also based on considerations of political prestige, a belief that there was a moral obligation to countries holding their reserves in sterling, and worries that the role of sterling as a trading and reserve currency, and the invisible earnings thought to depend on this, would be undermined.

The breakdown of the Bretton Woods agreement is discussed further on pp. 275–278.

Wider Bands and Crawling Peg Systems

In an attempt to preserve the virtues of pegged exchange rates, while avoiding the speculative pressure that can build up with the threat of devaluation, several schemes have been developed by economists which might make the adjustable peg system workable by introducing more flexibility into it. One such scheme is the *crawling peg*. Under the crawling peg a country would maintain its pegged exchange rate within agreed margins at a level equal to the moving average of the market exchange rate over an agreed previous time period. This would allow a country's currency to drift gradually lower if circumstances warranted, and at the same time would avoid both the upheaval of devaluation under the adjustable peg system and the possibility of excessive depreciation under free floating.

Other objective indicators, other than a moving average of the past rates of exchange, could be used to introduce more flexibility into exchange rates while preserving some semblance of order. Changes in the level of reserves, the domestic rate of inflation, the level of employment, etc., could all be used to trigger off exchange-rate changes according to agreed rules. All the proposals would involve automatic adjustment of a pegged rate according to some agreed formula.

(3) Managed Floating

Under managed floating there are no pegs and no parities that the authorities are obliged to preserve. Instead the currency is free to float but the authorities intervene to avoid what they regard to be undesirable consequences of excessive appreciation or depreciation. A weak currency may lead to excessive depreciation which the authorities may wish to avoid because of its repercussions on the domestic price of imports and the internal cost structure. Alternatively, countries with a strong currency may wish to avoid excessive appreciation. To operate a managed float requires that the monetary authorities add to the supply of or demand for foreign exchange as circumstances warrant in order to achieve the exchange rate desired. The limits to which a country can manage a floating rate depends on the volume of reserves it has (to defend a depreciating currency), and its ability to control the money supply, if need be, as it accumulates reserves (to prevent an appreciating currency). This latter effect occurs when, with a fixed rate and currency inflows the country is obliged to supply its own currency (thereby raising the local money supply) in exchange for foreign currency.

(4) Freely Floating Exchange Rates

Under freely floating exchange rates the exchange rate is left to find its own level in the market without any official intervention. Balance of payments equilibrium is supposed to be achieved automatically. In an economic system in which the authorities are indifferent to the exchange rate, there is no need for international reserves. In practice, however, countries are not indifferent to the value of their currency in relation to others, and in the recent past free floating has never been adopted for any length of time as an exchange rate regime (although it must be said that the behaviour of the dollar since 1979 does resemble a free float). This system stands at the other end of the spectrum to the rigidly fixed parities of the old gold standard.

THE BREAKDOWN OF THE BRETTON WOODS SYSTEM

The Bretton Woods agreements were intended to construct an international monetary system conducive to the growth of world trade and to growing international prosperity. To be efficient in this way the Bretton Woods system required three things: first, provision for the appropriate amount and growth of international "*liquidity*" (i.e. reserves of gold and foreign exchange), since countries needed reserves to stabilise their exchange rates against short-run fluctuations; secondly, a high degree of *confidence* in the arrangements made so that destabilising speculative capital movements could be minimised and thirdly an effective *adjustment* mechanism to remedy long-run balance of payments deficits and surpluses without countries being forced to adopt policies such as trade controls or domestic deflation which would be injurious to the growth of world trade and prosperity.

(1) The Liquidity Problem

Countries' rights to draw on the IMF were initially small and though quotas were subsequently increased they made only a small contribution to international liquidity. The addition to countries' reserves of gold was determined by the amount of new gold produced less the (additional) demand for gold to be used industrially or held privately for speculative purposes. In consequence it was essentially arbitrary, and small. Significant growth in world reserves could therefore come only from increased holdings of "reserve currencies" – national currencies (sterling and US dollars) held by the central banks of other countries. Because of the increasing weakness of the UK economy and recurrent fears of sterling devaluations, holdings of sterling made only a small contribution to the growth of world reserves. So the major source of new liquidity was increased holdings of dollars.

During the 1960s there were growing doubts about the system's role in the creation of international *liquidity* which had come, as discussed, to depend upon the US deficit channelling dollars into other countries' reserves. Some thought this an inadequate vehicle for the creation of sufficient liquidity to lubricate the growth of world trade, others that it was generating too much liquidity and with it inflationary pressures both outside as well as inside the US. A criticism made by the French in particular was that the US, as suppliers of reserve currency, could run balance of payments deficits without applying the stern internal corrective measures required in other countries. The United States' decision to finance its involvement in Vietnam by running successive payments deficits rather than raising domestic taxes, coupled with the rapid expansion of US ownership of companies in Europe, added further weight to this argument and a campaign began in the late 1960s in favour of raising the price of gold and giving it a larger role in the international monetary system. The US strongly resisted this, as they did anything which smacked of devaluation, particularly as the USSR and South Africa, which together produce about 75% of the world's new gold, stood to be the principal beneficiaries.

In 1964, dollar liabilities of the US to foreign official institutions exceeded US gold holdings for the first time and, despite the US commitment to redeem dollars for gold, the confidence of foreign holders of dollars that they had a gold-backed asset was undermined. Accordingly, a run on US gold stocks now became conceivable, so long as US balance of payments deficits were not corrected. However, as the Vietnamese War intensified, so the outflow of dollars increased, leading directly to the so-called problem of "dollar overhang" – the difference between the millions of dollars held in countries' reserves and the limited supply of assets (mainly gold) held by the US as backing for them. Partly because of this, exchange rate relationships became more shaky in the second half of the 1960s, when the par values of several major currencies were changed.

(2) The Confidence Problem

One aspect of what was called the "confidence problem" in the Bretton Woods system was that, with a system of fixed but adjustable exchange rates, speculation on exchange rate changes was a one-way gamble: if speculators moved their funds out of sterling in anticipation of a devaluation either they would make a profit, if devaluation did take place, or they would not make a loss, if it did not. A second, and ultimately more important, aspect of the problem was the coexistence of gold and the dollar as reserve assets. The system depended, as already discussed, on US balance of payments deficits for the growth of international liquidity but these deficits necessarily involved a decline in the gold backing of US dollar liabilities which would eventually lead to a decline in confidence in the dollar.

Nevertheless, by and large, it was not until the 1960s that confidence in the system began to wane. The change partly reflected concern that the arrangements might no longer succeed in promoting balance of payments equilibrium since the position of the dollar itself had altered. The gradual disintegration of the Bretton Woods arrangements was to some extent attributable to the success which had attended them. The liberal trade policies which they had encouraged, plus US aid, were certainly successful in sustaining the hoped-for recovery of Japan and Europe, but, almost inevitably, different countries experienced different rates of productivity, growth and inflation, and thus the relative competitiveness of countries changed. Indeed, with the benefit of hindsight, it is easy to see that an erosion of the US competitive position was implicit in the post-war changes: but in the event, the deterioration was more than the system could cope with. A series of large overall US balance of payments deficits in the 1960s undermined confidence in the dollar and brought to the surface the question of adjustment when the key currency itself was a weak one. If the link between the key currency and gold was to be preserved – a link seen as important to the dollar's role as such – the only alternative was for other countries to revalue against the dollar, an initiative they were reluctant to take.

A persisting lack of confidence in the dollar finally precipitated the suspension of dollar convertibility in August 1971. In effect, this removed the cornerstone of the system and all the major currencies then floated for the first time since the 1930s, with most of them appreciating quite sharply in terms of the dollar. The world at this stage was on a dollar standard. This episode concluded with the Smithsonian realignment of December 1971, which represented a final attempt to reverse the generalised trend towards floating. It incoporated a 7–9% devaluation of the dollar, and a consequent appreciation of other currencies, via an increase in the official price of gold (to US$38 an ounce). But a significant step towards greater flexibility was made by the wider (2¼%) margins of fluctuation permitted around the newly-set central rates. However, in an international economic environment characterised by widening inflation differentials and increased capital flows, the initiative failed when Britain, for one, decided not to maintain the value of sterling at its new level. In June 1972, the pound was allowed to float downwards. This, together with the more general adoption of floating following exchange rate problems early in 1973, marked the beginning of a new era of international monetary arrangements in which individual countries chose the exchange rate policies thought most appropriate to their domestic economic objectives from the variety of options available.

(3) The Adjustment Problem

During this period, other weaknesses in the basic apparatus of Bretton Woods began to show themselves. One of these was that the system did not provide effective enough pressures on countries with weak currencies to *adjust* their domestic economic policies to correct external deficits.

In principle long-run tendencies to balance of payments surpluses or deficits should have been adjusted by agreed changes in the exchange rate. However in practice the failure to define "fundamental disequilibrium" in quantifiable economic terms, US hostility to exchange rate changes, and the concept of the fixed parity as the "fulcrum of domestic stability" resulted in a heavy bias against exchange rate changes. Between 1949, when sterling and a number of other currencies were devalued against the dollar, and 1971, the only changes in the exchange rates of major currencies were the devaluations of the French franc in 1958 and 1969, the devaluation of sterling in 1967 and the revaluations of the Deutschmark in 1961 and 1969.

In practice, adjustment took place to a large extent through policy-induced changes in domestic income and employment, with deficit countries being compelled to accept high levels of unemployment. This deficiency in the adjustment mechanism was accentuated by the asymmetry of pressures on deficit and surplus countries – there was much more pressure on the former to contract their economies than on the latter to expand; and by the asymmetry of pressure on the United States and on other countries – because the dollar was a reserve currency the United States was not subject to the same pressures as other countries to correct its balance of payments deficits, since it was not losing gold and foreign exchange reserves (assets) but merely increasing the amount of dollars (liabilities) held in other countries.

THE IMPACT OF OPEC ON THE INTERNATIONAL ECONOMY

The activities of the Organisation of Petroleum Exporting Countries (OPEC) may be divided into several phases:

(1) The exploits of a widely dispersed group of countries to seize the opportunities given by the Yom Kippur war of 1973 to more than quadruple the price of crude oil from US$2.20 a barrel in October 1973 to US$9.84 a barrel in October 1974.

(2) The period of hostility in the consuming countries, against the background that OPEC was a cartel and like all cartels was inherently unstable and would eventually disappear. There was, of course, another view that oil was an exhaustible resource and price should be used to alert us to the need to conserve it.

(3) The general acceptance by the industrialised countries that OPEC, and in particular Saudi Arabia, was a new force of world importance and that their new found wealth provided great opportunities for the exports of the industrialised countries and further that some OPEC member states, with small populations (called low absorbers) had accumulated vast current account surpluses which could be recycled – generally through the financial institutions of the industrialised countries – to borrowing countries, and in particular to the countries of the Third World. The acceleration of exports to the OPEC countries resulted in an OPEC balance of payments surplus being converted to a deficit.

(4) Late 1979 early 1980 was characterised by a further doubling of the oil price. The OPEC surplus rose to $114 billion in 1980 necessitating further recyling.

(5) The early 1983 phase until the present starting with the downturn in the price of oil and the consequential dent in the confidence of the weaker members of OPEC due to the oil glut. This is further exacerbated by the fact that for the first time in decades the non-OPEC oil exporters are producing more oil than the 13-member nations of OPEC.

In 1973, the world was rudely awakened to the fact that one of the main pillars of its economic structure, low cost energy from petroleum, was under attack. The supply of such energy was no longer secure, and its price has been high ever since, following the realisation that the monopoly power possessed by the Organisation for Petroleum Exporting Countries (OPEC) could be exploited.

What has happened is that OPEC has in effect levied a tax on oil-consuming countries. After spending some of the revenues for imports or goods and services, the OPEC nations put the surplus into foreign assets that they find attractive. In the aggregate the process appears to be automatic; the countries in surplus have no alternative to the purchase of claims on other countries. The rub is that the types and locations of claims are chosen by the oil producers, and most of the countries that pay the oil tax do not attract any OPEC investments directly. These countries – or entities in these countries – have to go out into the international capital market and borrow to cover their deficits.

For these borrowing countries, recycling is not automatic at all. It is an eventually painful process of piling up debts just to cover the higher cost of the same quantity of imported oil – debts that allow their economies to keep going but do not, in the absence of other adjustments, create new productive capabilities out of which the debts can be serviced in the years ahead. As discussed below, the burden of debt incurred by developing countries has become increasingly onerous.

Countries that attract OPEC investments – the stronger industrial countries in general and the UK in particular – finish up in effect as financial intermediaries. The countries themselves, or private institutions within them, take on the risks involved, for which they are paid through lending margins charged. Some of this intermediation takes the form of increased bilateral and multilateral official financing, but most of the increased financing required in the 1970s came from US and from foreign commercial banks that, in turn, added to their short-term liabilities to members of OPEC.

The oil shock of 1973–1974 came at a time of unsustainable world-wide demand pressures causing an acute inflation problem (even apart from the escalation of oil prices). Moreover, the international monetary system was going through an uneasy transition from the apparent stability of the Bretton Woods framework to a set of arrangements on which agreement had not yet been reached.

The effect on this fragile situation of the jump in oil prices – from $2.20 per barrel in June 1973 to $9.84 in June 1974 (see Figure 9.4) – was devastating. Economic activity slumped severely in 1974 and 1975, especially in the United States. In fact, gross national product (GNP) growth rates have never recovered to the average rate of over 5% achieved in industrial countries in the 1963–1973 period. Inflation rates rose from an already high average 8% rate in industrial countries in 1973 to the double digit range in 1974. The OPEC surplus jumped from $8 billion in 1973 to $70 billion in 1974 while the current account balance of nations in the Organisation for Economic Co-operation and Development (OECD) shifted from plus $10 billion to minus $27 billion, and the non-oil developing countries saw their deficit rise from $7 billion and $24 billion.

Rising OPEC imports coupled with the declining real price of oil produced a fairly rapid reduction in the OPEC surplus. In fact, the OPEC surplus faded away much faster than many observers in 1974 thought possible. After the 1974 bulge, the surplus was in the $30–$40 billion range in 1975–77, and it dropped to less than $11 billion in 1978. The peak pressure on the external balance of the non-oil developing countries was in 1975, when they had a combined deficit of $32 billion. In the period 1976–78, their annual deficits averaged $20 billion – about 2.5% of their GNP and close to the average relationship prevailing before 1973. Industrial countries' current-account balances in the aggregate tended to vary with the cyclical situation – improving in 1975, registering moderate deficits in 1976 and 1977, and then moving into surplus in 1978. Within the total OECD, however, the US position deteriorated sharply with a cyclical upturn after 1975. Large US trade and current-account deficits in 1977 and 1978 helped to generate recurrent bouts of downward pressure on the dollar.

As the OPEC surplus declined, and the combined deficit of the non-oil developing countries stabilised, the financial stresses associated with the recycling problem seemed to ease. It also turned out that the international banking system was far more elastic than had been thought. The net size of the Eurocurrency market, through which much of the intermediation takes place, grew, from $160 billion in 1973 to $485 billion at the end of 1978. By June 1983 it had reached $945 billion (see further Chapter 11).

During the early part of the 1970s, the pressure on oil prices came mainly from the demand side, reflecting more than two decades of falling relative oil prices. Even after the 1973–74 quadrupling of oil prices many industrial countries, particularly the United States, failed to adjust effectively so that demand continued to be the major influence on oil prices. However, rising oil production from new areas (primarily the North Sea, Mexico, and Alaska) kept the rate of oil price increases in nominal terms quite moderate during 1974–78). In fact they declined by 20% in real terms. It was not until the second shock in the wake of the 1979 Iranian revolution, which resulted in a doubling of real oil prices, that a more fundamental adjustment in oil demand took place. This development is now known as the second oil shock. The average official OPEC export price for crude oil rose by 140% between the end of 1978 and the middle of 1980. The organisation for Economic Cooperation and Development has estimated that the rate of increase for consumer prices is about five percentage points higher in the 24 OECD member countries in 1980 than it would have been in the absence of the oil price increases.

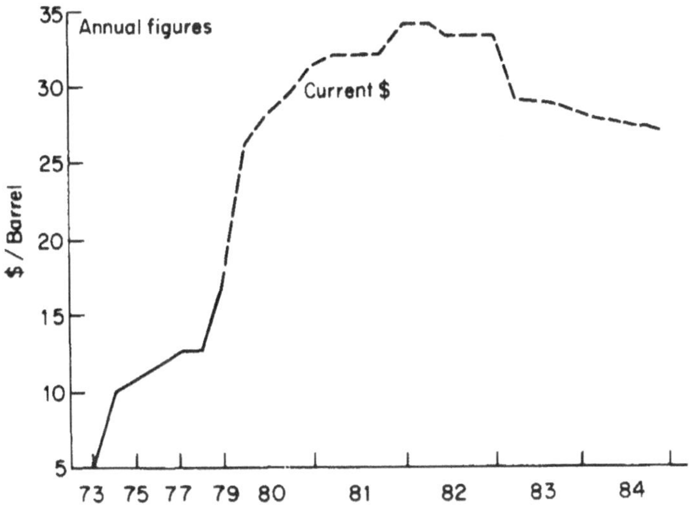

Fig. 9.4 Change in Oil Barrel Price
(Arabian Light)

The important difference between this oil shock and the original oil shock, is that money supply targets or objectives were almost universally adopted by the industrial countries between 1975 and 1978. Since the original increase in oil prices, in order to reduce inflation and/or inflationary expectations, targets had been maintained, and in some cases tightened. With intensified inflationary pressures, this inevitably led to higher interest rates. Naturally, this fed through into the foreign exchange market, with those countries adhering to their targets, receiving capital inflows, and thereby having stronger exchange rates (and vice versa).

FLOATING EXCHANGE RATES AND THE NEW ROLE OF THE IMF

One of the early purposes of the IMF was to promote foreign exchange market stability thereby avoiding competitive exchange rate depreciations. This policy was to be pursued alongside policies designed to facilitate the growth of world trade, promote high levels of employment and real income, and to reduce balance of payments disequilibria.

Members of the IMF (of which there are now 147) had to intervene in the foreign exchange market to maintain the value of their currencies within 1% of a centrally declared parity. Parity adjustments were only permitted if proof of fundamental disequilibrium could be established. When the fixed exchange rate rule book was thrown out in 1972 and 1973, the IMF found that it could no longer act as referee.

The IMF retained its important function of providing credit to countries that wished to intervene to support their currencies – most notably in the case of the UK in 1976 – and this enabled it to exert some influence over the economic policies of those countries. However, it was not until 1978, when everyone (including the IMF) recognised that there could be no return to the old system and at this stage member countries were able to agree on a new code of conduct. This was enshrined in the Second Amendment of the Articles of Agreement of the IMF.

It gave member countries freedom to choose their exchange rate arrangements, except for a prohibition against maintenance of the value of a currency in terms of gold. At the same time, each country undertakes, under Article IV, "to collaborate with the Fund and other members to assure orderly exchange arrangements and to promote a stable system of exchange rates", and the Fund is required to engage in continuous surveillance over members' exchange rate policies to ensure that they are consistent with this broad objective. In order to perform this function, the Fund adopted, in April 1977, a set of principles for the guidance of members' exchange rate policies, and principle and procedures for Fund surveillance over these policies, which became the basis for surveillance as soon as the Second Amendment came into Force on 1 April 1978.

The principles for the guidance of members' exchange rate policies were devised to ensure that each member country follows exchange rate policies that are compatible with its general obligations under Article IV:

> A. A member shall avoid manipulating exchange rates or the international monetary system in order to prevent effective balance of payments adjustment or to gain an unfair competitive advantage over other members.
>
> B. A member should intervene in the exchange market if necessary to counter disorderly conditions which may be characterised *inter alia* by disruptive short-term movements in the exchange value of its currency.
>
> C. Members should take into account in their intervention policies the interests of other members, including those of the countries in whose currencies they intervene.

The principles of Fund surveillance over exchange rate policies provide a list, which is not exhaustive, of developments that might indicate the need for discussions between the Fund and a member country. These developments include protracted large-scale intervention in one direction in the exchange

Table 9.2
Exchange Rate Arrangements as of March 31, 1984[1]

Pegged					
	U.S dollar	*French franc*	*Other currency*	*SDR*	*Other composite*
Antigua and	Lao People's	Benin	Bhutan	Burma	Algeria[3]
Barbuda	Democratic Rep.	Cameroon	(Indian	Burundi	Austria
Bahamas[3]	Liberia	Central African	rupee)	Guinea[3]	Bangladesh[3]
Barbados	Libya	Republic	Equatorial	Iran, Islamic	Botswana
Belize	Nicaragua[3]	Chad	Guinea	Rep. of	Cape Verde
Bolivia	Oman	Comoros	(Sp. Pta)	Jordan	China,
Djibouti	Panama	Congo			People's Rep.
			Gambia, The	Kenya[7]	
Dominica	Paraguay	Gabon	(£ stg.)	Rwanda	Cyprus
Dominican	St. Lucia	Ivory Coast	Lesotho	Sao Tomé and	Fiji
Rep[3]	St. Vincent and	Mali	(SAR)	Principe	Finland[7]
Egypt[1]	Grenadines	Niger	Swaziland	Seychelles	Hungary
El Salvador[3]	Sierra Leone	Senegal	(SAR)		Kuwait
Ethiopia	Sudan[3]	Togo		Vanuatu	Madagascar
				Viet Nam	
Grenada	Suriname	Upper Volta			Malawi
Guatemala	Syrian Arab Rep.[3]				Malaysia[7]
Haiti	Trinidad and Tobago				Malta
Honduras	Venezuala				Mauritania
Iraq	Yemen Arab Rep.				Mauritius
					Nepal
	Yemen, People's				
	Democratic Rep.				Norway
					Papua New
					Guinea
					Romania
					Singapore
					Solomon
					Islands
					Sweden
					Tanzania
					Tunisia
					Zambia
					Zimbabwe

No current information is available relating to Democratic Kampuchea. All members whose currencies are pegged to a single currency do so at present within zero fluctuation margin. Members whose currencies are pegged to the SDR or "Other Composite" maintain their exchange rates within zero or very narrow margins, seldom exceeding ± 1% about the peg. Within the "Flexibility Limited" category the "Single Currency" subcategory lists those members that are observed to maintain an exchange arrangement such that their exchange rate fluctuates with a variability equivalent to 2.25% margins with respect to another member's currency. The subclassification "Cooperative Arrangements" lists the countries participating in the European Monetary System (EMS). With the exception of Italy, which maintains margins of 6%, these countries maintain 2.25% margins with respect to their cross rates, based on the central rates expressed in terms of the European Currency Unit (ECU). Members with exchange arrangements listed under the "More Flexible" category are divided on the basis of the extent to which the authorities intervene in the setting of exchange rates. In some instances the exchange rate is allowed to move continuously over time; if the authorities intervene at all they do so only to influence, but not to neutralize, the speed of exchange rate movement; the exchange arrangement is classified as "Independently Floating." Alternatively, the exchange rate may be set for a short interval, usually one day to one week, and the authorities stand ready to buy and sell foreign exchange at the specified rate (the "Managed Floating" group).

Table 9.2 (*cont'd*)

Flexibility Limited Against a single currency or group of currencies		*More flexible*		
Single currency[2]	*Cooperative arrangements*	*Adjusted according to a set of indicators*	*Other managed floating*	*Independently floating*
Afghanistan[3]	Belgium[3]	Brazil	Argentina	Australia
Bahrain[4]	Denmark	Chile[3]	Costa Rica[3]	Canada
Ghana	France	Colombia	Ecuador[3,9]	Japan
Guyana	Germany, Fed. Republic of	Peru[3]	Greece	Lebanon
Maldives	Ireland	Portugal	Guinea Bissau	South Africa
Qatar[4]	Italy[6]	Somalia[5]	Iceland	United Kingdom
Saudi Arabia[4]	Luxembourg[3]		India[8]	United States
Thailand	Netherlands		Indonesia	Uruguay
United Arab Emirates[4]			Israel	
			Jamaica	
			Korea	
			Mexico[3]	
			Morocco	
			New Zealand	
			Nigeria	
			Pakistan	
			Philippines	
			Spain	
			Sri Lanka	
			Turkey	
			Uganda[3]	
			Western Samoa	
			Yugoslavia	
			Zaire	

[2] All exchange rates have shown limited flexibility against the US dollar.
[3] Member maintains dual exchange markets involving multiple arrangements. The arrangement shown is that maintained in the major market.
[4] Exchange rates are determined on the basis of a fixed relationship to the SDR within margins of up to ± 7.25%. However, because of the maintenance of a relatively stable relationship with the US dollar, these margins are not always observed.
[5] The exchange rate is maintained with overall margins of ± 7.5% about the fixed shilling/SDR relationship; however, the exchange rate will be re-evaluated when indicative margins of ± 2.25% are exceeded.
[6] Margins of ± 6% are maintained with respect to the currencies of other countries participating in the exchange rate mechanism of the EMS.
[7] The exchange rate is maintained within margins of ± 2.25%.
[8] The exchange rate is maintained within margins of ± 5% on either side of a weighted composite of the currencies of the main trading partners.
[9] Member maintains a system of advance announcement of exchange rates.

Source: IMF

market: an unsustainable level of official or quasi-official borrowing or lending for balance of payments purposes; various kinds of restrictions or incentives affecting current transactions or capital flows; abnormal encouragement or discouragement to capital flows through financial policies for balance of payments purposes; and exchange rate behaviour that appears to be unrelated to underlying economic and financial conditions.

When the Second Amendment came into effect all countries were required to notify the Fund of the exchange arrangements that they intended to apply after 1 April 1978. They were also required to notify the Fund promptly of any changes in their exchange arrangements. The Exchange Arrangements as of 30 June 1984 can be seen in Table 9.2.

Important as the floating currencies are (the principal ones being the US dollar, Japanese Yen, Swiss Franc, and pound sterling) the fact is that the vast majority of the world's currencies are still pegged in one way or another to one thing or another.

THE EUROPEAN MONETARY SYSTEM – THE INTERVENTION SYSTEMS

At its meeting in Bremen in July 1978, the European Council, composed of the heads of state and government of the member countries of the European Communities (EC), agreed that closer monetary co-operation between their countries should be promoted through the creation of the European Monetary System (EMS). The system went into operation on 13 March 1979. At the same time, the European common margins arrangement (the "snake") ceased to exist. All EC countries, except the United Kingdom, decided to participate in all aspects of the EMS, in particular the operational heart of the system, the exchange rate mechanism. Greece, which joined the EC in January 1981, is at present not a member of the EMS although the drachma is now part of the ECU (see Table 9.3).

According to the European Council, "the purpose of the European Monetary System is to establish a greater measure of monetary stability in the Community".

At the heart of the EMS is a system of fixed but adjustable exchange rates. Each currency has a central rate expressed in terms of the European Currency Unit (ECU). The ECU consists of a basket of fixed amounts of the ten currencies of all EC countries. These central rates determine a grid of bilateral central rates with fluctuation margins of plus or minus 2.25% (6% for the Italian lira). Intervention by the participating central banks to keep the exchange rates of their currencies within the margins is obligatory and unlimited, in principle, in EMS currencies.

The ECU is a basket of fixed amounts of EEC currencies – for example, it contains 8.78 pence sterling, which accounted on 18 September 1984 for some 14.90% of the basket (see Table 9.3). The amounts of each currency in the basket are changed by agreement of the Council of Ministers if, for instance, the percentage weight of a currency in the basket comes to diverge too far from the country's relative importance in the Community, as measured by gross domestic product. In fact the weights were changed on the 18 September 1984.

The ECU performs several functions within the EMS. Exchange rate parities for participating currencies are all set relative to the ECU. For example, in the rates set on 21 March 1983 ECU 1 = DM 2.24184, and ECU 1 = F.fr 6.87456. Central cross-rates are then derived by dividing these rates

Table 9.3
Composition of the European Currency Unit

	Amount of each currency in basket		*Approximate weight of currency at 18 September 1984*
Deutschmark	0.719		32.10
French franc	1.310		19.10
Pound sterling	0.0878		14.90
Dutch guilder	0.256		10.20
Italian lira	140.00		10.20
Belgian franc	3.71	3.85	8.60
Luxembourg franc	0.14		
Danish krone	0.219		2.70
Irish punt	0.00871		1.20
Greek drachma	1.15		1.40

*The exact weight of each currency depends on its current exchange rate, and changes continually.

against the ECU into one another. Therefore the F.fr/DM central parity is $6.87456 \div 2.24184 = 3.06648$. All central rates are similarly derived (see Table 9.5).

Intervention limits are calculated from these central rates. For most of the participating currencies (in fact all except the lira), the divergence limits are $\pm$ 2.25% (approximately) on either side of the central parity. For cross-rates against the lira, the intervention limits are set $\pm$6% from the central parities. Central banks are obliged to intervene to keep cross-rates within these limits, and there is a credit mechanism to help them do this.

The ECU performs two other functions:

(1) It is a denominator for expressing unit of account debts and claims as between central banks. An exchange rate risk is unavoidable whenever there is possibility of an exchange rate adjustment, but by denominating debt and claims in ECU, the EMS has introduced the concept of Community burden-sharing in respect of the exchange rate risk, in that the risk is no longer borne wholly by the debtor nor wholly by the creditor (this point is discussed below).

(2) It is an instrument of settlement between Community central banks. In this role the ECU is an asset, brought into existence by a procedure (described below) in which EMS members, including the UK, acquire ECUs as reserves. ECUs thus acquired are used primarily as a means of settling debts arising from official market intervention in Community currencies, with the proviso that a creditor central bank may not be obliged to accept ECUs over and above an amount equal to 50% of its claim.

Table 9.4 illustrates, using the example of sterling (not a full member of the EMS), how one calculates the ECU value of a particular currency.

Table 9.4
The European Currency Unit (ECU)

	Currency amount		*Sterling equivalent*	*Share of total value*
Deutschmark	0.719		18.69	31.47
French franc	1.310		15.35	25.84
Pound sterling	0.087		8.70	14.64
Italian lira	140.00		3.30	5.55
Dutch guilder	0.256		5.93	9.98
Belgian franc	3.71	3.85	4.96	8.35
Luxembourg franc	0.14			
Danish krone	0.219		1.58	2.66
Irish punt	0.008		0.71	1.19
Greek drachma	1.15		0.17	0.32
Sterling value 18.9.84			59.39	100

A grid of bilateral central rates and the agreed margins of fluctuation set the limits at which official exchange market intervention is obligatory. These rates are illustrated in Table 9.5. Thus, the Bundesbank will buy deutschmarks for French francs at FF 2.9985 per DM 1, and sells deutschmarks for French francs at 3.1363 per DM 1. In France, the Banque de France will buy francs for deutschmarks at DM .31885, per FF 1 and sells francs at DM 0.33350 per FF 1. Note that these intervention rates are calculated in such a way that when the deutschmark is weak, both central banks are intervening in the same direction. Similarly, for the other countries. This can be seen from the respective cross rates, i.e.

$$\frac{1}{2.9985} = \text{DM } 0.33350$$

$$\frac{1}{3.1363} = \text{DM } 0.31885$$

Changes in central rates are to be made by "mutual agreement" and in accordance with a "common procedure". The Committee of Central Bank Governors and the Monetary Committee of the Community, as well as the European Commission, are involved here. However, final decisions are taken by the ministers of the countries participating in the EMS, as has happened on several occasions (see Table 9.7). The European Council's resolution of December 1978 states that "there will be reciprocal consultation in the Community framework about important decisions concerning exchange rate policy between countries participating and any country not participating in the system"; hence the UK can participate in decision-taking.

In addition to the grid of central rates, there is a "divergence indicator", which serves as an early warning device that signals whether a currency diverges in its development from the average of the others. For this purpose, "divergence" is measured by the divergence of a participating currency from its central rate in terms of the ECU, not in terms of any of the other participating currencies.

Table 9.5
European Monetary System: Bilateral Central Rates and Intervention Limits (effective March 21, 1983)

		100 Belgian/ Luxembourg francs	100 Danish kroner	100 deutsch mark	100 French francs	1,000 Italian lire	1 Irish pound	100 Netherlands guilders
Belgian/ Luxembourg franc	U	...	564.10	2,048.35	668.00	33.970	33.2810	1,818.0
	C	...	551.536	2,002.85	653.144	31.9922	61.8732	1,777.68
	L	...	539.30	1,958.50	638.60	30.130	60.4965	1,738.0
Danish krone	U	18.54300	...	371.40	121.11	6.159	11.4735	329.6300
	C	18.1312	...	363.141	118.423	5.80057	11.2184	322.297
	L	17.72700	...	355.06	115.78	5.463	10.9687	315.13
Deutsche mark	U	5.106	28.165	...	33.350	1.696	3.160	90.770
	C	4.99288	27.5375	...	32.6107	1.59733	3.08925	88.7526
	L	4.882	26.925	...	31.885	1.504	3.021	86.780
French franc	U	15.650	86.365	313.63	...	5.2010	9.6885	278.35
	C	15.3106	84.4432	306.648	...	4.89819	9.47313	272.158
	L	14.97	82.565	299.85	...	4.6130	9.2625	266.10
Italian lira	U	3,318.9	18,305.0	66,473.0	21,677.0	...	2,053.53	58,997.0
	C	3,125.76	17,239.7	62,604.3	20,415.7	...	1,934.01	55,563.0
	L	2,943.8	16,236.0	58,960.0	19,227.0	...	1,821.45	52,329.0
Irish pound	U	1.6530	9.1168	33.1015	10.7964	0.549015	...	29.3832
	C	1.61621	8.91396	32.3703	10.5562	0.517061	...	28.7295
	L	1.5803	8.7157	31.6455	10.3214	0.486968	...	28.0904
Netherlands guilder	U	5.7535	31.7325	115.235	37.58	1.91100	3.5600	...
	C	5.62561	31.0273	112.673	36.7434	1.79976	3.48075	...
	L	5.5005	30.3375	110.1675	35.925	1.69500	3.4030	...

Legend: U = Upper limit.
C = Bilateral central rate.
L = Lower limit.

Source: Commission of the European Communities.

The indicator flashes when the market value of a currency crosses its "divergence threshold", expressed as a specified percentage divergence from its central value in terms of the ECU (see Table 9.6). The calculation of the ECU was illustrated in Table 9.4. Due to the wide intervention limits and to the presence of sterling within the ECU but not within the EMS it is necessary to adjust the ECU rate accordingly. This is the explanation for the column entitled "% change adjusted for divergence". (If sterling is stable against all the EMS currencies the two columns, as here, are identical.)

The rationale behind the device of the "threshold of divergence" is that one currency can be strong against all others and thereby exceed its threshold of divergence, without any other currency necessarily falling below its threshold. The symmetry which on the parity grid system dictates that for every sinner (i.e. a weak currency) there must be a saint (i.e. a strong currency) is broken. One country is singly to blame for divergence and the onus of adjustment is placed uniquely upon it.

Thus the alleged problem with the predecessor of the EMS, the currency snake, was that it usually placed the burden of intervention on the weakest currencies, even if the root cause of the divergence in cross-rates was that one particular currency (e.g. the DM) was strengthening against all the others. When the new rules were established for the EMS in 1979, it was felt by several countries (including the UK) that this situation should be remedied. As a result, the "divergence indicator" against the ECU was introduced. This works, as follows. Each currency has a central rate set against the ECU, and maximum deviations from this rate are also agreed. If any currency comes anywhere near these limits (within three-quarters of its maximum divergence), there is a presumption that the central bank concerned will take immediate action to hold its currency within the divergence limits. The idea is that if a single currency moves out of line with its EMS neighbours, then the presumption should be that the central bank responsible for the divergent currency should have the prime responsibility for rectifying matters. This was particularly aimed at the Bundesbank which, under the 1972–79 "snake" arrangements, often failed to take action to prevent upward pressure developing on the DM. This forced other currencies down to their intervention limits against the DM, and resulted in deflationary measures being introduced to protect weak currencies against the strengthening DM. Under the new system, the intention is to place the burden of adjustment onto the divergent "rogue" currency, whether it is for example a strong DM, or a weak lira.

When a currency crosses its "threshold of divergence", this results in a presumption that the authorities concerned will correct this situation by adequate measures, namely:

(a) diversified intervention;

(b) measures of domestic monetary policy (in particular interest rate changes);

(c) changes in central rates;

(d) other measures of economic policy (e.g. fiscal policy or incomes policy).

A country is not obligated to take immediate action when its divergence indicator flashes, but the early warning triggers consultations in the appropriate Community bodies – such as the Committee of Central Bank Governors, the Monetary Committee, the Economic Policy Committee, or the Council of Ministers.

Table 9.6

EMS ECU Rates and the Divergence Indicator

	Ecu central rates	*Currency amounts against Ecu September 14*	*% change from central rate*	*% change adjusted for divergence*	*Divergence limit %*
Belgian Franc	44.9008	45.1958	+0.66	+0.66	±1.5471
Danish Krone	8.14104	8.13506	-0.07	-0.07	±1.6419
German D-Mark	2.24184	2.24596	+0.18	+0.18	±1.1458
French Franc	6.87456	6.89382	+0.28	+0.28	±1.3699
Dutch Guilder	2.52595	2.53037	+0.17	+0.17	±1.5171
Irish Punt	0.72569	0.72483	-0.12	-0.12	±1.6673
Italian Lira	1403.49	1382.70	-1.48	-1.48	±4.0410

Changes are for Ecu, therefore positive change denotes a weak currency. Adjustment calculated by Financial Times.

Source: *Financial Times*, September 17, 1984.

The divergence threshold for each currency against the ECU is three-quarters of the theoretical maximum divergency which would result from its being 2¼% below the central parity for all other member currencies (6% for the lira). In practice, because each currency has a different weight in the ECU, this divergence indicator varies between currencies.

For example, the DM has a weight of roughly 32% in the ECU basket (see Table 9.4), so a maximum appreciation of 2¼% in the DM against all other currencies would increase the DM/ECU parity by only about 1.53% (i.e. $\frac{3}{10}$ of 2.25%). The divergence threshold is then set at three-quarters of this maximum divergence – approximately 1.14% for the DM. The formula is given below:

75.0% × ±INTERVENTION BAND × 1 MINUS the WEIGHTING

Applying this to the Deutschmark and Lira threshold gives:

DM divergence threshold:

$$\frac{75}{100} \times \pm 2.25 \times \left(1 - \frac{32.10}{100}\right)$$

$$= \pm 1.1458$$

Lira divergence threshold:

$$\frac{75}{100} \times \pm 6 \times \left(1 - \frac{10.20}{100}\right)$$

$$= \pm 4.0410$$

The EMS incorporates and expands the three previously existing EEC credit mechanisms, namely: the very short-term financing and the short-term monetary support (STMS), both of which are the responsibility of the central banks, and the medium-term financial assistance (MTFA), which is granted by the Council.

HAS THE EMS BEEN A SUCCESS?

Foremost among the objectives of the EMS is the achievement of a high degree of exchange rate stability as a basis for further economic integration within the EC.

The variability of EMS exchange rates appears to have declined since the system was introduced, compared with a number of non-EMS currencies

Table 9.7
Realignment of Central Rates (%) in Relation to the Group of Currencies whose Bilateral Parities were not Changed

	Dates of realignment						
	24.9.79	30.11.79	22.3.81	5.10.81	22.2.82	14.6.82	21.3.83
Belgian franc Luxembourg franc	0	+5	0	0	-8.5	0	+1.5
Danish krone	-2.9	0	0	0	-3	0	+2.5
German mark	+2	+5	0	+5.5	0	+4.25	+5.5
French franc	0	+5	0	-3	0	-5.74	-2.5
Irish pound	0	+5	0	0	0	0	-3.5
Italian lira	0	+5	0	-3	0	-2.75	-2.5
Dutch guilder	0	+5	0	+5.5	0	+4.25	+3.5

Source: European Economic Community.

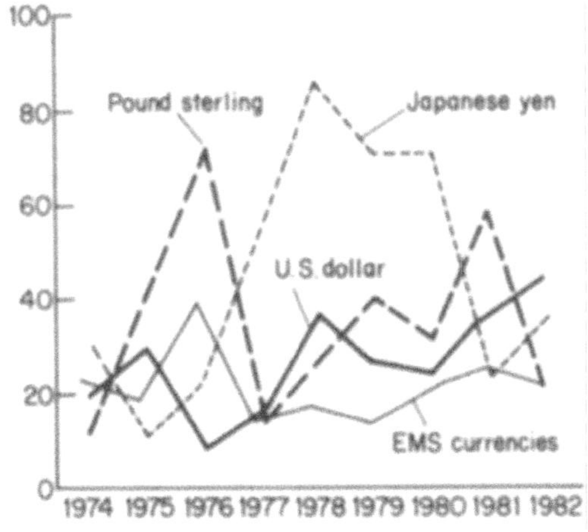

Fig. 9.5 Variability of Nominal Effective Exchange Rates

Source: IMF, World Economic Outlook (1983)

inside and outside Europe. For all EMS currencies, except the Danish krone, average variability in 1979–1981 was less than in 1974–78.

It appears that the operations of the EMS have had a moderating effect on the exchange rate variability of the participating currencies, with this influence spreading to those European currencies outside the system that have close economic and financial ties with the participants (see Table 9.7 and Figure 9.5). In contrast, the variability of nominal effective exchange rates of the US dollar, the Japanese yen and the pound sterling have risen sharply since 1979.

A second criterion of the system's success is less easily satisfied however. It is not good enough to merely preserve stable exchange rates if inflation rates continue to vary between the member countries, necessitating either large or frequent currency realignments.

Until 1983 there was no sign that inflation rates were "converging" – indeed Europe's inflation rates moved further apart in 1980 and 1981, since the oil crisis was met in Germany and the Netherlands with a tight fiscal and monetary policy, while the French and Italian governments embarked upon reflationary policies in order to expand their way out of the worldwide recession.

However, since late 1982, and particularly since the last EMS realignment on 21 March 1983, the French and Italian governments have shifted to clearly restrictive policies and their inflation rates have come down. Both Italian and French governments stated explicitly that the need to stay within the EMS was a major consideration in their new policies.

It is worth remembering that Europe's last attempt to co-ordinate exchange rate policy – the so-called Snake of 1972 – effectively fell apart within two years, when France withdrew. The very fact that the system still exists, after five of the most financially turbulent years in post war history, shows that European governments have begun to recognise the external constraints on their macro-economic policies – and to do so, in most cases, before the recognition was forced on them by the markets through crisis.

One little known success of the EMS has been the increased usage of the ECU. After the US dollar and the Deutschmark it has evolved into the most actively traded currency in the foreign exchange market. Pressure from the European Commission in favour of its wider use and the increasing willingness of a growing number of banks to offer current and deposit accounts have aided its progress. As a result it is now possible to invoice and pay for goods and services with ECUs worldwide.

The ECU's stability in times of exchange rate volatility has encouraged its use by a number of EEC based companies as an accounting unit. In addition it is now the third most important currency in the Eurobond market with total bond issues, by early 1984, of around ECU 5.25bn ($4.4bn) held by private investors.

SHOULD BRITAIN JOIN THE EUROPEAN MONETARY SYSTEM?

The current members of the EMS are West Germany, Denmark, Luxembourg, Belgium, the Netherlands, France, Italy and Ireland. Britain and Greece are the only common market members that do not belong to the EMS, although their currencies are part of the ECU.

If Britain joined the EMS the pound sterling, by a system of intervention points, would be locked into a firm relationship with the Deutschmark, the French franc and all the other EMS currencies.

The arguments in favour and against EMS membership are evenly balanced.

THE ARGUMENTS IN FAVOUR OF EMS MEMBERSHIP

(1) It has achieved a degree of exchange rate stability compared with the behaviour of non-EMS exchange rates. The movement of exchange rates within the EMS, since its inception, has been between 10% and 15% whereas outside it has been between 30% and 40%. This relative stability within the system, at least with respect to exchange rates, has had important consequences for forward planning in trade and industry – and therefore for employment prospects. In contrast, swings of between 30% and 40% in exchange rates outside the system are far greater than any profit or loss that could be made.

The IMF recently published a study entitled *The European Monetary System: The Experience, 1979–82*, by Horst Ungerer, with Owen Evans and Peter Nyberg. The study examines the variability of exchange rates before and after the establishment of the EMS. It concludes that the average exchange rate variability of EMS currencies has diminished since the system was introduced, and that this stabilising influence has spread to the exchange rates of European currencies closely tied to the EMS. In contrast, the exchange rate variability of the major currencies not tied to the EMS – the pound sterling, the US dollar, and the Japanese yen – appears to have increased significantly.

(2) Moreover, it could be advantageous to promote a currency link with Europe given Britain's increasing trade with the EEC. In 1983, 54% of Britain's trade was conducted with the "Deutschmark bloc" of the EEC, Austria, Switzerland and Scandinavia, compared with only 35% a decade ago.

(3) The policy of pooling reserves should make it easier to defend sterling if falling oil prices made it vulnerable. Thus the damaging effect on the cost of imports and thereby on domestic inflation could be mitigated.

(4) The consistent strength of the Deutschmark is another often canvassed reason for joining. Since the EMS currencies are tightly linked, a rise in the DM (the strongest currency) would tend to pull other member currencies upwards. As the United Kingdom conducts more trade using dollars as the medium of exchange than any other European country, then any upward influences in the exchange rate (brought about by EMS membership) would reduce further the threat of import-induced inflationary pressures deriving from a sterling fall against the dollar.

(5) It is argued that a depreciation of sterling has a greater effect on domestic inflation than the UK's international competitiveness. The argument is that following a devaluation the sterling cost of material imports and finished manufactured imports rises by the full amount of the devaluation. UK companies then take advantage of the higher manufactured import prices to raise the prices of their manufactured goods. Thus domestic prices rise initially by a much greater amount than the share of imports in GDP times the devaluation. Higher domestic prices are reflected in higher wages demands which in turn pushes up both domestic and UK export prices. Thus the domestic price level rises by the full amount of the sterling depreciation. On this basis the main "advantage" claimed for remaining outside the EMS namely the ability to vary the sterling exchange rate according to national economic policy is largely illusory.

(6) There is a political case for becoming a member in that as full members of the EEC we should be good Europeans and participate in all the European institutions. So belonging to the EMS would be an indication of a wider and more fundamental commitment to Europe.

(7) Finally, the EMS would be bound to have an important role to play in any move towards the reconstruction of a global exchange rate system. The United Kingdom would have a more influential role as a full member. What is true for EMS contributions to any global development is, of course, even more true for developments within the EMS itself. As a full EMS member the United Kingdom may be in a better position to influence its future developments.

THE ARGUMENTS AGAINST MEMBERSHIP

(1) One argument is that the United Kingdom has a different economic structure from the rest of the EEC, with its position as an oil producer, so that the pound sterling is subject to different economic forces from the other currencies. This was shown in the real trade-weighted appreciation of sterling by 24% from 1978 to 1981, and its corresponding fall since then. Thus the existence of North Sea oil and sterling's petro-currency

status, it is argued, make the pound fundamentally unsuitable to join a semi-fixed exchange rate regime.

This point should not be exaggerated. The volatility of sterling was also caused by the fact that this was a transitional period, when the vigorous use of monetary policy brought inflation down from 21.9% in 1979–80 to just less than 5% now.

(2) Membership of any stable exchange rate system precludes the use of the exchange rate itself as a means of adjustment, and thus takes away from countries one element of freedom. This may be a very important and relevant part of the adjustment process, if domestic and international costs are out of line. The economic history of Argentina and Chile in recent years shows spectacularly the damage that may be done by clinging to over-valued exchange rates.

The key exchange rate that industrialists concentrate on, given the importance of trade with Germany, is the sterling/DM rate. Using various measures of competivity this rate has been, for a long period, overvalued and industrialists fear that if the UK is an EMS member with an inappropriate exchange rate they will not be able to compete in the German market.

(3) Membership might require excessive Bank of England intervention in the foreign currency markets in order to satisfy the demands made by adherence to the EMS limits. Given the size and volatility of capital flows, combined with UK experience of joining the "snake" it is feared that we may, faced with speculative outflows, be unable to hold the rate. In the spring of 1972 Britain was a member of the forerunner of the EMS, the EEC currency "snake", for just six weeks, but had to withdraw after the Bank of England expended some $1 bn in intervention to defend the exchange rate. This occurred in the days when exchange controls, which were abolished in October 1979, were still in force.

(4) Some officials feel that membership would automatically result in a loss of monetary independence for Britain. Under EMS rules an economy which is expanding too rapidly in relation to the other members has to be reined in by its government. This is because an excessively buoyant economy tends to suck in imports or generate inflation, or both. If imports rise, the current account eventually moves into growing deficit. If inflation exceeds that of other member countries, then capital tends to move out of the country, other things being equal. Either way, the exchange rate comes under pressure unless the Government does something about it.

At the very least, the Government has to spend reserves on supporting its currency. Since this is unlikely to prove effective in anything but the short term, the Government has to raise interest rates or deflate by means of fiscal policy in order to prevent its exchange rate falling.

On the other hand, countries with appreciating currencies have to cut interest rates or sell their own currencies in the exchange markets so as to keep their parities down. These measures will tend to boost the domestic money supply, and could fuel inflation indirectly. More directly, a government which renounced a strengthening exchange rate loses a powerful weapon against inflation.

Thus ultimately UK interest rates and the inflation rate would be governed by that of the other EMS countries. We could not, due to the exchange rate pressures, risk being out of line. This is a lesson the French government under President Mitterrand was forced to learn rather painfully. Monetary policy would thus be geared to external objectives (the exchange rate) rather than domestic objectives (such as full employment).

(5) There is a natural anxiety within the British Government that an EMS exchange rate target could be a "hostage to fortune". Given that successive British governments have repeatedly failed to meet their domestic monetary targets, it could be politically embarrassing if it proved necessary to withdraw from the EMS after a short time, although it must be said this is a consideration that has never worried the French government!

(6) Firms can generally guard against short-term market exchange rate volatility by hedging in the forward exchange markets or by other ways. It must be stressed however that hedging techniques may not be available or may be costly.*

(7) The EMS has not always managed to bring about any great convergence of members' economic policies particularly in relation to national inflation rates. For example, between March 1979 and June 1982 the growth of the inflation rates of West Germany, France and Italy mushroomed by over 20%, 50% and 73% respectively. With such large differences in the growth of inflation rates, it is hardly surprising that the need for realignments of exchange rates has arisen.

Indeed it has been argued that far from helping the convergence of economic policies among the member countries the EMS does the opposite: it intensifies the divergence.

The reasoning runs as follows: because capital movements between EMS members are free; because there is reasonable assurance that their exchange rates will remain stable; because there is still great disparity in their inflation and interest rates: therefore capital will tend to flow from the low-inflation low-interest countries to the high-inflation high-interest rate markets. This will keep interest rates higher in the low-inflation countries than they ought to be and, conversely, lower than

*For a detailed examination of hedging techniques readers are recommended to consult Brian Kettell, *The Finance of International Business* (Graham and Trotman, 1979) and, by the same author, *A Businessmans' Guide to the Foreign Exchange Market* (Graham and Trotman, 1985).

they ought to be in high-inflation countries. Hence, the EMS, far from being conducive to the convergence of members' economic policies, does the very opposite: it strengthens deflationary forces in low-inflation countries and shelters high-inflation countries from the castigation of adequately high interest rates to which they ought to be subjected.

(8) A reservation arises whereby British membership would result in the system embracing three of the world's five leading currencies – the Deutschmark, French franc and sterling (the other two being the yen and the dollar). The mechanics of keeping three currencies aligned could prove to be much more difficult than maintaining stability between just two.

(9) In addition it is said that Sir Geoffrey Howe when Chancellor of the Exchequer (1979–1983) was won over to being anti-sterling EMS membership following his experience in the chair during two EMS exchange-rate realignments. None of the devaluing countries was allowed by the others to lower its exchange rate as much as it wanted, because of the implications for the common agricultural policy. Assuming that the "green" CAP exchange rates followed the market rates, farm produce prices would be lowered in the revaluing countries and raised in the devaluing ones. This led the revaluers to insist upon the smallest possible changes. Sir Geoffrey concluded that this was a bad way to run an exchange rate system. Although it must be said that the system was only supposed to have small changes. In addition, exchange rate fixing and intervention are against the Government's ideology of favouring free markets.

(10) Finally an argument has been put forward concerning the effect on oil revenues. A fall in oil prices cuts the revenues from the North Sea as naturally oil importers pay less. However, as oil prices are fixed in dollars, a fall in the sterling dollar exchange rate could restore that loss. The dollar is not an EMS member but sterling membership of the EMS could reduce the freedom to fall against the dollar, if for example, several major EMS currencies were appreciating against the dollar.

FIXED VERSUS FLEXIBLE EXCHANGE RATES

As illustrated in Table 9.2 only relatively few countries permitted and currently permit their currencies to float freely. Of the 147 countries comprising the membership of the International Monetary Fund, 37 peg their currency to the US dollar, 13 to the exchange rate of the French franc, 14 to the SDRs, 24 to some other composite unit, and 5 to some other currency. Eight countries, the members of the European Monetary System, peg their currencies to the European Currency Unit and to each other while floating freely against other currencies. Thirty-eight countries have miscellaneous arrangements. Only eight countries (including the United States) permit their individual currencies to float freely.

One can legitimately ask what arguments can be put forward in favour of fixed rates and in favour of floating rates.

THE ARGUMENTS FOR FIXED EXCHANGE RATES

These arguments are part of a more general argument for national economic policies conducive to international economic integration. Fixed exchange rates are equivalent to a single currency: they simplify profit-maximising calculations of traders, facilitate competition, and promote the integration of the whole area of fixed exchange rates into a connected series of markets. It may be argued that the need for economic integration and the benefits of connected competitive markets are sufficiently strong to justify fixed exchange rates among major industrialised countries.

Also, some economists believe that fixed exchange rates are a form of discipline over nations in the group of countries with fixed rates. A country's policy actions may be inhibited if it recognises that they are likely to cause a devaluation. Friedrich A. von Hayek, recent Nobel Prize winner in Economics, put the case bluntly:

> "Present unemployment is the direct and necessary consequence of what we have been calling a full employment policy . . . inflation is solely and entirely a question of the quantity of money . . . fixed exchange rates may be inferior to an ideal policy, but nonetheless may be absolutely essential to protect governments against a kind of pressure which is bound to be imposed upon them if they have freedom to act in these respects."

He argued that if the public believes that unemployment can be significantly reduced by tax cuts or expenditure increases, democratic governments cannot resist the pressure to take such measures, and central banks cannot resist the pressure to accommodate the added demand for funds by increasing the money supply.

In addition, those who favour fixed exchange rates argue that flexible rates cause undue risk and hardship for international trade and investment, because of the uncertainty of changes in exchange rates and the consequent uncertainty of revenues, costs and net returns.

On the other hand, there may be adverse consequences for business firms engaged in international transactions if fixed rates are accompanied by exchange controls or other restrictions.

Certain circumstances may particularly justify government intervention to stabilise exchange rates. These occur:

(a) when the government is capable of large-scale operations;
(b) when external benefits derive from government action.

Consider first the fact that a government's potential for intervention on the exchange is usually so large as to enable it to influence and even determine the course of the exchange rate *for a short time*. When the international market for goods or securities is subject to large and complex disturbances, uncertainty about the future course of the exchange rate grows among government officials and private individuals alike. In circumstances of little confidence about where the near or intermediate term equilibrium rate lies, market participants may become unduly influenced by movements of the rate, and, taking any movement as evidence of at least a direction in which the future equilibrium rate lies (or in which others might think it lies), execute transactions that anticipate continuation of the movement and by that action make the anticipation self-fulfilling. Once a dynamic process of this sort has begun, it can cause the exchange rate to move for a time away from the trend equilibrium level that the speculators in fact seek. Thus the destabilising speculation may have imposed uneconomic disruption on decisions about consumption and production. The government, as intervenor in the exchange markets, can by the scale of its operations break such a self-fulfilling chain when smaller and necessarily profit-motivated market participants would still hesitate to move against it. Government interventions for short periods can force market participants to pause to seek new information about the equilibrium rate.

A second case justifying government intervention to stabilise exchange rates occurs when external benefits derive from it. Thus it is argued stable exchange rates contribute to government policy goals such as price stability and stable aggregate output and employment. It has been argued by McKinnon* that too little rather than too much private speculation was responsible for the wide swings in exchange rates in 1973/74. Keynes† had also argued this view in connection with the early 1920s. So the limited private capital available should be increased by limited government speculation.

ARGUMENTS IN FAVOUR OF FLOATING EXCHANGE RATES‡

These include discussion of simplicity, continuous adjustment, independence of domestic policies, insulation from external inflation and reducing the need for official reserves. Opponents of flexible rates argue the force of arguments put forward by supporters of fixed rates.

Simplicity of Exchange Rate Determination

By simplicity of exchange rate determination is meant that there is no need for countries to decide what constitutes the appropriate exchange rate or for their general agreement on whether deficit or surplus countries are responsible for the adjustment burden. It is simply demand and supply pressures in

*Ronald J. McKinnon, "Floating Exchange Rates, 1973–74: The Emperor's New Clothes" Karl Brunner and Allen H. Meltzer, eds., *Institutional Arrangements and the Inflation Problem*, Carnegie-Rochester Conference Series on Public Policy, Vol. 3, a supplementary series to *Journal of Monetary Economics* (New York: North Holland, 1976), pp. 79–114.

†John Maynard Keynes, *A Tract on Monetary Reform* (London: Macmillan, 1923).

‡Some of the ideas and terms in this section are drawn from H. Carter and I. Partington, *Applied Economics in Banking* to whom grateful acknowledgement is made.

the foreign exchange market which determine the appropriate exchange rate for each currency. Disputes in the 1960s between the United Kingdom and West Germany as to altering the exchange rate were a source of continuous wrangling.

Continuous Adjustment

If a country is suffering balance of payments difficulties because of a long-run decline in its competitive position, then a floating exchange rate may allow a gradual depreciation of the home currency to come about, thus providing a continuous stimulus to exports and a continuous discouragement to imports. The post war fixed exchange rate system was characterised by periods of deflation and occasional, in the case of the UK, devaluations. Thus business was subject to uncertainty about the market size and following a devaluation was faced with overnight new information as to the need to restructure their organisation in favour of exporting and the seeking of domestic substitutes. Floating exchange rates permit new information to occur all the time and enable forward planning to build this in thereby enabling continuous balance of payments adjustment.

Independence of Domestic Policies

Under the post war system, deficit countries had to direct fiscal and monetary policies at the external situation since expenditure-reducing was the only way in which the balance of payments could be improved (devaluation, as already discussed, was difficult to get agreement to). In the UK for example, booms often had to be cut short by restrictive domestic policies as an increased demand for imports led to a deterioration in the balance of payments. Consequently internal policies were often dictated by the external situation. But if exchange rate variations are successful in bringing about automatic adjustment, then governments may have greater independence in the use of domestic policies.

As will be seen later in this Chapter this view ignores the fact that expectations of changes in monetary and fiscal policy can have very swift impacts on exchange rate movements.

Indeed a major argument for exchange-rate flexibility has always been that it may avoid the necessity of restricting demand and dampening economic activity in order to correct a balance of payments deficit. Of course, exchange depreciation at full employment also requires domestic demand contraction in order to release resources to improve the balance of payments, but provided resources can be switched easily and quickly into the traded goods sector to meet the demand for exports and import substitutes there is no reason why unemployment should rise. Flexible exchange rates possess the potential virtue, therefore, that they may be able to reconcile more easily the desire of most economies for simultaneous internal and external balance.

Insulation from External Inflation

One explanation for the transmission in the late 1960s of worldwide simultaneous accelerating inflation is to be found in the role played by fixed exchange rates. The reason for this is that monetary expansion in an individual country leads to a deficit in that country's balance of payments and puts inflationary pressure on the rest of the world. The mechanism whereby this equalisation would occur is most easily seen by considering the following experiment. Let the world economy initially be in a zero inflation equilibrium. Now assume that one large country begins to increase its money supply, and that members of the world economy rigidly maintain their fixed exchange rates. What will happen to prices, wages and balances of payments in the world economy? Initially, presumably, the "inflationary" country will have a balance of payments deficit and the rest of the world will have a surplus.

From this situation three things will occur which will raise the inflation rates in the surplus countries. First the movement into a surplus on the balance of payments (from the initial full equilibrium) will create excess demand, which, other things being equal, will cause prices to move upwards. This excess demand occurs as there are more buyers of the countries' goods abroad than there were before and, assuming a reasonable degree of capacity working, there will be inflationary pressures in the surplus country. Secondly, inflationary expectation will be revised upwards either directly as a result of the initial observation of an over-inflating overseas economy or as a consequence of initial price rises caused by excess demand. This will further add to the domestic inflationary pressure. Thirdly, the money supply of the surplus country will be increasing because of the additions to reserves arising from the payments surplus. Thus if the Bundesbank is selling deutschmarks in exchange for dollars in order to prevent the appreciation of the deutschmark it is thereby increasing the German money supply. So with a fixed exchange rate countries with surpluses import inflation. If the rate was flexible they would receive the low inflationary benefits of appreciation. There are three reasons put forward as to why flexible exchange rates, despite the above viewpoint, cannot fully insulate a domestic economy from external influences.

The first reason is that real activity in an economy will react to exchange rate changes only to the extent that relative costs adjust, and after the time lag that it takes for demand to respond to changes in these relative costs. It has long been recognised, of course, that exchange rate changes can only be effective if they lead to shifts in the costs of producing goods in one country as compared with others. To the extent, however, that devaluations set off movements in wages and prices that lead to offsetting increases in costs, while appreciations act in the direction of reducing costs, the effects of exchange rate changes can be limited in both time and amount.

The second reason lies in the high level of external trade in relation to domestic production in many countries (in particular the EMS countries).

Exchange rate changes cannot, especially given the lags we have mentioned, prevent the level of economic activity in one country from being affected directly by demand for its products in its principal trading partners. In this important respect, therefore, the flexible rate system has a good deal of similarity to a pegged rate system, and those responsible for economic policy need to continue to take a close interest in economic developments in other countries.

The third aspect of interdependence which is important concerns those countries whose currencies are widely used for international trade and held by other countries in their international reserves. The domestic monetary policies of these major countries are naturally reflected in the external value of their currencies, and if these policies result in sharp fluctuations or in widespread shifts in confidence then the functioning of the world's markets and the economies of other countries are invariably and directly affected.

These three reasons illustrate that even with freely floating rates there will be continued interdependence of national economies.

Conclusion

Although currencies probably would not fluctuate so much if the world switched back to fixed exchange rates it is almost certain that there would be a series of mini-crises as in the final days of Bretton Woods. The longer range distortions, such as the overvalued dollar and the undervalued yen which occurred in the early 1980s would be no easier to resolve.

The arguments for and against fixed and flexible exchange rates are finely balanced. An individual country must choose the system that serves it best consistent with its position and responsibilities in an interdependent world economy. After the experience of floating exchange rates since 1972, however, there can no longer be an overwhelming presumption that floating rates are superior to some form of adjustable peg system – contrary to the dominant academic view, during the Bretton Woods era of the 1950s and 1960s. Many of the presumed advantages of floating exchange rates have failed to materialise.

OVERSHOOTING – AN ARGUMENT FOR FIXED EXCHANGE RATES*

One powerful argument for fixed exchange rates revolves around the concept of "overshooting". In order to illustrate the way overshooting of the exchange rate can occur a simple example will be used. Consider the situation whereby a country wishes to reduce its underlying inflation rate by announcing a reduced target for monetary growth. This would eventually lead to a fall in

*Many of the ideas and terms in this section are drawn from articles in *The Economics Analyst* by David Morrison and Gavyn Davies of Simon and Coates to whom grateful acknowledgement is made.

prices and wages and an appreciation of the exchange rate. However, different markets will react at different speeds to the announcement of a new monetary target. In particular financial markets adjust faster than goods and labour markets. If this proves to be the case, then the exchange rate will react extremely quickly to any announced reduction in monetary growth, and will immediately rise to reflect the full extent of the expected long-term reduction in inflation. On the other hand, goods markets and labour markets will not immediately adjust to the new situation partly because of "sticky" expectations and partly because of the existence of long-term contracts which will have fixed wages and price levels ahead of the change in monetary conditions. As a result, commodity prices and wages do not adjust immediately to the reduced rate of monetary growth, and nor do they adjust immediately to the appreciating exchange rate. The level of output and employment will therefore be affected. In commodity markets, prices will continue to rise at rates which reflect the monetary conditions in operation before the announcement of the reduced monetary target: and this will result in commodity demand falling below productive capacity. The excess supply of commodities would, on its own, lead to unemployment; and addition unemployment would be caused by the fact that real wages do not adjust downwards to reflect reduced commodity demand, and a less competitive currency.

Overall, the early upward adjustment of the exchange rate is not matched by reduced prices and wages, so real competitiveness deteriorates, and this forces the economy into recession.

The different adjustment speeds between financial, commodity and labour markets therefore result in a prolonged interim period during which a reduction in monetary growth causes a recession in output and employment. This phenomenon is called exchange rate "over-shooting". After a while, perhaps after 2–5 years, price and wage inflation will begin to reflect the reality of excess commodity supply and high unemployment, and will adjust downwards towards the lower rate of monetary growth. The rise in the exchange rate will now be cost-justified, and real competitiveness will return to its original level, allowing employment and output to rise.

The history of sterling in 1979–81 can be explained with this theory. The overshooting of the real exchange rate was in addition exacerbated by the 1979–80 wage explosion when prices which were supposed to fall following the tight monetary policy and high exchange rate actually rose. This forced up interest rates and increased the attractiveness of sterling.

If we accept that in the interim period, mentioned earlier, that commodity prices and wages will be slower to adjust to a new situation than the financial markets would then there are broadly two ways in which governments can in principle overcome the problem of "over-shooting". First, the authorities can intervene in the foreign exchange markets to slow down the response of the exchange rate to the new monetary conditions, thus bringing the speed of adjustment into line with the slower commodity and labour markets. Alternatively, if foreign exchange intervention is deemed to have undesirable monetary consequences, the same overall effect can be achieved by imposing taxes or direct capital controls on foreign currency inflows. Either way, a temporary exchange rate target would be implemented to ensure that the foreign exchange market adjusted no quicker than the commodity and labour markets to reduced monetary growth.

In conclusion then, if we accept as a fact of life in the real world that commodity prices and wages cannot be made to adjust instantaneously to changes in monetary conditions, then one can argue that there could be a case for using exchange rate targets. In this case then we have monetary targets being used with temporary exchange rate targets (see pp. 189–190 where this idea is expanded).

FORECASTING EXCHANGE RATES

INTRODUCTION

A foreign exchange rate is the price of one currency in terms of another. Unlike most other prices, however, foreign exchange rates serve as the balancing mechanism for the complete spectrum of internationally traded goods, services and capital movements.

Since the exchange rate is a price it is determined by supply, demand and stockbuilding. Stocking or destocking occurs when the official authorities intervene to keep exchange rates higher or lower than they would otherwise have been.

The principal factors which influence sellers of foreign currency, buyers of foreign currency, and government intervention policy now need to be enumerated.

Day-to-day influences over foreign exchange rates can cause the rate to move in the opposite direction to that indicated by longer term fundamentals. This section discusses medium/longer term factors, day-to-day influences affecting exchange rates and will then discuss ways of forecasting exchange rates by the use of single variables viz, relative inflation rates and relative money supply growth.

THE MEDIUM/LONG TERM

In the medium/long term three factors influence exchange rates:

(1) the balance of payments;
(2) government economic policy;
(3) international monetary arrangements.

(1) The Balance of Payments

The need for foreign-exchange transactions arises because goods, services and capital are traded across national boundaries. As discussed in Chapter 8 these three items form a constituent part of a country's balance of payments.

When a country is in current account deficit, that is, when it buys more goods and services abroad than it sells, there will be an excess supply of its currency on the exchange markets. This excess will have to be absorbed either by inflows on capital account or by central bank intervention. The country's exchange rate will fall unless foreign investors are prepared to buy the excess currency at the prevailing rate, or the central bank is willing and able to finance the current account deficit by running down its foreign currency reserves or borrowing.

The current account is worth including in any forecast both for its direct effect on exchange rates and for its indirect effect on exchange market expectations. While a current account surplus causes some operators to buy a currency, the rate at which other operators will be willing to satisfy this demand by selling the currency in question depends, among other things, on their view of the future direction of the current account. If the surplus is expected to rise, existing holders will probably be unwilling to sell unless they are offered a higher rate (since they probably expect the exchange rate to move higher in the future). Conversely, if the surplus is expected to fall, existing holders will probably be willing to sell at the existing, or even at a lower, rate.

There are two variables which largely determine the nature of the trade accounts.

(i) relative prices;
(ii) relative incomes

The word "relative" is used because the absolute level of prices or incomes in a country are meaningless unless they are compared with the levels in the countries with which the country trades. Only those prices of goods traded in each country are relevant for comparison. Changes in prices of non-traded goods, such as service industries, affect prices of traded goods only indirectly.

As incomes expand, consumption and investment also tend to expand. Given an economy with full resource utilisation this leads to price increases. The impact on the trade account depends on how the increase in demand is channelled. An increased demand completely channelled into consumption increases the amount of goods imported. On the other hand, an increased demand completely channelled into investment, particularly if this is in the export industries, makes these industries more competitive and increases exports.

A good current account forecast is no guarantee of a good exchange rate forecast. The reason is fairly obvious. Exchange rates are also influenced by capital movements. When currencies are floating freely, a current account surplus (or deficit) must be offset by a capital account deficit (or surplus). The problem facing the forecaster is that of determining how much, if at all, the exchange rate will have to move to bring forth these off-setting capital flows.

It has already been suggested that the expected trend on current account is one of the factors international money-managers consider when buying or selling a currency. However, the capital account is subject to many other influences. Thus direct investment overseas may be for raw materials, cheaper production costs or to increase the size of the available market. Capital flows will depend on expected levels of profit and political stability. Portfolio investment and short-term capital flows depend on the relative returns, a combination of interest yield and exchange risk on these investments, again tied in with political considerations.

(2) Government Economic Policy

Governments, as we discussed in Chapter 7, are committed to several economic objectives. These include increasing the growth rate of the economy, full employment, price stability and improving the balance of payments. The problem is that policies designed to solve one problem may have adverse effects on other problems. Three major policies are available to the government to achieve their objectives; these are: (i) monetary policy, (ii) fiscal policy, (iii) other policies such as price and income controls. All these policies affect the balance of payments and income and ultimately exert an influence on the exchange rate. Assuming a fixed exchange rate it is useful to examine the way attempts to influence one objective ultimately influence other objectives and eventually exert pressure on the exchange rate. Table 9.8 summarises the problems faced by governments, the prescription to attack the problem, its effects and ultimately the pressure on the exchange rate.

Thus in case I the unemployment is reduced but there is a deterioration of the balance of payments and downward pressure on the exchange rate. In case II inflation falls but unemployment rises and there is upward pressure on the exchange rate. In case III the balance of payments deficit may be elimininated but unemployment rises and there is upward pressure on the exchange rate. In case IV the balance of payments surplus is reduced but the price level rises and there is downward pressure on the exchange rate.

It is necessary to emphasise what are known as the dilemma cases. If the high level of unemployment coincides with the problem of a persisting balance of payments deficit, the government must make a conscious decision as to which objective is most important. The outcome of such a decision will affect the foreign exchange market in diametrically opposite ways. Attention to the domestic problem of unemployment will tend to aggravate the problem of balance of payments deficits. Attention to the balance of payments deficits will tend to aggravate the domestic problem of unemployment.

A similar dilemma between the external position of the country and its domestic objectives is encountered when a persisting balance of payments surplus appears in conjunction with a high rate of inflation. We discussed on p. 301 the fact that a balance of payments surplus causes inflation by injecting more spending into the economy. The more the government combats domestic

Table 9.8

The Traditional Effect of Government Economic Policy on the Exchange Rate*

				Effects on other objectives		
Problem	*Prescription to attack the problem*	*Effects*	*Price level*	*Balance of Payments*	*Full Employment*	*Exchange Rate*
1. High unemployment	Reflation - Expansionary	Unemployment Falls	Rises	Deteriorates	-	Downward pressure
2. High Inflation	Deflation - Contractionary	Inflation falls	-	Improves	Not achieved	Upward pressure
3. Balance of payments deficits	Deflation - Contractionary	Deficit falls	Falls	-	Not achieved	Upward pressure
4. Balance of payments surplus	Reflation - Expansionary	Surplus falls	Rises	-	Achieved	Downward pressure

* It must be stressed that current economic thinking does emphasise that there may well only be short-run effects on unemployment of increased government spending (see Chapter 6). This has not however prevented some European governments from pursuing these policies.

inflation, the more competitive its goods become internationally, and the larger the balance of payments surplus. The more the government attempts to control the balance of payments surplus, the larger the inflation rate in the domestic economy.

As is evident from Table 9.8 there may be a dilemma for governments. If high unemployment exists, the solution to this (i.e. reflation) weakens the exchange rate. If at the same time high inflation exists the solution to this (i.e deflation) strengthens the exchange rate. This dilemma can be resolved by directly changing the country's exchange rate. The combination of high unemployment and a balance of payments deficit, with the government placing equal priority on these problems, is resolved by the policy of reflation and devaluation. Similarly, if high inflation corresponds with a balance of payments surplus, the traditional policy solution indicates deflation and revaluation.

The importance of government economic policy in influencing the exchange rate can clearly be discerned. In order to forecast its impact it is necessary to understand two factors: first, the likely response of government to changing economic conditions; and secondly, the eventual effect of these policies on the foreign exchange market.

(3) The International Monetary System

Having examined alternative exchange rate arrangements earlier in this chapter this section examines the implications of the international monetary system on the forecasting of exchange rates.

Between 1946 and 1971 the international monetary system was one of fixed exchange rates. The monetary authorities pledged, in the form of an agreement with the IMF, to maintain exchange rates within small margins around a target rate, called the "par value". This "par value" might be changed whenever a country's balance of payments moved into fundamental disequilibrium and after it became clear that various alternative policies such as internal deflation and/or controls were ineffective and/or politically not feasible.

Forecasting exchange rates in this environment consisted essentially of a three-step procedure. First, from an examination of a country's balance of payments trends and other fundamentals, such as relative rates of inflation and trade flows, a measure of the pressure on a currency was derived. Secondly, changes in the level of foreign exchange reserves (including borrowing facilities) of the central bank indicated when a situation would become critical. Finally, there was the crucial step of predicting which of the rather limited policy options the economic decision-makers of a nation would resort to in the crisis, i.e. reinforced attempts at internal deflation, intervention and exchange controls, devaluation or some combination of these policies.

The success or failure of the forecasting game depends on the final step. The difficulty in this was considerably eased by the fact that those who decided on devaluations and revaluations were, unlike private transactors, not guided by profit-maximising objectives. The motives of monetary authorities comprised the full spectrum from national prestige and domestic partisan politics to fears of post-devaluation unemployment. One particularly pleasant feature about this era of exchange rate forecasting for the foreign exchange market speculator was that the downside risk of actions taken on the basis of such forecasts was limited; either the exchange moved in the generally expected direction, or the central bank managed to hold it steady. Thus the risk of making a loss was virtually zero while the possibility of making a gain was quite high.

However, since 1971 the objectives of monetary authorities in their intervention policies have become less clear making the final step very difficult to predict. The motives for intervention were listed out at the Economic Summit Meeting held in Versailles in 1982. The various objectives of intervention since 1973 have included:

(A) Limited objectives related to short-term market conditions

(1) Countering disorder:

(a) Defined in terms of narrow technical considerations (e.g. size of bid-ask spreads, size of intra-day movements, "thin" and nervous trading.)

(b) Countering disorder precipitated by essentially non-economic shocks.

(c) Countering disorder of a short-term type-market psychology and "band-wagons". Resisting exchange rate movements that might gain a momentum of their own.

(2) Sending a signal of determination to the market, or testing the market.

(3) Attempts to hold a rate level for very short periods (e.g. to protect a psychological benchmark).

(B) Attempts to influence exchange rate levels over intermediate periods.

(1) Resisting large short-term movements or "erratic fluctuations" or smoothing day-to-day movements above a certain absolute size.

(2) Buying time for reassessment of economic policy.

(3) "Leaning against the wind", i.e. moderating the movements in the exchange rate.

(C) Attempts to influence exchange rate levels over long periods.

(1) Resisting rate movements "which bear no relation to the fundamentals".

(a) Resisting apparent "overshooting".

(b) Bridging operations to enable markets to realise that the fundamentals have already changed.

(2) Attempts to give some leeway to monetary policy by lessening the impact on domestic monetary conditions of monetary conditions abroad.

(3) Resisting depreciation out of concern over its inflation consequences or resisting appreciation in order to maintain competitiveness.

(4) Attempts to defend rate-level floors or ceilings over extended periods.

(5) EMS marginal and intra-marginal intervention by the participants in the European Monetary System to keep rates within the prescribed parity bands.

(D) Other objectives

(1) Attempts to acquire foreign currencies without re-igniting downward pressures on own currency.

(2) Dampening seasonality or off-setting very large transactions.

(3) Preserving the value of international holdings of assets denominated in the domestic currency in order to avoid the potential destabilizing impacts of widespread shifts in asset holdings by market participants.

As we discussed on p. 282 with effect from 1 April 1978, the Second Amendment to the IMF's Articles of Agreement came into effect. This involves the following significant provisions. First, a member country shall avoid manipulating exchange rates in order to prevent effective balance of payments adjustments, or to gain an unfair competitive advantage over other members. Secondly, a member should intervene in the exchange market, if necessary, to counter disorderly conditions which may be characterised, *inter alia*, by disruptive short-term movements in the exchange value of its currency. Thirdly, members should take into account, in their intervention policies, the interests of other members, including those of the countries in whose currencies they intervene.

Clearly, forecasting intervention points in the post-1971 situation is a much more complicated procedure than it was in the pre-1971 situation.

The introduction of money-supply targets has had a very significant impact on the foreign exchange market. If the money supply is controlled and inflation is reduced, this strengthens the exchange rate. However, as soon as expectations build up that the actual money-supply targets will not be met, this weakens the exchange rate. Thus the central bank must always be willing to raise interest rates when faced with money-supply growth higher than the targeted range. Faced with expectations of future interest rate rises capital inflows may be delayed. In the UK expectations of interest-rate rises reduce the demand for fixed coupon stocks, such as gilt-edged securities, and this in turn weakens the authorities' ability to control the money supply.*

It is important to draw a distinction between short-term currency forecasts and medium and long-term currency forecasts. In the short term, capital flows – precipitated by political developments, interest rate divergencies and currency expectations – are the key determinants of currency movements. They can lead to significant short-term fluctuations either side of a currency's medium and long-term trend. It is to this problem that we now turn.

SHORT-TERM INFLUENCES ON EXCHANGE RATES

Charles Coombs, former Senior Vice-President of the Federal Reserve Board whilst responsible for US Treasury and Federal Reserve operations in the gold and foreign exchange markets, described the foreign exchange market in the following terms:

> "By its very nature, the foreign exchange market is a nervous, high risk, ultra sensitive mechanism primarily geared to short-term developments. Of the tens of billions of dollars in daily transactions cleared through the market, only a fraction derive from such fundamental factors as foreign trade and long-term investment. On a day-to-day basis, the market is instead dominated by short-term capital movements in search of a quick profit or a hedge against exchange rate risks. For months at a time, short-term interest rate differentials between New York and Europe can have a far more decisive effect on exchange rates than do current trade figures. In such an international market traders are exposed to all the political and economic winds that blow from every quarter of the world. And as exchange rates move in response to the chattering stimulus of news ticker reports, there is an ever present risk that a rate movement in one direction will suddenly become cumulative. The market is characterised by sudden shifts of sentiment that send traders scurrying for cover and violently distort supply and demand relationships."†

Coombs is arguing that movements in the trade figures and capital accounts figures determine the behaviour of a currency over a long period of time. However, operators in the markets are very sensitive to short-term psychological and technical reactions, which may reverse temporarily the basic longer-term trend of exchange rates.

As Keynes once remarked about stock markets (and beauty contests): "it is not the objective facts but the way the majority of market operators act which shapes the demand and supply in financial markets".

What is it that causes these short-term movements?‡

*For a detailed examination of the way money-supply targets influence exchange rates see B. Kettell and S. Bell *The Foreign Exchange Handbook* (Graham and Trotman, 1983).
†C. Coombs, *The arena of International Finance* (John Wiley, 1976).
‡Some of the ideas here are more fully developed by J. Heywood, *Foreign Exchange and the Corporate Treasurer*. (Adam and Charles Black.)

(1) Economic News

Because of the widespread awareness of the importance of news items about the economy upon exchange rates, many foreign exchange dealers try to forecast economic news. Much economic data, such as balance of payments figures, retail price indices, key interest rate changes, money supply growth and so on are published in the news media on a definite schedule on dates known in advance; even at times of day known in advance. So dealers try to forecast what the numbers will look like when they are published at, say, 3 p.m. two days hence. If, for instance, US money supply figures are expected to be worse than previously, market operators may start to buy dollars in anticipation of US interest rates rising. Before the advent of money supply targets they would have sold dollars.

All this activity in discounting prospective economic news items and reacting to actual news items is a major contributor to day-to-day fluctuations.

(2) Official and Unofficial Forecasts

The publication of official forecasts of the economic prospects for particular countries can also have an impact upon exchange rates. Organisations such as the Treasury in the UK, the IMF in Washington and the OECD in Paris publish regular economic forecasts. The existence of the forecast often generates considerable comment in the financial press, all of which serves to highlight the particular economic problems and opportunities within the various economies and so influences the climate of opinion. Similar widespread publicity of an unofficial forecast, e.g by one of the better known private forecasting services has been known to influence markets.

(3) Political News Items

Political news items of all types may alter the prospects for an individual currency. Such items include:

(a) key announcements of policy changes;
(b) statements by senior politicians;
(c) appointments and resignations of key political figures;
(d) public opinion polls (popularity of leaders, policy priorities, voting intentions);
(e) general elections and by-elections;
(f) trends in international relations;
(g) trade agreements;
(h) threatened or actual war.

(4) Technical Market Factors

These provide a different source of day-to-day fluctuations in exchange rates. One source arises from isolated large transactions going through the market which temporarily upset the market's ability to balance supply and demand. Like ripples spreading across a pond, the impact of the original large transaction will react around the market until the full amount can be absorbed.

Similarly, some currencies are subject to regular monthly or weekly cycles due to the impact of large regular payments, typically for oil. During 1974 and 1975 there was a pronounced monthly pattern for sterling as oil companies purchased sterling for delivery on the 15th of each month to pay for oil from the Arabian Gulf. During the late 1970s and early 1980s sterling was also influenced on certain days by the need by certain oil companies, to pay petroleum revenue tax (PRT).

One example of technical factors influencing exchange rates is the close link between some currencies whereby if one rises/falls against a key currency the other must rise/fall against the same currency. An example of this is the close link between the Deutschmark and the Swiss franc, whereby if the Deutschmark rises/falls against the dollar then the Swiss franc must rise/fall against the dollar. An example will make this clear. Assume that the exchange rate between the Deutschmark and the Swiss franc maintained by the Swiss central bank is 1 DM = 80 Swiss cents (this is approximately correct) and that 1 DM = 80 Swiss cents = US$1. Now assume that the DM doubles in value against the dollar, i.e. 1 DM = $2. In order for 1 DM to be still equal to 80 Swiss cents then the Swiss franc must rise so that now 1 DM = 80 Swiss cents = US$2, i.e. the Swiss franc rises to 40 Swiss cents = US$1. So in this case as the Deutschmark appreciates against the dollar so does the Swiss franc.

It may be instructive to take the case where the DM halves in value against the dollar so that 1 DM is now worth only 50 US cents. Therefore it now takes 2 DM to purchase 1 US dollar. Since 1 DM is fixed at 80 Swiss cents then 2 DM must be worth 1 Swiss franc 60 cents. In other words the Swiss franc has halved in value against the dollar.

Another technical factor is that some currencies are used as world reserve currencies. These currencies are held as a store of value as well as a medium of exchange. Participants in the foreign exchange market who hold, e.g. the dollar, as a store of value may react very nervously to expectations that in the short run the dollar is expected to fall while in the medium term the fundamentals are in the dollar's favour. Since these arbitragists may need to convert their funds at short notice it is not surprising that fears of capital losses worry them. It is not much use to them to be told the market is over-reacting.

FORECASTING EXCHANGE RATES BY USING ONE SINGLE VARIABLE

Forecasting exchange rates by incorporating the various items already mentioned is a cumbersome process and is also prone to error in view of the number of variables which need to be estimated. It is for this reason that some forecasters prefer to base their predictions on a single variable. Two particular variables have been singled out:

(a) the rate of inflation via the concept of purchasing power parity;

(b) the relative money supply via the international monetary theory of the balance of payments.

(1) Purchasing Power Parity

The theory of purchasing power parity was put forward by Gustav Cassel at the end of the First World War. The purchasing power parity theory states that the exchange rate between two countries will reflect the relative buying power of the respective currencies. An example will clarify this. Assume a motorcycle costs £500 in the UK and $1,500 in the US. If the current rate of exchange is $3 = £1, the motorcycle will cost the same in either country, and the exchange rate reflects purchasing power parity. If however, the exchange rate moved until £1 was worth only $2, it would be cheaper for an American to buy a motorcycle in England because he could then buy it for $1,000 (ignoring transport costs). Assuming flexible prices, as the demand for motorcycles increased in the UK the price would rise and, as the demand for motorcycles in the US declined, their price would fall. With the increase in demand by Americans for UK motorcycles there would be an increase in the demand for sterling, which in turn, would raise the value of the pound and reduce the value of the dollar. This whole process would continue until exchange rates against reflected purchasing power parity i.e. $3 = £1.

Purchasing power parity theory is, therefore, an hypothesis about the equilibrium relationship between an exchange rate and a corresponding relative price index; it rests on the notion that the exchange rate and relative price index cannot diverge from their proportionate equilibrium relationship without setting in motion corrective forces that will act to restore equilibrium.

Two requirements are necessary to produce an exchange rate forecast under this approach. First, a base period when purchasing power parity existed between two countries, or when domestic price levels were equal when measured in a common currency, has to be established. Secondly, a run of actual and forecast inflation rates for the two countries in question must be obtained. Taking the exchange rate for the base period and adjusting it for any subsequent inflation differential allows a specific value for the exchange rate to be projected over future periods.

Purchasing power parity is, however, subject to several limitations, one of which is that changes in domestic prices need not cause a change in exchange rates because many goods are not traded internationally. Another criticism is that indirect taxes and tariffs make exchange rates deviate from purchasing power parity. Also, transport and other transactions costs, such as high information costs involved in finding the cheapest products, leave room for large purchasing power disparities.

Considerations other than price can also affect competitiveness. There are two broad aspects of non-price competitiveness. The first is the act of selling the goods, which includes the amount of advertising undertaken, whether to use agents or subsidiaries, the frequency and length of visits by salesmen to markets and their customer contact. The second aspect concerns the product itself, e.g. its design or fashion, ease of maintenance and operation, quality (including reliability and technical specification), delivery time, and after sales service.

Proponents of the theory often leave vague, or disagree over, which ratio of price indices should be compared with the exchange rate. Such vagueness and disagreement reflects the lack of a satisfactory model of the corrective forces that might prevent the exchange rate from diverging persistently from a proportionate relationship with an appropriate ratio of price indices. Another severe drawback with the theory as a forecasting tool is that it assumes causality runs from prices to the exchange rate and not the other way round. For some commodities, e.g. copper, it is clear that movements in the exchange rate determine the domestic price and not vice versa. Thus a movement away from the theory may imply a disequilibrium price level not a disequilibrium spot rate.

The outcome of these criticisms is that the theory is useful in indicating the long-term trend in a currency rather than in predicting exchange rates over a period as short as a year.

(2) The Monetary Theory of Exchange Rate Determination

The international monetary theory of exchange rate determination is an old idea, with Ricardo being an early exponent. The theory, which saw a resurgence in the 1970s can be applied to either fixed or flexible exchange rates. Suppose that the authorities in some country on fixed exchange rates increase the rate of monetary expansion: assuming that the economy is small and fully employed, individuals now find themselves with excess money balances. They will attempt to exchange them for goods and financial assets, i.e. aggregate demand will increase. Individuals in the country which has increased its rate of monetary expansion will, since the economy is fully employed, eliminate their excess money balances through the balance of payments, that is by exchanging them for foreign goods and securities. Thus as a result of the increase in its rate of monetary expansion the country will develop a balance of payments deficit which in turn will lead to a reduction in its foreign reserves.

In the opposite situation, when the money supply, or its rate of growth, is reduced, individuals and firms find that their real balances are below the desired level. They will, therefore attempt to accumulate money balances.

They can do so by exchanging goods for money balances from abroad, that is, the country will develop a balance of payments surplus.

Thus, under a system of fixed exchange rates, national monetary authorities lose control over the rate of expansion of their nominal money supply. Their freedom is limited to the ability to choose the level of foreign exchange reserves they desire to hold. If they want to increase their holdings of reserves they must reduce the rate of monetary expansion, and vice versa if they find that their foreign exchange reserves are in excess of the desired level.

Assume, in this case, that the economy under consideration is fully employed and that its government abstains from operations in the foreign exchange market, i.e. the country in question operates a system of flexible exchange rates. Now suppose that the rate of monetary expansion increases. This leads to an increase in the amount of real cash balances that individuals and firms hold. They now hold a volume of real cash balances in excess of that which they desire. Their response is to attempt to eliminate their excess cash balances. They will, therefore, try to exchange their excess cash balances for other assets, as well as for goods and services. Thus aggregate demand in the economy will increase. Producers cannot increase their output. Responding to the increase in the demand for their goods and services, they will attempt to hire additional labour to expand their production: but if the economy is already fully employed, all they achieve is to raise wages. Thus the excess demand created by the expansion in the money supply leads to a rise of prices and wages. As prices rise the real value of cash balances held falls. Prices rise until the excess real cash balances are eliminated with individuals now holding the desired level of cash balances. If the rate of monetary expansion is maintained at its new higher level prices will continue to rise, i.e. inflation will emerge.

However, an increase in domestic price inflation will not be the only consequence of the rise in the rate of monetary expansion. When individuals and firms attempt to eliminate their excess money balances they do so partly by offering, say, sterling, in exchange for goods produced abroad and for foreign financial securities. This increase in the supply of sterling in the foreign exchange market leads to a fall in the price of sterling in terms of all other currencies, assuming that the demand for the UK currency has not correspondingly increased. If the higher rate of monetary expansion is maintained, the international value of sterling will continuously fall. Thus an increase in the rate of growth of the money supply will lead to inflation and a falling international value for the currency in a fully employed economy on flexible exchange rates.

The outcome is that, if the money supply is higher than the money demand under fixed exchange rates, reserves fall and under flexible exchange rates the exchange rate falls until money supply equals money demand. A falling exchange rate raises domestic prices and increases the demand for cash balances. If the money supply is lower than the money demand under fixed exchange rates, reserves rise and under flexible rates the exchange rate rises.

A rising exchange rate lowers domestic prices and reduces the demand for cash balances. Again the process stops when money supply equals money demand.

The encouraging aspect about this approach is the way in which it analyses exchange rate changes within the context of the overall balance of payments. The theory recognises that a country with a large current account surplus can experience downward pressure on its exchange rate when its money supply is growing too fast; and that a country with a large current account deficit can experience upward pressure on its exchange rate, when its money supply is growing too slowly. This follows because excessive or deficient growth in cash balances can be eliminated by a movement on current account or capital account, or by a combination of the two.

The monetary theory has to be used carefully in a world characterised not by full employment but by unemployment. If there are free resources, monetary expansion can stimulate output and increase employment without necessarily producing inflation. The rise in national income might adversely affect the current account as imports are encouraged but the effect is likely to be moderate. An exchange-rate forecaster using the monetary theory must make an assessment, when attempting to predict the exchange rate movements, of whether a monetary expansion will raise output or prices.

In practice the situation is somewhat easier. If the economy is depressed, inflation will be moderating and the exchange rate will be reflecting this. The monetary expansion will reduce the tendency for inflation to drop even if the full impact is on output. Thus a monetary expansion produces downward pressure on the exchange rate even if the economy is depressed.

There are two major problems with the theory. Firstly, it is necessary to obtain accurate estimates of the future demand for money and supply of money. Secondly, given the existence of a world of managed floating exchange rates it becomes necessary to estimate the extent to which a monetary imbalance is corrected by a change in the reserves or by a change in the exchange rate or both.

Chapter 10

International Liquidity

INTRODUCTION

By international liquidity is meant the stock of internationally acceptable assets available for the settlement of debts between individuals, corporate bodies and trading nations. These international assets can take various forms, the qualifications for continuous use being that they be liquid, easily transferable, readily acceptable and that they have a stable and predictable value. International liquidity, like national money, serves at least three potential functions: it is a medium of exchange, a unit of account, and a store of value. Individuals and corporate bodies are likely to hold international money to finance trade, for investment and for speculative purposes. Central banks' demand for reserves are likely to be motivated by two conceptually separable forces, a desire to defend the value of their currency on the foreign exchange market and a precaution against the possibility that they will have to finance a balance of payments deficit. Private demand for international liquidity stems from transaction and speculative motives while central banks' demands stem from precautionary motives and transactions motives, e.g. the need to service foreign debts, etc.

Historically international monies have taken three broad forms; commodity money, fiat money and credit money. In the context of international trading relations gold has been the principal form of commodity money. As discussed in Chapter 1 commodity monies were used, both domestically and internationally, and among those commodities precious metals, and particularly gold, acquired pre-eminence and eventually drove out competitors. Gold, as a relatively scarce precious metal, was acceptable in international transactions because it fulfilled the function of a medium of exchange and store of value. Over time, however, with a continuous expansion in world trade and a shortfall in gold supplies, the need to economise on existing gold stocks became increasingly apparent. Despite the obvious advantages of paper money (cheaper to produce, more convenient to hold in cash form, etc.) international trust was not sufficient to accept it on its own. Money that has intrinsic value because it is made of a precious metal can be contrasted with fiat money which has value because the public has "faith" that it will be accepted as legal tender. It was quickly realised that the advantages of fiat money could be reaped if it were backed by something with intrinsic value. Consequently, fiat money backed by gold came to be used in international transactions. The countries whose currencies were used were those which were important trading nations, had a stock of gold with which to back their currency, and were prepared to run balance of payments deficits in order to supply the rest of the world with such liquidity. Thus, prior to the Second World War, the pound sterling was the principal form of fiat money, whereas since the Second World War the US dollar has dominated international monetary relations.

Increasing sophistication of, and confidence in, the domestic economy usually results in an increasing dependence on credit money. This is also the case with the international economy. Thus, over the past decade there have been increased attempts to develop a form of credit money as a further attempt to economise on the use of national currencies. This development has been particularly evident in attempts to increase the role of special drawing rights.

International reserves are conventionally defined as official holdings of gold, foreign exchange, and International Monetary Fund-related assets. Apart from gold, these reserves are made up of currencies suitable for intervention in the foreign exchange market and for direct payment of foreign obligations and also of financial assets that can be converted into such currencies on short notice at a generally moderate risk of loss (e.g. Treasury bills).

A broader concept of international liquidity includes, in addition to the holdings of international reserves, the capacity of borrowing from foreign sources. The concept of international liquidity is much less precise than that of international reserves, because the capacity to borrow abroad is in part determined by the terms on which a country is willing or able to borrow, including cost, maturity, and other conditions related to the loans.

Developments in official reserve holdings and in international liquidity are affected by the structure of the international monetary system, including the exchange arrangements adopted, by macro-economic policies, and by the responses of monetary authorities to the emergence of payments inbalances. Credit market conditions and interest rates also bear on the broader concept of international liquidity by affecting the borrowing possibilities of countries.

In understanding developments in international liquidity it is necessary to first understand the role and importance of the International Monetary Fund as a supplier of international liquidity. We will then move on to discuss other sources of international liquidity, foreign exchange, central bank gold holdings and special drawing rights.

THE INTERNATIONAL MONETARY FUND

When a country joins the Fund, it is assigned a quota the amount being determined by the member's economic characteristics relative to those of other members of comparable size. Large countries receive large quotas and vice versa. The size of the member's quota determines, among other things, the member's voting power, the size of its potential access to Fund resources, and its share in allocations of SDRs. Quotas are reviewed at intervals of not more than five years to take account of changes in the relative economic positions of members and the growth of the world economy. Initial subscriptions, and normally subscriptions associated with increases in quotas, are paid mainly in the member's own currency, and a small portion, not exceeding 25%, in reserve assets (SDRs or other members' currencies that are acceptable to the Fund).

The principle way in which the Fund makes its resources available to members is by selling to them the currencies of other members or SDRs in exchange for their own currencies. A member to which the Fund sells currencies or SDRs is said to make "purchases" (also referred to as "drawings") from the Fund. The purpose of making the Fund's resources available to members is to meet balance of payments needs.

As already mentioned the quota provides the basis upon which voting rights and drawing rights are assessed. Each member pays a subscription to the Fund equal to the value of its quota; 25% of this was originally paid in gold, the remaining 75% in the country's own currency. With effect from the ratification of the Second Amendment to the IMF's Articles of Agreement, in 1978, members were no longer required to pay gold to the Fund in connection with any transaction or operation. The IMF therefore acquires stocks of currencies from its members which can subsequently be lent to nations facing balance of payments difficulties. Any country facing payments difficulties can borrow an amount of foreign currency from the fund up to the value of its quota. The loan (plus service charges) is repaid over a specified time period (three to five years). The use of the Fund positions forms a relatively small percentage of total reserves.

In addition to these automatic drawing rights any member can further draw on its credit tranche. Here the member can borrow up to 125% of its quota in five slices or "tranches". The first drawing (the "reserve tranche") is unconditional. The remaining four tranches are, however, conditional, the conditions imposed becoming more stringent with each successive drawing (see Table 10.1). Because of the conditionality element these are not usually included in calculations of countries' foreign exchange reserves. A country's ability to draw on the IMF depends on the IMF's holdings of the drawing country's own currency.

In addition to the reserve and credit "tranches" other borrowing facilities are available to IMF members. First there is the Compensatory Financing Facility which was devised for countries which for various reasons, such as the

Table 10.1
Possible Tranche Drawings and Related Conditionality

Transaction	*IMF Holdings of Member's:*[1]		*Reserve position in the fund (RPF)*	*Conditionality*
	Domestic currency (% of quota)	*Reserves (% of quota)*	*(% of quota)*	
Deposit of quota	75	25	25	—
Drawings				
Reserve tranche[2]	100	—	—	None[3]
Credit tranche 1	125	—	—	Increasingly severe, involving programme agreed by IMF and member to overcome balance of payments disequilibrium[4]
Credit tranche 2	150	—	—	
Credit tranche 3	175	—	—	
Credit tranche 4	200	—	—	

[1] Assuming no drawing on special facilities of the Fund and no borrowing of relevant members' currency by other members.
[2] Formerly the gold tranche.
[3] Except balance of payments need.
[4] Performance criteria attached in credit tranches 2-4 only.

Source: G. E. J. Dennis, International Financial Flows, (Graham and Trotman, 1984).

weather, suffered temporary set backs in their export earnings. Secondly there is the "Extended Fund Facility" which was established to assist countries with longer term structural economic problems. Thirdly there is the "Trust Fund" which uses funds obtained from profits from the IMF's gold sales programme. Fourthly there is the "Supplementary Financing Facility" also called the "Witteveen Facility" which is designed to help members to cope with balance of payments problems caused by the rising oil price. Finally there is the "buffer stock facility" which provides loans for countries to finance commodity stocks.

The compensatory financing facility, which was established in February 1963, is to assist members, particularly primary producing countries, experiencing balance of payments difficulties attributable to shortfalls in earnings from merchandise exports and invisibles that are both temporary and due largely to factors beyond their control. In May 1981, the Fund decided to extent financial assistance to members facing balance of payments difficulties produced by an excess in the cost of their cereal imports. This assistance was integrated with assistance available under the compensatory financing facility in respect of temporary shortfalls in export receipts.

The buffer stock financing facility, which was established in June 1969, is to provide assistance to members with a balance of payments need related to their participation in arrangements to finance approved international buffer stocks of primary products.

The extended facility, which was established in September 1974, is to make resources available for longer periods and in larger amounts than under the credit tranche policies, to members that are experiencing balance of payments difficulties owing to structural imbalances in production, trade, and prices, or that are unable to pursue active development policies because of their weak balance of payments positions.

The oil facilities, which were set up in June 1974 and April 1975, were to assist members with balance of payments difficulties due to the rise in oil prices.

The supplementary financing facility was established in February 1979 to provide assistance to members facing payments difficulties that are large in relation to their economies and their Fund quotas.

Access to the different IMF credit facilities is illustrated in Table 10.2.

Table 10.2

Maximum access to the Fund's Resources under its Current Policies and Facilities

Per cent of quota

	Where regular access is through:	
	Stand-by arrangement[1]	*Extended arrangement*[1]
Regular facilities		
Reserve tranche	[2]	[2]
Credit tranches	100	25
of which:		
First credit tranches (3)	*25*	*25*
Upper credit tranches (3)	*75*	-
Extended Fund Facility (EFF)	-	140
Supplementary Financing Facility (SFF) Enlarged Access Policy (EAR)	350/500[3]	285/435[3]
	450/600	450/600
Special facilities		
Compensatory Financing Facility (CFF)	125[4]	125[4]
of which:		
Export shortfalls	*100*	*100*
Cereal import cost excesses	*100*	*100*
Buffer Stock Financing Facility (BSFF)	50	50
	175	175
Total	**625/775**	**625/775**

[1] For clarity, access is demonstrated as being entirely through one or the other of a stand-by or extended arrangement. In practice, a member can draw under one type of arrangement, while still indebted to the Fund for purchases made under a previous arrangement, but only up to an outstanding limit of 165% of quota for ordinary resources (ie through the credit tranches and the EFF), and up to 450% over three years and 600% cumulatively for both ordinary and borrowed resources.

[2] This will depend on the net cumulative total of each member's past reserve asset subscriptions, reserve tranche purchases and net use of its currency by the Fund.

[3] Maximum access to the SFF and EAR under stand-by and extended arrangements is limited to 350 and 285% of quota, respectively, over three years, or 500 and 435% cumulatively.

[4] While maximum access to each window of the CFF is set at 100% of quota, there is a combined limit of 125%.

Source: Bank of England, *Quarterly Bulletin* (December 1983).
Reproduced by kind permission of the Bank of England.

FOREIGN EXCHANGE

Foreign exchange includes monetary authorities' claims denominated in foreign currency on foreigners in the form of bank deposits, treasury bills, short-term and long-term government securities, and other claims usable in the event of a balance of payments deficit. (Relatively few currencies are used as foreign exchange.)

When currencies like sterling and the dollar act as international money they are often referred to as reserve currencies. The motivation for their increasing use is fairly well known. They are less costly to produce than gold, they are more convenient to hold for foreign exchange intervention purposes, they are easier to acquire, and they usually yield income in the form of interest payments.

The mechanism for creating convertible currency reserves differs from that for gold. With gold it is necessary to rely on increased production from South Africa or sales to the West from the USSR. With convertible currency reserves it is necessary to rely primarily on the key currency countries running current account deficits. In other words, the rest of the world runs a balance of payments surplus with the key currency countries by selling them goods and services in exchange for stocks of their currencies which, because of their international acceptability can then be used as reserves.

The major achievement of the dollar during the current century has been its displacement of sterling as the world's premier reserve and trading currency, a process which was complete by 1944. This transformation reflects the change in the relative economic importance of the two countries. As Figure 10.1 shows, between 1938 and 1949 the United States moved from having the

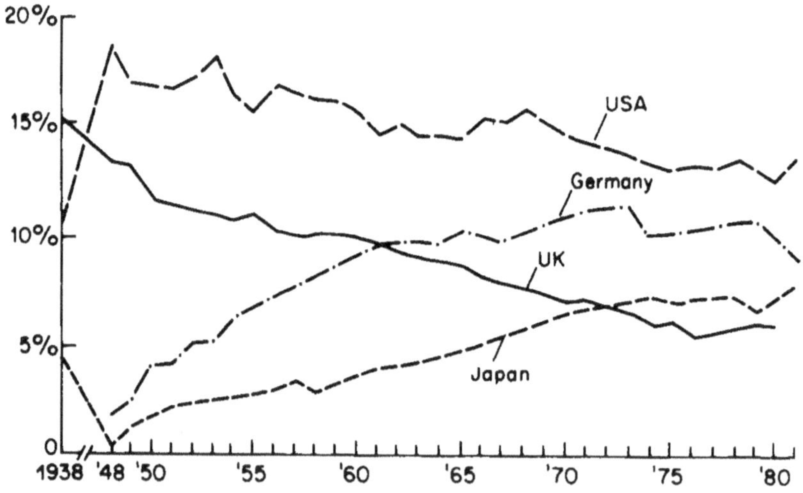

Fig. 10.1 Share of World Trade

Source: IMF

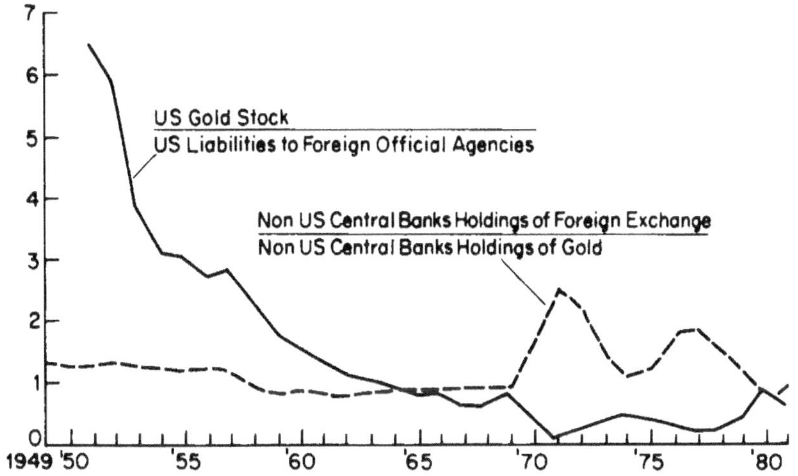

Fig. 10.2 Non-US World Reliance on Dollar Reserves and the changing nature of the US ability to back its official liabilities.
Source: IMF

Table 10.3
Share of National Currencies in Total Identified Official Holdings of Foreign Exchange, End of Selected Years 1973–83*

(In per cent)

	1976	*1977*	*1978*	*1979*	*1980*	*1981*	*1982*	*1983*	*Memorandum: 1983 ECUs Treated Separately†*
All countries									
US dollar	76.5	77.9	75.6	72.8	66.7	69.4	68.5	69.1	58.3
Pound sterling	1.8	1.7	1.7	2.0	3.0	2.2	2.5	2.6	2.4
Deutsch mark	9.0	9.2	11.0	12.6	15.1	13.2	12.5	11.9	10.6
French franc	1.6	1.3	1.2	1.4	1.7	1.4	1.4	1.2	1.0
Swiss franc	2.3	2.4	2.3	2.7	3.2	2.8	2.7	2.4	2.2
Netherlands guilder	0.9	0.9	0.9	1.1	1.3	1.2	1.0	0.8	0.7
Japanese yen	2.0	2.3	3.2	3.5	4.2	4.1	4.2	4.2	3.8
Unspecified currencies	5.9	4.3	4.2	4.0	4.8	5.7	7.2	7.8	20.5
	100.0	100.0	100.0	100.0	100.0	100.0	100.0	100.0	100.0

* The detail in each of the columns may not add to 100 because of rounding. Starting with 1979, the SDR value of European currency units (ECUs) issued against US dollars is added to the SDR value of US dollars, but the SDR value of ECUs issued against gold is excluded from the total distributed here.

† This column is for comparison and indicates the currency composition of reserves when holdings of ECUs are treated as a separate reserve asset, unlike the earlier columns starting with 1979 as is explained in the preceding footnote. The share of ECUs, amounting to 13.5% for the total and 25.0% for the industrial countries, respectively, has been added to that of unspecified currencies.

Source: Various IMF publications.

second largest share of world trade behind the United Kingdom to being the most important trading nation – accounting for 18.6% of world trade.

The effects of the second world War on the US economy were negligible compared with its impact on the European and Japanese economies, with the result that the relative economic importance of the United States increased dramatically. In financial terms, US dominance was even more complete: it owned 60% of the world gold stock. This superiority enabled the United States virtually to dictate the terms at Bretton Woods.

The post-war dominance of the dollar combined with the overall acceptance of fixed exchange rates ultimately led to the dollar collapse in 1971. As US liabilities increased, by 1964 (see Fig 10.2) they were greater than US assets. The process of stimulating the US economy and financing the Vietnam War had greatly expanded the number of overseas dollar holders.

The dollar was devalued in 1971 and has moved up and down in value considerably since then. It has however retained its role as the world's dominant currency. This is largely due to the liquidity of dollar denominated paper based on the lack of US exchange controls and on the depth of US financial markets. The dominance of the dollar in official reserves can be seen from Table 10.3, as can the reduction in the importance of the pound sterling.

CENTRAL BANK GOLD HOLDINGS

Following the demise of the international gold standard which had been adopted prior to the First World War the role of gold in international monetary relations went into secular decline. Gold's role at the Bretton Woods Conference (1944), however, was reasserted despite Lord Keynes' protestations about the metal being a "barbarous relic". Throughout the 1950s and early '60s, gold's role declined. However, the late '60s and particularly the late '70s saw a great resurgence in the importance of gold. Following the adoption of the basket measurement of the SDR (see Table 10.4) gold ceased to have any relevance as a unit of account; a state of affairs underscored, in 1976, by the abandonment of the official gold price. Gold remains a reserve asset but its price is allowed to fluctuate with the pressure of the free market supply and demand. Central banks are no longer prevented from buying or selling the metal on the open market.

SPECIAL DRAWING RIGHTS (SDRs)

The late 1960s were characterised by increasing uncertainty as to how future increases in the demand for international reserves could be satisfied. It was against this background that the International Monetary Fund decided to create a new international reserve asset. The supply of, and confidence in, this new asset would be independent of any one country's domestic economic policies. The new type of reserve asset which was created to help improve the functioning of the international payments system was the special drawing right (SDR), and came into existence in 1970. SDRs were created as bookkeeping entries and were essentially given to all IMF member countries electing to receive them. These bookkeeping entries were designed to be transferred directly between central banks in settlement of balance of payments deficits, with the IMF originally guaranteeing their value in terms of a fixed amount of gold. Actual holders of SDRs have included only the central banks and Treasuries of IMF member countries which have agreed to accept them, and the IMF itself.

Table 10.4
SDR Basket of Currencies

	1 July 1974		*1 July 1978*		*1 January 1981**
	Units of currency included	*Weight %*	*Units of currency included*	*Weight %*	*Weight %*
US $	0.40	33.0	0.40	33.0	42
D-mark	0.38	12.5	0.32	12.5	19
£ sterling	0.045	9.0	0.05	7.5	13
French franc	0.44	7.5	0.42	7.5	13
Japanese yen	26.0	7.5	21.0	7.5	13
Dutch guilder	0.14	4.5	0.14	5.0	-
Italian lira	47.0	6.0	52.0	5.0	-
Canadian $	0.071	6.0	0.07	5.0	-
Belgian franc	1.60	3.5	1.60	4.0	-
Saudi riyal	-	-	0.13	3.0	-
Swedish krona	0.13	2.5	0.11	2.0	-
Iranian rial	-	-	1.70	2.0	-
Spanish peseta	1.10	1.5	1.50	1.5	-
Austrian schilling	0.22	1.0	0.28	1.5	-
Norwegian krone	0.099	1.5	0.10	1.5	-
Australian $	0.012	1.5	0.017	1.5	-
Danish krone	0.11	1.5	-	-	-
South African rand	0.0082	1.0	-	-	-

* Units of currency unchanged since 1 July 1976.

Source: International Monetary Fund.

Prior to July 1974 the value of the SDR was fixed to the US dollar. From July 1974 the value of the SDR was determined daily by the IMF on the basis of a basket of currencies with each currency assigned a weight in the determination of that value. In the derivation of the SDR value, the currencies of the basket are valued at their market exchange rates for the US dollar and the US dollar equivalents of each of the currencies are summed to yield the rate of the SDR in terms of the US dollar. The method of calculating the US dollar/SDR exchange rate remains the same, although the number and weights of currencies in the SDR basket have changed over time.

Beginning January 1, 1981, and remaining so today, the SDR valuation basket consists of the currencies of the five members having the largest exports of goods and services during the period 1975–79, i.e. the US dollar, Deutschmark, French franc, Japanese yen, and pound sterling. The weights for the five currencies (US dollar 42%, Deutschmark 19%, French franc, Japanese yen and pound sterling 13% each) broadly reflect the relative importance of these currencies in international trade and finance, based on the value of the exports of goods and services of the members issuing these currencies and the balances of their currencies officially held by members of the Fund over the five year period 1975–79.

HOW HAVE INTERNATIONAL RESERVES GROWN OVER TIME?

The 1970s were characterised by a rapid rise in the amount of international reserves. Reserves had increased to $46 billion at the end of 1949 to $97 billion at the end of 1969, a compound annual increase of 2.75 per cent. In the ensuing years as can be seen from Table 10.5 reserve growth accelerated although it did slow down somewhat at the end of the 1970s. The major components of official international liquidity can be seen over the last 10 years to be gold and foreign exchange with Fund related assets playing only a minor role.

This reserve growth occurred at a time when the shift to floating exchange rates should, in theory, have lessened the need for international reserves. On the other hand, the main function of international liquidity is to enable countries to bridge temporary external payments shortfalls, without having to subject their economies to excessively onerous adjustment policies. Looked at from this point of view, the rapid growth of reserves during the 1970s would not appear to have produced a situation of excessive reserve ease. On the contrary, an increasing number of countries have recently been experiencing severe external payments constraints, which in the aggregate are acting as a brake on world economic recovery.

There are a number of reasons for this apparent paradox. The most important is that, while reserves are a very important element of the international liquidity position of each individual country and certainly the most amenable to quantitative measurement, there are others whose significance has greatly increased in the past 10 years or so: the size of the country's external debt, its maturity structure, the amount of unutilised credit facilities and, most importantly, the country's ability to borrow internationally. Secondly, global reserve totals are of limited significance; equally – or even more – important for the general state of reserve ease is their country distribution. Thirdly, the results of any review of reserve delopments over time can be strongly influenced by the choice of the base period, and the picture looks very different if end-1973 is taken as the reference point. Finally, reserve growth has to be viewed in relation to reserve needs; the 1970s saw a huge increase, particularly in value terms, in international exchanges of goods and services, as well as in the volume and volatility of international capital flows.

Table 10.5

Official Holding of Reserve Assets, End of Selected Years 1973–82 and End of March 1983[1] (In billions of SDRs)

	1973	%	1976	%	1977	%	1978	%	1979	%	1980	%	1981	%	1982	%	March 1983	%
All countries																		
Total reserves excluding gold																		
Fund-related assets																		
Reserve positions in the Fund	6.2	2.9	17.7	5.9	18.1	4.9	14.8	3.47	11.8	1.76	16.8	2.19	21.3	3.14	25.5	3.50	29.4	4.10
Special drawing rights	8.8	4.1	8.7	2.9	8.1	2.3	8.1	1.90	12.5	1.89	11.8	1.54	16.4	2.45	17.7	2.88	17.5	2.40
Subtotal, Fund-related assets	15.0		26.4		26.2		22.9		24.3		28.6		37.7		43.2		46.9	
Foreign exchange	102.7	48.1	161.7	53.2	203.6	55.0	223.8[2]	52.4	249.3	37.30	296.5	38.73	304.7	45.68	294.6	40.35	293.3	41.66
Total reserves excluding gold	117.7		188.1		229.8		246.7[2]		273.6		325.1		342.4		337.8		340.2	
Gold[3]																		
Quantity *(millions of ounces)*	1,022		1,015		1,030		1,038		945[4]		953		952		947		947	
Value at London market price	95.0	44.6	117.7	30.4	140.1	37.8	179.6	42.10	366.7	54.95	440.3	54.75	324.6	48.66	392.2	53.27	364.1	51.84
Total reserves (including gold)	212.7		298.1		369.8		426.3		667.3		765.4		667.0		730		704	

1 "Fund-related assets" comprise reserve positions in the Fund and SDR holdings of all Fund members and Switzerland. Claims by Switzerland on the Fund are included in the line showing reserve positions in the Fund. The entries under "Foreign exchange" and "Gold" comprise official holdings of those Fund members for which data are available and certain other countries or areas, including Switzerland. Figures for 1973 include official French claims on the European Monetary Cooperation Fund.

2 Beginning with April 1978, Saudi Arabian holdings of foreign exchange exclude the cover against the note issue, which amounted to SDR 4.3 billion at the end of March 1978.

3 One troy ounce equals 31.103 grams. The market price is the afternoon price fixed in London on the last business day of each period.

4 The decrease recorded in the quantity of countries' official gold holdings from the end of 1978 to the end of 1979 reflects mainly the deposit by the nine member countries of the European Monetary System of 20% of their gold holdings with the European Monetary Cooperation Fund. The European Currency Units (ECUs) issued in return for these deposits are shown as part of the countries' official foreign exchange holdings.

Source: International Monetary Fund, *International Financial Statistics.*

WHAT CHARACTERISTICS SHOULD A RESERVE ASSET POSSESS?

Having discussed the major sources of reserve assets it is important to assess what characteristics a reserve asset should possess. The suitability of a reserve asset should be assessed with regard to three broad considerations: "confidence", "stabilisation" and "seigniorage". The confidence problem arises from the simultaneous use of more than one form of reserve asset. In these circumstances whenever doubts arise regarding the acceptability of any one asset, the possibility exists that reserve holders (both official and non-official) may substitute that asset for another, placing strains on the system. As already discussed, given the post war strength of the US economy and its huge gold stocks, the US dollar was regarded as being "as good as gold". US dollar liabilities were after all backed by gold on a greater than one to one basis. Countries therefore accumulated dollar reserves supplied through a US balance of payments deficit. Since, however, the US was under no obligation to maintain a fixed relationship between its gold assets and its external dollar liabilities, her liquidity position steadily worsened. Eventually, this caused creditors to beome suspicious of the ability of the United States to meet its obligations, with the result that central banks, from the early 1960s started to cash in their dollars for gold at the official gold price resulting in the eventual collapse of the gold exchange standard in 1971.

One solution to the confidence problem would be to have a single reserve asset, namely gold. This solution would no doubt solve the confidence problem but two other considerations are important: stability and seigniorage. By stability is meant the ability of the supply of international money to facilitate a sustained growth in world trade. This supply ought not to be excessive otherwise world inflation may be generated and fuelled. Nor should it be deficient, in which case deflationary tendencies may predominate. Ideally the supply of international money should increase steadily in line with world trade and perhaps also should change in a counter-cyclical manner in order to stabilise the world economy. From the stabilisation point of view the liquidity arrangements of the post war Bretton Woods system seem to have been inadequate. With the "official" price of gold being held at $35 per ounce, and mining costs rising, gold supplies for monetary use increased very slowly. The supply of internatonal liquidity thus became primarily dependent on convertible currencies, principally the dollar, and thereby on the size of the US balance of payments deficit.

Another consideration in developing an international reserve asset is the siegniorage problem. Seigniorage accrues whenever paper money replaces commodity money. The production of commodity money has a genuine resource cost. Thus if the world were on a gold standard, increases in the world money supply could only be achieved by the surrender of real resources to the gold mining industry. Paper money can, however, be produced at a very low cost to society, and its face value is usually considerably in excess of the resources used in its production. This difference in the face value of paper money, and the cost of actually producing it, is referred to as seigniorage and accrues to the producer of the paper money. Seigniorage thus accrues to those countries issuing reserve currencies. Any country wishing to increase its stock of international reserves may have to do so by running a payments surplus with the reserve issuing country (i.e. the United States, or, in the past, the United Kingdom). In other words, a country has to export goods, i.e. give up the domestic use of real resources, in order to obtain paper money, the rate of return on which may be either zero, very low, or even negative. Many countries have objected to this seigniorage accruing principally to the world's richest nation, viz, the United States. Again the seigniorage problem would be resolved by the use of a commodity money such as gold. Presumably, however, against this, it is desirable to reap the available gain to society of substituting a medium of exchange which is easy to produce (paper money) for one which is difficult to produce (gold). Today most non-gold reserves are held in interest bearing financial assets. The seigniorage is correspondingly reduced.

GOLD VERSUS SDRs

With these criteria, i.e. confidence, stabilisation and seigniorage in mind, one can now examine the relative merits of gold and special drawing rights as mechanisms for supplying international liquidity for the future. Firstly, in an inflationary age there is no question of a once-for-all gold revaluation leading to a permanent solution of the need for steadily growing liquidity such as can be provided through regular SDR allocations at a controlled rate. This need for increase international liquidity occurs for two reasons. First, with world wide inflation, the simple rise in prices increases the need for more monies in order to undertake the same amount of international transactions. Secondly, as the world's capital and goods markets have become more integrated, thus increasing the volume of international transactions, there is a necessity for an increase in the amount of international money. These two factors act as multipliers on the value of financial transactions and thus on the demand for international liquidity. Under current institutional arrangements only the dollar or gold can act as the basis of an international currency system, as there are simply not enough alternatives. Despite the increased willingness of Germany, Switzerland and Japan to increase the importance of their own currencies, these still represent only a small portion of international liquidity.

The crux of the case against gold lies in the element of inflexibility, it introduces into the control of the world's supply of liquidity. Since the existing flow of gold production is very small in proportion to current monetary stocks, and production is relatively unresponsive with respect to price, the physical stock of monetary gold can be regarded as more or less given in the short or medium term. South Africa's annual production, which is about 73% of non-communist world output, represent a little over 2% of the world's monetary gold stock. The scope for increasing monetary gold from new production is therefore rather limited.

Some advocates of the reinstatement of gold see this inflexibility as a way of restoring financial discipline on governments as, it has been argued, occurred during the gold standard period. In fact, economic historians have thrown doubt upon whether the gold standard ever did impose this financial discipline.

Thirdly, SDRs are cheap to produce in contrast with gold mining. Finally, the distribution of the seigniorage benefits of SDR creation is at least roughly neutral, and could, with sufficiently general agreement, be varied to reflect any consensus that might be established on a desirable international redistribution of income. The distribution of the seigniorage benefits of gold revaluation has been at best capricious and at worst perverse, with the major gold producers (South Africa and the Soviet Union) and the gold hoarders benefiting substantially, and most of the developing countries gaining virtually nothing.

These defects of gold as a reserve asset compared with SDRs are well recognised, although the advocates of gold as an international reserve asset would minimise their importance. They would say that although gold-mining is an unproductive activity in so far as monetary gold does not satisfy intrinsic wants, the proportion of the world's resources currently devoted to gold-mining is trivial – less than one-tenth of one per cent. This could be considered an acceptable price to pay if the international economic system were more efficient as a result. The arbitrariness of the real income transfer resulting from gold-mining is also recognised; but this objection applies to the exploitation of all raw materials, and in a world where the price of oil (a vastly more important component of world trade) can be quadrupled in a few months, nobody would pay much attention to the income transfer aspects of gold, were it not for the policial fact that the two principal producers are South Africa and the Soviet Union.

THE "PRIVATISATION" OF THE CREATION OF NEW INTERNATIONAL LIQUIDITY*

Increases in international liquidity have become increasingly dependent on the private sector banking system. So official organisations, like the IMF, have been supplanted by the international capital markets as the primary sources of international liquidity. This is particularly true for less developed countries.

Lending through the international credit (capital) markets comes in three principal forms: (1) suppliers' credits, (2) bond issues, and (3) bank credits.

(1) Suppliers' credits occur when the manufacturer sells on deferred payments terms, borrowing from the home country bank to finance the period from shipment of the goods until payment is received. Official export credit agencies will often insure the exporter and, in many cases, additionally give a guarantee direct to the bank.

*The ideas in this section are more fully developed in B. Kettell and G. Magnus, *The International Debt Game* (Graham and Trotman, 1985).

(2) Bond issues represent fixed-term debt obligations issued by borrowers whose nationality is different from the country of the capital market in which an issue is made, and come in two varieties: (i) "foreign" bonds, which are issued in a single national market, and (ii) "Eurobonds", which are underwritten and sold in more than one market simultaneously. Foreign bonds and Eurobonds may be either "publicly offered" (i.e. offered for sale to investors at large), or "privately placed", and their maturities tend to be relatively long-term – usually more than three to five years, frequently as long as ten to 15 years. Eurobonds issued with variable coupons are known as floating rate notes.

(3) Bank credits consist of loans and lines of credit granted by banks to non-residents, either out of funds borrowed in the Eurocurrency market (Eurocurrency credits), or from domestic currency resources (domestic currency credits).

Until the 1970s, banks' involvement with LDCs (see Table 10.6) was limited to the provision of short-term trade finance facilities, a few term loans to governments extended mainly in conjuction with IMF stabilisation programmes often with gold as collateral, and a few project-related loans. Most of the finance raised by LDCs was acquired from governments (official development assistance), the World Bank (for economic development projects) and, as necessary, from the IMF (for balance of payments adjustment purposes). As of 1971, less than one-third of LDC debt was owed to banks and much of that took the form of suppliers' credits. In the preceding years, banks financed little more than 7% (on average) of the LDC's net external borrowing.

Table 10.6

Financing the Non-Opec LDC's 1968–73 ($bn)

	1968	*1969*	*1970*	*1971*	*1972*	*1973*
Current account deficit	6.8	5.9	8.7	11.4	9.2	9.9
Net external borrowing	5.0	3.8	7.1	8.2	10.5	10.2
of which, banks	0.3	0.4	0.4	1.2	2.1	3.7
suppliers credits	0.7	0.8	0.7	0.2	0.3	0.3
other private sources	–	-0.1	0.8	1.2	2.0	0.5
official sources	2.6	2.8	3.1	3.3	3.6	5.1
IMF	0.2	–	-0.4	–	0.4	0.2
short-term*	1.2	-0.1	2.5	2.3	2.1	0.4

* Including errors and omissions

Source: IMF, *Annual Reports*

In the immediate years before the first oil price shock, it can be seen that the role of banks in lending to LDCs was still rather small though beginning to become more important. Let us look at some of the reasons why banks and LDCs were beginning to form closer financing relationships.

First, during and after the second half of the 1960s, a number of LDCs began to open up their economies to foreign investment and trade and generate rapid economic growth and investment opportunities. To support the dynamism in these economies, governments and the multinational companies to which they played host now began to require increasing amounts of foreign debt.

Secondly, the growth of aid from official sources had begun to slow down and had, in any case, been redirected towards those LDCs with the lowest per capita income and the least flexible economies. As a result, the "better-off" LDCs turned to private commercial banks for more trade – and project-related financing. The fact that the gap between commercial and official interest rates was narrowing made commercial borrowing less unattractive and the fact that banks, unlike the IMF, could not impose conditions and could arrange loans rather more quickly made commercial borrowing more appealing.

Thirdly, the rapid growth in international banking and of the eurocurrency market in particular, allowed the supply of loanable funds to rise substantially. More and more banks were becoming active in international lending – around 60 new banks a year started to participate, including, it should be noted, many that had little or no experience in lending to LDCs or managing country risk.

Fourthly, the development and expansion of the syndicated loan market allowed more banks to become involved in lending to LDCs, to spread their risks geographically and to share in the perceived rewards resulting from the strong economic performance of the borrowers.

The banks were not passive agents in the formation of relationships with LDCs. It was part of, a perhaps informal, strategy to grow worldwide, to service their major customers in the developing world and to reap the rewards from an expanding economic environment in which LDCs were playing an increasingly important role. Though it was not the only concern, the drive to increase assets was the prevailing influence in bank strategies in the 1970s.

LENDING FROM THE FIRST OIL SHOCK TO 1981

The first watershed in international lending to LDCs arrived, as we discussed in Chapter 9, with the first oil price shock in 1973/74, which created a massive imbalance in the international balance of payments (see Table 10.7). The current account balance of oil exporting countries jumped from $7 billion in 1973 to $68 billion in 1974 and remained between $30 and $40 billion until 1977, while the current account balance of the non-oil LDCs deteriorated from –$11 billion in 1973 to –$37 billion in 1974 and –$46 billion in 1975.

At the time of the oil shock, there were dire predictions that the world would never be able to live with such large payments imbalances and that a major economic depression was likely since the oil price increases were seen as a sort of tax on the rest of the world that would not be offset by additional spending from the OPEC countries. The IMF and World Bank did not have the

Table 10.7
Current Account Balances 1973–78 ($billion)

	1973	1974	1975	1976	1977	1978	1979	1980	1981
Industrial countries	20	-11	20	1	-2	33	-6	-40	1
Oil exporting countries	7	68	35	40	30	2	69	114	65
Non-oil LDC's	-11	-37	-46	-33	-29	-41	-61	-89	-108
Centrally planned Economies	-2	-2	-9	-7	-3	-5	-3	-4	-4

Source: BIS, OECD, IMF

resources to lend to the rest of the world and the governments of the industrial countries had neither the willingness nor the ability to take the steps necessary to help the world economy to adjust. Almost by default, international banks took on the job of recycling the surpluses of the OPEC countries to the rest of the world, notably the non-oil producing LDCs.

As it happened, OPEC nations did spend rather more than had been expected and, being for the most part conservative investors, they deposited substantial funds at relatively short maturities in the eurocurrency market. Private financial institutions now found themselves awash with liquidity at a time when there was a large-scale demand for credit on the part of LDCs and when mechanisms existed to intermediate those surplus funds to LDCs. In recent years there have been frequent criticisms that after 1973/74 banks "overlent" and/or that LDCs "over borrowed". Such criticisms are really rather academic and meaningless in the absence of qualification and are made with the benefit of hindsight. There is little question that the banks lacked proper tools and mechanisms for evaluating sovereign government risk and that LDCs borrowed partly, but not exclusively, for the purpose of sustaining consumption. However, had the banks not intermediated the so-called petrodollars in the way they did, LDCs would have been forced to curtail their development programmes sharply and economic activity in industrial countries would have fallen more dramatically and for much longer.

The most important development to be noted in and immediately after the 1973/74 period was the major change in LDC financing between private and official sources (see Tables 10.8 and 10.9). Banks were now the most important players in the game, encouraged in part by the governments of industrial countries which at the very least, did nothing to interfere. Multilateral official institutions, notably the IMF, became in effect the lender of last resort to LDCs if private markets were unwilling to lend or accept the risks involved.

In 1979/80, the second oil shock generated new upheavals in the international economic system. The OPEC surplus rose from $2 billion in 1978 to $114 billion in 1980 and remained over $60 billion in 1981, while the non-oil LDCs increased their deficit from $41 billion in 1978 to $108 billion in 1981. This created a renewed major demand for recycling, which banks duly fulfilled but this time, the warnings of more serious problems were gathering. In 1979 Turkey was obliged to renegotiate its foreign debt and the Iranian crisis sent

Table 10.8
Financing the LDC's[1] in the 1970s

	1971	*1976*	*1978*	*1980*
Total external debt[2] ($bn)	90	220	345	465
- financed by (%):				
Bank loans	12.2	29.1	30.4	33.3
Other private lending	10.0	7.3	8.4	7.6
Total private	22.2	36.4	38.8	40.9
Official sources	26.7	16.8	14.2	12.3
Multilateral sources	11.1	11.8	11.6	12.0
Exports credits	30.0	23.2	24.6	24.5
Other[3]	10.0	11.8	10.7	10.3

[1] Including OPEC
[2] External term debt
[3] Includes lending by OPEC countries

Source: OECD, *Development Co-operation 1982 Review*
Reproduced by kind permission of the OECD, Paris.

shock waves through the banking system. In both cases, however, the conventional wisdom was that these were isolated incidents and the result of specific domestic political upheavals. In the few years before the debt crisis finally "broke" bank lending continued at a rapid pace.

There are two important aspects of banks' lending activities in this period which need to be highlighted. The first is the concentration of banks' exposure among a small group of countries. The second is the steady growth in the proportion of short-term debt, i.e. debt that falls due for repayment within 12 months.

Table 10.9
Bank Lending to Non-Oil LDC's, 1976–81

	1976	*1977*	*1978*	*1979*	*1980*	*1981*
Lending to all non-oil LDC's ($bn)	21	15	25	40	49	50
- as % current account deficit	64	52	61	66	55	46
Increase in bank claims (%)	28.7	14.9	19.3	26.6	26.2	22.2
Share of non-oil LDC's in total net bank lending (%)	30	21	28	32	31	30

Sources: BIS, IMF

From after the first oil price shock to just after the second one, the outstanding bank loans to the major LDC borrowers* grew at an average annual rate of 30 per cent, compared with just over 22% for all LDCs. By 1982, this group accounted for 84% of all debt owed by LDCs to BIS banks. For US banks alone, the group accounted for 88% of LDC bank debt owed to the 9 largest US banks and 90% of the debt owed to all US banks. An increasing proportion of the debt contracted in the last few years was of a short-term character. This was

*21 in all, comprising, Argentina, Brazil, Chile, Columbia, Ecuador, Mexico, Peru, Venezuela, Indonesia, Korea, Malaysia, Philippines, Taiwan, Thailand, Algeria, Egypt, Israel, Ivory Coast, Morocco, Algeria, Turkey.

deemed to be less risky than longer-term commitments to which lenders would be "locked-in", but the rapid growth in short-term debt increased the vulnerability of borrowers to a sudden drop in the willingness of lenders to roll over that debt – an ominous development that occurred in 1982–83 – and it also made it more difficult for banks to extricate themselves from particular debt situations on the grounds that if all lenders withdrew credit lines, they would precipitate the very liquidity crisis they sought to avoid.

Chapter 11

The Eurocurrency Markets

WHAT ARE EUROCURRENCIES?

The Eurocurrency market is the market in which Euro-banks accept deposits and make loans denominated in currencies other than that of the country in which they are located. Like domestic savings banks, Eurobanks provide depositors with safe, interest-bearing and relatively short-term financial assets, while they lend for considerably longer maturities to borrowers.

Like the Holy Roman Empire, which was neither Holy, Roman, nor an Empire, the so-called Eurodollar market is neither European nor a market for dollars. It is rather, the market for bank deposits which are denominated in foreign currencies. The list of foreign currencies includes the dollar, the pound sterling, the Swiss franc, the Deutschmark, the Dutch florin, the French franc, the Japanese Yen and the Italian lira. The basis for the appellation, "Eurodollar", lies in two aspects of the market. First, most of the banks who accept these non-resident funds in the form of foreign currency deposits are located in Europe. Second, the great preponderance of such deposits is denominated in US dollars. Transactions in the Eurodollar market consist primarily of purchases and sales by European banks of the demand liabilities of US banks (this is discussed further below).

The origin of the market is attributed by some to the placement by various state banks in the Soviet Union and elsewhere in Eastern Europe of US dollars with two Soviet banks, the Moscow Narodny Bank of London, and the Banque Commerciale pour l'Europe du Nord, of Paris. These state banks apparently preferred to place their holdings of US dollars with the Soviet banks as a means of reducing the risk of having their funds blocked. Since then, a number of factors, discussed later, may be cited as contributing to the development of the Eurodollar market.

Although eurodollars are *held and used outside* the United States, they *remain in* the US banking system. Commercial banks operating outside the

Table 11.1

Eurocurrency Market Size based on foreign currency liabilities and claims of banks in major European countries, the Bahamas, Bahrain, Cayman Islands, Netherlands Antilles, Panama, Canada, Japan, Hong Kong, and Singapore billions of dollars (rounded to nearest $5 billion), at end of period

	1973	*1974*	*1975*	*1976*	*1977*	*1978*	*1979*	*1980*	*1981*	*1982*	*1983 June*	*1984 March*
Estimated size												
Gross	315	395	485	595	740	950	1 235	1 525	1 860	2 050	2 056	2 257
Liabilities to nonbanks	55	80	90	115	145	190	260	350	460	505	489	603
Liabilities to central banks	40	60	65	80	100	115	145	150	130	90	84	90
Liabilities to other banks[1]	220	255	330	400	495	645	830	1 025	1 270	1 455	1 483	1564
Net	160	220	255	320	390	495	590	730	890	960	945	
Claims on nonbanks	70	105	130	165	210	265	330	425	530	595		
Claims on central banks and on banks outside market area[2]	70	95	105	130	150	185	200	230	275	270		
Conversions of Eurofunds into domestic currencies by banks in market area[3]	20	20	20	25	30	45	60	75	85	95		
Eurodollars as % of gross liabilities in all Eurocurrencies	74	76	78	80	76	74	72	75	78	79	80	78

[1] includes unallocated liabilities
[2] includes unallocated claims
[3] in European market area only

Source: *World Financial Markets* (August 1984 and earlier issues).
Reproduced by kind permission of Morgan Guaranty Trust Company.

US which accept eurodollar deposits, will normally credit these dollars to their own account with a major "money centre bank" in the United States. The US bank acts as correspondent for its foreign counterpart, for all its business in US currency. As and when these same dollars are used for a particular transaction (e.g. deposit with another non-US based bank or loan to a client), the foreign bank will instruct its US correspondent to debit its account and transfer the funds, for instance to another bank's account, again through the intermediary of that bank's US correspondent. Demand deposits, maintained by foreign banks with their US correspondents, constitute external liabilities of the US banking system. This anomalous practice (it exists in equivalent forms for all offshore currencies) finds its justification in the fact that the US financial system is best equipped to clear US dollar transactions between banks, *regardless of their nationality*.

Table 11.1 gives an indication of the size and growth of the Eurocurrency.

WHY DO EUROCURRENCY MARKETS EXIST?

The answer to this is quite simple. They exist because of government regulations. Remember that Eurodollars are time deposits, denominated in US dollars, in a bank or branch located outside of the United States. In other words it is an external market for credit. Here one must ask why a market for (in this case dollars) developed outside the United States. Three preconditions are necessary for the existence and growth of an external market for credit. First, since all Eurocurrency transactions are international transactions from a legal point of view, a sufficient number of borrowers and lenders must be free to transfer funds internationally. Secondly, since the payment of Eurocurrency loans and deposits ultimately takes place through the clearing system of the country whose currency is being used to denominate the credit, non-residents must have free access to clearing balances. Thirdly, and most importantly, domestic banking must represent a cost disadvantage. Eurobanks must enjoy sufficient cost advantages to be able to reward customers for bearing the perceived risk of engaging in banking in the "external" market.

Eurocurrency banking is always carried out in jurisdictions which provide Eurobanks with a systematic competitive advantage over those banks that pursue financial intermediation in a national market. The authorities of these "offshore centres" allow banks a great deal of freedom with respect to those credit activities that are denominated in foreign currencies, especially when the counterparts in the transactions are non-residents, because such transactions do not affect domestic credit conditions. Thus systematic differences between national and external markets in the regulation of financial intermediaries are the decisive factors in explaining the reasons for the existence of the Eurocurrency market. The competitive advantage of Eurobanks is a result of the competitive disadvantages of banks in the national market.

The disadvantages arise almost exclusively from existing or anticipated banking regulations of the following types:

(1) regulations which restrict the banks freedom to lend, e.g. the existence of quantitative and qualitative lending guidelines. These were discussed in Chapter 7 and have the affect of reducing the potential profitability of bank lending.

(2) regulations which burden financial intermediation activities with special costs; in several domestic markets, bank loans are subject to certain fees and taxes which can considerably increase their cost. For instance, in the United States, it is customary for commercial banks to demand that their borrowers should maintain "compensating balances" of up to 20 per cent of the loan amount. These balances must be kept on account, free of interest, as a notional safeguard against the borrower's default. At equal nominal rates of interest, eurodollar loans therefore represent a saving of 25%. Deposit insurance can also be costly.

(3) rules and regulations which limit interest rates on both deposits and loans;

(4) rules and regulations which force intermediaries to maintain reserves which do not yield a market return:

(5) all other rules and regulations which restrict competition among banks in one way or another.

Of course not all regulations create a competitive disadvantage for banks in national markets. For example, regulations promoting disclosure of financial conditions, and those activities of the supervisory authorities that further the safety of the institutions, will tend to attract depositors, and banks, to certain jurisdictions. Yet these are the exceptions. By and large, domestic rules and regulations tend to be a burden on financial intermediaries, since banking laws are frequently designed to further political and economic objectives other than the efficiency and security of the banking system. The unique character of Eurobanking is that it allows banks to choose among jurisdictions. Since the banking authorities of offshore centres are thus in effect forced to compete with one another, the regulations that evolve tend to be those that favour banks and their depositors.

STRUCTURE OF EUROCURRENCY INTEREST RATES

Examination of the Eurocurrency interest rates taken from the *Financial Times* (Table 11.2) gives an indication of the range of Euro-currencies regularly traded. In each case the first rate quoted is the bid, or borrowing rate, i.e. the rate which the banks pay for deposits. The second rate quoted is the offer, or lending rate, i.e. the rate at which the banks will lend the currency. Clearly, the difference between the borrowing and lending rate, the spread, is the bank's profit on the deal.

Table 11.2
Euro Currency Interest Rates (Market closing rates)

Sept. 10	Sterling	*U.S. Dollar*	*Canadian Dollar*	*Dutch Guilder*	*Swiss Franc*	*D-mark*	*French Franc*	*Italian Lira*	*Belgian Franc Conv.*	*Belgian Franc Fin.*	*Yen*	*Danish Krone*
Short term	$10\frac{1}{2}-10\frac{3}{4}$	$11\frac{3}{8}-11\frac{1}{2}$	$11\frac{5}{8}-12$	$6\frac{1}{16}-6\frac{3}{16}$	$3\frac{1}{4}-3\frac{1}{2}$	$5\frac{1}{4}-5\frac{3}{8}$	$10\frac{3}{4}-10\frac{7}{8}$	$14\frac{1}{4}-15\frac{1}{4}$	$11-11\frac{1}{2}$	$11\frac{1}{8}-11\frac{3}{8}$	$6\frac{3}{16}-6\frac{5}{16}$	$11\frac{7}{8}-12\frac{3}{8}$
7 days' notice	$10\frac{5}{8}-10\frac{3}{4}$	$11\frac{9}{16}-11\frac{11}{16}$	$11\frac{3}{4}-12\frac{1}{8}$	$6\frac{1}{16}-6\frac{3}{16}$	$2\frac{5}{8}-2\frac{7}{8}$	$5\frac{5}{16}-5\frac{7}{16}$	$10\frac{3}{4}-10\frac{7}{8}$	$14\frac{1}{8}-15\frac{1}{8}$	$10\frac{3}{4}-11\frac{1}{4}$	$11\frac{1}{8}-11\frac{3}{8}$	$6\frac{3}{16}-6\frac{5}{16}$	$11\frac{3}{4}-12\frac{1}{4}$
Month	$10\frac{13}{16}-10\frac{7}{8}$	$11\frac{11}{16}-11\frac{13}{16}$	$12-12\frac{3}{16}$	$6\frac{1}{8}-6\frac{1}{4}$	$4\frac{5}{8}-4\frac{3}{4}$	$5\frac{5}{16}-5\frac{7}{16}$	$10\frac{7}{8}-11$	$14\frac{3}{8}-14\frac{7}{8}$	$10\frac{3}{4}-11\frac{1}{4}$	$11-11\frac{1}{4}$	$6\frac{5}{16}-6\frac{7}{16}$	$11\frac{3}{8}-11\frac{7}{8}$
Three months	$10\frac{3}{4}-10\frac{13}{16}$	$11\frac{13}{16}-11\frac{15}{16}$	$12\frac{1}{8}-12\frac{5}{16}$	$6\frac{5}{16}-6\frac{7}{16}$	$4\frac{13}{16}-4\frac{15}{16}$	$5\frac{1}{2}-5\frac{9}{16}$	$11\frac{1}{4}-11\frac{3}{8}$	$14\frac{3}{4}-15\frac{1}{4}$	$10\frac{3}{4}-11\frac{1}{4}$	$11-11\frac{1}{4}$	$6\frac{5}{16}-6\frac{7}{16}$	$11\frac{3}{8}-11\frac{7}{8}$
Six months	$10\frac{3}{4}-10\frac{13}{16}$	$12\frac{1}{16}-12\frac{3}{16}$	$12\frac{3}{8}-12\frac{9}{16}$	$6\frac{5}{8}-6\frac{3}{4}$	$5-5\frac{1}{8}$	$5\frac{7}{8}-6$	$11\frac{13}{16}-11\frac{15}{16}$	$15\frac{1}{4}-15\frac{5}{8}$	$11-11\frac{1}{2}$	$11-11\frac{1}{4}$	$6\frac{5}{16}-6\frac{7}{16}$	$11\frac{5}{8}-12\frac{1}{8}$
One year	$10\frac{13}{16}-10\frac{15}{16}$	$12\frac{9}{16}-12\frac{11}{16}$	$12\frac{3}{4}-13$	$6\frac{13}{16}-6\frac{15}{16}$	$5\frac{1}{16}-5\frac{3}{16}$	$6\frac{3}{16}-6\frac{1}{4}$	$12\frac{3}{4}-12\frac{7}{8}$	$15\frac{3}{4}-16\frac{1}{4}$	$11\frac{3}{8}-12\frac{7}{8}$	$11\frac{1}{8}-11\frac{3}{8}$	$6\frac{7}{16}-6\frac{9}{16}$	$12-12\frac{1}{2}$

Asian $ (closing rates in Singapore): Short-term $11\frac{1}{2}-11\frac{3}{4}$ per cent; seven days $11\frac{5}{8}-11\frac{7}{8}$ per cent; one month $11\frac{3}{4}-11\frac{7}{8}$ per cent; three months $11\frac{7}{8}-12$ per cent; six months $12\frac{1}{8}-12\frac{1}{4}$ per cent; one year $12\frac{5}{8}-12\frac{3}{4}$ per cent, Long-term Eurodollars; two years $13\frac{3}{8}-13\frac{1}{2}$ per cent; three years $13\frac{1}{2}-13\frac{5}{8}$ per cent; four years $13\frac{5}{8}-13\frac{3}{4}$ per cent; five years $13\frac{3}{4}-13\frac{7}{8}$ per cent nominal closing rates. Short-term rates are call for U.S. dollars and Japanese yen; other two days' notice.

Source: *Financial Times*, September 11, 1984.

A striking feature of the interest rate structure, or yield curve, is that in normal circumstances, in order to allow for the fact that money now is worth more than money in the future, interest rates tend to be higher the more distant the maturities. Another striking characteristic is that interest rates on weak currencies, notably the French franc, the Italian lira are higher than on strong currencies such as the Swiss franc and the Deutschmark. Weak currencies have high Eurorates since speculators attempt to acquire a liability in a weak currency which they hope will decrease in value enabling them to repay the debt and make a profit. Strong currencies have low Eurorates since speculators have bought these currencies with the hope that they will be revalued thus giving them a profit. As the Euromarket is a free market, if demand exceeds supply, prices, i.e. Eurorates, rise and if supply exceeds demand prices, i.e. Eurorates, go down.

THE RELATIONSHIP BETWEEN EUROCURRENCY INTEREST RATES AND DOMESTIC INTEREST RATES

The clearest way to appreciate the relationship between Eurocurrency (in particular Eurodollar) interest rates and domestic interest rates is to ask some practical questions about the reasons for the growth of the Eurodollar market. For instance, why would a depositor entrust his dollar-denominated time deposit to a financial institution outside the United States when the natural choice is a bank in the United States?

Although familiarity, similar business hours, and in special circumstances the desire for political anonymity may occasionally account for such deposits being offered to financial institutions outside the United States, in the vast majority of cases a Eurobank could not offer lower deposit rates than are offered by US banks without losing the deposit. In other words, the supply of deposits to Eurobanks becomes infinitely elastic at the US deposit rate. This is illustrated in Figure 11.1.

On the lending side, similar considerations apply. Since borrowers consider a loan from a US bank to be as good as, if not better than, a loan from a Eurobank, foreign institutions can compete successfully only if they offer loan rates that are no higher than the effective rates charged by US banks. Factors such as familiarity, business hours, and communications may again play a role. But in a world of sizeable transactions (seldom in units of less than $1 million), where the transactors are large banks, public entities, and corporations that have resident operations in many countries, modern communications technology makes the impact of such factors minimal. Figure 11.1 shows how the demand for Eurodollar loans becomes infinitely elastic at the US loan rate, thus serving as an upper boundary for the movement of the Eurodollar loan rate.

With deposit rates higher and effective lending rates normally lower in the Eurodollar market than in the US market, as shown in Figure 11.1, financial

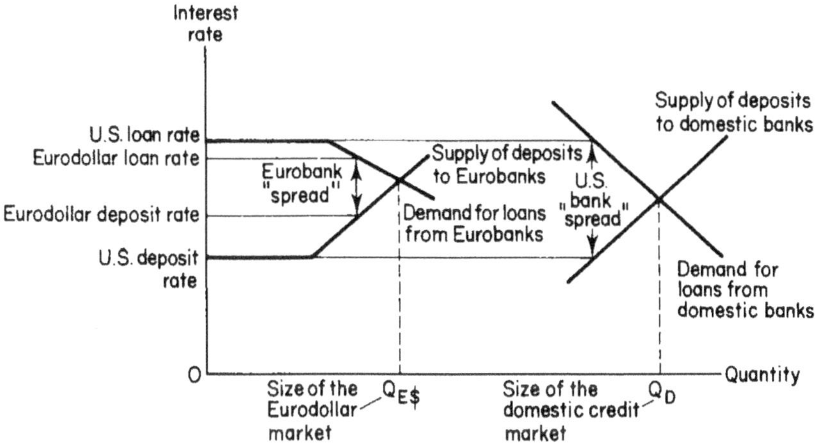

Fig. 11.1 Demand-and-Supply Curves in the Domestic and External Credit Markets
Source: Gunter Dufey and Ian H. Giddy, *The International Money Market* (1978), p. 52
Reproduced by kind permission of Prentice-Hall, Inc., Englewood Cliffs, N.J.

institutions outside the United States that offer similar deposits and loans must be able to operate on a lower spread. Out of a smaller margin between the deposit and lending rate each Eurobank must cover its various costs and earn a return sufficiently large to justify remaining in this kind of banking business. Eurobanks are able to do so largely as a result of the more competitive and less regulated framework in the Eurodollar market.

More specifically, Eurobanks are able to operate profitably on narrower margins than are domestic banks because of (i) the absence of statutory reserve requirements, deposit insurance fees, and official constraints on the allocation of funds that lower effective returns on domestic banks' portfolios; and (ii) the absence of either official restrictions (such as Regulation Q in the United States) or private restraints (such as banking cartels) on the level of interest rates offered.

THE EFFECTS OF CONTROLS ON CAPITAL FLOWS

Legal restrictions on international transactions come in many different forms, shapes, and sizes. But they all have the same effect on the relationship between internal (domestic) and external (Euro-) markets: they cut the external market off from its internal base. So domestic borrowing rates for instance can be lower than euro-borrowing rates as domestic residents may not be free to transfer funds into the euromarket thereby equalising interest rates. Similarly domestic lending rates can be above eurolending rates as domestic residents may not be free to borrow in the euromarkets. Such controls, to the extent that they are effective, insulate the Eurodollar market from the influence of domestic credit conditions and make exchange rate expectations in conjunction with foreign conditions the essential determinants of Eurodollar rates.

Let us take a closer look at this relationship. In the absence of tight controls on international financial transactions, there will be arbitrage between the external and internal segments of the market for dollar credit. This keeps Eurodollar lending and deposit rates within a margin determined by effective domestic lending rates (the upper limit) and domestic deposit rates (the lower limit).

In a similar fashion, controls limiting depositor arbitrage may cause rates in the external market to fall below corresponding domestic deposit rates, when effective capital controls prevent an inflow of funds. Germany and Switzerland have provided excellent cases illustrating such effects. Both countries at various times during the 1970s imposed controls on the inflow of foreign funds, promptly causing the external deposit rate to fall below the equivalent deposit rate, which would otherwise represent an effective "floor" for the EuroSwiss franc or EuroDeutschmark rate.

The growth of the Euro-dollar market has paralleled the growth of controls on the US banking system. In 1959–60, the United States imposed no restriction on capital movements, set modest reserve requirements on commercial banks, and ran a highly developed international market for primary securities of all kinds (including a huge stock of short-term Treasury bills, in which foreign central banks held much of their exchange reserves). The decline of sterling finance in London and the restoration of dollar convertibility for European currencies left the United States well placed to be the dominant world financial centre, based on the techniques of traditional foreign exchange banking. But this idyllic development, as seen through the eyes of the New York banking community, was soon to be disrupted by the American government.

First, restraints were imposed on the flow of both long-term and short-term capital from the United States by (i) the Interest Equalization Tax (IET), introduced by President Kennedy in 1963, which imposed a substantial levy on the sale of foreign bonds and equities in the United States; (ii) guidelines imposed in 1965 on American commercial banks that limited their acquisitions of foreign assets (i.e. curtailed short-term lending to foreigners); and (iii) the 1968 requirement that American multinational corporations raise funds for new direct investment (reinvestment) outside the United States.

The introduction of IET had a three-fold effect. First, the cost to non-US residents of raising funds through bank loans or bond issues from the US market was increased, by an average of 0.79% p.a. Secondly, purchases, by US residents, of non-US securities diminished sharply. Thirdly, as overseas subsidiaries of US corporations were assimilated to non-residents (with the result that parent company loans to such subsidiaries were classified as foreign securities), it provided an incentive for the financing of foreign ventures with funds raised overseas viz. in the euro-dollar market.

The second type of restraint was that interest ceilings were imposed on time and savings deposits in US banks. These "usury" restrictions became more onerous as nominal rates of interest rose in the uncontrolled open market because of heightened inflationary expectations, while the ceilings on nominal deposit rates of interest remained relatively inflexible.

Hence, on both the lending and the deposit sides, traditional foreign exchange banking in the United States became distinctly less attractive in the early 1960s. While these regulatory distortions were intensified throughout the later 1960s, most were eventually terminated. In 1974, as concern for specific balance-of-payments targets diminished, the controls and levies on capital outflows were lifted entirely. Although now much less onerous, these American controls undoubtedly did much to shift international finance to the Eurocurrency market during its period of rapid adolescent growth.

While the American financial system was thus tying itself in knots, the British authorities began separating deposit and loan transactions in foreign currencies from those in sterling. An important class of British merchant banks – many of which are British residents but American-owned – could accept deposits and make loans in dollars (or any currency but sterling, and this regulation was lifted in October 1979) completely free of regulatory constraint. Neither interest ceilings nor reserve requirements are imposed, and only informal monitoring of these transactions is undertaken by the Bank of England. The big British clearing banks, on the other hand, were initially confined to sterling transactions and to traditional foreign exchange banking because of their customary cash and liquidity requirements. Eventually, however, even the clearing banks were allowed to undertake Eurocurrency transactions, which are exempt from these requirements.

THE RELATIONSHIP BETWEEN EUROMARKETS AND FOREIGN EXCHANGE MARKETS – THE FORWARD EXCHANGE MARKET

The forward exchange market is the market in foreign currencies whereby one currency is exchanged for another currency at some time period in the future (normally up to one year ahead). The important point here is that the exchange rate is agreed upon now while the currencies are exchanged in the future.

Under normal market conditions, the forward market is determined by international interest rate differentials. Interest rate arbitrage is the process of moving funds from one currency to another currency in order to take advantage of higher rates of interest. Uncovered interest arbitrage is where an investor transfers funds from one currency to another and ignores the fact that currencies with high interest rates tend to be prone to devaluation. Covered interest arbitrage is where an investor transfers funds and takes out a corresponding forward contract which, at a cost, guarantees that he has no exchange risk. In this case the investor has, as is seen below, to decide whether the interest differential in his favour outweighs the loss on the forward deal.

Whether or not it is profitable to move short-term funds from one centre to another depends not only on the additional interest that might be gained by so doing, but also on the relation of the two currencies in the spot and forward markets. If, for example, a US investor is considering investing money in UK Treasury bills because the interest rates are higher than on US Treasury bills, it is necessary first to convert dollars into pounds. While he holds sterling Treasury bills he runs an exchange risk in that at the end of three months the pound may be worth a lot less than at the beginning of the period and this could wipe out any increased interest he receives.

In order to eliminate any exchange risk the US investor could sell pounds forward, i.e. buy dollars forward. The forward exchange market is dominated by supply and demand. Whenever the amount of a currency being sold forward outweighs the amount being bought forward the price of that currency will go down, and whenever the amount of a currency being sold forward is less than the amount being bought forward the price of that currency will go up.

If a currency is at a discount this means that the forward value of that currency is lower than the spot value. If a currency is at a premium this means that the forward value of that currency is higher than the spot value. In the above example, since there are more forward sellers of pounds sterling the pound is at a discount and the dollar is at a premium. By definition, if two currencies are quoted against each other and one currency is at a discount the other currency must be at a premium.

The theory of forward exchange holds that under normal conditions the forward discount or premium on one currency in terms of another is directly related to the difference in interest rates prevailing in the two countries. The currency of the higher interest-rate country should be at a discount in terms of the currency of the lower interest-rate country. Similarly, the currency of the lower interest rate country should be at a premium in terms of the higher interest-rate currency. The forward exchange rate is said to be at interest parity whenever the interest differential and the forward discount or premium (expressed in per cent per annum) are equal. This relationship is explained diagrammatically in Appendix 1.

In practice, forward rates are determined under normal conditions by differences in Euro-rates. Thus, the forward rate of sterling against the dollar depends on the difference between the rate on Eurosterling and the rate on Eurodollars. Essentially the Euromarkets are free markets and can be freely used by non-residents. This means that banks can freely cover any forward market commitments. The way this works goes along the following lines.

Assume that many market users believe that the dollar will weaken in three months time against the UK pound. They react to this by selling dollars three months forward for pounds. In order that the bank buying the dollars and thereby supplying the pounds forward possesses the pounds it will borrow 3-month Eurodollars now (thereby forcing up Eurodollar rates) and in turn will sell them spot for sterling and in turn (in order to get a return from the sterling) will place the sterling in the Euro-sterling market (thereby forcing down Eurosterling rates).

In this way the bank possesses the pounds it needs in the future. So in three months time the bank sells the pounds it has had on deposit and with the dollars it receives, repays the Eurodollar loan. In this sense, the bank is said to be square. Naturally, the cost of buying the dollars forward for the bank will be the cost of borrowing the Eurodollars minus what it receives from depositing the sterling. The wider the differential between the cost of borrowing the Eurodollars and what it receives on Eurosterling the wider the discount on the dollar (and vice versa).

Consequently, any domestic money market development which raises the Eurodollar rate and/or lowers the Eurosterling rate will widen the cost of forward cover. Naturally, it follows from this that any development which lowers Eurodollar rates, and/or raises Eurosterling rates will reduce the cost of forward cover.

The Relationship between Euromarkets and Forward Exchange Markets: An Example

It is useful to give an example here. (Note that in this case the pound sterling, and not the dollar as was the case above, is at a discount.) If the interest differential in favour of a given currency is higher than the discount in the forward market for that currency, there is an incentive to invest funds in the high interest rate currency and to cover the investment in the forward market. If the interest differential in favour of a given currency is lower than the discount in the forward market for that currency, there is an incentive to invest funds in the low-interest currency and to cover the investment in the forward market.

An example illustrates both these situations. If the money markets are in equilibrium this is termed "interest parity". For simplicity, it is assumed here that bid and offer rates are identical.

	Eurocurrency Rates (Three month maturity)	
Eurosterling	=	9%
Eurodollar	=	6%
	Forward exchange market	
Three month forward pound sterling	=	3% discount against the dollar

In this example the high interest currency, the pound sterling, is at a 3% per annum discount in the forward market against the dollar and this fully reflects the interest differential between the Eurocurrency rates. A company or a bank would be indifferent between investing in sterling at 9% and covering forward, giving a total return of 6%, or of investing in dollars at 6%. In other words interest parity prevails. However, assume now that the cost of forward cover is 2%. In this case there is an advantage to be derived from investing in sterling at 9% and covering forward at 2%, giving a return of 7%. This gives a better return than the 6% available by investing in dollars. In this example the interest differential (3%) is greater than the cost of forward cover (2%) giving an incentive to invest in the high interest currency. However, this situation will not last long as the increased investment in sterling reduces sterling interest rates and increases dollar interest rates. Similarly, the increase in forward sales of sterling causes the discount to widen. Eventually, interest parity again prevails.

Assume now, that the Euro-rates remain the same but the cost of forward cover has risen to 4%.

	Eurocurrency rates (Three months maturity)	
Eurosterling	=	9%
Eurodollar	=	6%
	Forward exchange market	
Three month forward pound sterling	=	4% discount

In this case, investing in sterling and covering forward gives a total return of 5% (9–4%) which compares unfavourably with investing in dollars. The interest differential is lower than the discount in the forward market and this gives an incentive to invest funds in the lower interest currency and to cover the investment in the forward market. Thus an investor could borrow covered sterling for 5% and invest in dollars for 6%. Yet again this situation is unlikely to last for long. Continued sterling borrowing combined with large placements into dollars soon raises sterling rates and reduces dollar rates until interest parity prevails. Arbitrage along these lines always ensures that the Eurocurrency interest rate differential equals the forward premium, or discount.

THE EURODOLLAR CREDIT MULTIPLIER

Control or regulation of the Eurocurrency market continues to be called for by those who regard the market's rapid growth as an important cause of inflation in both the United States and abroad. Discussion upon the importance of this phenomenon revolves around what is known as the Eurodollar credit multiplier.

The mechanism of multiple credit in the Eurodollar banking system can be illustrated with the help of a simple example. Suppose the owner of a dollar deposit in New York transfers it to Eurobank 1, that the deposit is re-lent to Eurobank 2, who then extends a dollar loan to a German borrower; suppose that, instead of converting the dollars into Deutschmarks, the German borrower uses the dollars to extinguish a debt to a Dutch supplier who in turn redeposits the dollars with Eurobank 3. The latter may now lend the dollars to an Italian borrower and so on. The re-deposit of the original dollar deposit with Eurobank 3 has started a new chain of Eurodollar transactions and thus is part of a process of multiple expansion of deposits and credit in the Eurodollar market. As long as the process of re-depositing with Eurobanks continues, the flow of credit and the stock of money in national banking systems need not be affected: the deposit originally transferred to the Eurodollar market remains also as a deposit with the United States banking system. Appendix 2 gives an example of the multiplier.

Redepositing with Eurobanks gives rise to multiple deposit creation in the Eurodollar maret, while the fact that Eurobanks keep their reserves in the United States explains why this process need not occur at the expense of credit creation elsewhere. Eurobanks taken together constitute a private banking system that keeps as reserves, deposits with another private banking system – that of the United States.

The size of the Eurodollar deposit multiplier is inversely related to leakages from the re-depositing process into the acquisition of assets other than Eurodollar deposits, that is, principally, into dollar deposits in New York and into foreign-currency assets. In brief, the size of the Eurodollar deposit multiplier is directly related to the system's loan-retention ratio and inversely related to the Eurobanks' reserve ratio.

The expansion process of the Euromarkets can be fuelled in several ways. Multi-national companies, foreign affiliates of American corporations, and non-bank financial institutions abroad may maintain Eurodollar accounts from which disbursements are made and into which some of the proceeds of Eurodollar loans may well be paid. The proceeds of medium term dollar loans may be placed in the Eurodollar market. Finally, some of the dollars put into the market by central banks may have originated in Eurodollar loans.

In trying to estimate the value of the credit multiplier in such a market it is necessary to know by how much the market would grow given some initial inflow of funds. If the total size of the market increased by only the size of the inflow, then the multiplier would be one. If it expanded as a result of credit multiplication by twice the amount of the inflow, the multiplier would be two. In fact, what limits the expansion to little more than the amount of the inflow, apart from the low deposit ratio, is the fact that it has to compete, in regard to interest rates with the US market. An inflow of funds tends to reduce interest rates, and the resulting fall in the differential in favour of Eurodollars vis-à-vis US domestic deposits and other domestic deposits tend to cause other funds to flow out of the market. Effectively the banks, in order to loan out the additional funds, have to make loans more attractive, which means lowering the loan rate as well as the deposit rate. The market suffers heavy leakages when borrowers convert from Eurocurrencies into domestic currencies. In practice, given the low deposit ratio and the interest-rate effect discussed above, the multiplier in the market is unlikely to be much more than one.

There are two theoretical objections to the textbook description of a multiple expansion of credits and deposits on a given reserve base. The first objection is put forward by Friedman who observed:

> "For example, if Euro-dollar banks held zero prudential reserves 100 per cent of outstanding deposits would be created deposits and the potential multiplier would be infinite. Yet the actual multiplier would be close to unity because only a small part of the funds acquired by borrowers from Euro-dollar banks would end up as additional time deposits in such banks."*

The second objection is that the multiplier is misleading even in a national system under a regime of reserve requirements. Tobin has pointed out:

> "an individual bank is not constrained by any fixed quantum of reserves; depositors' performance preferences do matter, so that an increase in reserves does not lead automatically to an expansion of deposits."†

To sum up, the application of bank reserve multipliers to the Eurocurrency market is not a realistic approach because the reserve multipliers can only show potential creation processes which say nothing about actually created deposits.

Despite these criticisms of the credit creation process there is no doubt that the Eurodollar system has gone a long way towards meeting increased liquidity requirements for routine financing of international trade in normal conditions. The Eurodollar market does tend to make for expansion through increasing the velocity of circulation of deposits. Formerly idle deposits become active deposits. By changing hands more frequently they finance a larger volume of trade.

SHOULD THE EUROCURRENCY MARKETS BE CONTROLLED?

Three broad issues underline the controversy about the Euromarkets:

(1) Have the Euromarkets contributed to worldwide inflation by complicating efforts at monetary control for national authorities or by providing a too ready source of financing for expenditures?

(2) Have the Euromarkets contributed to exchange rate instability?

(3) How safe are Eurobanking operations?‡

*M. Friedman, "The Euro-Dollar Market: Some First Principles" in *The Morgan Guaranty Survey* (New York, 1969), p. 11.

†J. Tobin, "Commercial Banks as Creators of Money", in Deane Carson, ed. *Banking and Monetary Studies* (Homewood, Ill., 1963), p. 417.

‡This latter controversy is discussed further in B. Kettell and G. Magnus, *The International Debt Game* (Graham and Trotman, 1985).

(1) Have Euromarkets Fuelled Inflation Worldwide

The first view claims that growth of the Euromarket mentioned earlier has complicated efforts by domestic monetary authorities to control inflation. It has long been recognised that a shift of deposits from a banking system to the corresponding Euromarket (say from the United States to the Eurodollar market) usually results in a net increase in bank liabilities worldwide. This occurs as already discussed because reserves held against domestic bank liabilities are not diminished by such a transaction, and there are no reserve requirements on Eurodeposits. Hence, existing reserves support the same amount of domestic liabilities as before the transaction. However, new Euromarket liabilities have been created, and world credit availability has been expanded. Critics of this view point out that Euromarket expansion does not create money, because all Eurocurrency liabilities are time deposits (albeit of short maturity) and not demand deposits. Hence, they should be treated as investments serving the store of value function of money but cannot act as a medium of exchange. Again, against this view one could argue that the existence of Eurocurrency deposits allows depositors to economise on the money balances. Consequently the rate of utilisation, or velocity of circulation, of the domestic money stock may increase. Any given level of economic activity can then be transacted with less money. That can have inflationary consequences if the increase in velocity is not offset in time by the authorities.

The important general point is that accepted concepts of money are being changed by practices in the Euromarkets, and not just domestically. This recognition that financial markets are undergoing rapid structural change underlines much of the official concern about Euromarket growth. Potentially, such change can disrupt traditional relationships between money stock measures and expenditure flows. As a result, monetary authorities may end up either seeking to control an inappropriate money measure or finding it difficult to decide how much weight to give alternative measures of the money stock.

Morgan Guaranty Bank argue that the contention that the Euromarkets have fuelled inflation is riddled with pitfalls. First they point out that the statistical fact there is often a mistaken comparison of Eurocurrency liabilities with the narrowly defined domestic money supplies. This they claim is like comparing apples with oranges. More than three-quarters of the gross European liabilities are inter-bank deposits and most of the remainder consist of time deposits, whereas narrowly defined domestic money supplies include only transactions balances held by non-banks. For meaningful analysis, the focus (they argued) should be on the Eurodeposits of non-banks and on comparable domestic monetary aggregates such as M_3 which includes large denomination time deposits and term re-purchase agreements at banks. (US M_3 now includes Euro$ deposits owned by US residents.)

Secondly, Morgan Guaranty claim that the inflationary impact of the Euromarkets is exaggerated. The amount of outstanding Eurocurrency deposits held by non-banks is still quite small in relation to domestic monetary aggregates. This fact undoubtedly helps to explain why numerous quantitative studies have failed to find that the growth of the Euromarket could help to explain US inflation or changes in the velocity of circulation of the US domestic money supply.

Morgan Guaranty believe that the real issue about the Euromarkets is that Eurocurrency deposits held by non-banks have grown more rapidly than comparable domestic monetary aggregates in the principal countries. The average annual change in the 1970s has been around 25% (this can be compared with a figure of 15% for domestic monetary growth). There is thus the possibility that the Euromarket, given its competitive advantage over domestic banking markets will grow more rapidly than comparable domestic monetary aggregates.

A related charge against the Euromarkets is that they contribute to inflationary pressures by increasing credit availability to deficit countries and thereby impeding adjustment of international payments imbalances. Specifically, deficit countries are said to be able to obtain balance-of-payments financing from banks operating in the Eurocurrency markets without having to take actions to reduce their deficits. As a result, worldwide expenditures – in particular, consumption expenditures – are maintained at high levels, putting upward pressure on prices in world markets.

In this view, Eurocurrency loans serve to displace credits that carry with them conditions on national economic policies – most importantly, borrowings from the International Monetary Fund (IMF). On the demand side, borrowing countries are seen as reluctant to submit to Fund involvement in their policies. As a result, they have a marked preference for bank financing of balance-of-payments deficits. On the supply side, banks are seen as wary of exerting leverage against borrowers by withholding new loans since such a step might jeopardise prospects for repayment of earlier loans and because they are naturally reluctant to get involved in domestic political arguments. In fact banks have competed aggressively in recent years in extending new Eurocredits and, at least until very recently, at terms increasingly favourable to borrowers. In any case, individual commercial banks have no mandate for tailoring their lending activities to promote international balance-of-payments adjustment.

At heart, these criticisms apply to international bank lending practices generally. They become specific charges against the Euromarkets only because the bulk of bank lending to sovereign borrowers takes place in those markets (especially the Eurodollar market). However, the Euromarkets do have a natural comparative advantage in handling this business. This is based on three Euromarket characteristics.

First, sovereign borrowers frequently need large amounts of funds at once. The most convenient, and often the only, way to accommodate such large loans is the syndicated bank credit. This financing technique has reached its fullest development in the Euromarkets.

Secondly, both borrowers and lenders often prefer that loans be syndicated across a network of banks from different countries. In that way, borrowing costs may be minimised while the risk of the transaction is spread as widely as possible.

Thirdly, from the point of view of the commercial banks, there are often tax advantages in Euromarket lending, compared with strictly domestic lending. In some cases, earnings on loans shifted from the Euromarkets to bank head offices would become subject to additional domestic taxes, which would serve at the margin to discourage banks from extending such loans. For example, earnings on loans booked through the overseas branches of New York City-based banks would be subject to state and local taxes if shifted to the home office books.

Consequently, while international lending could in principle be made from domestic offices instead of Euromarket branches, in practice the transition would be uneven. Thus, it is argued, regulation of the Euromarkets could result in less balance of payments financing, smaller deficits, and a possible reduction in inflationary spending.

This line of argument is sharply criticised by many bankers as well as officials of a number of deficit countries. To them, the problem is not that financing deficits is too easy. Rather, the problem is that, because of successive oil price shocks, international payments imbalances have become so large and intractable that reasonable stability for the world economy requires adequate financing through the Euromarkets. Moves to restrict growth of the Euromarkets would inevitably raise the cost of funds to borrowers. But countries borrowing to offset the impact of higher oil prices or of a recession in the industrial world are not in a strong enough position to be very sensitive to borrowing costs in the short run. Hence, such restrictive measures would do little to promote adjustment and would simply make recycling a more costly proposition for borrowing countries. In short, those who make this argument say that, without provision of alternative private and official financing sources, measures to restrict Eurolending would disrupt the recycling of oil funds, cause added difficulties for deficit countries, and contribute little or nothing to the reduction of oil-induced inflation.

(2) Increased Foreign Exchange Market Instability

The next major charge against the Euromarkets is that its rapid growth, discussed earlier, has resulted in increased foreign exchange crises.

The arguments can commonly be broken down into a number of propositions. First, is the claim that the Euromarkets serve as a source of finance for exchange market speculation or hedging activities. Although this proposition has frequently been advanced, it is practically impossible to confirm or deny empirically. Apart from that, however, the proposition has no clear policy implication unless it is assumed that no other source can replace the Euromarkets in financing currency speculation. It must be stressed that there are many ways to finance speculation and hedging activities, notably through leads and lags in commercial transactions.

A commonly voiced criticism is that Euromarket operations, by virtue of their technical efficiency, have increased the international mobility of capital. As a result, any factor influencing the exchange market in a particular way may induce destabilising capital flows and greater swings in rates than would occur without the Euromarkets.

It is difficult to know what to make of this charge. It is certainly true that the Euromarkets are highly efficient. That is one reason they have grown so fast in recent years. It is also true that the Euromarkets have enhanced international capital mobility, both between countries and between currencies. However, to speak of what might have happened in the absence of the Euromarkets is not helpful. After all, the Euromarkets grew to maturity as a response to the various types of barriers that were put in place in the 1960s to impede international capital movements. Since then, these barriers have been widely relaxed. The conclusion must be that the Euromarkets are less important in facilitating capital movements now than they once were.

(3) How Safe Are Eurobanking Operations?

The last broad area of argument about the Euromarkets covers questions regarding the safety of banking operations. The most obvious issue is whether banks are adequately assessing the creditworthiness of borrowers to whom they are making loans. After many years of experience, both banks and supervisory authorities have found that standards of evaluation commonly applied at home can be usefully applied in international lending as well. But, in addition, some characteristics of international banking complicate prudential oversight. Consequently, several issues are seen to deserve special attention:

(a) maturity mismatching and interest rate risk;
(b) "country" risk;
(c) capital adequacy and bank earnings;
(d) foreign exchange risk;
(e) ultimate responsibility for "lender of last resort".

The maturity mismatching of Eurobanking operations is singled out by some observers as an object of concern. The structure of Eurobank liabilities is dominated by short-dated money. Bank of England data indicate that about 40% of Eurobank liabilities in London is of one-month maturity or shorter, with half of this at eight days or less. The weighted average maturity of total liabilities in London is probably between three and four months. By comparison, the typical syndicated bank loan in the Euromarkets calls for the interest rate to be adjusted at six-monthly intervals.

Country risk identifies a set of banking problems dealing with the exposure of Eurobanks to official or private borrowers and lenders from countries other than the banks' home countries. The general focus of concern is whether banks have made an excessive amount of loans to countries that are likely to repudiate debt, to impose controls on outflows of funds, to delay repayments, or to take other actions to jeopardise the capital value of bank assets or the earnings on loans. The specific country borrowers that are sources of concern change with economic and political events. In principle, however, payments difficulties may arise with any borrower, so that the problem is a general one and not confined to any group of countries.

Another prudential concern is the adequacy of returns to banks on international lending and the associated implications for bank capital.

Banks assume foreign exchange risk in their operations when the currency composition of their assets does not match that of their liabilities, thereby leaving them vulnerable to losses from unanticipated changes in exchange rates.

One of the traditional responsibilities of any central bank is to act as lender of last resort – to supply funds to a solvent bank or to the banking system generally in an emergency that threatens a sharp contraction of liquidity. This role normally has been framed with respect to commercial banks in the domestic banking system. But the emergence of the extra-territorial Euromarket created ambiguities about which central bank would be responsible for providing lender-of-last-resort support for overseas operations.

APPENDIX 1

INTEREST ARBITRAGE AND THE DETERMINATION OF THE FORWARD EXCHANGE RATE

Plotted on the vertical axis of figure, are interest rate differentials, with a plus (+) differential indicating a higher interest rate in the "foreign" country than in the "home" country.

Plotted on the horizontal axis are the discounts (minuses) or premiums (pluses) on the forward exchange of the "foreign" country, expressed in per cent per annum. Any combination of these two variables can be expressed as a point on the chart. The "interest parity" line joins together those points where the forward exchange rate is in equilibrium with the interest rate differential. Moving along the interest parity line, if interest rates in the foreign country are 2% higher than in the USA, the currency of that country is at a 2% per annum discount in the forward market; if foreign interest rates are 1% below US rates, the foreign currency is at a 1% premium. When the forward exchange rate is at its interest parity, movements of short-term funds between the two centres with exchange risks covered are not profitable, since the gain to be made from the higher interest rate abroad is exactly offset by the cost of covering the exchange risk in the forward market.

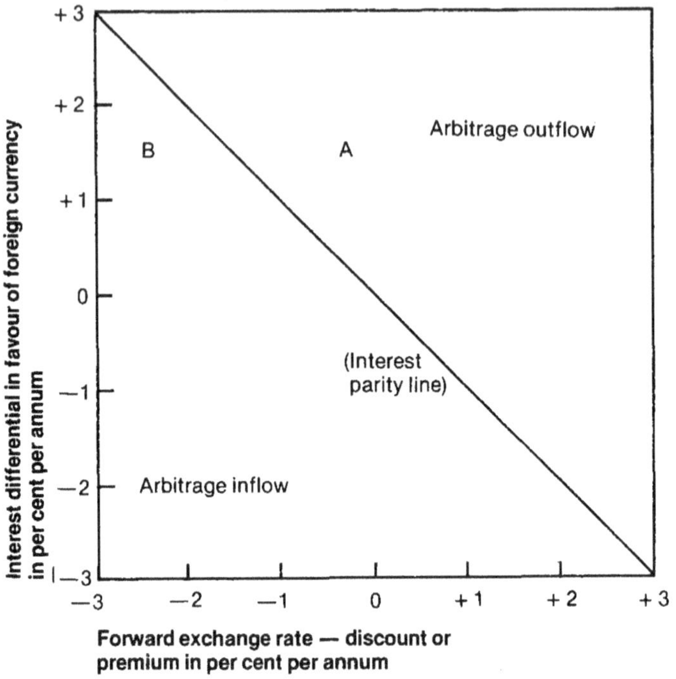

Fig. 11.2
Source: A. Holmes and F. Schott, The New York Foreign Exchange Market (Federal Reserve Bank of New York, 1965).

When the forward exchange rate gets out of line with its interest parity (either because of speculative or other developments in the exchange market or because of changes in interest rates) it becomes profitable for short-term investors to shift funds from one centre to another, i.e. an "interest arbitrage incentive" emerges.

Point A on the chart indicates a position where interest rates in the foreign country are 1.5% higher than in the home country, while the forward discount on the foreign currency is only 0.5%; a transfer of funds abroad with exchange risks covered would consequently return an additional yield of 1% per annum.

The actual movement of funds abroad tends to restore interest parity by: (a) increasing the forward discount on the foreign currency as a result of the demand for spot exchange and the offering of foreign currency forward by the arbitragers; and (b) lowering the interest rate differential as funds are transferred from one market to another.

Point B also illustrates a position where interest rates abroad are 1.5% above those in the home country, but in this case the forward discount on the foreign currency is 2.5% per annum. Despite the higher interest rates abroad, there would be no incentive to move funds there for investment with the exchange risk covered. On the contrary, it would be profitable to move funds from abroad despite the fact that the investment of these funds would bring a lower yield, since the interest loss of 1.5% would be more than compensated for by the 2.5% gain on the forward exchange transaction. The movement of funds from abroad would again tend to restore interest parity, however, by: (a) reducing the forward discount on the foreign currency as the result of an increased supply of spot exchange and the demand for forward foreign exchange by the arbitrager abroad; and (b) lowering the interest rate differential as funds are transferred from the foreign money market to the home market.

This theory indicates that forward rates fluctuate closely around their interest parities. However, there are several reasons why this theory may not work in practice; the supply of funds able to arbitrage freely may not be unlimited; there may be a shortage of suitable short-term investments in some countries. In the case of potential institutional investors there may be legal restrictions on investing abroad with exchange control limiting the ability of residents to move funds to where they wish. Finally investors may have psychological reasons to fear that funds may become blocked if they are placed in certain currencies.

APPENDIX 2

THE EURO-DOLLAR CREDIT MULTIPLIER REVISITED

In order to demonstrate an example of multiple deposit creation with respect to the Eurodollar market an example of monetary expansion as a result of a transfer of funds from a US bank to a London bank is examined. An Arab sheik transfers $1,000,000 from his New York bank, Morgan Guaranty in Friedman's example, to his London bank, Bank H. Bank H will then show an increase of deposit liabilities of $1,000,000. At the same time, it will gain an asset, i.e. a claim on a US bank for $1,000,000. For simplicity Friedman assume that Bank H's correspondent bank is Morgan Guaranty. As Morgan Guaranty will decrease its liabilities to the Arab sheik by $1,000,000 and increase its liabilities to Bank H by $1,000,000, the change in their accounts can be numerised as follows:

Morgan Guaranty		*Bank H*	
Assets	Liabilities	Assets	Liabilities
	−$1,000,000 to Arab Sheik +$1,000,000 due to Bank H	+$1,000,000 due from M.G.	+$1,000,000 to Arab Sheik

The total deposit liabilities of Morgan Guaranty have not changed while both total assets and total liabilities of Bank H have gone up by $1,000,000. If Bank H normally retains 10% of its assets and prudential preserves, it now will have an additional $900,000 to lend out, while keeping $100,000 on demand at Morgan Guaranty. Assuming the recipient of the loan, a British import company, UK Ltd., requires the funds for future use in the USA and so holds the money in a demand deposit at a US bank, conveniently, Morgan Guaranty, Bank H has now replaced its $1,000,000 deposit with Morgan Guaranty by a $100,000 deposit with Morgan Guaranty, and a $900,000 loan to UK Ltd. The total liabilities of Morgan Guaranty are again unchanged.

Morgan Guaranty		*Bank H*	
Assets	Liabilities	Assets	Liabilities
	−$900,000 due to Bank H +$900,000 to UK Ltd	−$900,000 due from Morgan Guaranty +$900,000 loan to UK Ltd.	

A quick summary of the total change is now in order. Morgan Guaranty's position is fundamentally unchanged: it had a $1,000,000 liability to the Arab Sheik; now it has a $100,000 liability to Bank H and a $900,000 liability to UK Ltd. However, Eurodollars are up by $1,000,000. There has been no balance of payments deficit and no monetary expansion. The increase in Eurodollars occurred as a result of a transfer of funds. However, because these funds were transferred from a non-bank to a bank (from an Arab Sheik to Bank H) there is a potential for expansion. The expansion will take place if the borrowed funds are redeposited in the system, i.e. redeposited in a Eurobank.

Suppose that UK Ltd., rather than holding the $900,000 in the USA, uses it to purchase timber from a Russian company, and this company chooses to hold the money in dollars at Bank R, another bank in London which again conveniently holds its dollars on deposit with Morgan Guaranty in New York. Again Morgan Guaranty's position is fundamentally unchanged with a $100,000 liability to Bank H and a $900,000 liability to Bank R rather than a $1,000,000 liability to Bank H. There have been 900,000 more Eurodollars created in this instance as Bank R's liabilities are up by $900,000

Morgan Guaranty (MG)		*Bank H*		*Bank R*	
Assets	*Liabilities*	*Assets*	*Liabilities*	*Assets*	*Liabilities*
	−$900,000 due to Bank H +$900,000 due to Bank R	−$900,000 due from Morgan Guaranty +$900,000 loan to UK Ltd		+$900,000 due from Morgan Guaranty	+$900,000 to Russian company

If this process continued, the proceeds of Eurodollar loans always being re-deposited in Eurobanks, the final volume of obligation of Eurobanks denominated in dollars would be $10,000,000 all based on the $1,000,000 liability of Morgan Guaranty. The Eurodollar multiplier (the rate of the increase in Eurodollar deposits to the initial primary deposit) in the first case is one and in the second case, ten. In the first example, there was a maximum leakage and in the second, zero.

Source. Adapted from M. Friedman, "The Euro-Dollar Market: Some First Principles", in *The Morgan Guaranty Survey* (New York, 1969), p. 11.

Additional Reading

CHAPTER 1

G. E. J. Dennis, *Monetary Economics* (Longmans, 1981).
D. G. Pierce and D. M. Shaw, *Monetary Economics* (Butterworths, 1974).

CHAPTER 2

A. D. Bain, *The Economics of the Financial System* (Martin Robertson, 1981).
D. T. Llewellyn *et al*, *The Framework of U.K. Monetary Policy* (Heinemann, 1982).

CHAPTER 3

E. R. Shaw, *The London Money Market* (Heinemann).

CHAPTER 4

D. T. Llewellyn *et al. op cit.*
T. Congdon, *Monetary Control in Britain* (Macmillan).

CHAPTER 5

T. Havrilesly and R. Schweitzer *Contemporary Developments in Financial Institutions* (Harlan Davidson, 1983).
Barclays Review:
February 1982 A. Davies, "Living Without the Minimum Lending Rate".
May 1980 A. Davies, "Money, the Base and Interest rates".
November 1981 Centrespread, "The UK Monetary System".

The Banker:
Financial Times, Business Publishing, February 1984 P. Dunkley, "Base Rate: the random factor in clearing bank profitability".
B. G. Malkiel, *The Term Structure of Interest Rates: Expectations and Behaviour Patterns* (Princeton University Press, 1966).

CHAPTER 6

G. E. J. Dennis, *op cit.*
P. Wonnacott and R. Wonnacott, *Economics* (McGraw Hill, 1979).
H. R. Vane and J. L. Thompson, *Monetarism: Theory, Evidence and Policy* (Martin Robertson, 1979).

CHAPTER 7

M. J. Artis and M. K. Lewis, *Monetary Control in the United Kingdom* (Philip Allen, 1981).
T. Congdon, *Monetary Control in Britain* (Macmillan 1981).
D. T. Llewellyn *et al.*

CHAPTER 8

L. B. Yaeger, *International Monetary Relations* (Harper and Row, 1976).
R. E. Caves and R. W. Jones, *World Trade and Payments* (Little, Brown and Co. Inc., 1973).

CHAPTER 9

Yaeger, *op cit.*
B. Kettell and S. R. Bell, *Foreign Exchange Handbook* (Graham and Trotman, 1983).

CHAPTER 10

B. Kettell, *Gold* (Graham and Trotman, 1982).
A. D. Crockett, *International Money* (Thomas Nelson, 1977).

CHAPTER 11

B. Kettell and G. M. Magnus, *The International Debt Game* (Graham and Trotman, 1985.

Index

Debits include expenditure abroad by British airlines on airport charges, crews' expenses, charter payments, etc., together with payments to overseas airlines by UK residents for passenger fares, freight on UK imports and the carriage of mail.

Travel

This covers personal expenditure by UK residents in overseas countries and by overseas residents in the United Kingdom.

Financial Services

Items recorded under this heading are the earnings, net of expenses, of financial and allied institutions for services, including brokerage, merchanting, arbitrage, banking charges and commissions, underwriting of capital issues, risk underwriting, and other insurance.

Other Services

This, statistically very large component, consists of:

(a) agent's commissions;
(b) overseas receipts and expenditure from telecommunications and postal services;
(c) film and television payments and receipts;
(d) royalties, licence fees;
(e) expenditure by overseas students;
(f) consulting earnings, etc.

Interest, Profits and Dividends (IPD)

Interest, profits and dividends (IPD) are the returns on the credit side on overseas investments, banking flows, and foreign investment in the United Kingdom. In 1983 they accounted for around 33% of invisible earnings. These current account flows are directly related to entries in the capital account. For example, where a UK subsidiary overseas makes a profit which is reinvested in that subsidiary, the profit will be recorded as an IPD earning while the investment is recorded as a capital outflow which increases the value of the UK's external assets. When the profit is not reinvested overseas, the balance of payments benefit will usually be received in the form of a dividend paid to the UK company by the overseas subsidiary. Interest on borrowing and lending abroad by UK banks in foreign currency is recorded net (interest received less interest paid) to reflect the close link between banks' borrowing and lending.

All interest flows between UK residents and non-residents are included in IPD. These include payments and receipts of interest by UK banks; interest payments by the public sector on that part of its debt held by overseas residents; interest receipts by the public sector on its loans abroad and on holdings of foreign currency assets; interest payments by companies on their

GPSR Compliance

The European Union's (EU) General Product Safety Regulation (GPSR) is a set of rules that requires consumer products to be safe and our obligations to ensure this.

If you have any concerns about our products, you can contact us on ProductSafety@springernature.com

In case Publisher is established outside the EU, the EU authorized representative is:

Springer Nature Customer Service Center GmbH
Europaplatz 3
69115 Heidelberg, Germany

Batch number: 10824729

Printed by Printforce, the Netherlands